RHETORIC CONCORD AND CONTROVERSY

Antonio de Velasco
University of Memphis
Melody Lehn
University of Memphis

Long Grove, Illinois

For information about this book, contact:
Waveland Press, Inc.
4180 IL Route 83, Suite 101
Long Grove, IL 60047-9580
(847) 634-0081
info@waveland.com
www.waveland.com

10-digit ISBN 1-57766-735-2
13-digit ISBN 978-1-57766-735-3

Printed in the United States of America

7 6 5 4 3 2 1

Contents

Section IV
Invention, Ambiguity, and Rhetorical Constraint 181

Section V
Interdependence, Identity, and the Rhetoric of Dissent 233

Editors' Introduction

Antonio de Velasco and Melody Lehn

We started with a question posed to each of the contributors to this volume: "Where do diversity and sameness meet on the human tongue and in the human condition?" For some readers, the question might presume too much, or seem overly broad. Rhetoricians are trained to attune themselves to history, contingency, and context. The question, however, asks us to imagine a universal "where" for rhetoric that lives beyond a particular locale. In its asking, the question evokes a scene of human action in which we find bodies and histories, motives and symbols, all tied together in ambiguous, contradictory, and transmutable arrangements. Multiplicity and uniformity, the divisive and the irenic. The question prompts readers to see how such apparent opposites are, in reality, intertwined, and thus open to imaginative and cunning manipulation by friend and adversary alike.

More questions: "Does rhetoric civilize? Or does it repress and control? Or both? Does it express the self? Or dissolve it into a cultural miasma? What is the price of community gained through the language of social control? What is the limit of dissent expressed through the language of difference and personal liberation?" Such questions seem wicked in their sharp bifurcation of the predicates that routinely attach themselves to "rhetoric"; however, they accumulate salutary force, even coherence, on the basis of their form. Through the author's use of a steady, almost rhythmic antithesis, rhetoric's identity is shown, on the one hand, to defy neat resolution (surely, there is no single answer to any of these questions). And yet, on the other, a different sort of resolution emerges: the "where" touched on above, the human place at which "diversity and sameness meet," becomes the primal site at which rhetoric sustains its integrity, coordinates its power, and reveals its place in history. To ground the study of rhetoric in this Janus-like domain is to define rhetoric *itself* as more than a strategic activity, as more than a shadow forever cast by some brighter truth. It is to set before our eyes a distinct drama of human existence, and then to place rhetoric at its ethical and aesthetic core. From this move, follows another: rhetoric study exists to help humans recapture from dogma and abstraction the concrete resources they need to survive, both when they find themselves on the brink of drifting apart *and* when they find themselves driven toward conformity.

Seen from this vantage, acts of definition and allegiance, of naming and of pledging loyalty to names, will always anticipate an audience, a community, indeed a pedagogy. Rhetoric study becomes, at last, a labor of perpetual responsibility to ourselves and to others, a call to teach and to study, continually and in a fashion that will, by definition, take form amid many voices and for many reasons. Nevertheless, it is the appeal of such a vigorous, humane multivocality—a *multiplex ratio disputandi*—that has brought countless people together throughout rhetoric's 2,500 year history. Together and apart, sometimes for fun, sometimes for keeps. The study of rhetoric finds its dwelling in the space between.

At one such crossroads, the Rhetoric Society of America (RSA) gathered more than 1,100 scholars from across the globe at its fourteenth biennial conference to address the theme "Rhetoric: Concord and Controversy," which serves as the title for this collection. We gathered for four days, from May 28–31, 2010 at the Marriott City Center in Minneapolis, Minnesota, a city Michael Leff (author of the above questions and the conference theme) aptly called "a space between the coasts." At the close of the introduction, we will return to this absent author and to his lasting contributions to our Society. Traces of his presence, however, appear from the start, for it was he who selected Sharon Crowley and Jack Selzer to deliver the meeting's two marquee talks. In each discussion we find distinct perspectives on what Selzer calls the "necessary symbiosis" of concord and controversy.

In her plenary address, "What Shall We Do with the White People?" Crowley recounts how a most pernicious (and evolving) form of concord, white supremacy, has contributed to centuries of violence and marginalization. For Crowley, the "ersatz unity" of white supremacy, its powerful and continuing ability to organize and permeate the social imaginary, masks a proven deficiency, one she sees plainly in the rise of the "Tea Party" protests of 2010: "our race privilege has not demonstrably helped white people to become markedly better citizens." In his luncheon address, Selzer also speaks to the legacy of America's racial and political struggles, albeit from a very different angle. When he takes readers back to August 28, 1963, the day Martin Luther King Jr. gave his "I Have a Dream" speech, Selzer does so with a particular mission—to show how those famous words "were embroidered within larger networks of discourses that were in play, often in competition, in the summer of 1963." Selzer reconstructs various forms of dissensus, fragmentation, and debate to define the backdrop of the March on Washington, and then shows how attending to these controversies—within the civil rights movement itself, in particular—can reveal a rhetorical situation that is "highly complex, as full of dissonance as consonance. . . ."

Crowley and Selzer offer imaginative applications of the conference theme. They clear distinct yet intersecting paths that help us to ponder the questions found above. Indeed, as is appropriate, and as was intended, the conference theme opened itself to a variety of rhetoric scholarship, while still anchoring participants in a common space. Of the hundreds of papers delivered, *Rhetoric: Concord and Controversy* offers readers just a sample of the fine work produced in this common space.

Our criteria for selection—innovative, edifying, and polished rhetoric scholarship suited to the theme—steered what became a longer and more difficult editorial process than expected. Of those papers accepted, most had to be abridged. And all were edited for matters of style and consistency. *Rhetoric: Concord and Controversy* represents, in other words, not a transparent reflection of the 2010 meeting, but the product of hundreds of editorial choices that might have been otherwise. Indeed, the twenty-nine essays that make up the core of the volume could have been organized in any number of ways. The conference featured several perspectives active in contemporary rhetoric study. Each could have been allowed to stake its own "territory" in the volume. Out of a desire to stress possibilities for overlap and shared purpose in the field, however, we elected to provide five thematically oriented sections, each of which brings together papers by rhetoricians from across the disciplinary spectrum.

In the second section, "Publics, Pedagogies, and Rhetorical Tensions," Cezar M. Ornatowski, Michael S. Kochin, and M. Karen Powers each examine the contours of specific public controversies, and in each case discover different ways in which, as Powers puts it, rhetoric can contain "the capacity for legitimating as well as contravening present-day ideals of democratic citizenship." To speak of rhetoric, democracy, and citizenship, in turn, raises questions of training, of how effective and sensitive rhetors are capacitated for the arena of concord and controversy. Zachary Dobbins explores how such training happens when students learn to approach narrative rhetorically, while J. Blake Scott offers an excellent example of how rhetoric study can deploy technology to organize and open discursive possibilities for students in ways we never imagined. Approaching the theme directly, Donald Lazere offers a timely critique of America's failure to prepare students for the agon of civic life—and then proposes a series of practical and specific curricular solutions, indeed "a coherent curriculum, or at least a sequence of general education requirements, that would foreground study of political controversy."

And yet, as revealed in the volume's third section, "Freedom, Ethos, and the Rhetoric of Rights," civic agency will always find its limit in the blind spots and contradictions that mark human subjectivity. Lynn Clarke and Ira Allen each offer fruitful ways to conceive of these limits by turning our attention to the dynamic psychic terrain of rhetorical action, while Alex C. Parrish argues, in a related vein, for a need to complicate traditional notions of "ethos" by removing them from the realm of "human exceptionality." Of course, to understand civic agency at all in the modern era is to come to terms with the discourse of rights. We are therefore happy to feature essays by Jennifer Keohane, Megan Foley, and Rebecca A. Kuehl that each approach rights with sophistication, that is, as rhetorical productions embedded in circumstance.

Claudia Carlos leads off the fourth section, "Invention, Ambiguity, and Rhetorical Constraint," with a revealing analysis of *insinuatio*, a complex yet understudied figure of invention that offers a "nuanced understanding of what it means to speak boldly to those who hold power over us" even as we may seem, perhaps, to be doing otherwise. Nancy Myers and Ellen Quandahl each probe the history of rhetoric and come away with insight into how gender tensions and ambiguities ground rhetorical context and performance. For Rebecca Lorimer and Kyle Schlett, ambiguities—of translation, of style, of history—provide grounds from which to assess rhetoric's distinctive character. As Lorimer, glossing Burke, eloquently puts it, "the slippage between linguistic concord and controversy is pronounced in translation, highlighting just how rhetorical the activity may be." Likewise, for Timothy Henningsen, a version of this kind of "slippage," troubled by the history of colonialism, not only defines the setting of Anglophone Caribbean literature, it brings forth a complex literary art that rhetoric is uniquely situated to appreciate.

The fifth section, "Interdependence, Identity, and the Rhetoric of Dissent," starts with Paul Lynch's study of a recent case of rhetorical "apostasy" on the left. Lynch examines the interdependence of concord and controversy by focusing on how "the apostate and the group both reject and need each other" as they struggle to negotiate and define their newly formed roles. Homing in on a quite different case of interdependence, Heather A. Roy follows activists using innovative rhetorical strategies to counter the anti-gay and anti-military media spectacles of the Westboro Baptist Church. Kelly M. Young and William Trapani offer critical commentary on the erasure of controversy in museum display—and why the politics of identity tied to these effacements should concern us. Through her case study of the rhetoric of the nineteenth-century Mormon leader Eliza R. Snow, Rosalyn Collings Eves shines light on how "even as Snow encourages her listeners to identify with one another, she encourages them to withdraw spiritually and economically from the outside world" as a means to reaffirm their collective identity. Recapturing the value of apocalyptic rhetoric from its many critics, Keith Miller probes the contexts and nuances of Malcolm X's "tragic frame" to show its potential for rearranging dominant perspectives and founding alternative visions of political and moral order.

In the sixth section, "Argument, Reason, and Rhetorical Theory," Beth Innocenti looks to Richard Whately's account of the pragmatics of argument to explore the relationship of norms to rhetorical force. Innocenti opens a path for seeing how argument, even amid circumstances of clear discord, can be judged reasonable and practically effective. And yet, as David C. Hoffman shows in his analysis, although appeals to "reason" may seek to transcend the plane of controversy, they are always themselves engaged in a struggle for definitional authority. Sometimes, as Jon Leon Torn argues, that struggle is internal. Asking whether concord and controversy can "be located within rhetoric itself, within the very textual movement of rhetorical action," Torn tracks nuances in Joseph Addison's imperial rhetoric that help to explain its mixed political character. While Patrick Shaw calls for more attention to Richard Weaver's influence on twentieth-century rhetorical theory, Ethan Sproat and Ann George each offer interesting ways to reconsider Kenneth Burke's already powerful influence. Providing useful commentary on a heretofore unexamined meeting of the minds, Sproat goes into the archives to explore the correspondence of Burke and the literary theorist Paul de Man. Ann George, on the other hand, examines Helen Keller's thinking alongside Burke's, and in the process reminds readers how the best rhetorical theory often comes from the most unexpected places.

While unexpected discoveries are often causes for joy, they are as often tied to bad news. So it was with the news on February 5, 2010, that Michael C. Leff, then-president of the RSA and author of the conference theme, had died rather suddenly. In the volume's afterword, Steven R. Edscorn explores one of Leff's final essays, while honoring his mentor with one of the finest compliments a rhetorician can receive: a well-drawn comparison with Isocrates. Like Isocrates, Leff saw in rhetoric study a way of life and learning revealed, a human legacy of practical and artistic significance. Tenaciously, he held to this vision, even as he shared it with others. If our work is done, the following pages will succeed in sharing it with you.

Section I

Plenary Perspectives

1

What Shall We Do with the White People?[1]

Sharon Crowley

I begin with Will Counts' famous photograph of Elizabeth Eckford, taken as she tried to enter Central High School in Little Rock, Arkansas, in the fall of 1957 (see figure 1). Elizabeth was fifteen years old that August. Behind Elizabeth and to her right is Hazel Bryan. Hazel is accompanied by her best friends: Sammie Dean Parker, who has turned away from the photographer to address her father, and Mary Ann Burleson, who is at the left edge of the picture. Counts' photograph pointedly conveys the fact that Elizabeth is utterly alone on the street in front of Central High. Although she is surrounded by a crowd of people, she is not part of it; unlike Hazel and Sammie Dean, Elizabeth has no girlfriends or relatives nearby to whom she can turn for help or solace.

The evening before this picture was taken, Daisy Bates, the local NAACP representative, had arranged for the black students who were to integrate Central to travel to the school in a group the next morning. Elizabeth did not get the message because the Eckfords had no phone.[2] And so she found herself all alone in front of Central High, where a hostile crowd began to follow her. Across the way, members of the crowd brutalized L. Alex Wilson, editor of the *Tri-State Defender.* Elizabeth knew she was in danger, so she hurried toward a bus stop. Angry whites followed, still verbally harassing her. Concerned passersby offered her rides home, but she was too shy or too well-bred to accept them. As she waited for the bus, she was sheltered by Benjamin Fine, education editor for *The New York Times,* who endured the crowd's taunts for his trouble, and a white woman named Grace Lorch helped her find and board the correct bus (Roberts and Klibanoff 162). Although she got home safely on that day, Elizabeth has been haunted by its memory all her life (Margolick).

Like Elizabeth, I was also fifteen in 1957; I remember being impressed, when first I saw Counts' photographs, by the pretty full-skirted dress with the gingham trim that Elizabeth made for her first day of school, along

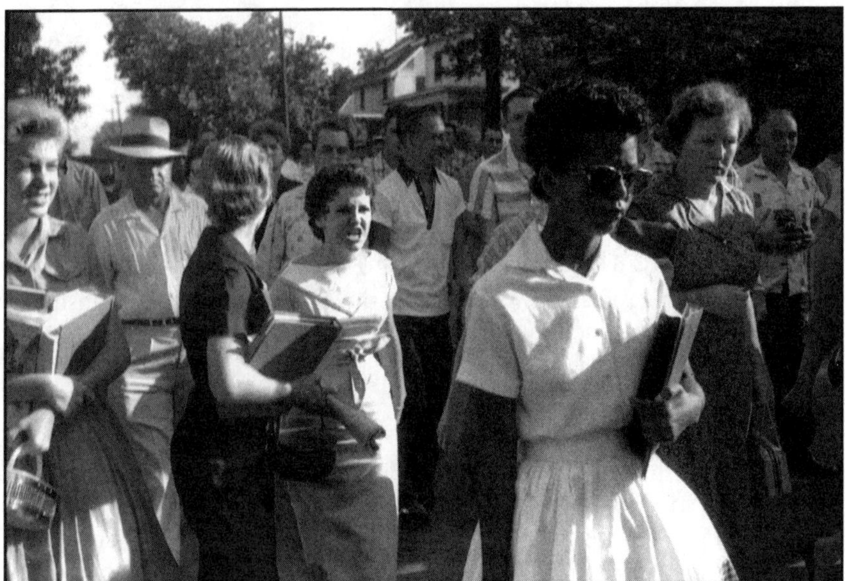

Elizabeth Eckford arriving at Central High School, Little Rock, Arkansas, 1957. Will Counts Collection: Indiana University Archives.

with her fashionable tennies and popcorn socks. My fifteen-year-old eye judged Hazel's fitted dress somewhat less favorably; according to the fashion standards of the fifties it was just a little too tight, which suggested to me that Hazel was not quite respectable. Incredibly, I was so interested in appraising the fit of her dress that I missed the hatred twisting Hazel's face.

I was not alone in my fixation on fashion and the moral status it conveyed. Historian Elizabeth Jacoway, who grew up in Little Rock, was thirteen when Elizabeth Eckford enrolled at Central High. Here is her memory of those years:

> I lived through the 1957 desegregation crisis with my eyes closed. My "Uncle Virgil" Blossom was superintendent of schools, but I was more interested in the fact that my cousin was a cheerleader and "popular" than that her father was instituting a dramatic social revolution in my city. I knew of course that Orval Faubus was governor of my state, but I was more impressed by the fact that my older brother made fun of Farrell Faubus's socially unacceptable, "country" white socks and blue jeans than that the governor was resisting integration. (xi)

We can add Sammie Dean Parker to this list of clueless white girls. According to one of Elizabeth's biographers, Sammie Dean has since complained that "because of the troubles at Central . . . she never got to be Miss Little Rock" (Margolick).

In August 2007, a blog entry in the *Arkansas Times* (Brantley) reminded readers of the chaos that had erupted at Central High fifty years earlier. It included the following comments by and about Ralph Brodie, who was president of the student council in 1957. Brodie has apparently "crusaded for years for a more sympathetic view of white students," and he "is angry at how the media have depicted whites at Central. He says 95% did not harass the black students."

> "I'm sure they were bullied . . . but that's history," Brodie says. . . . "When there are people you know who are having those problems, you got to mind your own business, and that's what most of us did." (Brantley)

While Brodie minded his own business, the black students were insulted, harassed, and threatened during their entire stay at the school. Imagine for a moment how different the history of these events might have been had the president of the student council offered to walk with Elizabeth to class.

White Blindness, White Supremacy

How could Ralph Brodie, along with Elizabeth Jacoway and Sammie Dean Parker and me, remain so blind to what was happening right in front of us? Our youth cannot excuse us, because Elizabeth saw reality only too clearly on that August day in 1957. No; we did not see because we are white. As whites, we were—and still are—in the grip of a pervasive ideology that confers many benefits on white people over and above the privilege of remaining blind to brutality. This point was powerfully made long ago by W. E. B. DuBois in his monumental *Black Reconstruction*, where he writes that during the late nineteenth and early twentieth centuries:

> [Whites] were given public deference and titles of courtesy because they were white. They were admitted freely with all classes of white people to public functions, public parks, and the best schools. The police were drawn from their ranks, and the courts, dependent upon their votes, treated them with such leniency as to encourage lawlessness. Their vote selected public officials, and while this had small effect upon the economic situation, it had great effect upon their personal treatment and the deference shown them. White schoolhouses were the best in the community, and conspicuously placed, and they cost anywhere from twice to ten times as much per capita as the colored schools. The newspapers specialized on news that flattered the poor whites and almost utterly ignored the Negro except in crime and ridicule. (700–01)

DuBois published *Black Reconstruction* in 1935. But African American citizens still suffer from the "public and psychological wages" paid to white people by white supremacist ideology. In 2006, Joe Feagin claimed that

> African Americans and other Americans of color are expected to defer to whites in regard to the values and operative norms imbedded in the society's major institutions. . . . From this white perspective . . . the phrase "American society" typically means white-controlled social

> institutions; the phrase "social values" (or "family values") typically means white-determined values; and the word "Americans" typically means "white Americans." (30)

These beliefs and assumptions are seldom articulated quite as clearly as they are by scholars such as DuBois and Feagin; that they are not a regular part of our civic discourse suggests to me that white supremacy is a hegemonic discourse in America. That is to say, most whites are unaware that they hold or practice white supremacist beliefs until some challenge, such as the integration of Little Rock Central High, forces their articulation.

I prefer the term "white supremacy" to "racism" because the former locates the trouble where it resides: not in some amorphous "race problem" but squarely among white people.[3] Used in this way, that is, to name a set of beliefs that can erase the interests of African Americans from white thought, "white supremacy" is not confined to a few radicals and nuts, but is widely distributed among white Americans.

Currently this ideology supports and maintains a state of near-apartheid in some parts of our country. While the civil rights movement achieved truly momentous legal and policy changes at the midpoint of the twentieth century, enforcement of those laws and policies has been difficult and uneven. Today, many American towns and cities remain effectively segregated, thanks to white flight and unwillingness to enforce open housing legislation. Because of *de facto* segregation, voting districts are easily gerrymandered to exclude minority voters from local and state elections. Public schools all over the nation are also segregated. Indeed, Peter Irons claims that "there has not been a single year in American history in which at least half of the nation's black children attended schools that were largely white" (338). And where residential patterns do not guarantee segregation, white people have created private "charter" schools and funded them with vouchers or tax credits so that their children may attend whites-only schools. Currently, then, the workplace and university campuses may be the only sites in American society where people of all backgrounds regularly meet and socialize. It is not a coincidence that affirmative action was once seriously enforced at both of these sites.

White Supremacy and Slavery

The ideology of white supremacy was articulated very early in American history. Common sense assumes that it developed in connection with the institution of slavery—but this assumption may not be quite right.[4] Slavery is far older than white supremacy; probably as old as humanity itself, or at least as old as the first conquest of one group by another (Davis 58). Slavery is of course a labor practice, part of an economy, and enslavement is not necessarily tied to any racial, religious, or geographical distinction between slavers and their victims. In ancient times, for example, conquering armies enslaved captured enemies, no matter who they were

(Garnsey 5). But a new form of slavery emerged with the dawn of capitalism: in ancient times, most slaves worked in households or on family farms, while on modern plantations gangs of anonymous slaves labored in huge rice or tobacco fields to produce commodities for people they would never meet (Evans 14–24). In the Old World, slavery was not necessarily a permanent condition: in ancient Rome, slaves were sometimes able to earn their way out of slavery, and during the Middle Ages Muslims enslaved in Europe could become free if they converted to Christianity. Under capitalism, however, people were permanently enslaved, and slaves knew that their children would be condemned to slavery as well.

In 1968, historian Winthrop Jordan investigated the origins of white supremacy in America. He assembled evidence establishing that white settlers in the American colonies certainly brought a set of xenophobic beliefs with them from England.[5] Africans were, of course, not Christian—such a condition denoted paganism or "heathenism" to the English. But, as Jordan notes, "heathenism was treated not so much as a specifically religious defect but as one manifestation of a general refusal to measure up to proper standards, as a failure to be English or even civilized" (24). In other words, the English reacted negatively to Africans because the latter were insufficiently English. But this does not explain how xenophobia devolved into white supremacy once English colonists emigrated to America.

The historical record of the early years of the tobacco colonies is scanty and confusing. We do know that a few Africans arrived in Virginia as early as 1619.[6] However, there is much disagreement among historians concerning the status of these early arrivals. Hugh Thomas notes that a "list of the living in Virginia" in 1624 included "twenty-two blacks, several of them presumably personal slaves of certain passengers on ships" (174). But Lerone Bennett Jr. asserts that Anthony Johnson and his family, like many other immigrants to the American colonies, were indentured servants: "the first black settlers fell into a well-established socioeconomic groove which carried with it no implications of racial inferiority. That came later" (35). Certainly, a few Africans and their descendants remained free, particularly in the northern colonies, throughout the colonial period. But Alden Vaughn assembles evidence to suggest that "the black men and women brought to Virginia from 1619 to 1629 held from the outset a singularly debased status in the eyes of white Virginians" ("Blacks" 129). Given the slim evidence available, Vaughn is unwilling to assert that these men and women were enslaved, but he does claim that "black Virginians were at least well on their way to such a condition" in these very early days of white settlement in the New World.

According to Edmund Morgan, as early as the 1640s in Virginia, "the courts clearly recognized property in men and women and their unborn progeny" (297). That "property" refers here to slaves rather than to indentured servants is suggested by the mention of progeny. If so, the notion of slavery as a permanent and inheritable condition was in use by white settlers only twenty years after the establishment of the first colonies. Morgan also notes court records that suggest that African Americans were enslaved in Virginia as early as the 1640s and 1650s (154). Jordan agrees that "between 1640 and 1660 there is evidence of enslavement, and after 1660 slavery crystallized on the statute books of Maryland, Virginia, and other colonies" (44). So we know that the practice of slavery was in place in American colonies by 1640, and was lent the authority of law after 1660.

Coincidently or not, between roughly 1660 and 1680 a series of laws were enacted that severely limited the social mobility of free Africans and African Americans. In 1661, for example, children born to African fathers and European mothers were condemned to servitude until the age of twenty; any white woman bearing such a child "would suffer severe public whipping and see her own service extended by as much as seven years" (Roediger, *How Race* 6). Maryland and Virginia both outlawed interracial sex in 1662 (Jordan 77–78). In 1668, lawmakers declared that free African American women "ought not in all respects be admitted to a full fruition of the exemptions and impunities of the English" (Allen 187).

Late in the seventeenth century the records begin to articulate connections between slavery and white supremacy. In 1670, the Virginia House of Burgesses passed legislation that mandated that non-Christians imported into the country by shipping (that is, captive Africans) were to become slaves for life (Morgan 329). The "shipping" clause exempted captive Native Americans from lifetime slavery. But the Burgesses closed this loophole in 1682, mandating that all non-Christians imported into Virginia were to be designated slaves. And, as Morgan writes, since they had "already decided in 1667 that conversion to Christianity after arrival did not alter the status of slave" and "since only Indians and Africans fitted this description . . . the act of 1682 set the further development of slavery on a squarely racial foundation" (329). Morgan summarizes: although "slavery might have come to Virginia without racism, it did not. The only slaves in Virginia belonged to alien races from the English. And the new social order that Virginians created after they changed to slave labor was determined as much by race as by slavery" (315).

So the available evidence suggests that in the American colonies white supremacy was articulated very early on—perhaps by 1640, probably by 1660, and surely by 1680. Jordan offers support for this reading when he notes a suggestive linguistic shift that occurred during the seventeenth century: while colonists had referred to themselves early on as "Christians," at midcentury "there was a marked drift toward 'English' and 'free.' After about 1680, taking the colonies as a whole, a new term appeared—'white'" (95). So linguistic evidence also suggests that by the mid-seventeenth century, colonists could make an ideological distinction among themselves based not on religion but on place of origin or culture; by the last decades of the century they could distinguish white people from everyone else.

Using this sort of evidence, contemporary historians have put forward a new reading of the origins of white supremacy.[7] They argue that the ideology was articulated by means of a series of conscious decisions made by wealthy planters, which were then enacted into law. That these laws were supremacist, rather than merely a means to protect property, becomes clear in the early eighteenth century. Theodore Allen cites a law passed by the Virginia Assembly in 1723 that disenfranchised all people of color: "No free negro, mulatto, or indian whatsoever, shall have any vote at the election of burgesses, or any other election whatsoever" (241). When free African Americans asked why the Assembly denied them this basic right of citizenship, the governor responded that the Assembly wished to "fix a perpetual Brand upon Free Negros and Mulattos" (242). Allen argues that this "was a deliberate act by the plantation bourgeoisie; it proceeded from a conscious decision in the process of establishing a system of racial oppression, even though it meant replacing an electoral principle that had existed in Virginia for more than a century" (242). In other words, the articulation of white supremacy was no accident; the law disenfranchising African Americans was preceded by a series of others enacted over a period of sixty or seventy years, laws that effectively discriminated African Americans from other inhabitants of the colonies. Thus the elite classes—which in Virginia, Maryland, and later in South Carolina, included planters and owners of huge tracts of land—deliberately wrote white supremacy into the laws of their colonies. Allen thinks they did this because they were afraid of rebellion by slaves and poor whites, as had occurred in Jamaica and on the continent in Bacon's Rebellion of 1676.

By 1730, Africans and African Americans constituted roughly 30% of the population of the eastern seaboard (Jordan 103). Planter William Byrd noted in 1736 that there were 10,000 African American men capable of bearing arms in Virginia, and hence he worried "in case there should arise a Man amongst us, exasperated by a desperate fortune he might . . . kindle a Servile War" (Allen 245). In 1749, two members of the Virginia Council warned that "convict bond-laborers . . . who are wicked enough to join our Slaves in any Mischief . . . in all Probability will bring sure and sudden Destruction on all His Majesty's good subjects of this colony" (Allen 245). So planters exploited the available racial distinctions to ensure the loyalty of poorer white people to their aims and desires. As David Roediger puts it, "the turn to racial slavery was a response to sharp social divisions among settlers and sought to create an ersatz unity among whites, indeed by creating 'white' itself as a social and legal category" (*How Race* 3). The roots of white supremacy, then, lay in "popular protest and in the elite's recognition of the rage of the poor" (3).

I want to dwell on this point for a moment because it is crucially important to understanding how white supremacy took hold in this country. American colonists discovered early on that great profits could be had in growing tobacco on a large scale. Planters also learned that they could not maintain a reliable labor force consisting of indentured servants from England who, once they completed their contracts, were free to develop unclaimed land and found plantations of their own. And so the planters turned to African captives, whose children would be born enslaved, in order to insure continuity of the labor force. The growth of unfree labor was exponential: between 1673 and 1725, just one slave-trading company sold 75,000 slaves in the English colonies, and in that era dozens of slave ships regularly visited our shores (Thomas 203). While there were about 180,000 enslaved persons in the colonies in 1650, by the end of the century there were well over half a million (Evans 31). Thanks to the growth of plantations enabled by slave labor, and the wealth they produced, unclaimed land became scarce and wealthy planters began to squeeze small householders out of business in other ways as well (Morgan 216ff). And so the danger arose that land-poor English colonists might join with slaves to foment disturbances against rule by the wealthy (Blackburn 322). In order to forestall social unrest or outright rebellion by an alliance of slaves, indentured servants, and landless whites, members of the planter class consciously and deliberately created an "ersatz unity" among white people, chiefly by means of proscriptive legislation against social interaction between blacks and whites. Robin Blackburn puts it like this:

> The slave trader and slaveholder introduced to the colonies a category of person who—they themselves insisted—was dangerous, capable of any atrocity if not closely watched and controlled. Once it reached a certain threshold, the introduction of Africans as slaves stimulated a racial fear and solidarity which helped to secure the slaveowner in possession of his property. Racial fear was probably as important as white privilege in rallying the support of independent white smallholders. Fear and privilege, both constituted with reference to black slaves, possessed the ability spontaneously to interpellate white people, making them see themselves as slaves might see them—that is, as members of a ruling race—and thus to furnish them with core elements of their social identity. (323–24)

Of course white supremacy was never universally accepted among whites; early laws against miscegenation establish that blacks and whites indeed socialized and married one another. Whites who opposed slavery early on did so primarily on religious or moral grounds. In 1689, for instance, Cotton Mather denounced slave owners who refused knowledge of the gospel to slaves (Aptheker 20). And in 1700 Samuel Sewell, a justice of the Massachusetts provincial court, published a tract that equated slavery to man-stealing. He was answered in 1701 by a fellow justice named John Saffin, a slave holder who apparently took Sewell's pamphlet as "a personal affront" (Tise 17). Even at this early date, Saffin's defense of slavery is rife with white supremacist arguments that I will not rehearse here but which were repeated, ad nauseam, by proponents of slavery throughout the eighteenth century and beyond.[8] I will say that neither

Saffin nor the hundreds of slavery sympathizers who echoed his sentiments down through the years noticed or admitted that the characteristics they attributed to African Americans were among the only available defenses slaves possessed against their oppressors.

The ideology undergirding slavery required more highly elaborated defenses during the Revolutionary period, when the discourse of civic republicanism became commonplace. Citizens who waged a violent revolution to achieve liberty and equality had to somehow reconcile their denial of those same privileges to a large portion of the population. Free African Americans used civic republican rhetoric throughout the late eighteenth century to mount powerful arguments against slavery and white supremacy (Bay 20). In 1792, for example, Benjamin Banneker wrote to Thomas Jefferson, asking Jefferson to acknowledge that "however variable we may be in society or religion, however diversified in situation or color, we are all in the same family and stand in the same relation to [God]" (Aptheker 16). Needless to say, Jefferson was not impressed (Bay 17).

White Supremacy After Slavery

Slavery was outlawed in 1863 by the Emancipation Proclamation. If the ideology of white supremacy was established to protect slavery, and if that were its only use, it should have disappeared after the Civil War. But it did not. After emancipation, wealthy and powerful white people resisted sharing their property and status with newly freed persons, and they marshaled the old belief in an "ersatz unity" among whites in order to insure that black families could not prosper. Belief in white supremacy grew so fierce, and its associated practices so violent, between Reconstruction and the First World War that historian Rayford Logan called this period "the 'nadir' of the African-American experience" (qtd. in Fredrickson 81). During the late nineteenth century and into the twentieth, entire communities of relatively prosperous African Americans were simply wiped off the map by arson and mass murder. To be sure, the Black Codes and the midnight rides of the Klan, and later, Jim Crow, served to segregate black Americans from white.[9] But I suspect that another motive for this fifty-year reign of terror was to insure that black people did not accrue wealth or civic power. Certainly, the effects of a long history of legal and financial deprivation are still being felt in black communities.[10] Had black families received the fabled "forty acres and a mule" when they were promised to them in recompense for a century of enslavement, their descendants might have been able to practice the sort of entrepreneurship that is associated with the fabled American dream, despite the level of violent harassment they endured. I would also like to note that the "ersatz unity" forged by white supremacy nearly always benefits powerful whites at the expense of those less well off; no corporation was charged with slavery during the late nineteenth century when black men accused of minor legal infractions were sold into debt peonage to work in mines and mills for no wages at all, nor were any wealthy Alabama businessmen jailed during the civil rights era for instigating the Klan atrocities carried out by so-called "poor whites" (Blackmon; Sokol).

White supremacy was not disarticulated by civil rights legislation, despite bogus claims that we now live in a post-racial society.[11] This claim is itself a manifestation of white supremacy—skin color is a matter of indifference in this country only among whites dealing with other whites. Furthermore, very public examples of supremacist thought appear regularly in the media: spectacular examples include Don Imus' infamous reference to the Rutgers' women's basketball team and Chris Matthews saying after a State of the Union address that he forgot for a moment that Obama is black. But white blindness is not limited to the famous. Ordinary Americans who say they are "tired of hearing about race" are ignoring the widespread nature of white supremacy and the intensity with which it is felt and expressed; those who plaintively ask, "Why is everything always about race?" are ignorant of American history, which, as I hope I have suggested here, is *all* about race.

Surely the disgusting displays that accompanied protests against health care reform can be taken as nothing other than expressions of white supremacist rage. The incoherent demands of the Tea Party suggest to me that the so-called "conservative revolution" of the past 40 years is as much a reaction to legislative gains made by the modern civil rights movement as it is to taxes or health care reform or anything else. These people have never gotten over the *Brown* decision, much less the Civil Rights Acts of 1964 and 1965. The angry demonstrations bring to mind the words of William J. Wilson, writing in the *Anglo-African Magazine* as "Ethiop," from whose essay I borrow my title:

> If we look into [whites'] social state, we shall discover but strife, bitterness, and distraction. Not those honest and frank differences of opinion that beget and strengthen sound opinion, but low petty captiousness and cowardly vindictiveness, everywhere pervade. On looking over the county as a whole, we see section divided against section and clan pitted against clan, and each cheered on by fierce leaders and noisy demagogues on the one side; while compromises and harmony and quiet are sued for on the other. (62)

Wilson wrote these apt words 150 years ago. Apparently, in the meantime, our race privilege has not demonstrably helped white people to become markedly better citizens.

Notes

[1] I borrow my title from William J. Wilson, whose 1860 essay is conveniently reprinted in Roediger, *Black on White*, pp. 58–66.

[2] Accounts of this event can be found in Jacoway, Margolick, Roberts and Klibanoff, Sokol, participant autobiographies, and in general histories of the twentieth century civil rights

movement. Many years later Mary Ann Burleson recalled that on the day the photograph was taken, Hazel Bryan "was 'rather pleased with herself'—so much so that two days later, she was in front of Central again, telling reporters that no way would she attend an integrated Central High School. 'Whites should have rights, too!' she said, into a television camera" (Margolick). Sammie Dean was later suspended from Central High for harassing the black students, and when one of the nine, Minniejean Brown, was expelled by the school board for "failure to adjust," Sammie Dean distributed cards that said "One down, eight to go."

3 White supremacy negatively affects the lives and prosperity of many Americans: Native Americans, African Americans, Asian Americans, Latinos, and most recently, Americans of Middle Eastern origin. But even though white supremacy plays out differently in each of these relations, they share in common the belief among white people that America is primarily a white nation. See Rittenhouse for a useful study of how the ideology of white supremacy is instilled in children.

"Race" and "racism" are notoriously difficult to define. The first term has no biological referent; that is to say, "race" does not exist outside of the ideologies within which it is wielded. Scholars tend to define these terms in ways that serve their aims, so there is little agreement among them. For useful discussions of the definitional issues, see Isaac (pp. 15–39) and Fredrickson (pp. 6–10). Feminist philosopher Shannon Sullivan suggests that white supremacy may be distinguished from white privilege insofar as the former is conscious while the latter is unconscious (190). Sullivan does not mean "unconscious" in a determined or fully Freudian sense wherein the unconscious is inaccessible to rational reflection, but in the sense that it is literally embodied in habit. This distinction has the advantage of rendering habit subject to change. I am not sure what Sullivan gains by making this distinction; it might not have been necessary had she based her model of belief on the work of Pierre Bourdieu or Judith Butler, who begin their accounts of habit with the social, rather than on a Freudian account that she is forced to surround with qualifications and emendations.

4 The relation of white supremacy to slavery is a contentious issue among academic historians, who regularly complain about the shortcomings of those who have previously addressed the issue. See, for example, Eric Foner's excoriation of the Dunning School in the preface of *Reconstruction,* and the last chapter of Theodore Allen's *The Invention of the White Race*. Clearly there are grounds for this complaint; white historians are no more free of the grip of white supremacy than are other white Americans. For historiographic overviews of work on the relation of white supremacy to slavery, see Kolchin and Vaughn, "The Origins Debate."

In one of the first historical essays to reflect the philosophy of the burgeoning civil rights movement, Mary and Oscar Handlin argued that slavery was in place well before white supremacy was invented. This claim infers that the degraded condition of slavery itself eventually led colonial whites to believe in their superiority. A few years later Winthrop Jordan argued, to the contrary, that slavery grew and flourished because a set of xenophobic beliefs was in place among white colonists prior to their acceptance of slavery. While this version of history is not necessarily conservative as long as its proponents perceive that xenophobia and white supremacy are cultural constructs, as Jordan does, the claim that supremacy preceded the institution of slavery does appeal to conservatives and libertarians whose worldview is based on the notion that a natural hierarchy exists among humankind. Needless to say, the hierarchy argument was very popular among slave owners. See Tise for examples.

5 Xenophobia and racism are not the same thing (Fredrickson 6). Xenophobia (fear of the other) refers to the apparently widespread tendency among human groups to see themselves and their culture as different from, and perhaps superior to, those of other groups. Benjamin Isaac distinguishes xenophobia from "proto-racism" as follows: when a group presumes that its superiority to another is due to "heredity or unalterable exterior influences, it is possible to speak of proto-racism" (37). That is to say, racism introduces a notion of determinism, whether biological, psychic, or environmental. As Isaac notes:

> If we find that a people is described as having the mentality of slaves because they are ruled by a king, then this is not racism, but ethnic prejudice. If, however, we read that people are stupid and courageous because they live in a cold climate, then it can be argued that this is a form of proto-racism, since there is an implicit assumption that these people are stupid through physical factors beyond their control. Their descendants will remain stupid, because the climate of their country will not change. (37–38)

Capitalism was perhaps instrumental in altering Anglo-American xenophobia into racism; as David Harvey remarks, "Capitalism did not invent 'the other' but it certainly made use of and promoted it in highly structured ways" (104).

[6] Historians of this issue focus on Virginia—and Maryland to a lesser extent—because their inhabitants had little contact with the Spanish and Portuguese colonies in the Indies, where slavery and the slave trade had flourished for almost a century prior to their founding. This was not true of say, South Carolina, where the principal crop was rice, and whose planter class assumed from the beginning that they had to rely on slave labor in order to make a profit. According to Jordan, the unique history of the tobacco colonies makes it possible to trace the development of slavery and "the shadowy, unexamined rationale which supported it" (72).

[7] This group includes Allen, Blackburn, Evans, Nash, and Roediger. Allen's reading rethinks Jordan's assumption that the articulation of white supremacy with slavery was incidental or "an unthinking decision." William McKee Evans writes that "the planter class wove these racial laws and court decisions into the new social fabric" (43). And Gary Nash claims that during the late seventeenth century, "southern colonizers were able to forge a consensus among upper- and lower-class whites . . . race became the primary badge of status" (244–45).

[8] Saffin included a poem of his own composition in his reply:

> Cowardly and Cruel are those Blacks Innate,
> Prone to Revenge, Imp of inveterate hate.
> He that exasperates them, soon espies
> Mischief and Murder in their very eyes.
> Libidinous, Deceitful, False and Rude,
> The Spume Issue of Ingratitude. (qtd. in Tise 18)

[9] For histories of the depredations wreaked on African Americans during this period, see, for starters, Blackmon, Foner, Kennedy, Wade, Wells, and White.

[10] Feagin's research establishes a firm connection between centuries of economic deprivation and current levels of poverty among African Americans. See Feagin, "Documenting" and *Systematic*, pp. 18–20.

[11] See D'Souza, for example. What has changed is that overt expressions of white supremacy have gone underground, at least in polite society. Sociologist Eduardo Bonilla-Silva has helpfully identified a few of the discursive dodges that whites currently use to assure ourselves that we are not white supremacists—see *Racism Without Racists*, pp. 28–52.

Works Cited

Allen, Theodore. *The Invention of the White Race*. Vol. 2. London: Verso, 1997.

Aptheker, Herbert. *Anti-Racism in U.S. History: The First Two Hundred Years*. Westport, CT: Greenwood P, 1992.

Bay, Mia. *The White Image in the Black Mind*. New York: Oxford UP, 2000.

Bennett, Lerone, Jr. *Before the Mayflower: A History of Black America*. New York: Viking, 1961.

Blackburn, Robin. *The Making of New World Slavery*. London: Verso, 1997.

Blackmon, Douglas. *Slavery by Another Name: The Re-Enslavement of Black Americans from the Civil War to World War II*. New York: Doubleday, 2008.

Bonilla-Silva, Eduardo. *Racism Without Racists: Color-Blind Racism and the Persistence of Racial Inequality in the United States*. 2nd ed. Oxford: Rowman & Littlefield, 2006.

Brantley, Max. "The Great Chili Incident." *Arkansas Blog. The Arkansas Times,* 30 Aug. 2007. Web. 7 Jan. 2010.

Davis, David Brion. *Inhuman Bondage: The Rise and Fall of Slavery in the New World*. New York: Oxford, 2006.

D'Souza, Dinesh. *The End of Racism: Principles for a Multicultural Society.* New York: The Free P, 1995.

DuBois, W. E. B. *Black Reconstruction*. New York: The Free P, 1935.

"Ethiop" (William J. Wilson). "What Shall We Do with the White People?" *Black on White: Black Writers on What It Means to Be White*. Ed. David Roediger. New York: Shocken Books, 1998. 58–66.

Evans, William McKee. *Open Wound: The Long View of Race in America*. Urbana: U of Illinois P, 2009.

Feagin, Joe. "Documenting the Costs of Slavery, Segregation, and Contemporary Discrimination: Are Reparations in Order for African Americans?" *National Coalition of Blacks for Reparations in America*. 2000. Web. 7 Jan. 2010.

———. *Systematic Racism: A Theory of Oppression*. New York: Routledge, 2006.

Foner, Eric. *Reconstruction: America's Unfinished Revolution, 1863–1877*. New York: Harper and Row, 1988.

Fredrickson, George. *Racism: A Short History.* Princeton: Princeton UP, 2002.

Garnsey, Peter. *Ideas of Slavery from Aristotle to Augustine*. Cambridge: Cambridge UP, 1996.

Handlin, Oscar, and Mary Handlin. "Origins of the Southern Labor System." *William and Mary Quarterly* 3rd ser. 7 (1950): 199–222.

Harvey, David. *The Condition of Postmodernity: An Enquiry into the Origins of Social Change*. Cambridge, MA: Blackwell, 1989.

Irons, Peter. *Jim Crow's Children: The Broken Promise of the "Brown" Decision*. New York: Viking, 2002.

Isaac, Benjamin. *The Invention of Racism in Classical Antiquity.* Princeton: Princeton UP, 2004.

Jacoway, Elizabeth. *Turn Away Thy Son: Little Rock, The Crisis that Shocked the Nation*. New York: The Free P, 2007.

Jordan, Winthrop. *White Over Black: American Attitudes Toward the Negro, 1550–1812.* Chapel Hill: U of North Carolina P, 1968.

Kennedy, Stetson. *After Appomattox: How the South Won the War.* Gainesville: UP of Florida, 1995.

Kolchin, Peter. "Review Essay: Putting New World Slavery in Perspective." *Slavery and Abolition* 28.2 (Aug. 2007): 277–88.

Margolick, David. "Through a Lens Darkly." *Vanity Fair* 24 Sept. 2007. Web. 6 Jan. 2010.

Morgan, Edmund. *American Slavery, American Freedom: The Ordeal of Colonial Virginia*. New York: Norton, 1975.

Nash, Gary. "Social Development." *Colonial British America: Essays in the New History of the Modern Era*. Ed. Jack P. Greene and J. R. Pole. London: Johns Hopkins, 1984. 233–61.

Rittenhouse, Jennifer. *Growing Up Jim Crow: How Black and White Southern Children Learned Race.* Chapel Hill: U of North Carolina P, 2006.

Roberts, Gene, and Hank Klibanoff. *The Race Beat: The Press, the Civil Rights Struggle, and the Awakening of a Nation*. New York: Vintage, 2007.

Roediger, David, ed. *Black on White: Black Writers on What It Means to Be White*. New York: Shocken Books, 1998.

———. *How Race Survived U.S. History from Settlement and Slavery to the Obama Phenomenon*. London: Verso, 2008

Sokol, Jason. *There Goes My Everything: White Southerners in the Age of Civil Rights, 1945–1975*. New York: Vintage, 2007.

Sullivan, Shannon. *Revealing Whiteness: The Unconscious Habits of Racial Privilege*. Bloomington: Indiana UP, 2006.

Thomas, Hugh. *The Slave Trade: The Story of the Atlantic Slave Trade: 1440–1870*. New York: Simon and Schuster, 1997.

Tise, Larry. *Proslavery: A History of the Defense of Slavery in America, 1701–1840*. Athens: U of Georgia P, 1987.

Vaughn, Alden T. "Blacks in Virginia: Evidence from the First Decade." *Roots of American Racism: Essays on the Colonial Experience*. New York: Oxford UP, 1995. 128–35.

———. "The Origins Debate: Slavery and Racism in Seventeenth-Century Virginia." *Roots of American Racism: Essays on the Colonial Experience*. New York: Oxford UP, 1995. 136–74.

Wade, Wyn Craig. *The Fiery Cross: The Ku Klux Klan in America*. New York: Oxford UP, 1987.

Wells, Ida B. *The Red Record: Tabulated Statistics and Alleged Causes of Lynching in the United States. Project Gutenberg*. 2005. Project Gutenberg Literary Archive Foundation. Web. 7 Jan. 2010.

White, Walter. *Rope and Faggot: A Biography of Judge Lynch*. New York: Knopf, 1929.

2

Concord and Controversy on August 28, 1963

Jack Selzer

I want to begin by thanking you all for bringing such intelligence and energy to our conference this week, and for staying around to listen to me speak today.[1] The biennial conference of RSA has been especially challenging this year because of the circumstances that arose as it was being framed this past winter—we lost a large portion of our collective heart and soul and mind when Michael Leff died so suddenly on February 5—and the quality of our meeting is especially notable given those circumstances. You have already heard me recognize so many people who came together to make the conference come off well, especially Mike's colleagues at Memphis—but I thank everyone in this room as well for your patience as the conference program was being constructed and even more for the wonderful papers that you have been offering, many of which will be appearing in our conference book and in other publications to come. It's been a team effort, hasn't it?

My topic today has everything to do with team effort too. It's the product of my attempt to think seriously about the theme of our conference, dreamed up by Michael Leff: "Rhetoric: Concord and Controversy." Invoking Kenneth Burke and Cicero, wouldn't you know it, and attentive to the rhetorical currents swirling in contemporary culture, Mike called attention to one of his favorite professional paradoxes. There are, he noted,

> two opposing dimensions of rhetoric, the one divisive and conflictive, the other irenic and unifying. . . . Rhetoric simultaneously divides and unifies, separates as it identifies; and it dwells most naturally in the in-between space where sameness and difference ambiguously embrace one another. . . . Where do diversity and sameness meet on the human tongue and in the human condition?

Mike wanted us to meditate together on this foundational paradox, the fundamental tension between concord and controversy that seems at the same time so natural and inevitable; the imperative toward concord emerges from and assumes the presence of controversy, and the presence of controversy, it seems, breeds (as long as we are patient) a drive toward concord. A necessary symbiosis, if you will. And while citing my professional hero, Burke, Mike challenged us to attend always to this paradox as we make the link between our professional calling as rhetorical scholars and our personal duty as public rhetors and citizens. How do these two impulses—division and consubstantiation, Burke called them—inevitably coexist? To what extent is it true that the conflicting and the irenic must accompany each other? Ever since Mike extended to me the honor of giving this luncheon plenary talk, I have been trying to think of how this paradox might and might not be so, in rhetorical life and in the life of our profession, as a kind of test of Mike's hypothesis.

A natural testing ground on which to study the issue would seem to be the landscape before the Lincoln Memorial, site of our most canonical national rhetorical performance, Martin Luther King's "I Have a Dream" oration, delivered on August 28, 1963. In the process of considering King's speech, I will be highlighting the tensions between concord and controversy as they developed before and during that day. But I will also be offering my own modest recommendation for how to *study* rhetorical action, for that is the real point of what I offer today. My method has been inspired by Kenneth Burke, refined by the work and example of many people at this conference, and is rooted in the metaphor of conversation—because in that metaphor, I am convinced, lies one means of recovering both concord and controversy in a way that can be as consistently telling for analysis as it is for production.

So I'm not promising anything terribly telling or original concerning King's trademark speech. I really can't hope to teach the people here anything especially new about what King said, because many of you have taught the speech at one time or another and because we have a number of experts in this room who have commented tellingly upon it already. (Two of them, Keith Miller and Keith Gilyard, are sitting right in front of me as I speak; Bob Hariman is here too; and my new colleague Kirt Wilson will be sharing Penn State space beginning in August. Among others.) But I do hope to illustrate the *method of analysis* that I am recommending, enriching along the way (if all goes well) your understanding of King's performance. What I'll be doing is recapturing some of the conversations, the discourses, that were swirling about it on that sultry August afternoon, as a way of illustrating how King's words were embroidered within larger networks of discourses that were in play, often in competition, in the summer of 1963. I will be attentive in particular to the voices of dissensus that were operating within the civil rights movement, although you'll be hearing about expressions of concord too. And in reconstructing that conversation, I will be looking to recover lost and forgotten voices in particular. Our collective task, as Mike Leff reminded us, is to attend to both concord and controversy, and that goes too for interpretations of the civil rights movement, which is still too frequently viewed as unrelievedly triumphal, unrelievedly unified and cohesive, the happy crusade of dedicated heroes sacrificing and subordinating themselves and working in harmony to win out against intractable Evil and oh-so-easy-to-recognize Villains.

Let's start with two images.

Abraham Lincoln at the dedication of the Gettysburg National Cemetery, November 19, 1863. Library of Congress.

Martin Luther King Jr., "I Have a Dream" speech, March on Washington, August 28, 1963. AP Images.

These are the two iconic moments in American public oratory, aren't they? According to conventional lore, Lincoln's speech changed American history—the subtitle of Garry Wills's prize-winning book on the speech is *The Words That Remade America*. Single-handedly on that November day in 1863, the legend holds, Lincoln invented a new national identity by informing Americans that the promise of the Declaration of Independence, in particular the words "all men are created equal," could be realized only through a commitment to a "new birth of freedom" made on civil war battlefields and in the hearts and minds of Americans. But we know now, through the work of several scholars (e.g., David Zarefsky and Linda Selzer), that Lincoln did not alone invent those words or create independently any summons to a new birth of freedom—his references to the Declaration of Independence were part of a long tradition stretching back decades that included women arguing for equal rights; Harriet Beecher Stowe's amazingly popular *Uncle Tom's Cabin*; Lincoln's own speech of July 7 that same year; and Frederick Douglass's 1852 Fourth of July oration; among many others. So we know better than to over-aggrandize the power of individual rhetors; we understand emancipation *not* as a revolutionary act by A Great Individual, but as an evolutionary and continuing change accomplished communally over time; and nowadays, rather than sitting him on a lonely throne upon a pedestal, we put Lincoln into group portraits, as is the case (for instance) in Doris Kearns Goodwin's popular recent book *Team of Rivals*.

My point today is very simple and, as I indicated, not especially original: I want to offer a reminder that in our scholarship and in our teaching we must do the same with "I Have a Dream" and with all the other rhetorical exchanges that we teach. It's about teamwork. August 28, 1963, was not just King's day, King's words did not emerge independently or without discord or challenge. "I Have a Dream" was only one instrument being played in 1963 within an uneasy orchestra of often contending discourses.

I have time today to make my point by concentrating on two moments.

The first occurred in mid-June 1963, the period when the March was being formally authorized. June 11, 1963, to June 25, 1963, was one of the most fantastic fortnights in American history. As I think back on those weeks in my own life, there was on the one hand a normalcy to it all—I had just completed my freshman year at almost-all-white McNicholas High School in an almost-all-white suburb of mostly segregated Cincinnati, Ohio. Having played center field as a freshman on our excellent high school team (on May 10 we lost in the district finals to Elder, a team we had already beaten twice that year), I had the summer baseball season, the upcoming football season of my sophomore year, and my first girlfriend on my mind, and I would be spending that summer playing baseball games for Murphy's Tugboats or doing informal football workouts two or three evenings and afternoons a week with teammates I had been playing with since third grade (and who in some cases remain my friends today). My family was an overwhelming influence: My parents had my seven brothers and sisters locked into safe rhythms of life—doing outside chores around the house, preparing and consuming and cleaning up after meals, enjoying together the regular festival of whiteness known as network TV (Walt Disney and *Bonanza* on Sunday, *The Andy Griffith Show* on Monday, *The Dick Van Dyke Show* on Wednesday, *My Three Sons* on Thursday, *Gunsmoke* on Saturday), all within the predictable cycles of churchgoing and schooling and growing up. Judging from the letters in The Kenneth Burke Papers that I have examined, the times were on the surface unremarkable for Burke as well: you have to look very hard to find even indirect references to civil rights in Burke's 1963 correspondence and in the publications he was producing. During that fortnight in June, he had been reestablishing himself at his Andover homestead, working in his garden, reconnecting with his extended family (the height of the three growing Chapin boys is to this day recorded on a door frame at Andover: "June 12, 1963"), and (having recently retired from Bennington College) resettling his writing schedule after a busy ten-week semester teaching a graduate seminar in literary criticism at Penn State. It seems that on June 3 he had left the State College home he had rented on Glenn Road, right down the street from where I would live with my family from 1986 to 1996—but now I'm getting off the subject. . . .

And yet oblivious and as unengaged as I was, there was really no way of ignoring the spectacular events taking place that June. If TV was still very white, top 40 music most decidedly was not: the Beach Boys, Bobby Vinton, and The Four Seasons were now sharing time with The Crystals and Stevie Wonder; the Ronettes may have looked white (particularly their beehive hairdos), but their music sounded like R&B and Motown; Martha and the Vandellas were singin' about a heat wave; and Bob Dylan's answer was already blowin' in the wind. If *Lawrence of Arabia, Dr. No,* and *How the West Was Won* were the hit movies that I was seeing (I passed on *Cleopatra,* starring Liz Taylor and Richard Burton, which opened in Cincinnati on June 22), I would also be taking in *To Kill a Mockingbird* with Gregory Peck, which unveiled at Cannes on May 19. I've consumed the daily newspaper since I first learned to read because it fed my interest in sports, and the *Cincinnati Enquirer*[2] and the *Cincinnati Post and Times-Star* (one arriving in the morning, one in the afternoon), insular as they were, were emphasizing the turmoil around the world—and so I still remember the sensational headlines: liberation political actions in Africa; speculation about the prospects for the Second Vatican Council since the astounding Pope John XXIII had died on June 3; Gordon Cooper's orbit around the earth in mid-May, and the Soviet answer, a launch of the first woman into space on June 16; David Ben-Gurion's resignation as prime minister of Israel; the Supreme Court ruling outlawing prayer and Bible-reading in public schools on June 17; and political and military developments in a place called Vietnam, where Buddhists were resisting the corrupt Diem regime, setting themselves aflame, and forcing *Life* magazine consumers like me to turn their thoughts to Indo-China.

If school had just let out for the summer in Cincinnati, one school elsewhere was gripping national attention because on Monday, June 11, Governor George Wallace finally ended his lengthy resistance to the integration of the University of Alabama in the face of strong federal pressure (embodied in Bobby Kennedy and federalized National Guard troops). During May and June, most notably in Birmingham, Alabama, but in 185 other communities as well (according to Taylor Branch [825]), at least 758 demonstrations had taken place related to civil rights, almost 15,000 people had been arrested, and countless acts of violence had been perpetrated on African Americans. Some of that turmoil had touched Cincinnati. The local NAACP chapter announced a drive to get 50,000 additional Negroes onto the voting rolls in the Cincinnati area, and I still remember well that my school had been embroiled in nothing less than a race-related riot that I witnessed during a basketball game in March 1962. Integration was in progress, in other words, but very fitfully, and my friends who worked at the amusement park swimming pool three miles from my house were reporting occasional difficulties enforcing the segregation conventions that African American Cincinnatians were challenging: the Coney Island park, rides, and amusements were desegregated in 1952, but not its pool.

On the evening of June 11, flush with the triumph over Wallace but chastened and sobered by all that civil unrest, President Kennedy was moved suddenly to address the nation, and I recall watching television with my parents and older siblings in our family room as he used the Alabama incidents as the occasion to announce plans for civil rights legislation that would ensure desegregated facilities and schools, as well as voting rights. Departing at several points from his semi-prepared text, from the heart Kennedy offered ringing endorsements of freedom, a word he used a dozen times in his twelve minutes on television—for informally, but very widely, the slogan for that summer had already become "Free in '63." [At this point a clip of part of Kennedy's speech was shown; the entire speech is available on YouTube.]

Let me repeat a few of those words:

> This nation was founded on the principle that all men are created equal, [and] one hundred years have passed since President Lincoln freed the slaves, . . . yet their heirs are not fully free. . . . Now is the time for this nation to fulfill its promise.

Three hours later NAACP leader Medgar Evers was murdered at his home in Jackson, Mississippi.

I wasn't shocked at the murder in the sense of being surprised, to be honest. There was lots of big talk and furtive whispering in my respectable, segregated suburb about acquiring guns and guarding access to our community, and while I never saw or heard any gunplay myself, I read about it in the papers; and in the following summers, National Guardsmen would patrol the peaceful streets that I walked home from school on with a show of force to discourage vigilantism. The Evers funeral took place in Jackson on June 15 (he was then buried in Arlington National Cemetery on June 19), and on the days before and following, as John Doar was facing down a potential riot in Jackson, Kennedy was convening a June 22 meeting at the White House that would include King, representing the Southern Christian Leadership Conference (SCLC); 74-year-old A. Phillip Randolph, the venerable labor-leading head of the Brotherhood of Sleeping Car Porters; John Lewis, newly elected chair of the Student Nonviolent Coordinating Committee; Walter Reuther of the United Auto Workers; Bobby Kennedy; LBJ; Whitney Young of the Urban League; and of course Roy Wilkins, leader of the NAACP.

The assembled leaders discussed the particulars of the civil rights legislation, the bipartisan support it had attracted, the means of overcoming the likely Senate filibuster opposing it, as well as the advisability of a march on Washington in support of that legislation. Kennedy, though skeptical, did not oppose the march, but others certainly did. One of those opponents was someone not invited to the meeting: Malcolm X claimed many times that the meeting was simply an effort to co-opt the liberation movement by integrating and domesticating it. But another opponent of the march *was* present, Roy Wilkins. "Fresh" from a stretch in the Jackson jail himself, Wilkins vociferously objected to the march partly out of a continuing rivalry with King, partly out of a concern that financial resources dedicated to the NAACP would end up elsewhere, partly because of rumors that communists were behind the march, and partly out of his concerns about a violent backlash from the white community (as realized in the murder of Evers). Should the NAACP retain its leadership position, or share it with (or even yield it to) unruly but impassioned grassroots marching-in-the-streets movements? (Recall that the NAACP and SNCC had openly ridiculed and mocked King's actions during the Albany Movement of 1962, that the most recent issue of *The Saturday Evening Post* had accused King of "arrogance and opportunism," and that the "triumph" we now understand as the Birmingham campaign had by no means been yet secured—as the murders of four little girls, among others, would prove on September 15.)

Randolph meanwhile had already been planning an October march of his own in support of job opportunities, having, well, dreamed of such a thing since at least 1941. As Malcolm X related in his *Autobiography*, a grassroots movement for a march had been percolating that spring in concert with Randolph's plans. And so when Randolph accepted leadership of an August march instead, its agenda was expanded: it would be "a march for jobs *and* freedom."

The next day after that June 22 meeting, Kennedy left for Europe. On June 23, he was greeted in Bonn by a half million cheering Germans. Toward the end of his trip, on June 26, he gave the most ringing freedom speech of his public life, the memorable "I am a Berliner" address. Fifteen of the 671 words Kennedy used that day were "free" or "freedom" in his challenge to the world, which Ronald Reagan reprised in 1987 and that Barack

Obama knew all too well when he spoke in the same city in the summer of 2008. Kennedy's speech is conventionally remembered as a cold war call for the end of the Berlin Wall and for political openness in East Berlin and East Germany, but his words were constructed as much by events in Africa, Birmingham, Jackson, Albany, and throughout the segregated north and south.

And they were constructed in part by words spoken in Detroit as well. While Kennedy was being welcomed in Bonn (and Klansman Byron Beckwith was being arrested for the murder of Medgar Evers), King was being welcomed in Detroit, appearing at a huge, effervescent, and peaceful rally and march—twenty years to the day after a bloody Detroit riot claimed thirty-four lives and required, even during wartime, the installation of federal troops. Over 125,000 people took part in the march down broad Woodward Avenue on that Sunday, June 23—but not with the support of the NAACP and not without all kinds of local feuding, documented authoritatively by Taylor Branch (842–43) and many others. The Detroit march was organized not by the NAACP, but by the legendary Reverend C. L. Franklin—son of Mississippi sharecroppers and pastor of New Bethel Baptist Church in Detroit—famous as "The Million Dollar Voice" because his sermons were carried on the radio and because of his wonderful singing voice. (You may have heard of his daughter, Aretha.) Supporters of Franklin, who had invited King, were calling NAACP leaders "a bunch of Uncle Toms"; NAACP leaders publicly boycotted the rally, and for another month, Roy Wilkins would remain suspicious and unsupportive of such popular uprisings unless they were explicitly sanctioned by his NAACP. The Detroit march was also opposed by a growing body of black nationalists, impatient with nonviolence and integration, who ridiculed Franklin and regarded King himself as a Tom. Five months later, after all, on November 10 at another Detroit rally (this one publicly opposed by Franklin), Malcolm X would rip and ridicule the March on Washington—in his famous anti-King diatribe, "Message to the Grassroots"—as a white-managed conspiracy and "sellout," the Farce on Washington (281).

But let me resist the temptation to digress too much further from June 23. At the end of the Detroit march, King offered his full support to Kennedy's proposed legislation, concluding his 48-minute speech this way [here was played a three-minute excerpt, including this peroration]:

> And if we will do [all] this we will be able to bring that new day of freedom into being. If we will do this we will be able to make the American dream a reality. And I do not want to give you the impression that it's going to be easy. There can be no great social gain without individual pain. And before the victory for brotherhood is won, some will have to get scarred up a bit. Before the victory is won, some more will be thrown into jail. Before the victory is won, some, like Medgar Evers, may have to face physical death. But if physical death is the price that some must pay to free their children and their white brothers from an eternal psychological death, then nothing can be

more redemptive. Before the victory is won, some will be misunderstood and called bad names, but we must go on with a determination and with a faith that this problem can be solved. [*Applause*]

And so I go back to the South not in despair. I go back to the South not with a feeling that we are caught in a dark dungeon that will never lead to a way out. I go back believing that the new day is coming. And so this afternoon, I have a dream. It is a dream deeply rooted in the American dream. I have a dream that one day, right down in Georgia and Mississippi and Alabama, the sons of former slaves and the sons of former slave owners will be able to live together as brothers.

I have a dream this afternoon that one day, little white children and little Negro children will be able to join hands as brothers and sisters. I have a dream this afternoon that one day men will no longer burn down houses and the church of God simply because people want to be free. I have a dream this afternoon that there will be a day that we will no longer face the atrocities that Emmett Till had to face or Medgar Evers had to face, that all men can live with dignity. I have a dream this afternoon that my four little children will not come up in the same young days that I came up within, but they will be judged on the basis of the content of their character, not the color of their skin. I have a dream this afternoon that one day right here in Detroit, Negroes will be able to buy a house or rent a house anywhere that their money will carry them and they will be able to get a job. [*Applause*]

Yes, I have a dream this afternoon that one day in this land the words of Amos will become real and "justice will roll down like waters, and righteousness like a mighty stream." I have a dream this evening that one day we will recognize the words of Jefferson that "all men are created equal, that they are endowed by their Creator with certain unalienable rights, that among these are life, liberty and the pursuit of happiness." I have a dream this afternoon. [*Applause*]

I have a dream that one day "every valley shall be exalted, and every hill shall be made low; the crooked places shall be made straight, and the rough places plain; and the glory of the Lord shall be revealed, and all flesh shall see it together." I have a dream this afternoon that the brotherhood of man will become a reality in this day.

And with this faith I will go out and carve a tunnel of hope through the mountain of despair. With this faith, I will go out with you and transform dark yesterdays into bright tomorrows. With this faith, we will be able to achieve this new day when all of God's children, black men and white men, Jews and Gentiles, Protestants and Catholics, will be able to join hands and sing with the Negroes in the spiritual of old: Free at last! Free at last! Thank God almighty, we are free at last! [*Applause*]

That was Detroit, June 23, 1963. The words still electrify, don't they, especially with their anticipation of King's assassination, especially if you've not heard them before, and especially of course because of their not-so-rough anticipation of August 28.

So you get my point. From the beginning of the March on Washington preparations, there was plenty of concord, but also plenty of dissent within the movement, controversy amid the concord; the good guys were sometimes hard to tell from the bad; and many lines in "I Have a Dream" were already written by the end of June, so to speak, by a number of others. The apparent disjuncture that so many have commented on in King's "I Have a Dream" speech, the internal conflict between the first half's emphasis on jobs and the "Let Freedom Ring" peroration, was not really so much a conflict at all as an inevitable consequence of the two themes of the march. Kennedy's "promise" at the end of his TV address would morph easily into King's "promissory note." And indeed the first section of King's speech mirrors in many ways (and for very good political reasons) the phraseology of Kennedy's addresses on TV and in Berlin. "I Have a Dream" includes not just King's formulations rehearsed in Detroit (and in an August speech in Chicago), but phrases owing to Scripture, to Randolph and Franklin, to Lincoln and Gandhi, to Malcolm X (remember that King spoke to the "marvelous new militancy which has engulfed the Negro community"), to "The Battle Hymn of the Republic" and the Declaration of Independence, and to who knows who and what else. Marion Anderson famously sang "My Country 'Tis of Thee" on the steps of the Lincoln Memorial in 1939, so no wonder King recited the words of the song in the same place in 1963. Did King pinch his "I have a dream" phrase from activist Prathia Hall in the 1962 Albany campaign, and his "let freedom ring" refrain from Chicago preacher Archibald Carey's address at the 1952 Republican National Convention, as Michael Eric Dyson has contended (citing Keith Miller as his authority)?

For my second episode, let's flash forward quickly—I realize that my time is short—to August 28, 1963, itself, a day which, while legendarily peaceful thanks to the organizational genius of Bayard Rustin, did not lack for moments of discord. Not that the intervening months did not have their own discords—with King vacillating over whether he should purge two of his closest advisers on account of their communist ties; with Wilkins arguing with Randolph over Bayard Rustin's involvement; with James Meredith and J. H. Jackson in Chicago opposing the march; with Mississippi governor Ross Barnett proposing a resettlement of blacks in Africa and George Wallace and William F. Buckley publicly denouncing the march (Wallace because it was part of a communist conspiracy, Buckley because it represented "mobocracy"); and with JFK negotiating his way between supporting civil rights leaders and placating the obstructionist Democrats within his own party, most of them southerners, for the sake of his broad legislative program. (For King's relationships with white moderates, see Cox; for King's predicament as a leader attentive to various subgroups within the African American community, in a circumstance directly relevant to the theme of "concord and controversy," see Hariman. A Gallup poll, incidentally, showed Americans solidly behind Kennedy's civil rights legislation, but it also showed Kennedy trailing Republican presidential candidate Barry Goldwater in the southern states.)

MARCH ON WASHINGTON FOR JOBS AND FREEDOM

AUGUST 28, 1963

LINCOLN MEMORIAL PROGRAM

1. The National Anthem	*Led by* Marian Anderson.
2. Invocation	The Very Rev. Patrick O'Boyle, *Archbishop of Washington.*
3. Opening Remarks	A. Philip Randolph, *Director March on Washington for Jobs and Freedom.*
4. Remarks	Dr. Eugene Carson Blake, *Stated Clerk, United Presbyterian Church of the U.S.A.; Vice Chairman, Commission on Race Relations of the National Council of Churches of Christ in America.*
5. Tribute to Negro Women Fighters for Freedom Daisy Bates Diane Nash Bevel Mrs. Medgar Evers Mrs. Herbert Lee Rosa Parks Gloria Richardson	Mrs. Medgar Evers
6. Remarks	John Lewis, *National Chairman, Student Nonviolent Coordinating Committee.*
7. Remarks	Walter Reuther, *President, United Automobile, Aerospace and Agricultural Implement Wokers of America, AFL-CIO; Chairman, Industrial Union Department, AFL-CIO.*
8. Remarks	James Farmer, *National Director, Congress of Racial Equality.*
9. Selection	Eva Jessye *Choir*
10. Prayer	Rabbi Uri Miller, *President Synagogue Council of America.*
11. Remarks	Whitney M. Young, Jr., *Executive Director, National Urban League.*
12. Remarks	Mathew Ahmann, *Executive Director, National Catholic Conference for Interracial Justice.*
13. Remarks	Roy Wilkins, *Executive Secretary, National Association for the Advancement of Colored People.*
14. Selection	Miss Mahalia Jackson
15. Remarks	Rabbi Joachim Prinz, *President American Jewish Congress.*
16. Remarks	The Rev. Dr. Martin Luther King, Jr., *President, Southern Christian Leadership Conference.*
17. The Pledge	A Philip Randolph
18. Benediction	Dr. Benjamin E. Mays, *President, Morehouse College.*

"WE SHALL OVERCOME"

March on Washington for Jobs and Freedom program of events. August 28, 1963. National Archives.

Here is the program for that day. As you scan this document, note that this was a very full schedule of presentations; each person was consequently given just seven minutes to speak. So the consequent (and uncharacteristic) brevity of King's speech was assured by Rustin's insistence on that limitation. Note also that the uneasy coalition addressing the assembled multitudes before the Lincoln Memorial had many and sometimes conflicting goals, reflected not just in the full title of the March on Washington for Jobs and Freedom, but also embodied by the people gathered for the event: black workers, farmers, and disenfranchised citizens; and black and white entertainers, students, and clergy. Speakers represented a fragile "popular front" coalition including Wilkins' NAACP, Young's Urban League, James Farmer's Congress on Racial Equality (CORE), Lewis's SNCC, Reuther's United Auto Workers, and King's SCLC (not to mention the Catholic, Protestant, and Jewish religious leaders). All of them negotiated multiple needs and aims and opportunities; and they uneasily accommodated all kinds of difference in the interest of an important show of concord. Very few, if any, could subscribe to all ten of the official demands that were presented to President Kennedy after the march—one of them a demand that congressional seats be reduced in states still practicing segregation.

You probably know about the increasing impatience and radicalism during the summer of 1963 of the SNCC. SNCC chair John Lewis had to be toned down in his presentation as the result of vigorous negotiations that were occurring even as the first speeches were being given, negotiations that required the insertion of another speaker to fill the resulting gap in the person of the mercurial Reverend Fred Shuttlesworth, the man long in the middle of the Birmingham campaign, firehosed during May and since 1961 shuttling between that city and my Cincinnati as the pastor at Revelation Baptist Church, located at 1556 John Street, near Crosley Field. Lewis, under pressure from his elders, finally agreed not to use charged terms like "the masses" and "revolution" and "Sherman's March to the Sea" in order to keep the peace. (Incidentally, according to the August 28 *Cincinnati Enquirer*, 497 of my fellow Cincinnatians, black and white, some of them perhaps religious nuns who taught at my high school, traveled together to the march on a special overnight train, organized by an interfaith and interracial committee of church leaders. The march happened to take place while the Ohio Valley Jazz Festival was attracting to Cincinnati the likes of Cannonball Adderley, Oscar Peterson, and Thelonius Monk—and one fan from Louisville, still named Cassius Clay, whose photo in the *Cincinnati Enquirer* on August 30 quoted him as saying, "If Liston gives me any jive, I'll take him in five.")

And you won't be surprised at the gradualism that still prevailed within the SCLC and NAACP on August 28. White leaders such as Archbishop Patrick O'Boyle, who delivered the invocation once he was satisfied that Lewis wouldn't overstep, and black activist Benjamin Mays, who offered the benediction, did not really share a great deal of common ground. And not everyone was real pleased, either, by the succession of remarkable women who were either excluded from the roster of speakers or simply honored in a brief special tribute (e.g., Rosa Parks, Diane Nash) or invited simply to perform (e.g., Mahalia Jackson and Marian Anderson). Almost all white congressmen and senators boycotted the march, carrying on their usual business (the three from Cincinnati certainly did); but so did Congressman Adam Clayton Powell (who thought whites should be kept out of the movement) and Malcolm X, who continued to refer to the whole show as "The Farce in Washington," who indicated on August 25 that "no Muslims will be involved" (*Enquirer*), and who nevertheless couldn't resist attending the march unobtrusively, on the edges. Robert Shelton, imperial wizard of the Ku Klux Klan, had planned to "observe the March" (*Enquirer*) but in an act of divine intervention (you might say) was prevented from doing so when he was injured in a plane crash en route.

In short, the rhetorical situation faced by King and the others gathered that day before the Lincoln Memorial was highly complex, as full of dissonance as consonance, controversy as much as concord. And why wouldn't it be so? Concord and controversy always travel together, inseparable. Like Mr. Lincoln enthroned behind him, King spoke on August 28 for (and against) many others, not just in his own words but channeling the words of others, and he spoke in a way that only imperfectly and incompletely muted dissent. I don't just mean that it is our responsibility as rhetorical scholars to understand the broad social dimension of King's personal performance—how it was instigated and even articulated by many others, including Mahalia Jackson, who is said to have goaded King into leaving his script and concluding "by telling about the dream," or how it took place as whispers circulated through the crowd that "the old man" (W. E. B. DuBois) had passed away just hours before in Ghana. I mean that we have to acknowledge the voices of many others in that speech—the voices of

Civil Rights March at the Washington Monument, August 28, 1963. National Archives.

Kennedy and Shuttlesworth, Lewis and Evers, Wilkins and Anderson, Randolph and Rustin and Carey, voices heard in Berlin and Detroit, Jackson and Birmingham.

Let's therefore encourage students and the public to see the March on Washington not as a stage for the heroic King to address anonymously assembled passive masses but as a People's Movement. When we do, we will not at all be diminishing the achievement of Martin Luther King Jr., but attending to the fullness of his genius, courage, and savvy. And when we do, we will be doing rhetorical analysis in a way that does justice to Kenneth Burke's and Michael Leff's knowing insight: consensus never comes without controversy, and concord is always accompanied by criticism. As much as possible we must recover the full conversation when we do contextual rhetorical analysis. And we should probably remember all that not just when we are in the act of analysis, but also when we are advising prospective rhetors too. Let's teach our students that no act of rhetoric really ends the discussion, that it is a rare moment indeed when someone will say, "Thanks for clearing that up!" and that they can always expect criticism of one kind or another when they enter into public discourse. Rhetoric is a rough-and-tumble contact sport (as well as a team sport) and it takes people with a thick skin to play it.

That's the point of my talk. But rather than open myself to your comments and dissents at this point—for I too can dish out criticism far better than I take it—let me instead send you back to our conference sessions with a personal note.

Where was I on Wednesday, August 28, 1963? I sure wasn't in Washington, and I wasn't at the Ohio Valley Jazz Festival either. I was practicing football. My school team would play our season opener ten days later, on September 6—where I scored the first and only touchdown of my varsity career in our 35–0 win over neighborhood rival Anderson. On August 24, four days before the march, we played a preseason practice scrimmage against a mostly black team from Central High in the Cincinnati Public High School League, and I got a lesson related to white supremacy: while trying to win a first-team defensive backfield job, I gave up a couple of embarrassing touchdowns on long pass plays. So it goes. (Years later I finally felt better about this episode when I learned that the player who beat me that day was probably Al Moore, who went on to star at Miami.) I've mentioned my teams in this talk, and maybe I tend to see King and Burke as members of teams, because all my life I've enjoyed being on teams of one kind or another. Baseball, football, and later softball teams, yes—remind me to tell you sometime how Jerry Springer was once on my summer softball team—but a team called "family" too. School teams and church teams and community teams as well. And now, of course, professional and academic teams. This is an opportunity for me to acknowledge my great good fortune at being associated with them throughout my career. My Penn State colleagues come first to mind of course (after my family)—we've always operated as a team, and that has always given us an advantage whenever it came to developing students or competing for scarce institutional funds. So thanks to fellow Penn Staters Marie and Stuart and Cheryl and Keith; Rosa and Suresh and Debbie and Mike; Jeremy and Steve and Rich and especially Linda. And to Don and Davida, Jeff and Sharon, Anne and Jennie and Jeanne and Chris, among others, once and always Penn Staters no matter where they go, and to all the fantastic grad students who have come through Paternoville and been with me at Camp Rhetoric and the Kenneth Burke farm and various other gatherings and left your indelible marks.

RSA has been my team too, and this conference has surely been a team effort as well, hasn't it? What a pleasure it has been, having a chance to get involved in this great organization more generally. I've been on the executive board for about a decade now, working with tremendous teammates and making new relationships. And without a doubt, having had the privilege and pleasure of serving as president of this organization has been, by far, the greatest honor of my professional life. From the bottom of my heart, I thank you for it.

Notes

1 In this essay I strive to preserve the oral and informal nature of my RSA presentation. I note in brackets, for instance, two points in the presentation where I offered audio clips: one by John Kennedy and one by Martin Luther King Jr. in Detroit. I want to thank Bill Schraufnagel for outstanding assistance with the video and audio parts of this presentation, and for his assistance with my research. I also want to thank Tony de Velasco and Melody Lehn for helping with the images that appear in this essay. My original talk used additional and often different images, and Tony and Melody have found inventive and effective ways to retain the flavor of my RSA presentation.

2 In my account of events of 1963, I have drawn extensively from my scrutiny of the *Cincinnati Enquirer* archives in the Cincinnati Public Library; I also consulted contemporary news magazines and popular magazines. For their assistance I thank the librarians in the newspaper archives there. Because the events are easily available in multiple sources and in order to serve the convenience of the reader I have chosen not to document my specific sources in greater detail.

Works Cited

Branch, Taylor. *Parting the Waters: America in the King Years.* New York: Simon & Schuster, 1988.

Cox, J. Robert. "The Fulfillment of Time: King's 'I Have a Dream' Speech (August 28, 1963)." Ed. Michael C. Leff and Fred J. Kauffeld. *Texts and Contexts*. Davis, CA: Hermagoras P, 1989. 181–204.

Dyson, Michael Eric. *I May Not Get There with You: The True Martin Luther King, Jr.* New York: Touchstone, 2000.

Goodwin, Doris Kearns. *Team of Rivals: The Political Genius of Abraham Lincoln.* New York: Simon & Schuster, 2005.

Hariman, Robert. "Time and the Reconstitution of Gradualism in King's Address: A Response to Cox." Ed. Michael C. Leff and Fred J. Kauffeld. *Texts and Contexts*. Davis, CA: Hermagoras P, 1989. 205–17.

Malcolm X with Alex Haley. *The Autobiography of Malcolm X.* New York: Grove P, 1964.

Miller, Keith. "Voice-Merging and Self-Making: The Epistemology of 'I Have a Dream.'" *Rhetoric Society Quarterly* 19 (1989): 23–32.

———. *Voice of Deliverance: The Language of Martin Luther King, Jr.* Athens: U of Georgia P, 1998.

Selzer, Linda. "Historicizing Lincoln: Garry Wills and the Canonization of 'The Gettysburg Address.'" *Rhetoric Review* 16 (1997): 120–36.

Wills, Garry. *Lincoln at Gettysburg: The Words That Remade America.* New York: Simon & Schuster, 1993.

Zarefsky, David. *Lincoln, Douglas, and Slavery: In the Crucible of Public Debate.* Chicago: U of Chicago P, 1990.

Section II

Publics, Pedagogies, and Rhetorical Tensions

My particular approach . . . incorporates elements of critical thinking and semantics in a model for analyzing argumentative rhetoric, combining the factual knowledge and critical skills that students need to make informed judgments about the partisan screaming matches and special-interest propaganda that permeate current political and economic controversies.

—Donald Lazere

How does a body politic reconstitute itself?

—Cezar M. Ornatowski

The epideictic rhetoric shaping Kent State University's commemorations embodies the capacity for legitimating as well as contravening present-day ideals of democratic citizenship.

—M. Karen Powers

If politics is action, to say that politics is ideally conversation—that is, to take the norms for politics from the norms for conversation—is to confuse a metaphor for a description.

—Michael S. Kochin

Electronic databases can provide students with rich resources for rhetorical invention and can function as important forms of arguments themselves.

—J. Blake Scott

Narrative can complement other modes of argumentation, and thereby enhance rhetorical education and practice, by foregrounding our conflicts, dramatizing the experiences and values that give them shape, and providing readers the opportunity to engage more fully in the processes of inquiry, deliberation, and judgment.

—Zachary Dobbins

3

Constructing Pluralism

Identification and Division in the Political Transformation of Poland

Cezar M. Ornatowski

Introduction

How does a body politic reconstitute itself?

This summer marks the thirtieth anniversary of the historic "Gdansk Accords" signed between the striking Polish workers and the communist authorities in Gdansk shipyard on August 31, 1980. The talks began the process of change motivated by the need for what was referred to at the time as a "new social contract," a process that led, over the course of the following decade, to a reconstitution of the body politic culminating in the dramatic political transition of 1989.

In the following essay, I offer a brief rhetorical account of the originary moment of this reconstitution, drawing on Kenneth Burke's categories of identification and division and his reflections on constitutionality. My aim, however, is not so much to narrate a significant moment in rhetorical history, but rather to interrogate that moment to learn something about both rhetoric and the nature of constitution, and especially about their relationship. I will focus on the August 23–31, 1980 negotiations between striking workers and the government delegation as my "representative anecdote," which, in the Burkean spirit, I take to represent a reduction[1] of complex subject matter, "wherein human relations grandly converge" (324). This approach will allow me, within limited space, to evolve a "terminological structure" conducive to some insights into the nature of rhetoric as grounded (my term will be *instituted*) in constitutional relationships, thus as an *institution* rooted in a *constitution*.

I take "constitution" as a verb: "the act or process of constituting" (Burke 341), where *con-* designates a relationship, in fact, implies a dialectical relationship, both a "with" (as in *con*cord, *con*forming, *con*sort, *con*voy) and an "against" (as in *con*trary, *con*trast, *con*troversy). Constitution thus occurs, by definition as it were, on the "wavering line" (Burke) between identification and division. The *-stitute* part of *constitute* (from Latin, *-stituere, -stitui, -stitutum*) means to cause to stand, to set up, place, establish, settle, as well as to found (as in *a foundation*). Hence, *constitutus* implies something (a "form of being, or structure and connection of parts, which constitutes and characterizes a system or body" [340]) that has been arranged, settled, or agreed upon (University of Notre Dame).

Following Burke, I conceive constitution as an "enactment arising in history" (365) involving an agonistic calculus of motives (that is, as the outcome of a dramatistic process involving agents, purposes, agencies, and so on) that creates community by proclaiming a "common substance" (343).[2] My analysis thus focuses on the transformation in the "calculus of motives" involved in the redefinition of this common substance as it may be discerned from my "representative anecdote": the reconstitutive historical moment of the August 1980 negotiations in the Gdansk shipyard between striking workers and the government commission.

Talking (Re)Constitution

In "real-socialist" Poland, as in other iron curtain countries, the state was constitutionally identified with an ideology. Article 1 of the Constitution of the Polish People's Republic (the so-called "Stalinist constitution," ratified by parliament on July 22, 1952) defined the country as a "state of people's democracy," while Article 2 further defined the "people" who were this "democracy's" proper subjects and putative political agents by specifying that "power belongs to the *working people of towns and villages*" (Office of the Polish Constitutional Tribunal; my translation, emphasis added).

The "working people of towns and villages," ritually invoked as both addressees and subjects in official Polish regime discourse, constituted the "common substance" of the real-socialist body politic. The "structure and connection of parts" that comprised this body consisted of "comrades," "workers and peasants," "party members and non-members," and "believers and unbelievers" (note specific groupings and lines of identification/division) in "moral/political unity" (in the words of a ubiquitous slogan) under the (constitutionally asserted) "leading role" of the communist party. Since this structure was largely a function of the identification of the state with ideology, it was characterized by an interpenetration of the party apparatus and state administration, which had two aspects: one was the duplication of many key administrative state organs and functions within the party structure; the other was the practice of "nomenklatura," the selection of candidates for key administrative positions according to party affiliation or ideological identification, rather than "technical" expertise. The result was what the opposition referred to as the ideological "appropriation of the state."[3]

Since the regime ideologized and penetrated the entire space of the "lifeworld," the citizen confronted the state in every area of daily life, social as well as, to some extent, private life (bear in mind that most people were employed by the state; rented their dwellings from the state; got their education, medical care, and all basic services from the state; and so on). Since all organizations and associations, practically all forms of public life (except for religion, which helps explain its role as the only refuge from and alternative to the state, as well as its role as a neutral "witness" in the political negotiations throughout the 1980s), were also appropriated by the state, the citizen confronted the state at every step, directly and without mediation. To ordinary daily consciousness, therefore, the body politic appeared rather to be defined by the division between the individual citizen and the state, a division enacted in daily rhetorical practice in terms of "us" and "them," a distinction that was reversible: for most citizens, "they" designated the state and its "owners"; for the authorities, the people were "they."

It was this adversary relationship between the citizen and the state that was the focal issue that dominated and defined the specific character of the Polish transformation. Every confrontation over any issue whatsoever, whether political, economic, legal, or any other—down to such minutiae as the availability of fertilizer or meat, the price of sugar, store opening hours, conditions of schooling, the content of textbooks, work safety and pay, or the provisions of the economic plan—all occurred along this diving line. It was along this line that the crisis of public confidence in the state, which took more local and fragmented forms and was brutally suppressed in 1956, 1968, and 1970, accumulated by the late 1970s to precipitate the massive (and as it turned out, transformative) strikes of August 1980.

The strike and the resulting creation of the free, independent, self-governing "Solidarity" labor union challenged the constitutive calculus of identifications and divisions at the roots as a prelude to the eventual advent (after 1989) of pluralism. The workers declared openly that the putative "moral/political unity" of the people was "compelled with a police baton." They rejected the categorizations of citizens underlying official discourse as part of the regime's strategy of "divide and rule," and insisted instead on talking with the government delegation along the line of "Pole to Pole" (pun unintended): a broad "generic" national identification that subsumed and rendered irrelevant other divisions (*Gdansk-Sierpien 1980* 102).[4] They thus rejected the basic "structure and division of parts" that "constituted" the real-socialist state and the "appropriation of the state," and protested against what they saw as the specifically state-socialist version of the paradox of constitutionalism: the derogation of the constitutional "sovereignty" of the "working people of town and villages," especially of the urban proletariat and the peasants, by the very agency (the communist party) that designated itself (constitutionally) as their representative.[5] Finally, they pointed out that, for all of the above "constitutive" reasons, in the dealings vis-à-vis the state in every aspect of the "lifeworld" the citizen was deprived of effective voice and agency and reduced to an object of administrative fiat with no effective recourse. Thus, the bottom line (the word "line" seems uniquely appropriate here, since it represents precisely Burke's "wavering line" between identification and division) was what it meant to be a "subject" (Polish, *podmiot*) and therefore, also, by entailment, the meaning of "citizenship," of which the workers felt deprived.

Most of the famous "21 postulates" presented to the authorities by the Gdansk Interfactory Strike Committee (headed by Lech Walesa) concerned mundane matters of life and work; their political significance lay not in their substance or coherence (many were patently impossible to implement, such as an enormous across-the-board pay increase for *all* working people of Poland or the provision of consumer goods that were simply unavailable; some postulates also "technically" contradicted others, such as simultaneous demands for pay raises and controlling prices), but in their exploitation of a major weakness of the real-socialist version of the totalitarian state.[6] The state or system that seeks to control every aspect of life is responsible for, and thus vulnerable in, every aspect of life (which, by the way, may explain why regimes that aim at a radical reinvention of society tend toward increasing authoritarianism, since broad responsibility for every aspect of life implies broad vulnerability to public opinion, their coalescence spurring the need for increasing control). It is that vulnerability that the strikers exploited in underscoring the major line of division that ran through the political community and that made every aspect of life—including the content and meaning of citizenship—dependent on the ability or willingness of the state to provide.

Burke defines "transformation" as "a change in substance or principle, a qualitative shift in the nature of *motivation*" (357, emphasis added). The negotiations over the 21 postulates and the accompanying events indeed affected what amounted to a core transformation in the constitution of the body politic.

The "change in substance" was the redefinition of the nature of the sovereign people themselves. While the authorities insisted that they spoke in the interests of and in the name of the "working people," the striking workers insisted that they spoke not only in their own name, but in the name of all the people of Poland; hence their insistence on talking as "one Pole to another." As one of the members of the Interfactory Strike Committee put it: "We are fighting in the name of all the people and the entire population, workers, employees, farmers. . . . Because all are here among us . . ." (*Gdansk-Sierpien 1980* 38). The "name of the people" thus became "the Polish people," in contrast to "working people of towns and villages."

The "change in principle" was represented by a key, and politically pivotal, demand: postulate number 1, the demand for the legalization of "free, independent, self-governing labor unions." Such independent unions would function as the rudiment of civil society, a "mediating" body between the citizens and the state (hence, fundamentally changing the political location and meaning of citizenship), one capable of performing independent analyses of social issues and equipped with independent means of mass communication. Even more importantly, from a "constitutional" standpoint, such a union, in embodying the principles of free association and popular representation, broke the party's monopoly on representing the "working people of towns and villages" and thus on speaking "in the name of," as well as in the place and in effect despite of, the constitutionally sovereign people (which, again, was the real-socialist version of the paradox of constitutionalism).

Finally, the central element in the transformation of the constitutive "calculus of motives" (following the change in the character of "agent," affected by the redefinition of the people and relocation of citizenship, and of "agency," affected by the creation of independent labor unions), the "qualitative shift in the nature of *motivation*," was the emergence of the social relationship that underpinned, defined, and was emblematic of the entire movement: solidarity. This relationship—which was also the name of the strike bulletin and would shortly become the name of the new union—emerged not as a function of ideology or theory but as a function of the pragmatic situation "on the ground."[7] Only by being solidary—solidary with each other, as well as with workers from over 400 enterprises[8] all over Poland who went on strike in solidarity with them—could the strikers hope to gain anything but harassment, dismissal, or arrest. Indeed, the Gdansk strike was a "solidarity" strike by definition, as it were.[9] Critical to the success of the strike was also the solidarity of the general population of the city of Gdansk and the entire region. Crowds numbering in the thousands surrounded the shipyard day and night, preventing an assault by troops, supplying the strikers with food and other necessities, and serving as a conduit for communications in the face of an official news blackout and severance of phone communications with the rest of the country.

The shipyard became in effect a self-governing "republic" while much of the city of Gdansk came voluntarily under the authority of the Interfactory Strike Committee. Workers and others who kept the city going wore white-and-red armbands (Poland's national colors), stores flew national flags, and private taxis that served the transportation needs of the strike (the entire region's transit systems were on strike) displayed white-and-red ribbons on their antennae. The change of colors from red to red and white symbolized and helped enact (alongside the workers' rhetoric) the ongoing reconstitution of the body politic in terms of ordinary, street-level reality, the realm that Vaclav Havel called the "here and now" and designated as the heart of the "political." Havel emphasizes that the dissident movements in Poland and Czechoslovakia did not have as their point of departure any grand plans for systemic changes or any blueprints for change in any traditional "political" sense; rather, their actions were local and anchored in an "everyday struggle for a better life 'here and now'" (88). The "here and now" represents the level that Havel labels as that of the "aims of life": the level of genuine human needs, wants, and relationships—the level out of which, according to Havel, society's spontaneous self-organization arises and in which it takes place (77). Writing in 1979, a year before the watershed events in Gdansk, Havel concluded that meaningful change in central/eastern Europe could only come through a "fundamental *reconstitution* of the position of people in the world, their relationship to themselves and to each other, and to the universe" (52, emphasis added) (for another, complementary take on the rhetorical mechanisms of this reconstitution in the "here and now," see Ornatowski). The constitutive relationship of solidarity remained critical after the successful resolution of the Gdansk strike; as Lech Walesa put it at the conclusion of the negotiations, "we have the 21 postulates agreed on and their realization depends on *us*, on our *solidarity* . . ." (*Gdansk-Sierpien 1980* 151, emphasis added).

The "us" of the participating public melded first pragmatically, "on the ground" during the course of the events of August 1980, and then rhetorically, through the negotiations of the Interfactory Strike Committee with the Government Commission and the resulting agreements. Consequently, the new union was instituted (as a labor union, thus an institution) not out of theory, doctrine, or on paper but "on the ground," as speaking *in the name of* and, perhaps even more importantly, *on the tangible authority of* the people (an authority tangibly granted by the risks involved and demonstrated by the undertakings of ordinary individuals along with the trust of the people in the project and its leaders). The constitutive "substance" ("us") enacted during the events of August 1980 was thus constituted by a relationship (solidarity), with the two *existentially* constituted each as a *function* of the other. This functional connection involved and implied "trust" and formed the foundation for a rhetoric that spoke "in the name of" the people thus constituted. In the case of the Gdansk strike, this "name" became the name of the new labor union and eventually of a mass movement: "Solidarity," a name that lent authority to Lech Walesa and other leaders in their talks with the authorities through the rest of the 1980s (it is for that reason that Walesa insisted on the legalization of "Solidarity" as the precondition for talks after it had been delegalized in the wake of the imposition of martial law on December 13, 1981; without a legally recognized union, of which he was an elected leader, Walesa could speak only in his own name as a "private" individual,[10] which he consistently refused to do). The fact that the mass movement adopted the name of the union, or perhaps that the union morphed into a mass movement that went beyond just "working people," is further evidence of popular trust, a trust that was not granted to the authorities.

It is significant that the authorities, in arguing against the creation of free, independent, self-governing labor unions, insisted on "standing on the ground" of the Polish Constitution. This raises a dual question: what is the foundation (or ground) for the legitimacy of constitutions and of rhetorics (what each "stands" on)?

"Solidarity" the union drew its existence and political meaning (as well as its name) from the fact that it embodied and represented the social relationship (solidarity) that gained the workers their own independent voice and in effect, in the words of one of the strikers, their "full citizenship" (*Gdansk-Sierpien 1980* 87). That relationship was ultimately founded on trust; under the circumstances, overcoming fear and trusting others constituted (I use the term "constituted" here with all of its constitutional implications) the condition of participation, and of success. The "us" represented by "Solidarity," its constitutive *substance*, was constituted as a function of the *relationship* of solidarity; the two were conjoined dialectically in the heat, so to say, of the experience of the events of August 1980. It is thus that "Solidarity" spoke "in the name" of the people; it is that its rhetoric was *in*-stituted: on an *act* of *con*stitution (*con* = with/against). The material embodiment of this in-stitution was, initially, the shipyard strike bulletin, entitled *Solidarity* (which became the official publication and, thus, the voice of the new union after the successful conclusion of the strike), and subsequently the name of the union itself and, further, the name of the mass movement.

By contrast, the formal state constitution on whose "ground" the authorities wanted to "stand" was not "grounded" in anything more than ideology and administrative procedure: it was originally, at the height of Polish Stalinism in 1952, written by a hand-picked committee of "experts," presented to Stalin for editing (Stalin in fact hand-edited portions of it), and then given to the Polish parliament for endorsement. Its "originary" act was not only a mere bureaucratic one, but a fundamentally fake one, in contrast to the existential act of "Solidarity's" founding "in the heat" of genuine—not staged or manipulated—events.[11] The 1952 communist constitution could, thus, provide no "ground" for "authoritative" rhetoric because it lacked social trust and provided neither legitimacy nor authority to speak "in the name of" the people it putatively represented; in effect, it amounted to nothing but so much (idealistic, but empty) "rhetoric."

The Gdansk strike of August 1980 and the subsequent creation of the "Solidarity" union redrew the constitutive calculus of motives on which the political body of People's Poland was founded, becoming, in the long term, the cornerstone for a new social contract, one that was only codified in a proper legislative manner in the new Constitution of the Republic of Poland in 1997. It also laid the foundation for the eventual (after the transition of 1989) advent of pluralism. In this sense, the Gdansk talks may be considered to have played the role of a de facto constitutive assembly, not dissimilarly to the role played by the Assembly of the Estates General at the beginning of the French Revolution (see Lefebvre; Schama).

Conclusion

I have tried to suggest here the notion of effective (authoritative) rhetoric as *standing on and rooted in* an act or process of *constitution* that provides the source of rhetoric's legitimacy to those who answer to the "name" in which it speaks (hence, rhetoric as instituted). Rhetoric (*a* rhetoric, for instance, religious rhetoric) emerges as an *institution* rooted in a *constitution*, the latter defining both substance and relationship, or a set of relationships (Burke's with/against). This relationship is "figured" not through, or not sufficiently through, the Constitution as a document but, most importantly, through rhetorical (and only rhetorical) *action*. The relationship between rhetoric as *institution* (standing on) and the act of *constitution* (its foundation in substance/motivation) is dialectical: the document itself is meaningless if it is not grounded in and arises out of pragmatic relationships in the "here and now," which in turn are often rhetorically mediated (as the rhetoric of "Solidarity" was rooted in the events and relationships of a particular struggle). (This rootedness, or, as I am calling it, *institution*, explains why constitutions as documents get outdated and have to be periodically renewed.[12])

A critical element of a rhetoric's institution is the "name" in which it speaks, which designates the "common substance" that is a function of constitutive *relationships*. The Polish 1952 "Stalinist" constitution was not properly constituted; Poland itself (unlike the Soviet Union, for instance) never had a popular communist revolution and thus "real-socialism" was installed by proclamation by a small Moscow-appointed group to a country at the time still occupied and administered by the Soviet army. Hence, the regime's rhetoric was not instituted, although it was "institutionalized" in a shallow sense of having been derived from the ideology of class struggle and established as "official" by fiat and practice. Thus, the "name" *in* which it spoke was not grounded in any relationship that *spoke to* the people of Poland (in contrast to "Solidarity"). Perhaps that is ultimately what "rhetoric" in its "empty" sense is: a rhetoric that has been institutionalized, but not instituted, and attempts to speak *in the name of*, but that "name" is not grounded in a functional relationship (i.e., a relationship that is felt as legitimately representing the lived conditions of existence, and thus one that also speaks *to* the audience it putatively names). (Such is the rhetoric of "administration"; it embodies formal administrative structures, relationships, and divisions, as well as administrative rationalities, and speaks in administrative jargon, but often feels alien to those to whom it would speak, because the name in which it speaks is not their "name.")

The outcome of the process of *reconstitution* I briefly traced here was aptly captured in a comment made by an opposition member of parliament at the outset of a meeting between newly elected opposition MPs and representatives of the still-communist government soon after the transitional June 4, 1989, parliamentary elections: "The representatives of the people greet the representatives of the authorities" (qtd. in Dubinski 28). The comment foregrounds the rhetorical foundations of "authority," which appears to be rooted in a constitutive act (literally: an act of *con-stitution = standing together with/against*) and bound up with trust. The "representatives" of the authorities, however, by that time indeed represented nothing but "authority" in the abstract, in a purely hierarchical and administrative sense, bereft of constitutive (and thus ideational) content: of both substance (the "name of" those, and on whose authority, they "represented" and to whom they spoke) and principle or motivation (the constitutive relationship that underwrote the community they presumably represented). Central to this relationship, and to the rhetoric of "authority," is trust. And trust was something the real-socialist regime had lost over the years, although initially, at least among some people, it enjoyed a measure of it, vested less in the existing system (that was imposed by the Soviet Union, as it were, from the "outside") than in an ideal vision that promised a rebuilding and renewal on new foundations amid the destruction of World War II; many of the most prominent Polish dissidents during the 1970s and 1980s, among them Adam Michnik and Jacek Kuron, belonged to the party in the post-war years and were committed to the project—or at least the vision—of socialism.

My final point is that the rhetorical spaces we designate as "democracy" or "totalitarianism" are actually discontinuous and nonhomogenous. While democracy generally and by definition depends on "instituted" rhetoric, it is permeated locally with pockets of merely "institutionalized" rhetoric, to which participants may or may not pay lip service for a variety of reasons as if it were still "instituted." Similarly, real-socialist Poland contained areas of instituted rhetoric, even within, or perhaps especially within, the higher ranks of the regime itself; surprisingly candid discussions occurred within the Politburo—for many members what appeared to be merely institutional rhetoric ("mere rhetoric") to most ordinary people was indeed instituted rhetoric, rooted in constitutive relationships forged through common revolutionary and wartime struggles and experiences. It was perhaps *in the name of* these relationships, and, thus, of the putative community of "class comrades" that was a function of these relationships, that they spoke. It was not, however, a name *to* which many ordinary people in Poland were still willing to answer by August 1980. Most of the workers who spearheaded the Gdansk shipyard strike were young, many in their early twenties (Lech Walesa himself was 37 and among the senior members). None of them were formed by the memory of pre-war Poland or the post-war struggles that to some extent shaped at least some of their elders. It was thus in relation to a different reality, a different "here and now," that they stood, and stood up, in August 1980.

Notes

[1] A representative anecdote, according to Burke, is synecdochic (a figure of reduction), representing part for the whole (326).

[2] Constitution as a noun, as "the fundamental, organized law or principles of government of a nation, state, society or other organized body of men, embodied in written documents, or implied in the institutions and usages of the country or society . . ." (Burke 341), is thus the outcome of enactment.

[3] Every constitution contains an "ideological layer" and a formal juridical layer. Every state is a realization of some underlying general "philosophy" and some specific values that render that philosophy into terms of citizenly attitudes and social practice. State institutions, in turn, and, further down the line, the law, are an expression of those values translated into political/administrative practice (Zakrzewska). In "real-socialist" Poland, however, this "expression" took, following Leninist principles, direct, "literal," and rigid forms.

[4] I would contend that it is this need, throughout the 1980s, to emphasize "national" identification as a foundation for citizenship as opposed to an ideological one that accounts in large part for the apparent resurgence of "nationalism" in Poland and other post-communist countries after 1989 (on that resurgence, see for instance, Tismaneanu). Once communism fell, this national identification became "orphaned," unmoored from its political purpose and foundation, and started taking virulent, xenophobic forms (often in tandem with another "unmoored" identification that under communism was largely politicized and played political functions: religion).

[5] The paradox of constitutionalism, well known to constitutional theory, lies in the question whether those who have the authority to make a constitution—who have the "constitutive power"—can do so without effectively surrendering that authority to the institutional sites of power "constituted" by the constitutional form they enact. In particular, is the constitutive power exhausted in the single constitutive act or does it retain a presence, acting as a critical check on the constitutional operating system and/or an alternative source of authority to be invoked in moments of crisis? (Loughlin and Walker). For instance, Harry L. Witte notes that in the United States today, rights "are largely the business of the courts and the legislature. The sovereign people, and the rich diversity of their voices, are at the sidelines of the process of giving contemporary meaning to rights" (385).

[6] The original postulates, painted in red and black on wooden boards and preserved in the "Solidarity" museum in Gdansk, have been placed on UNESCO's "Memory of the World" World Heritage list. The English version of the postulates is available at http://www.archiwa.gov.pl/memory/sub_listakrajowa/index.php?va_lang=en&fileid=022.

[7] Ironically, vigilant attention to the situation "on the ground" forms one of the foundations of Leninist revolutionary strategy, as one of the striking workers in Gdansk pointed out to the government commission during the August 1980 negotiations.

[8] The figure of "over 400" is given by two Polish journalists who were eyewitnesses to the strike (Gielzynski and Stefanski). One of the participants in the negotiations, however, gives the number of striking enterprises represented by the Interfactory Strike Committee to be 382 (*Gdansk-Sierpien 1980* 23).

[9] The initial strike, from August 14 to August 16, 1980, ended with the authorities agreeing to the shipyard workers' list of demands, which were mostly pay and work-conditions oriented. The strike took another, much more serious and, as it turned out in the end, "transformational" turn after the shipyard workers were accused by other, smaller striking enterprises of having "betrayed" them and left them to be "squashed" by the authorities. At that point, while most of the workers were already leaving the shipyard to go home, Lech Walesa declared a "solidarity" strike, which, eventually, turned into the massive, national-scale protest that brought about the "Gdansk Accords" and the creation of the "Solidarity" labor union and social movement.

[10] After the imposition of martial law, the authorities in fact insisted that "citizen Walesa" was only a "private person" and thus had no authority to speak out, or be spoken to, on public matters.

[11] Here, it is important to remember that, in contrast to the Soviet Union, Polish real-socialism was not the result of a revolution, popular or not, but was installed following the Soviet liberation of Poland from Nazi occupation.

[12] That is perhaps why Thomas Jefferson suggested that the US Constitution should be rewritten by each new generation (Jefferson suggested the time frame of every 20 years) (Witte). Along the same lines, one of the striking workers in the Gdansk shipyard suggested during the negotiations that putatively "representative" institutions have an inescapable tendency to "rot" and become "corrupt" and thus have to be periodically replaced by new ones (*Gdansk-Sierpien 1980*).

Works Cited

Burke, Kenneth. *A Grammar of Motives*. Berkeley: U of California P, 1969.

Dubinski, Krzysztof. *Okragly Stol*. Warsaw: KAP, 1999.

Gdansk-Sierpien 1980: Rozmowy Komisji Rzadowej z Miedzyzakladowym Komitetem Strajkowym w Stoczni Gdanskiej (23–31 Sierpnia 1980 r.) [Gdansk-August 1980: The Talks between the Government Commission and the Interfactory Strike Committee in Gdansk Shipyard (August 23–31, 1980)]. Warsaw: Instytut Wydawniczy Zwiazkow Zawodowych, 1981.

Gielzynski, Wojciech, and Lech Stefanski. *Gdansk Sierpien 80*. Warsaw: Ksiazka i Wiedza, 1981.

Havel, Vaclav. "The Power of the Powerless." *The Power of the Powerless: Citizens against the State in Central-Eastern Europe*. Ed. John Keane. London: Hutchinson, 1985. 23–96.

Lefebvre, Georges. *The Coming of the French Revolution*. Trans. R. R. Palmer. 1947. Princeton, NJ: Princeton UP, 1976.

Loughlin, Martin, and Neil Walker. *The Paradox of Constitutionalism*. New York: Oxford UP, 2008.

Office of the Polish Constitutional Tribunal. *Polish Constitutional Tribunal*. Web. 20 May 2010. <http://www.trybunal.gov.pl/wszechnica/akty/konstytucja_prl.htm>.

Ornatowski, Cezar M. "Rhetoric and the Subject of/in History: Reflections on Political Transformation." *Advances in the History of Rhetoric* 9 (2006): 187–207.

Schama, Simon. *Citizens: A Chronicle of the French Revolution*. New York: Knopf, 1989.

Tismaneanu, Vladimir. *Fantasies of Salvation: Democracy, Nationalism, and Myth in Post-Communist Europe*. Princeton, NJ: Princeton UP, 1998.

University of Notre Dame. *Latin Dictionary and Grammar Aid*. Web. <http://www.catholic.archives.nd.edu>.

Witte, Harry L. "Rights, Revolution, and the Paradox of Constitutionalism: The Processes of Constitutional Change in Pennsylvania." *Widener Journal of Public Law* 3 (1993): 384–428. Web. 15 May 2010.

Zakrzewska, Janina. *Spor o Konstytucje* [Struggles Over the Constitution]. Warsaw: Wydawnictwo Sejmowe, 1993.

4

Rhetoric, Dialectic, and Public Discourse

Michael S. Kochin

What is the place of dialogue or conversation in politics? One view common in academic discussions of politics is that, ideally, political discussion takes the form of a conversation, a conversation conducted according to rules for seeking the truth. Without too much difficulty we can formulate rules of reasonable behavior in conversation, and from the Greek word for speaking with another person in conversation, or *dialegein,* we get *dialektikē,* or dialectics.

One version of this view, hopefully well enough known that I do not have to summarize it, is Habermas's "discourse ethics," which the Amsterdam school of pragma-dialectics of van Eemeren and collaborators attempts to formulate as a technically precise ethics of speech acts.[1] Out of local patriotism I could cite my sometime Tel Aviv colleague Charles Blattberg and his distinction between negotiation leading to compromise and conversation leading to reconciliation (xi, 29).

In my work, by contrast, I have tried to understand politics as a field of action, and political speech as an action that both reproduces and alters political customs and institutions.[2] If politics is action, to say that politics is ideally conversation—that is, to take the norms for politics from the norms for conversation—is to confuse a metaphor for a description. We can learn something from the claim that politics is conversation, just as we can learn something from the claim that politics is theater.

Yet in this essay, I want to consider the limitations of the conversation or dialogue metaphor for politics by examining the ancient distinction between rhetoric and dialectic.[3] "Dialectic" I am going to take in the strictly Aristotelian sense as conversation aimed at clarifying the merits and demerits of a given thesis. "Rhetoric" I will take in the modified Aristotelian sense, as a reflection on the available means of persuasion. I will give an example of philosophical conversation or dialectic, and two examples of public speaking or rhetoric. In each situation, we will examine a similar move, pointing out what is sometimes called an *ad populam* fallacy. In an *ad populam* fallacy, public opinion is taken as evidence for an inference about the contents of that opinion, as if the fact that most Americans oppose the recent health care reform legislation were to be taken as evidence that the scheme was not only unpopular, but also unworkable. The claim that a fallacy has been committed has very different meanings in the dialectical situation compared to the rhetorical situation. I want to use this difference to understand the difference between the dialectical situation and the rhetorical situation, and thus the difference between conversation and political argument.

The Dialectical Situation

According to Aristotle's manual of dialectics, *Topics*, dialectic aims to find what can be said in critique or defense of a given philosophical thesis.[4] Consider the thesis "What is good for human beings is pleasure" (8.9.160b20 ff).[5] Having read Plato's *Gorgias* we know one promising line of attack on this thesis: pick a pleasure that is great (according to those who enjoy it) but disgraceful (494c–495b).

Here, I propose to put aside Socrates' original conversation with Callicles and instead analyze the following fragment from the very late antique pastiche of Plato, *Diogenes, or On Pleasure*, generally ascribed to the otherwise obscure Ireneaus of Jaffa:

Socrates: Now Diogenes, you say that the good is pleasure?
Diogenes: Yes.
Socrates: And the greater the pleasure the greater the good.
Diogenes: Yes.
Socrates: And whatever is pleasant for a man is good for him?
Diogenes: Yes.
Socrates: Do not some men find very great pleasure in being anally sodomized by dogs?
Callicles: Socrates, how dare you speak of such vile practices!
Socrates: Why, Callicles, do you not have an Internet connection? In any case, it is Diogenes here who is attempting to defend his claim that pleasure is the good.
Diogenes: And defend it I will. Indeed, Socrates, there are such men, some who prefer dogs, others who prefer rams or even horses. Ever wondered why I am called a cynic?
Socrates: Then if a man finds the greatest pleasure in being anally sodomized by dogs, is that not the greatest good for him?
Diogenes: Surely, Socrates, that is a correct inference.
Socrates: Under the rules I have discovered in this marvelous book called *Topics*, Diogenes, you have failed to defend your thesis adequately, for you have said something that is con-

trary to the opinion of all human beings in all places, Greek or barbarian.

Diogenes: But Socrates, what do you care what other people think?

The aim of the questioner in a philosophic conversational exercise, on Aristotle's account, is to silence the answerer, to reduce him or her to *aporia,* or the absence of argumentative resources. Socrates has forced Diogenes to utter a statement contrary to common opinion. The answerer is expected to grant the suppositions of the questioner if the suppositions are true and conform to accepted judgments (Slomkowski 31; *Topics* 8.8.160a39f).

Diogenes immediately finds a way out of the corner into which Socrates has painted him. Legitimately, according to the rules laid out in Aristotle's manual, Diogenes appeals from common opinion to the opinion of the wise, in this case by an *ad hominem* appeal to the view of Socrates himself, thereby dissolving Socrates' appeal to common opinion (*Topics* 8.10.161a3–4). Socrates was generally considered, at least by some of the contemporaries of Ireneaus of Jaffa, to be the very paradigm of a wise man.

One could also characterize Diogenes' move as a claim that Socrates committed an *ad populam* fallacy. In pointing out the fallacy, Diogenes attempts to prevent Socrates from finding a way out, a *poros*, that will enable him to continue to press this line of questioning. In claiming that the other participant has made a fallacious move, each side is appealing to the (fictional) audience of their conversation.[6]

Note also the subtle claim of a performative self-contradiction: if Socrates really does not care what other people think, why is he so interested in questioning Diogenes as to Diogenes' own opinion about whether pleasure is the good? It is probably not accidental that Ireneaus has written a Socratic dialogue despite his explicit references to Aristotle. Plato's Socrates, we should recall, presents in the *Phaedrus* an account of the soul and its ante-natal perception of the highest things (245c–250c). This wild flight of metaphysics is intended to explain why one can reasonably expect to learn the truth by examining someone dialectically as long as they answer according to their own judgment. Making one's inferences strictly from the opinions of the answerer is, according to Aristotle, what characterizes dialectical arguments (*Sophistical Refutations* 2).

Socrates does not, in fact, care what Diogenes thinks. Socrates cares whether the good is pleasure. For the Platonic (and presumably the Irenaean) Socrates, Diogenes' view that pleasure is the good is, as long as that view is sincere, a kind of imperfect reflection of the idea of the good. Socrates wants to exploit such an imperfect reflection of the good in his own quest to set his own thoughts in order about the good for man. The questioner in a dialectical exercise aims to refute the answerer's thesis not in order to change the answerer's mind about the thesis, but in order to clarify the status of the thesis in his own mind.[7] Similarly, the audience listens to the conversation in order to clarify its own mind about the thesis, or simply because for certain sorts, listening to dialectical examinations is pleasant (Plato, *Apology of Socrates* 23c). Unfortunately, limitations of space force us to leave for another day the conclusion of Ireneaus' dialogue, in which Diogenes gets Socrates to agree that the greatest pleasure is in fact *épater le bourgeois*.

Rhetoric as Mobilizing—or Demobilizing

For rhetorical examples, I want to look at the controversy in Israel surrounding the outcome of the 2006 Israel–Lebanon war. I want to look at one short but crucial passage in the April 30, 2007 "Preliminary Report" of the official Israeli Commission of Inquiry, generally known as the Winograd Commission, which looked into the conduct and the outcome of that war.

The stated goals of the preliminary report, in the face of Israel's perceived tactical and strategic failures in that war, were:

1. To assess the performance of the cabinet, the statutory cabinet committee known as the "Security Cabinet," and other decision making bodies.
2. To assess the performance of three specific individuals:
   a. Prime Minister Ehud Olmert
   b. Defense Minister Amir Peretz
   c. Wartime Chief of the General Staff Lt. Gen. Dan Halutz

What did the preliminary report want its readers to do? In the first place, as is clear from the formal conclusions, to mobilize the necessary efforts to make what the commission saw as the needed organizational reforms in the prime minister's office, the defense minister's office, the cabinet, etc. *Sotto voce* (but not *pianissimo*), the commissioners aimed to drive Olmert and Peretz from office, Halutz having already resigned. The preliminary report (and the final report as well) were careful to hold themselves out as presenting only the facts and leaving the public to make a decision.

In my view, the whole argument of the report hinges on an *ad populam* fallacy. The report takes Israeli public sentiment as its central evidence of the consequences of the Second Lebanon War: "If the results of the war were positive in the opinion of most [of the public], the commission of inquiry would not have investigated."[8] At least in the unclassified version of the report, the commission shows no sign of exploiting its ample staff and full access to decision makers and classified materials to make its own inquiry into the consequences of the war. I pointed this out in a piece I drafted immediately following the release of the preliminary report. There I concluded:

> . . . on the basis of a logically flawed inference "the public believes the war was a failure, therefore the war was a failure," the Winograd com-

> mission has plunged Israel into a political crisis. There is only one healthy way out of the crisis: the Israeli public, but especially opinion makers in politics, journalism, the army, the wider intelligence community, and academia, need to hold a factually informed public debate as to the actual consequences of the war, focusing principally on events in Lebanon during and subsequent to the war and their wider ramifications. Only should we come to agree with the hidden but implied premise of the Winograd report that the Olmert Government's decision to go to war and the mode in which it conducted that war failed to achieve sufficiently worthy ends, can we consider whether the personal "conclusions" and structural "recommendations" proposed in the preliminary version of the Winograd report are generally justified, and whether their application is desirable.

I was unable to get this piece published in a newspaper, but I circulated it on the Israel Political Science Association e-mail list, from which it achieved a certain readership among academics in relevant fields like public policy, political science, and Middle East studies. Readers included commission member (and Hebrew University emeritus professor of public policy) Yechezkel Dror (see Dror).

But consider the difference between my purpose in pointing out a fallacy and Diogenes' purpose in the dialogue I quoted above. Diogenes points out Socrates' *ad populam* fallacy to close off a line of inquiry to Socrates. My aim was demobilizing—I wished to answer the report in order to thwart the attempted mobilization against Olmert and Peretz. That was because, for political purposes of my own, I wanted to rehabilitate deterrence as a policy alternative for Israel in dealing with her enemies.

The Norms of Public Speaking and the Norms of Conversation

Yet is it even reasonable, as the pragma-dialecticians or the discourse ethicists suggest, to take the norms for political speech from the norms for conversation?

There is, in the first place, the matter of the temporal occasion (or kairos) that distinguishes public speaking from dialogue. Conversation is terminated either by accident or when its possibilities are exhausted. In a dialectical encounter conducted according to "Philosopher of Stageira" rules, the conversation is terminated when the thesis is either maintained or overthrown. Political deliberation, however, is occasional, and is terminated by the need to respond to the occasion before it passes. Contrast Socrates' statement in the *Theaetetus*, where it is contended that philosophical conversation cannot, inherently, be limited in time:

> Socrates: Look at the man who has been knocking about in law courts and such places ever since he was a boy, and compare him with the man brought up in philosophy, in the

life of a student. It is surely like comparing the upbringing of a slave with that of a free man.

Theodorus: How is that, now?

Socrates: Because the one man always has what you mentioned just now—plenty of time. When he talks, he talks in peace and quiet, and his time is his own. It is so with us now: here we are beginning on our third new discussion; and he can do the same, if he is like us, and prefers the newcomer to the question in hand. It does not matter to such men whether they talk for a day or a year, if only they may hit upon that which is. But the other—the man of the law courts—is always in a hurry when he is talking; he has to speak with one eye on the clock. (Burnyeat 172c–e)

Philosophical conversation is interminable because, and this is my second point of distinction, it is theoretical, aiming at understanding and explanation. Political deliberation is finite, essentially finite, because it is practical. It does little good to deliberate so long that one misses the proper opportunity for action. In consequence, rhetoric is to practice as dialectics is to theory. This is what is oxymoronic about the Amsterdam school's term "pragma-dialectics"—compare the contrasting neologism: "Theore-rhetorical."[9]

Thirdly, conversation makes use of opinions, while rhetoric, as I have argued elsewhere, presents facts.[10] Philosophical conversation is examination of opinions, in which the opinions of the questioner are compared with the opinions of the many or the wise, and as Aristotle says, "a syllogism is dialectical when drawn from generally accepted judgments" (*Topics* 1.1.100b; tr. Kennedy in Aristotle, *On Rhetoric*, 289–90). Consider, for example, the abortion debate as it appears in the academic ethics literature, where the pro-lifer is refuted by showing that his position contradicts the general opinion that abortion ought to be permitted in cases of rape.[11]

Philosophical argumentation seems to be able to get off the ground when all issues of fact are settled, often by ruling out some facts as indeterminable or irrelevant. If the facts are relevant, they are to be determined by political deliberation or by scientific demonstration. It is not for political philosophers, we might think, to decide whether the Iranians are pursuing nuclear weapons in order to use them in a "bolt from the blue" first strike, but for citizens, politicians, intelligence operatives, and nuclear scientists. Political philosophers can discuss the application of just war concepts to the "Iranian threat" once the facts of the situation are agreed upon, or at least the relevant alternative scenarios are postulated.

To quote Gilbert Ryle, dialectical inquiry "rules out a lot of types of questions" (9) (contrast Hintikka 6–7).[12] Aristotle is faithful to the Platonic insight that there is something special about the examination of judgments of the wise or the many. Aristotelian dialectic, as J. D. G. Evans says, can demolish claims to knowledge but positively it is unable itself to produce knowledge.[13]

Political deliberation—and here I depart from Aristotle (see Kochin, *Five Chapters*)—is about presenting and clarifying views of the facts. Facts give a speech the particularity required to convince the audience that the speaker has concrete knowledge of the matter at hand: as William Hamilton put it in his celebrated manual of *Parliamentary Logic,* "without some degree of particularity, a speech is pointless and ineffectual" (53, and cf. 61).

Fourthly, philosophical conversation is normatively equal, while the rhetorical situation is normatively deferential. Philosophical conversation is equal because neither participant has authority denied to the other, and neither knows any facts the other, or the audience, does not. The rhetorical situation is deferential: few speak, many listen. These few are heard, I have shown elsewhere, because they claim to know something, some relevant facts, that the many do not.[14]

Note that modern scientific inquiry is not dialectical. It is inegalitarian, with a sharp division between scientists and nonscientists. Scientific discourse aims at establishing facts rather than refuting theses, and aims to change things in the world, rather than clarify the questioner's or the audience's understanding—it is about "intervening" and not "representing," to use Ian Hacking's well-known vocabulary. Scientific interlocutors have limited time, like the forensic pleaders in the *Theaetetus,* thanks to the fact that science is competitive: it is not enough to present true and important scientific facts or effects—one has to present them first!

In conclusion, we need to keep in mind that neither dialectic nor rhetoric aims to change minds—to change what people think about certain claims. Rhetoric aims to change things by mobilizing the audience—or keep things from changing by demobilizing the audience. Dialectic aims to clarify the questioner's (and the audience's) understanding by examining what the answerer has to say in defense of his or her position (see Krabbe 32). In neither rhetoric nor dialectic do interlocutors aim at persuading each other.[15]

Speaking to change minds is preaching, or the subgenre of preaching, prophesy. Preaching is a nonclassical pursuit—albeit one that (after the encounter between Judaism and Hellenism that produced Christianity) incorporated many of the tools of Greek rhetoric and dialectic.[16] A political speech or a philosophical cut-and-thrust may indeed change minds, but changing minds is ancillary and often epiphenomenal to rhetoric or dialectic's respective goals. Rhetoric mobilizes aims to secure agreement, but this is agreement in the practical sense, agreement in the sense of joint action.

Notes

1 See van Eemeren and Grootendorst, *Speech Acts,* and "Rules for a Critical Discussion" in *A Systematic Theory,* pp. 123–57.

2 Kochin, *Five Chapters,* "The Superhero Next Door."

3 Gary Remer uses Cicero's distinction between conversation and oratory rather than Aristotle's distinction between dialectics and rhetoric to critique Habermas and other theorists of deliberative democracy. Remer attacks the theorist of deliberative democracy for neglect-

ing the constructive uses of emotion in politics as emphasized in Cicero's theory of public speaking (42–43). I turn to Aristotle rather than Cicero because Aristotle gives a more detailed account of the norms of conversation, and a richer conceptualization of rhetoric in which ethos is more than just another mode of "nonrational proof" (contrast Remer 48).

[4] It is worth pondering that we have an Aristotelian manual for conducting philosophical conversations, but we have no Aristotelian examples of philosophical conversations conducted in explicit adherence to those rules (Brunschwig 40–41).

[5] All translations from the Greek are my own, except as noted.

[6] Contrast F. H. van Eemeren and Peter Houtlosser, who speak of "the objective of the parties [in dialectic] . . . to decide jointly whether the protagonist can maintain his standpoint in the light of the criticisms maintained by the antagonist" (139). In Aristotelian dialectic, the judgment is made by the audience or the reader—according to the pragma-dialectics school, in a reasonable conversation it is the speakers themselves who must judge each speech act according to the relevant norms.

[7] See Frogel. Cf. Robert Nozick's account in the defense of his own mode of proceeding in the preface to *Philosophical Explanations*: "What is philosophically interesting . . . is the domestic problem presented for our own beliefs. Because this is what creates the philosophical interest, it is on this explanatory issue we shall concentrate, rather than on the philosophically pointless task of attempting to convince the other person" (18).

[8] Commission of Inquiry, ch. 7, par. 132, p. 135 (my translation); cf. ch. 7, par. 147, p. 138.

[9] Of course the Amsterdammers will say that they mean "pragmatics" in the sense of "speech-acts" (van Eemeren and Grootendorst, *A Systematic Theory* 22).

[10] See Kochin, "From Argument to Assertion," *Five Chapters*, ch. 3, "Things."

[11] For efforts to separate the abortion debate from the social and physiological facts of human reproduction see Zarefsky (*Argumentation*, Lecture Twenty-Two, "Arguments among Experts"); and Schiappa.

[12] Compare also Hintikka, pp. 12–13, where Hintikka admits that for Aristotle the only source of answers for the answerer is common opinion (to which Hintikka should have added the opinions of the wise). Hintikka's confusion comes from his assimilating Aristotle's essentialist logic of assertions to our modern nominalist logic of propositions (an error discussed in Kochin, "From Argument to Assertion"; see also Toulmin, p. 166 and Kimhi). Because Hintikka thinks that logic and dialectic deal with propositions, he thinks that one can understand a dialectical answerer as potentially emitting any type of proposition. He thus cannot understand why, in dialectic, Aristotle restricts the questioner and answerer to "dialectical" syllogisms, which take their premises from the many or the wise.

[13] Evans, p. 12, citing Aristotle, *Sophistical Refutations* 11.172a17–27; Aristotle, *Metaphysics* Γ2.1004b22–6.

[14] Kochin, *Five Chapters*, ch. 1, "Character," "The Superhero Next Door." Of course, the dialectical situation is egalitarian because both participants and audience are presupposed to belong to the elite. The many, Aristotle writes, cannot be expected to follow a long series of dialectical questions and answers (*Rhetoric* 3.18.4.1419a).

[15] Leff, p. 57; and see Walzer.

[16] On preaching as a new genre of rhetoric, see Yunis, pp. 229–32.

Works Cited

Aristotle. *On Rhetoric: A Theory of Civic Discourse*. Trans. George A. Kennedy. New York: Oxford UP, 1991.

Blattberg, Charles. *From Pluralist to Patriotic Politics: Putting Practice First*. Oxford: Oxford UP, 2000.

Brunschwig, Jacques. "Aristotle's Rhetoric as a 'Counterpart' to Dialectic." *Essays on Aristotle's Rhetoric*. Ed. Amélie Oksenberg Rorty. Berkeley: U of California P, 1996.

Burnyeat, Myles. *The Theaetetus of Plato*. Trans. M. J. Levett. Indianapolis: Hackett, 1990.

Commission of Inquiry into the Events of the Campaign in Lebanon 2006 (Winograd Commission). *The Second Lebanon War: Preliminary Report, April 2007* (in Hebrew). Web.

Dror, Yechezkel. "Literature on Evaluating War Results: An Academic List." Politicsplus. 4 May 2007. Web.

Evans, J. D. G. *Aristotle's Concept of Dialectic*. Cambridge: Cambridge UP, 1977.

Frogel, Shai. "Who is the Addressee of Philosophical Argumentation?" *Argumentation* 23 (2009): 397–408.

Hacking, Ian. *Representing and Intervening: Introductory Topics in the Philosophy of Science*. Cambridge: Cambridge UP, 1983.

Hamilton, William. *Parliamentary Logic*. London, 1808. Cambridge: W. Heffer and Sons, 1927.

Hintikka, Jaako. "Socratic Questioning, Logic, and Rhetoric." *Revue Internationale de Philosophie* 47 (1993): 5–30.

Kimhi, Irad. "Thinking and Being: The Two Way Capacity." Unpublished ms., 2010.

Kochin, Michael. *Five Chapters on Rhetoric: Character, Action, Things, Nothing, and Art*. University Park: Pennsylvania State UP, 2009.

———. "From Argument to Assertion." *Argumentation* 23 (2009): 387–96.

———. "The Superhero Next Door." The 2009 Karl Ritter Lecture in Political Rhetoric, Texas A & M University. May 2010. Web.

Krabbe, Erik C. W. "Meeting in the House of Callias: An Historical Perspective on Rhetoric and Dialectic." *Dialectic and Rhetoric: The Warp and the Woof of Argumentation Analysis*. Ed. F. H. van Eemeren and Peter Houtlosser. Dordrecht, Netherlands: Kluwer, 2002.

Leff, Michael. "The Relation between Dialectic and Rhetoric." *Dialectic and Rhetoric: The Warp and the Woof of Argumentation Analysis*. Ed. F. H. van Eemeren and Peter Houtlosser. Dordrecht, Netherlands: Kluwer, 2002.

Nozick, Robert. *Philosophical Explanations*. Cambridge: Harvard UP, 1981.

Remer, Gary. "Political Oratory and Conversation: Cicero versus Deliberative Democracy." *Political Theory* 27 (1999): 39–64.

Ryle, Gilbert. "The Academy and Dialectic." *Collected Papers*. Vol. 1. London: Hutchinson, 1971.

Schiappa, Edward. *Defining Reality: Definitions and the Politics of Meaning*. Carbondale: Southern Illinois UP, 2003.

Slomkowski, Paul. "Aristotle's *Topics*." *Philosophia Antiqua*. Vol. 74. Leiden: Brill, 1997.

Toulmin, Stephen. *Return to Reason*. Cambridge: Harvard UP, 2001.

van Eemeren, Frans H., and Rob Grootendorst. *Speech Acts in Argumentative Discussions: A Theoretical Model for the Analysis of Discussions Directed towards Solving Conflicts of Opinion*. Amsterdam: Foris, 1983.

———. *A Systematic Theory of Argumentation: The Pragma-Dialectical Approach*. Cambridge: Cambridge UP, 2004.

van Eemeren, Frans H., and Peter Houtlosser. "Strategic Maneuvering: Maintaining a Delicate Balance." *Dialectic and Rhetoric: The Warp and the Woof of Argumentation Analysis*. Ed. F. H. van Eemeren and Peter Houtlosser. Dordrecht, Netherlands: Kluwer, 2002.

Walzer, Michael. "Deliberation, and What Else?" *Politics and Passion: Toward a More Egalitarian Liberalism*. New Haven, CT: Yale UP, 2004.

Yunis, Harvey. *Taming Democracy: Models of Political Rhetoric in Classical Athens*. Ithaca, NY: Cornell UP, 1996.

Zarefsky, David. *Argumentation*. The Teaching Company, 2005. Audio Download.

5

Feminist Historiography, Epideictic Rhetoric, and the Kent State Shootings

Controversy, Commemoration, and Culpability

M. Karen Powers

Feminist scholars who write history typically flout traditional understandings of historiography as a straightforward, unbiased, and uncontested intellectual practice. Committed to resisting monolithic standard stories about relationships between past and present and to mitigating dominant views such stories preserve, these historiographers permit controversy to disrupt concord, as Cheryl Glenn explains, by "revisit[ing] the fruitful and necessary tension between history and history writing, a tension that scholars have been grappling with for decades as they read, reread, write, and rewrite histories of various discourses and practices" (388). Glenn claims that those of us who engage in this profoundly rhetorical act "do so in response to intellectual and ethical questions (of evidence, power, and politics) at the same time we resist received notions of both history and writing history" (388). Just as deep-seated disagreements about historiography linger in rhetorical studies, vexed intellectual and ethical questions remain in regard to (re)presenting one of the most disquieting episodes in U.S. history: the thirteen seconds on May 4, 1970, when the Ohio National Guard opened fire during a Vietnam War protest on the Kent State University campus, killing four students and injuring nine others.

A critical examination of the evidence, power, and politics concomitant with the university's discursive (re)construction of this tragic event is illustrative, both in terms of rhetoric's debates about historiography and also in regard to the discipline's shifting definitions of *epideictic,* particularly ways this genre functions to shape existing ideologies of democratic citizenship. Gerard A. Hauser, for example, points out the telling trajectory of several pivotal studies in the 1980s that focused on "sophists and rhetoricians of Greek antiquity"; as he notes, these analyses collectively "move beyond the definitional concerns that were at the center of scholarly discussion for at least the first half of the 20th century" to demonstrate how "epideictic discourse was understood to play an important role in the public realm beyond simple commemoration" (5). Hauser's reading of "these explorations into epideictic's premodern constitutive possibilities" persuades him to formulate a salient conclusion: "In important ways, the occasion for praising or blaming significant public acts and actors also afforded the opportunity to address fundamental values and beliefs that made collective political action within the democracy more than a theoretical possibility" (5). More recently, Robert Danisch elaborates on Hauser's observations by showing how Michel Foucault's "focus on discourse, power, and the subject . . . revises key issues in the history of epideictic rhetoric, suggests the importance of epideictic for questions of human agency and subjectivity and recommends epideictic practices for contemporary social affairs" (292). Within the context of Hauser and Danisch's shared supposition that epideictic transcends unambiguous ceremonial rhetoric to present possibilities for political intervention, I investigate feminist historiography's efficacy for epideictic's revitalization in a contemporary context as one of what Jim W. Corder terms "the old categories," one that could be "more useful, not as laws but as sources of questions, loci of observations" (96).

I couple a particular and contested methodology with a specific and reinvented rhetorical genre to offer a politicized interpretation of a controversial historical event that raises questions about protest and dissent as requisites of democracy. I reread and rewrite the Kent State shootings as an ineffaceable piece of my university's past, specifically as that history is recorded in the brief institutional text titled "May 4, 1970," which has been published in the Kent State University *Undergraduate Catalog* since 1978. I subject to rhetorical scrutiny two versions of this pivotal self-history. I read the 1978 original and the 1994 major revision in juxtaposition, as well as against a theoretical backdrop that insists "histories *do* (or should do) something" (Glenn 388). To elucidate the cultural work epideictic rhetoric ostensibly accomplishes by means of this pair of historical artifacts, or at least to examine what it is these histories might do, I entertain classical notions of the genre but complicate those understandings with recent redefinitions to speculate about ways epideictic performs as intricate argumentation to belie deprecating labels such as "empty display" and "artificial ritual." I posit this feminist rhetorical history that is—like all histories—partial, fragmented, and interested to consider the political ramifications of tacit relationships between words, beliefs, and actions and to participate in potentially transformative debates that turn on intersections between epideictic rhetoric and the formation of democratic ideologies.

Admittedly, a brief rhetorical study of just one incident, albeit strikingly definitive, in this university's 100-year history as that incident is recorded in just two short documents can make only the most limited contribution to debates about feminist rhetorical historiography, to conversations about reinventions of the epideictic genre, and to discussions of dissent as a mode of civic engagement in uncertain times. On the other hand, if the US university's legacy of complicity with state-sponsored, antidemocratic agendas is observable across the history of higher education, "the great tragedies at Kent State University in Ohio and Jackson State College in Mississippi" designate the most reprehensible type of such government coercion.[1] In effect, the "May 4, 1970" rewritings of a particularly ignominious history offer provocative insights into institutional inscriptions of the past by evoking the rhetorical implications for fixing deep-seated assumptions about tenets central to democracy within wide-ranging discursive realms: first, in terms of the US university as a geopolitical and discursive site of historical conflicts between citizens and government; second, as witness to the suppression of First Amendment rights despite putative protection; and third, as palimpsest on which disputed meanings of *democracy* have been written, partially erased, and rewritten. In this instance, Kent State University's epideictic rhetoric precipitated by the shootings exceeds ritual remembrance to signify as contested narrative, disputed interpretation, and challenged representation. Such commemorations write into the official record particular versions of the past that cannot circumvent historiographic corroboration of specific sets of "ideological differences that have defined the nature of the debate over cause, culpability, and appropriate commemoration and remembrance" (Bills 251). These institutional texts underscore epideictic rhetoric as oblique argument that continues to sculpt presumptively democratic precepts even four decades after thirteen seconds of rifle fire shattered collective assumptions about protest and dissent on that fateful day in May. In general, "May 4, 1970" does more than memorialize a historical tragedy: this public rewriting of the past works in rhetorical tandem with other discourses circulating in the public sphere to negotiate ideological differences constitutive of multiple and competing understandings of democracy.

Since the 1978–79 Kent State University *Undergraduate Catalog* published the original "May 4, 1970" statement, this official self-history has reappeared annually to acknowledge the lives tragically lost, the lives irrevocably changed, and the history regrettably made on that day. In a cursory sense, "May 4, 1970" reflects aspects of the traditional threefold definition J. Richard Chase recapitulates in "The Classical Conception of Epideictic": "simply the oratory of praise and blame"; "non-deliberative, non-forensic oratory"; and oratory "synonymous with display" such as "[c]eremonial [o]ratory" (293). For example, the title that has been replicated and ensconced at a prominent and public rhetorical site since 1978 reassures the audience with the terse yet evocative phrase "May 4, 1970" that this date, this tragedy, and these victims will not be forgotten. The similar and evident function of both the 1978 and 1994 texts as commemoration is further reflected in their collective rhetorical move to summon a repertoire of terms reminiscent of elegies—*loss, pain, memorial, vigil, tragedy, sorrow,* and *healing*—a strategy reiterated in the revision's explicit use of the very word *commemoration.*[2]

In like manner, the texts consecrate the historical event and recognize the losses wrought by the shootings with an enumeration of particular university tributes. The Kent State Library Memorial Room contains "books, papers, studies, and other materials relating to the events." In 1978 the Center for Peaceful Change was heralded as "an academic program designed to help students and others employ peaceful conflict resolution to resolve disputes." (The center was renamed the Center for Applied Conflict Management the same year the original "May 4, 1970" statement was extensively revised.) Another overt symbol of commemoration is the university's vow "to remember the four students who died—Allison Krause, Jeffrey Miller, Sandra Scheuer, and William Schroeder—through scholarships in their names." Similarly, a permanent May 4 Memorial inscribed with the words "'Inquire, Learn, Reflect'" sanctifies the scene of the shootings. The "May 4, 1970" text recognizes yet another display of remembrance in the annual May 3 candlelight service and subsequent May 4 vigil.

As a rhetorical act of commemoration, "May 4, 1970" exemplifies Aristotle's general categorization of the genre. One of the "three occasions, or species, of civic rhetoric" George Kennedy offers in *Aristotle on Rhetoric* pertains to "what he calls *epideictic,* or speeches that do not call for any immediate action by the audience but that characteristically praise or blame some person or thing, often on a ceremonial occasion such as a public funeral or holiday" (7). In this case, the statement stands in for the "ceremonial occasion," functioning as a recurring "public funeral" during which praise and blame are ritualized and imprinted on public memory. In regard to praise, "May 4, 1970" delineates a wide range of university tributes, but records few other overt instances, with only two exceptions notable in the 1978 text: first, the recognition of "many students, faculty, staff, and friends" who regard this "pivotal moment in the history of Kent State" as "a moment deeply felt"; and, second, the concluding point that expresses appreciation for "the many ways members of the Kent State community have chosen to express their feelings toward this tragedy." Praise plays an equally minimal role in the 1994 revision. One indirect designation of approval is presumably embedded in the statement, "Not every student was a demonstration participant or an observer," while a second instance more directly commends "some students who assisted with the downtown cleanup."

Generally speaking, both documents heap blame on actors and acts, contexts and circumstances. Citing a wide range of national issues and local situations that set the stage for the bloodshed that occurred, both versions of "May 4, 1970" hold responsible the Vietnam War, the escalation of the conflict into Cambodia, property damage to businesses in downtown Kent, and fearful community residents. The 1994 text calls attention to several additional players and factors ostensibly deserving of rebuke: the city's mayor for initiating the involvement of Ohio's governor, the governor for activating the National Guard and for declaring that "the University would remain open," students who set fire to the campus ROTC headquarters, the anti-war rally that "brought 2,000 to 3,000 people to the University Commons area," "some in the crowd" who disobeyed the "order to disperse" and "responded with verbal epithets and stones," and even the "spring winds" for rendering tear gas ineffective.

For the most part, however, ritualized blame is reserved primarily for two sets of actors involved in the deadly confrontation: the Ohio National Guard and Kent State University students. In both versions of "May 4, 1970," the Guard is sorted into two groups, one who fired their weapons and, by implication, one who did not. This detail is significant to the 1978 text in which the first sentence places direct blame on "a contingent of Ohio National Guardsmen [who] opened fire for a period of thirteen seconds, striking thirteen Kent State University students." At the same time, the unequivocal first line sets up a discursive parameter that sustains the Guard's fault to some degree in the second and third sentences as well, despite the shift to passive constructions in these sentences that tend to displace blame from the implied subject, the group who fired: "Four students were killed, one was permanently paralyzed, and the others were wounded in varying degrees of severity" and "[t]he students were shot as the Guard was responding to a demonstration on the campus." This originary articulation of Kent State University's post-May 4 history stops short of openly condemning the Ohio National Guard's lethal response to an anti-war protest by underplaying the troops' imperative role in the government's unwarranted use of force against unarmed citizens participating in a political rally. Then again, if the 1978 statement ultimately softens any critique of the Guard, it also stresses the pivotal point that students were shot and killed, as well as refrains from impeaching students for expressing vehement disagreement with controversial national and state policies and politics.

In evident ways, the 1994 revision of "May 4, 1970" offers a similar censure of the Guard, but this text differs markedly due to its series of telling rhetorical choices that suggest a less-restrained mitigation of that blame. First, rather than leading with the point that would reasonably seem to be the key purpose for remembrance and commemoration—the Ohio National Guard killed and wounded college students at an anti-war rally—this version withholds the crucial aspect of the tragedy, diffusing the effect of this overarching detail by relegating it to the second sentence. In other words, the first and seemingly fundamental detail announced is that "Kent State University was placed in an international spotlight after a tragic end to a student demonstration against the Vietnam War and the National Guard on May 4, 1970." This sentence's emphasis on the institution rather than on students' deaths and injuries invites the interpretation that one of the victims is the university itself, a casualty of a tarnished reputation that now compromises its status in the eyes of the world. The foregrounding of the state entity in terms of a particular loss suffered—presumably the university's creditable identity as it existed before May 4—seems to constitute a primary reason for remembrance. More troubling yet, the "student demonstration" itself, rather than the Guard's violent reaction to the protest, is apparently responsible for the "tragic end" and subsequent injury to the university.

This implication is reinforced by the same sentence's positioning of students. The Kent State student body is only indirectly mentioned, and that allusion is subtly negative in its function as a modifier for "demonstration." Further, the students' deaths and injuries are not introduced until the second sentence, leaving the meaning of "a tragic end" ambiguous, at least momentarily. Not only does the critical first line of the revised "May 4, 1970" text hold up the university for consideration as the injured party, the sentence distances the institution from the students by acknowledging them solely in terms of their protest that culminates in tragedy. The choice of words and their arrangement in the 1994 statement's initial sentence combine to tacitly renounce the connection between university and students by limiting the latter to a function that merely adds meaning to "demonstration." Similarly, rather than blaming the lethal response to the demonstration for "a tragic end," the terms used and the sentence structure incriminate the demonstration itself, and presumably the students' beliefs and actions that led to it. A related rhetorical strategy names and judges students via their demonstration as not only "against the Vietnam War and the National Guard," but also as against the university, permitting the institution to disown them and their behavior.

In contrast, the first line of the 1978 statement offers an almost antithetical perspective. Not only does this sentence site the university squarely within a local rather than global context, one noteworthy discursive move literally unites the institution and the students by referencing the university solely to describe the students. If "student" modifies "demonstration" in the 1994 text, "Kent State University" modifies "students" in the 1978 text. Naming students "Kent State University students" claims them, positions them as integral to the university rather than against it. If the two "May 4, 1970" statements indicate the time of the tragedy with identical words, "[s]hortly after noon," the dissimilar placement of students in relation to the university lends different meaning to that detail. The earlier text intimates the tragedy's repercussions for the local community by beginning with the fact that Kent State students were killed and injured and by linking the time of the tragedy with other specifics of place, such as the local landscape and local landmarks. Describing the "grassy knoll between Taylor Hall and the Prentice Hall parking lot" invokes a visual and likely familiar setting for a particular university audience. This appeal to local community is especially pertinent in terms of the tragedy that results from the rifle fire "striking thirteen Kent State University students": clearly, the victims are these students; clearly, the university's loss is these students.

If the implicit argument in the 1978 "May 4, 1970" text hinges on remembering and commemorating students whose lives were lost or permanently altered, the 1994 revision largely turns on assuaging the Guardsmen's culpability. When the latter statement does mention student casualties, "rifle fire" rather than the Guard is identified as the principal offender: "Thirteen seconds of rifle fire by a contingent of twenty-eight Ohio National Guardsmen left four students dead, one permanently paralyzed, and eight others wounded." The subtle shift in syntax strategically assigns the "Guardsmen" to a less conspicuous slot as an object of the preposition "by," whereas a more straightforward sentence structure would position them as the subject responsible—in two senses of the word—for the action in the sentence. This choice carries more evidentiary weight when considered in a slightly broader context; that is, juxtaposing the opening assertion, "Kent State University was placed in an international spotlight after a tragic end to a student demonstration," with the main point in the second line, "rifle fire" caused deaths and injuries, suggests how the two ideas work together, not only to limit blame directed at the Guard but to reinforce blame directed at the protestors. The "student demonstration" is conjoined with "rifle fire" to signify that these two acts, as corresponding counterparts, led to the eventual "tragic end." In this version of history, the Guard is reproached for the tragedy, to be sure, but this group's culpability is moderated by casting both major sets of actors in this rhetorical reenactment as duly blameworthy. The student demonstration, as a forum for the protestors' dissent, precipitated the rifle fire as a catastrophic consequence that brought disrepute to the university and instigated students' deaths and injuries. Rather than depicting the students as committed citizens who were exercising their constitutional rights to express their resistance to a nationally unpopular war, students were tacitly characterized as deserving of censure.

A more nuanced reading of the 1994 "May 4, 1970" statement reveals that students, or, more accurately, some students, are blamed in other implicit ways. In contrast to the original text, in which students are named throughout as "Kent State University students" or as simply "students," the revised text categorizes them according to two main divisions: as "students" and as "demonstration participants." The latter grouping is further bifurcated into "some in the crowd [who] responded with verbal epithets and stones" to the Guard's "order to disperse" and, by implication, some who did not. Equally important, the text makes a rhetorical move to unite the "demonstration participant" and the "observer" in the first paragraph: "Not every student was a demonstration participant or an observer." Although the students who were most forcefully involved in the clash with the Guard, those who hurled words and rocks, are most stringently chastised, those who merely observed the conflict are also implicated simply by virtue of association. What would appear to be two wholly different roles—"demonstration participant" and "observer"—are nearly conflated by pairing them in a single sentence and linking them with a coordinating conjunction that intimates their equivalent emphasis.

An alternative and equally logical relationship would seem to exist between observers of the rally and the "students [who] were walking to and from classes," the final category the 1994 text differentiates. The authorial reason for coupling the "demonstration participant" and the "observer," while setting apart students "walking to and from classes," renders somewhat unclear the blame attached to "observer[s]." Less ambiguous, however, is the text's strategy to criticize the category of students who are cast as eminently culpable, the "demonstration participant" whose beliefs and acts presumably necessitated the Guard's presence on campus. At the same time, this "May 4, 1970" version deems entirely blameless only those students who were not participants or even observers of the "student demonstration," those who eschewed participation altogether in a political protest that was not an uncommon occurrence in the late 1960s and early 1970s. As the document concedes, "The divisive effect of the Vietnam War on American society was especially evident on campuses throughout the country." In general, the 1994 text attaches some level of disapproval and some degree of blame to "demonstration participants," although this group of students might be just as persuasively considered dissenters who were acting to resist threats to democratic ideals.

Neither text reserves blame strictly for the Ohio National Guard, but the 1994 commemoration differs from the original in its subtly negative assessment of students deemed "demonstration participants." In a sense, like "some Guardsmen [who] turned toward the Taylor Hall parking lot" in which direction "between sixty-one and sixty-seven shots were fired," this class of students is also held accountable. In fact, this sentence provides yet another telling example of the text's effort to displace blame from the Guardsmen, namely by again removing them from pivotal subject positions that entail directly assigning fault. In its entirety, the sentence reads as follows: "As the Guard approached the crest of Blanket Hill, some Guardsmen turned toward the Taylor Hall parking lot, and between sixty-one and sixty-seven shots were fired." This complex sentence works assiduously to avoid rebuking the Guard for the actual firing of more than sixty bullets into a crowd of unarmed students. If the odd contortion of language is problematic in terms of syntax and parallelism, the awkward sentence's tacit meaning is most disconcerting. A more grammatically precise sentence, as well as a more forthright one, might read this way: "As the Guard approached the crest of Blanket Hill, some Guardsmen turned toward the Taylor Hall parking lot and fired between sixty-one and sixty-seven shots." Yet the "May 4, 1970" revision manipulates language to unobtrusively shift the meaning in such a way that the liability for killing four students and injuring nine others is less emotionally palpable, less logically tangible.

The eleven-sentence paragraph that contains the clumsy and unexpected shift to passive voice offers eight sentences in which the Guard is placed in a subject position five times: "The National Guard arrived Saturday night," "the Guard gave the order to disperse," "the Guard answered first with tear gas," "the Guard attempted to enforce the Ohio Riot Act with raised bayonets," and "the Guard then changed line formation." Similarly, in the paragraph's ninth sentence, an additional two phrases in this pivotal line feature the Guard as active participant: "The Guard approached the crest of Blanket Hill" and "some Guardsmen turned toward the Taylor Hall parking lot." At this critical point in the chronology of events, the text makes what is, at first glance, a perplexing shift to passive voice: "and between sixty-one and sixty-seven shots were fired." Just as this phrase indicates no agent, the stand-alone sentence that immediately follows—"Four students were killed and nine wounded"—designates no executor. Significantly, in every other instance in which the Guard is mentioned, they are the doers of the action. In this example, the passive constructions bury the blame for four students' deaths and nine students' injuries, a rhetorical agenda akin to the apparent effort from the first paragraph forward to name the "demonstration participants" as eminently if not equally culpable. In effect, the 1994 "May 4, 1970" text refrains from incontrovertibly denouncing the Guard, choosing instead to hold back unequivocal condemnation of the state's egregious use of deadly force to silence dissent—despite the conclusion reached by the President's Commission on Campus Unrest nearly a quarter of a century earlier that "the indiscriminate firing of rifles into a crowd of students and the deaths that followed were unnecessary, unwarranted, and inexcusable" (289).

Both versions of "May 4, 1970" aim to remember and commemorate the tragedy borne of this bleak historical moment; accordingly, the most immediately noticeable characteristic of the institutional text is its conventional performance as ceremonial rhetoric. A more scrupulous examination, however, raises questions about the texts' repertoire of functions, especially when considered in light of assertions such as Chaïm Perelman's that "the epideictic genre is not only important but essential," given its potential to prompt "a consensus in the minds of the audience regarding the values that are celebrated in the speech" (339). Considering "May 4, 1970" as reconfigured epideictic rhetoric and through the politicized lens of feminist historiography suggests that these texts work as implicit persuasion to reflect and construct pivotal values and beliefs, particularly in terms of the affiliated roles of protest and dissent that are central to the practice of democracy. It is perhaps in this capacity that "May 4, 1970" operates most powerfully. The newer version, especially, calls on the university's authoritative presence to adjudicate the Kent State shootings by assigning blame to specific acts and actors and by dispensing disapproval to certain beliefs and behaviors. In the process, the text constructs an epideictic rhetoric capable of instilling and cementing beliefs that tacitly dissuade citizen resistance to oppressive government. If as Kent State English professor Martin Nurmi noted in 1980, "The words 'Kent State' now refer to a signal historical event," his observation signifies all the more insistently under the accruing weight of the tragedy's subsequent remembrance and commemoration (qtd. in Bills 245).

Forty years after the Ohio National Guard resorted to deadly force that silenced protestors, at least for a moment, conflicting memories and contested interpretations of an event integral to the intersecting histories of the nation, the US university, and Kent State University continue the discursive and ideological endeavor to redefine the role of dissent within democracy. As epideictic artifacts engaged in this public discourse, the "May 4, 1970" texts offer glimpses of a history of controversy, commemoration, and culpability. One such perspective to emerge from the tragedy's political aftermath is James Munves' sobering conclusion:

> Nothing that grew out of the Kent State shootings will discourage another national administration or governor from seeking, when expedient, another bloody confrontation. Nothing that grew out of the shootings affirms that our liberties remain intact. The real victims of Kent State are all of us. (494)

The "May 4, 1970" revision, in particular, lends some measure of credence to these disturbing words. Yet the epideictic rhetoric shaping Kent State University's commemorations embodies the capacity for legitimating as well as contravening present-day ideals of democratic citizenship. These texts reveal a paradoxical locus where promise for political change persists even as dissent is discouraged. If "May 4, 1970" invokes pressing intellectual and ethical issues, Cynthia Miecznikowski Sheard's reconfigured epideictic opens space for political debate and transformation, since this "epideictic discourse allows speaker and audience to envision possible, new, or at least different worlds" (770).

Kent State University President Lester Lefton intimates just such a possible, new, or different world with his remarks delivered during a recent epideictic occasion: the listing of the May 4 site on the National Register of Historic Places. Lefton insists that

> we've learned a great deal from May 4. We've gone beyond May 4, and what we are going to do is respect what happened in the past and try and put it in a historical context so that people recognize that our democracy grew stronger because of what happened on May 4 at Kent State. ("Kent State Dedicates")

Lefton's assumption that the events of May 4, 1970 could ever be left behind runs counter to a conviction at the core of feminist rhetorical historiography, since "history is not frozen, not merely the past" (Glenn 389). But if the truism that couches history in fixed and invariable contexts is replaced with an understanding of the past as a rhetorical site that "provides an approachable, disruptable ground for engaging and transforming traditional memory or practice in the interest of both the present and the future," the epideictic rhetoric displayed in "May 4, 1970" might be rewritten to commemorate this terrible tragedy with a redefined epideictic fashioned expressly to strengthen democracy (Glenn 389). The year 2010 marks a singular epideictic point in Kent State University's history: the coinciding celebration of the one-hundredth anniversary of the institution's founding with the commemoration of the fortieth anniversary of the Kent State shootings. This timely epideictic moment presents a preeminent opportunity to rewrite "May 4, 1970," given that this existing historical fragment continues to shape the most definitive time in the university's past in ways that suggest epideictic rhetoric's potential to perform its ideal "visionary function" is yet to be realized (Sheard 770).

Notes

[1] Ten days after the Kent State shootings, Mississippi state police "fired a fusillade into a girls' dormitory," killing two and injuring twelve (President's Commission 18).

[2] Material that refers to "May 4, 1970" appears in the Kent State University *Undergraduate Catalog, 1978–79* and the *Undergraduate Catalog, 1994–95*.

Works Cited

Bills, Scott L., ed. *Kent State/May 4: Echoes through a Decade.* Kent, OH: Kent State UP, 1988.

Chase, J. Richard. "The Classical Conception of Epideictic." *Quarterly Journal of Speech* 47 (1961): 293–300.

Corder, Jim W. "From Rhetoric Into Other Studies." *Defining the New Rhetorics.* Ed. Theresa Enos and Stuart C. Brown. Newbury Park, CA: Sage, 1993. 95–105.

Danisch, Robert. "Power and the Celebration of the Self: Michel Foucault's Epideictic Rhetoric." *Southern Communication Journal* 71 (2006): 291–307.

Glenn, Cheryl. "Comment: Truth, Lies, and Method." *College English* 62 (2000): 387–89.

Hauser, Gerard A. "Aristotle on Epideictic: The Formation of Public Morality." *Rhetoric Society Quarterly* 29 (1999): 5–23.

Kennedy, George A. *Aristotle on Rhetoric.* New York: Oxford UP, 1991.

"Kent State Dedicates May 4 Site's Designation on National Register of Historic Places and New May 4 Walking Tour." *Kent State University, May 4 Online Newsroom.* 22 Apr. 2010. Web.

Kent State University. *Undergraduate Catalog, 1978–79.* Kent, OH: Kent State U, 1978.

———. *Undergraduate Catalog, 1994–95.* Kent, OH: Kent State U, 1994.

Munves, James. "More Than People Died at Kent State." *The Nation* 26 Apr. 1980: 492–94.

Perelman, Chaïm. "The New Rhetoric: A Theory of Practical Reasoning." Trans. E. Griffin-Collart and O. Bird. *The Rhetoric of Western Thought.* Ed. James L. Golden et al. 8th ed. Dubuque, IA: Kendall/Hunt, 2004. 336–55.

President's Commission on Campus Unrest. *The Report of the President's Commission on Campus Unrest.* Washington, DC: US Government Printing Office, 1970.

Sheard, Cynthia Miecznikowski. "The Public Value of Epideictic Rhetoric." *College English* 58 (1996): 765–94.

6

Conflict, Inquiry, and the Narrative Imagination

On the Art of Empathic Reasoning

Zachary Dobbins

Many of us who teach argumentation no doubt find disheartening the fact that not everyone shares in the following belief, one that underwrites, perhaps, our pedagogical practices, philosophies, and goals: often the best way to achieve (or at least to approximate) concord (here defined as mutual understanding) is to confront, head on and full steam ahead, controversy, that is, disagreement, conflict, and *mis*understanding. This fact might especially be disheartening to the many of us who seek to advance two of rhetorician Wayne Booth's efforts: (1) to reclaim rhetoric on behalf of practical reasoning and (2) to enhance the quality of our public debate and deliberation by expanding our definition of reasoning to include imagination and the so-called sentiment of empathy; in short, to find ways of noticing and discussing why exactly we disagree in the first place.

Booth's goal for reasoning—one he advances perhaps most compellingly in *Modern Dogma and the Rhetoric of Assent*—is to improve communication, to find the means by which we can most ethically and effectively negotiate our differences through discourse, reason, and imagination. In trying to understand one another, he reminds us, we cannot always aim for certainty or consensus, or true concord; sometimes the best we can do is remove misunderstanding with the hope of reducing unnecessary hostility and violence. And the surest route through these obstacles and toward these goals, he tells us, is through inquiry:

> The supreme purpose of persuasion . . . could not be to talk someone else into a preconceived view; rather it must be to engage in mutual inquiry or exploration. . . . Whatever imposes belief without personal engagement becomes inferior to whatever makes mutual exchange more likely. . . . The *process* of inquiry through discourse thus becomes

> more important than any possible conclusions, and whatever stultifies such fulfillment becomes demonstrably wrong. (137, emphasis added)

That is to say, the only way we can ensure we are vigilant in our efforts to understand one another is to keep inquiry open and the conversation going. Inquiry, Booth might add, is a process that thrives on controversy, one that protects against dogmatism and coercion, and one without which democracy will surely falter. For a lack of inquiry, especially when coupled with a lack of empathy, affects negatively not only the quality of our public discourse and deliberation, but also the quality of our judgments and, in turn, the scope of justice.

These are familiar challenges of rhetorical education and practice—how to promote inquiry into and reasoned deliberation over competing views, how to negotiate ideological conflict, how to use words and ideas instead of threats and epithets, coercion, fists or bombs. The challenge to keep the conversation going is made all the more difficult, of course, when we cannot even agree about the value of disagreement, and when inquiry is too narrowly defined or altogether abandoned. For pundits, politicians, and zealots, to the hard-core dogmatists among them, inquiry no doubt sounds like so much hogwash: indecisiveness, a lack of confidence, blasphemy, and the fast track to losing constituents, congregants, and votes. As I hope to demonstrate, however, this is a problem hardly limited to these easy targets . . . and assured culprits. Within the halls of the academy there is also dissent. ("Appropriately enough," one might chide, in jest or otherwise, since the author promotes disagreement, and here he's got it. To which the author responds, "Not all disagreement is the same; and sometimes we really should agree to disagree. Let me explain.")

This conflict over controversy is well dramatized, for instance, in a recent *Newsweek* article entitled "Harvard's Crisis of Faith," wherein Lisa Miller reports on a division among faculty over whether the university should reform its core curriculum—specifically, whether all undergraduates should be required to take a course in a category called "Reason and Faith," which would interrogate issues and debates about and within world religions. Successfully leading the case against this general education requirement is evolutionary psychologist Steven Pinker. Summarizing his position, Miller writes that Professor Pinker believes that the "primary goal of a Harvard education is the pursuit of truth through rational inquiry, and that religion has no place in that." In other words, according to Pinker, reason precludes faith.

Elsewhere, I have challenged Pinker's definition of rational thought, arguing that it too narrowly focuses on scientific proof and thus delimits what constitutes a good reason. In short, my argument is that he fails to consider the diverse ways we make sense of the world, and that his narrow view of reason poorly equips us for negotiating and debating our many conflicts of values that cannot easily be settled through appeals to objectivity. Here, I want to push this argument a little further by suggesting that by shooting down this course, Pinker is very possibly thwarting his own pedagogical goals, foreclosing the conversations such a course might yield. Specifically, he avoids cultivating precisely the critical thinking skills that might most closely resemble what he calls "the pursuit of truth through rational inquiry" and what some of us might prefer instead to call dialectic, deliberation, or practical reasoning.

At the very least, then, he is thwarting the pedagogical goals of *other* faculty, including those of us rhetoricians who would jump at the chance to teach the controversies surrounding "reason" and "faith." For instance, Pinker's colleague and professor of English at Harvard, Louis Menand, defends the course in Lisa Miller's article: "College is a time 'to unsettle presumptions, to defamiliarize the familiar, to reveal what's going on beneath and behind appearances.'" Supporting Menand's view, Miller herself offers an example of the kind of defamiliarization students might expect in such a course. As she states, "Forcing kids to grapple head-on with the worldview of a Christian or Muslim fundamentalist, say, would be a part of this unsettling."

I want to suggest that Pinker's resistance to this course in certain ways resembles another curricular debate that hasn't entirely been settled, namely the arguments against teaching literature in our first-year writing courses—arguments given their fullest articulation by compositionist Erika Lindemann, who in a 1993 article published in *College English* too narrowly set the terms for what constitutes rhetorical education. I believe that Lindemann, like Pinker, also thwarts her own pedagogical goals, chief among them her efforts to confront students with different ways of making meaning, thereby enhancing not only their rhetorical education but also, arguably, their *civic* education. As I will argue, perhaps most crucial to this education is cultivating our students' abilities to engage in reasoned deliberation: a process that requires they exercise their cognitive capacities to empathize with others while interrogating their own assumptions and beliefs—intellectual capacities that literature (and narrative in general) seems especially well-suited to help cultivate.

According to Lindemann, "We cannot usefully discuss the role of imaginative literature (however defined) in freshman English without first asking what the purpose of a first-year writing course is" (312). In my experience, the purpose of such a course is threefold: (1) to introduce students to academic writing, (2) to give them practice in the writing process, and (3) to develop their skills in critical thinking and reading. When the course is explicitly rhetorical, as mine tend to be, these three goals perhaps necessarily overlap, easily subsumed under a larger category we might simply call argumentation. Consequently, it seems Lindemann saddles us with an arbitrary constraint regarding *how* we cultivate these skills when she unnecessarily jettisons imaginative literature from first-year composition. As she states:

> Such courses have as their subject matter the *processes* whereby writers and readers enter the conversation of the academy and begin to contribute to the making of knowledge. . . . Interpreting texts presents only one way of knowing, a process of knowledge-making peculiar to the humanities. Other disciplines value different methods of making meaning. (313–14)

And yet, the process of interpreting literature (which Lindemann later pokes fun at) is not the only way one can use literature. Indeed, there are other ways to teach literature to foster the kind of rhetorical training she seems to favor—where students grapple not only with the unsettling worldviews represented in the texts themselves (for instance, a character's Christian or Muslim fundamentalism), but also with the unsettling ways in which these views are represented, at least in some works of literature, where readers are challenged to negotiate among competing views and where the author refuses to advocate explicitly for one over another.

One such way to teach literature rhetorically—and one that avoids the kind of traditional critical essay that Lindemann (with good reason) fears might dominate a lit-focused first-year writing course—is an approach to argumentation called "teaching the controversies," a now-familiar method of teaching critical thinking developed over the past twenty years by Gerald Graff. Graff argues that students require better instruction in the skills of analyzing and evaluating others' arguments and synthesizing these arguments in the thoughtful construction of their own. This approach requires that whatever discipline they are working within, students consider their essays as contributions to a larger conversation: one they enter into by responding to others' arguments, situating themselves in the position of ally as well as opponent. More recently, with the publication of the rhetoric and writing handbook *They Say/I Say*, Graff (along with his coauthor Cathy Birkenstein) has illustrated that his approach to academic writing can prepare students to explore and argue *any* controversy, including, for instance, public debates over obesity, nationalism, or economic inequity. Since teaching the controversies is hardly limited, then, to literary texts and the discipline of English, this approach to argumentation seems perfectly aligned with Lindemann's own rhetorical aims for first-year writing.

Though Graff himself does not explicitly make this connection, I want to suggest we bridge his early focus on literature and his recent focus on public debate in order to examine some other ways we can use literature rhetorically to foster the critical thinking skills that Lindemann and Pinker both seem to promote. Of course, we can begin by encouraging our students to see a work of literature as a form of proof in argumentation—a piece of textual evidence, say, of intellectual history or cultural practice—for example, *Uncle Tom's Cabin* as an artifact of, and perspective on, slavery. Further, and more to my purposes here, we can use literature as a mode of reasoning in itself.

One advantage of the narrative fiction I have in mind—and perhaps much narrative in general, fictional or otherwise—is that, as a form of meaning making, it often does a good job of dramatizing conflicts and raising questions without necessarily resolving or answering them. Narrative is also useful in generating opposing views and then requiring readers to negotiate among them, often without the author's guidance as to which view is correct. What is more, and what Lindemann seems to overlook, as does Pinker in his own way, is that literature can help aid in the process of defamiliarization that Menand argues is a crucial component of a college education; and it can aid in this process in part by introducing students to unfamiliar, if not also unpopular, perspectives and by encouraging them to take these views seriously (e.g., by placing readers in the consciousness of individuals they might have difficulty identifying with). In fact, according to scholars across disciplines—including philosopher Martha Nussbaum, political theorist Iris Marion Young, and cognitive scientists who study what they call "perspective taking"—narrative is an invaluable means of exercising our intellectual capacities to empathize with others, to try to understand more fully and also more compassionately the different values and experiences that give shape to our conflicting worldviews.

Consider, for instance, the novel *Cloudsplitter* by Russell Banks. Published in 1998, Banks's novel examines the turbulent life of abolitionist John Brown. Rather than asserting that Brown was either a lunatic or a saint, as have most historians and biographers for the past century and a half, Banks represents the abolitionist with flaws intact. Banks thereby provides readers with an opportunity that other authors largely deny them: that is, the challenge to interrogate for themselves, without encountering much overt bias, the question of how a person of faith can become an extremist—indeed, can become so motivated to redress a perceived injustice that he could murder his ideological opponents in cold blood and then mount a massive terrorist campaign, in this case a failed effort to incite an armed slave insurrection.

To further complicate our image of the abolitionist, Banks narrates the story from the perspective of Brown's son Owen, who gives voice to his own mixed emotions and ambivalence regarding his father's beliefs and actions. The novel not only requires that readers engage in the process of deliberation, it also models that very process in its form, in the consciousness of the son who struggles to reconcile his and his father's Christian faith with their acts of terrorism and violence. Consequently, father and son come across as individuals with complex reasons for what they believe and how they act—that is, individuals whose reasons for choosing one path over another are no doubt as intricate as they are for the rest of us.

Any number of courses might benefit by including this text on its reading list, most apparently those that examine debates over slavery, the Civil War, or the abolitionist movement. More generally, though, one could use the novel to explore any number of thorny ethical questions hardly limited to the nineteenth century—questions especially relevant in the wake of 9/11, and questions that would naturally arise in the Harvard course that Pinker rejects. For instance: How do we define terrorism? Are there religious justifications for the use of violence? How do we negotiate claims to competing (if not incommensurate) conceptions of "Truth," even competing conceptions of "God"? How do we distinguish a noble cause from a reprehensible one, democracy from demagoguery, or reason from faith?

Like many other works of narrative fiction, *Cloudsplitter* only obliquely raises these questions and certainly never settles them. Avoiding clear answers, the novel instead proliferates plausible interpretations, offering hypotheses while dramatizing the very process of inquiry required of critical thinking. That is to say, readers are left to grapple with these questions and competing explanations, to puzzle them out for themselves in the process of meaning making that Lindemann rightly celebrates as a chief goal of rhetorical education. As a mode of reasoning, then, narrative seems especially well-suited to fostering deliberation, perhaps even more effectively than proposition-driven arguments. For the latter mode often encourages readers to pledge their allegiance to the author's explicit position on an issue, thus directing their judgment toward more certain ends, often with the consequence, if not the goal, of discouraging inquiry into the merits of competing views. Thus, at the very least, narrative can complement other modes of argumentation, and thereby enhance rhetorical education and practice, by foregrounding our conflicts, dramatizing the experiences and values that give them shape, and providing readers the opportunity to engage more fully in the processes of inquiry, deliberation, and judgment.

If our goal is to enhance rhetorical education and practice by fostering reasoned inquiry and informed judgment, and through these means enhance also *civic* education and practice, then there's no good reason to quarantine our students from literature, nor from the controversies that literature can help dramatize and complicate. A crucial tool for exploring debates and an invaluable mode of reasoning in its own right, narrative can help cultivate skills in empathy and deliberation—that is, habits of thought—the intellectual and ethical value of which extends well beyond the walls of the academy. The controversies that narratives richly bring to life remind us that sometimes the closest we can come to achieving concord—however we define it—is by understanding more fully both how it's so difficult to achieve and how greatly we require inquiry, imagination, and empathy to get us there . . . or at least nearer to it.

Works Cited

Banks, Russell. *Cloudsplitter.* New York: Harper Collins, 1998.

Booth, Wayne. *Modern Dogma and the Rhetoric of Assent*. Chicago: U of Chicago P, 1974.

Graff, Gerald, and Cathy Birkenstein. *They Say/I Say: The Moves That Matter in Academic Writing*. New York: Norton, 2006.

Lindemann, Erika. "Freshman Composition: No Place for Literature." *College English* 55.3 (1993): 311–16.

Miller, Lisa. "Harvard's Crisis of Faith." *Newsweek* 11 Feb. 2010. Web. 23 Feb. 2010.

Nussbaum, Martha. *Cultivating Humanity: A Classical Defense of Reform in Liberal Education*. Cambridge: Harvard UP, 1997.

Young, Iris Marion. "Communication and the Other: Beyond Deliberative Democracy." *Democracy and Difference*. Ed. Seyla Benhabib. Princeton: Princeton UP, 1996. 120–35.

7

Argument Building from Databases

Remediating Invention in a First-Year Writing Course

J. Blake Scott

Describing it as a "defining characteristic" of digital media (35), Jay David Bolter and Richard Grusin define remediation as the process "by which new media refashion prior media forms" (273). In applying this concept to rhetorical as well as media refashioning, this essay will explore the remediation of an argument-building assignment in my first-year composition course. Designed to help students further research a kairotic civic issue, assess various arguments about it, arrive at a position, and begin to build an informed response, this assignment asks students to produce an electronic database of rhetorical proofs, a database that then functions as an important invention tool for subsequent assignments. My assignment, requiring a simple database created in a Google Docs spreadsheet, constitutes a modest refashioning of an earlier assignment that involved an annotated bibliography and argument diagram. As Bolter and Grusin explain, remediation can vary from merely using new media to access older media forms to more aggressively repurposing or even absorbing these forms (45–47). Creating and using a rhetorical database taps into students' creative logic of selection and compositing conditioned by new media, and it has the potential to encourage what Collin Brooke calls "proairetic" invention, or the associative, open-ended exploration and building of connections and patterns (85). Although my students' databases, and their uses of them, could be said to modestly refashion older rhetorical modes of invention, the assignment has the potential for other levels of remediation as well.

Before I go any further, let me clarify how I am using the term database, especially since databases and spreadsheets are viewed by many as somewhat different tools. Following Lev Manovich, I am defining a database generally as a structured collection of data that enables the user to manipulate data (numerical, rhetorical, or otherwise) through modular selection and variable compositing, or merging disparate parts or modules. As Manovich explains, databases have no predetermined order, but rather are given order when acted upon by users (101).

Because databases, as more general constructs, are not exactly new, I will briefly discuss a larger trajectory of rhetorical databases (or rhetorical technologies with database-like qualities) used to aid memory and invention. I will also explain some capabilities and operations (e.g., automated sorting) more specific to electronic databases. I will then further show and discuss student examples of my assignment, relating it to the processes of proairesis and, from Jeff Rice, chorography. I will end by briefly discussing future possibilities for the assignment, including using more powerful databases and enabling students to build arguments that are themselves databases of sorts. I argue, then, that electronic databases can provide students with rich resources for rhetorical invention and can function as important forms of arguments themselves.

A Brief History of Rhetorical Databases

One place to begin a Western history of rhetorical databases, especially as they relate to narrative forms, is with the aoidoi or bards who wove or stitched together epic heroic tales through oral mnemonic formulas. Bards drew on mental databases of such formulas, which Ong refers to as "prefabricated parts" and "clichés," to create and adapt their extended songs or chants (22). Following Manovich's definition of databases, the bards' oral formulas were modal and enabled variable selection and additive, aggregative composition in response to the exigencies of specific rhetorical situations. As Richard Enos explains, these singers of tales evolved into a formal guild of rhapsodes who recorded elements of the formula-driven narratives in writing in order to aid oral performances and store the cultural memory they conveyed (9). Although Manovich acknowledges the encyclopedias created by the ancient Greeks as examples of early databases, he *contrasts* them to narratives rather than acknowledging how narratives were also created through databases (233).

Later, the early rhetoricians, whose art was related to the poetic tradition of the rhapsodes, developed what we might call oral and written databases of arguments or proofs. According to George Kennedy, the first rhetorical handbooks (small books on papyrus) included collections of proofs and refutations, including emotional appeals, on which rhetors could draw to compose oral arguments in judicial settings. The sophists and other teachers and performers of rhetoric began to write handbooks for other occasions, too. These handbooks, such as those by Theodorus of Byzantium (a contemporary of Gorgias), were used as resources or starting points for arguments and also included collections of commonplaces and examples of rhetorical techniques. Later, Aristotle and others, such as Theophrastus, would further document in writing these databases, or collections of rhetorical elements and techniques used as invention resources.

Commonplace books, which changed and grew in popularity in early modern England and remained in widespread use through the Victorian age, have also been traced back to the sophists, namely Protagoras (Macintyre). Although they later came to include various types of collections and take on more readerly than writerly functions, commonplace books functioned as another type of rhetorical database used as an inventional resource for composition and declaration, and one that included premises, proofs, quote-worthy expressions or sayings from readings, and other rhetorical elements. In his description of how commonplace books were used in early modern England, Robert Darnton points to some of the qualities (e.g., modularity and variability) and uses of databases discussed by Manovich. Users of commonplace books, Darnton explains, "broke texts into fragments and assembled them into new patterns by transcribing them in different sections of their notebooks. Then they reread the copies and rearranged the patterns while adding more excerpts."

Rhetorical databases continued to change along with shifts in literacy and what Ong terms secondary orality, the latter of which can be additive and formula-driven (37, 134). Some have compared commonplace books and the journals that followed them to blogs, which Brooke describes as hybrids of databases and narratives, that act as platforms for more personal interactions with databases. Blogs, wikis, social networking pages, and other new media forms are also typically *created* by users from databases, and this process has conditioned our students' composing processes. In arguing that electronic databases are important new cultural forms and metaphors for cultural memory, and in discussing how electronic databases have evolved with new media technologies such as CD-ROMs (e.g., as virtual museums) and web databases, Manovich emphasizes some of the unique qualities of such databases, to which I now turn (214, 219).

Remediating Rhetorical Invention

Although I have been suggesting that the modularity of electronic databases is not necessarily new, Manovich explains how this modularity is more pronounced and combined with variability (including scalability) and automation. The modular elements stored in an electronic database can be quickly searched, filtered, or sorted, variously assembled, and otherwise acted upon by both the user and computer. According to Manovich, the extreme modularity, variability, and automation enabled by electronic databases changes the creative process, though perhaps not as radically as he suggests. Manovich contrasts the database logic of menu selection and compositing (or combining and seamlessly merging, 136) with a more sequential narrative impulse, though he, like Brooke, discusses hybrid new media forms, including narratives organized as databases (237). In their composing of various new media or new media-enabled texts, our students perform such operations as copying and pasting, sorting, searching, and compositing, operations that depend on computer databases. Some of these texts—such as iTunes playlists, Flickr albums, and Facebook accounts—look and function like database-narrative hybrids themselves; indeed, Manovich defines a new media object as "one or more interfaces to a multimedia database" customized for a specific set of purposes and users (37). As with the examples just mentioned, we often create interfaces from databases through a series of technological filters, ranging from basic code to user-friendly application software, that shapes our creative (and rhetorical) possibilities (117). Pointing to blog software, Brooke explains how these filters or platforms, as he calls them, allow users to create and interact with databases on a more "intimate scale" (108). In addition, some of these filters enable us to compose collaboratively by easily linking to, sharing, and contributing to one another's texts or interfaces.

Brooke and Rice have also discussed new processes of composing enabled by new media, explaining them in terms of remediated rhetorical concepts such as the five canons. Rice, for example, extends Gregory Ulmer's reconceptualization of invention as the composition and recognition of connections and patterns from unexpected juxtapositions of elements (such as argument parts) (34–35). Offering the website Everything2.com as an example, Rice describes chorography, part of his rhetoric of cool, as the associative creation of new meanings through experimenting with various connections and juxtapositions (131). Rice further extends this notion of associative invention through his concept of appropriation, which requires the rhetor to not only associatively rearrange and combine, but also to reimagine the logic of any underlying rhetorical structures and goals, including those of hierarchical organization, clarity, and coherence (58–60).

In *Lingua Fracta*, Brooke more systematically repurposes the five canons in building a rhetoric of new media. Most importantly for my analysis, Brooke develops a notion of invention as proairesis, which, like Rice's rhetoric of cool, manifests as the associative, open-ended building and exploration of patterns. Using the "associational network of sources" created through social bookmarking sites as an example (83), Brooke explains how proairetic invention creates interfaces that "allow patterns and relationships to emerge" (107). Just as Rice contrasts appropriation to the goal of clarity, Brooke contrasts proairesis to the hermeneutic impulse to fix meaning; he also explains how new media can enable an iterative process through which hermeneutic and proairetic impulses fuel each other. In discussing how the canon of arrangement works in relation to electronic databases (such as the Amazon website), Brooke argues, in contrast to Manovich, that the move away from a sequential progression does not mean arrangement is less relevant to new media but that it must be redefined in terms of selection, linking, and ordering (91). As he points out, the arrangement of databases themselves is crucial to creating databases and generating meaning from them (91). If arrangement is more about nonsequential connection- and pattern-making, then memory is about the perception of these connections and patterns (157), what Brooke calls a "persistence of cognition" that enables the recognition and retention of "particular ideas, keywords, or concepts across multiple texts" and sources (157). Thus, in remediating older memory and invention devices, electronic databases foreground new processes of argument recognition and building and enable new argument forms.

Although my students frequently use new media research tools and create visual and multimedia arguments for various civic forums, my first-year writing pedagogy admittedly could further explore the unique potential of new media forms and operations. Some of the composing strategies I have typically emphasized, including outlining a sequential argument and beginning with a claim or proposition, are hardly associative or proairetic. My database assignment is only a modest remediation of my earlier argument-building assignment, and one that still values the goal of creating more traditional civic arguments, but it has the potential to tap into students' undervalued new media-composing processes and to energize their invention.

Teaching Electronic Databases of Rhetorical Proofs

As I mentioned earlier, this assignment remediates parts of an earlier assignment designed to enhance students' research and argument-building skills. In the earlier assignment, students wrote annotated bibliographies that assessed various arguments about a kairotic issue (e.g., "To what extent should the Florida legislature enable universities to raise tuition?"), designed a diagram or concept map that included their tentative position or claim about the issue and assembled rhetorical proofs that could support their claim, and finally wrote a brief explanation of how they might adapt their argument to two specific rhetorical situations. Like this previous version, my database-building assignment follows issue analysis and rhetorical analysis assignments and serves as a bridge, if you will, to students' composing their own informed contributions to a civic debate in the last two assignments. In moving from analyzing civic debates and arguments to more directly contributing to them, students use their databases to compose different types of arguments (e.g., evaluative, proposal) for a specific issue's stakeholders and decision-makers. To enable students' collaborative work on the assignment, students must choose among three or four issues (each with multiple versions of issue questions) agreed upon by the class.

In addition to using the library's electronic databases of media and scholarly sources (databases that automate searching, indexing, and retrieval), students work together to create annotated bibliographies comprised partly of web bookmarks and notes (using the social bookmarking site Delicious.com). This part of the assignment helps students arrive at a tentative position on the issue through associative explanation. Instead of a diagram or concept map, students then create electronic databases of rhetorical proofs to support their position or claim. These databases, which both draw on (and link to) students' earlier research and include intrinsic proofs, are comprised of cells detailing reasons, underlying premises or assumptions, commonplaces, appeals to reasoning, appeals to credibility or character, appeals to emotion, appeals to authorities or data, examples, and/or other elements we learned about in the previous two assignments. As explained by the assignment description (see appendix A), students can organize their database columns in a number of ways, such as primarily around major reasons or types of proof. I also ask students to include a variety of appeals, to include references and links to sources where appropriate, and to include a section focusing on refutation of possible counterarguments. Some students additionally include possible audiences in their databases. Through Google Docs, students can work together in this part of the assignment, too, to share and comment on database elements (through the comment function). After students workshop and revise their databases, they write short papers (as before) explaining how they could use their database to create two different types of arguments (i.e., evaluative and proposal) for two different rhetorical situations (i.e., exigencies, audiences, purposes, and forums) that they identify.

Before I further discuss and show examples of these databases, let me explain why I used spreadsheets. Designed more for manipulating and creating various types of reports from numerical data, spreadsheets can be clunky, redundant, and less powerful than other types of databases, such as Microsoft Access. But they are a more familiar database form for many students and, through Google Docs, they enable web-based storage, sharing, and real-time collaborative composing (including a comments function and way to track multiple versions). Although I admit that spreadsheet databases function largely as glorified tables in my assignment, they still foreground an invention process around selection and compositing, and they still enable automated sorting and filtering, updating, reorganizing, and web searching.

To illustrate what these databases can look like, let me direct you to appendices B and C, which show parts of two students' databases or spreadsheets (exported from Google Docs as PDF files). The first sample database was constructed around a student's claim that major league baseball should impose a salary cap. As you can see in appendix B, this student organized his database columns around various types of proofs, including Aristotle's three artistic appeals, his situated ethos, and examples, and he includes fairly elaborate explanations, including some extrinsic data, in the cells under each column. The rows are organized around the major reasons that could be marshaled to support his claim to impose a salary cap, and, in the larger version, each reason is aligned with a corresponding audience, source, counterclaim, and refutation. In the two subsequent arguments he constructed from this database, one for a sports blog and the other in a letter to MLB Commissioner Selig, the student emphasized different reasons and included different combinations of appeals.

The second example, see appendix C, shows another student's database around her claim that the Florida legislature should not lift the ban on offshore drilling. This database contains some of the same categories as the previous one, but the columns are organized around major reasons and counterarguments and the rows around types of proof and their sources. Note the links to web articles identified in the social bookmarking stage of the assignment. This student went on to compose antidrilling arguments for her hometown newspaper and state representative, each argument a unique combination of database elements.

Other databases were organized still differently. Some students organized their columns more simply around types and examples of proofs, sources, and possible audiences, for example, while others dedicated larger parts of their databases to possible counterarguments and refutation or to extrinsic proofs and source links.

Although I ask students to begin to construct their database around a tentative position or claim about the issue, I also encourage them to qualify or otherwise adjust their positions if they develop sometimes unexpected observations or associations (and many of them do just this). When they design their database, I ask students to experiment with various designs (sets of columns and rows) that juxtapose rhetorical elements in different ways. Some students compose their versions in multiple sheets. As with the previous stage of annotating and assessing various arguments about the issue, this stage of the assignment asks students to work associatively and collaboratively to discover various patterns or lines of argument (merging extrinsic and intrinsic proof). Students can link their databases to their Delicious.com tags and others' databases. At this point, students can use the spreadsheet filtering and sorting functions, which automates pattern-forming to some degree. But the focus of this stage is not on recording patterns, following Brooke's notion of proairesis, it is on creating a structure that "allows patterns and relationships to emerge" (107).

The selection and compositing operations enabled by the database become more important later, when students experiment with merging different combinations of elements in response to two rhetorical situations. Students often find some overlap, but the parameters I give them for assignments four and five suggest a heavier reliance on extrinsic proof for one of the audiences and forums. At this point, too, some of the spreadsheet's automated functions, such as list view, sort, and search, can come in handy, enabling students to foreground and juxtapose different parts of their database. Later yet, when students actually compose the final two papers for the course, they can also sort and merge different combinations of examples, citations, and other elements from their databases.

This assignment, like the use of electronic databases more generally, does not abandon or completely automate the canons of arrangement and memory, but differently imagines and operationalizes them. Arrangement becomes more about open-ended, associative pattern formation, and memory becomes more about pattern recognition.

As I have taught it thus far, the assignment could do more to enable proairetic invention, perhaps by *not* asking students to start their database creation around a claim or proposition. In addition, the assignment does not follow Rice's process of appropriation, since it does not ask students to radically reimagine the basic structures of the arguments they compose from their databases. Let me conclude with a few remarks about how I plan to adjust the assignment in future classes to better tap into the power of databases and their remediation of rhetorical processes.

Possibilities of Rhetorical Databases

One of the first adaptations I want to try is to encourage students to use a more proper database such as Microsoft Access, and help them figure out more productive ways to sort, filter, and rearrange the parts of their argument. Using a more powerful database might require more technology training but would make it easier to organize the rhetorical elements in an even more modular, open-ended way, perhaps removing the need to start with a claim or proposition and thereby further enabling students' proairetic invention. I additionally will encourage students to include visual components in their databases, particularly since my course's fourth assignment asks them to accompany their written argument with an editorial cartoon.

Although I have mostly asked students to create more traditional enthymeme-based arguments from their databases, they could also use them to construct arguments, at least in one of the last two assignments, that are themselves database hybrids (e.g., blogs, wikis, Facebook pages, or Everything2.com websites) with more associative organizational logics. Such arguments would remain, like the argument-building database from which they would draw, modular, associative, and, to some degree, open-ended. Such arguments might not be well-suited to some decision-making audiences, such as policy makers, but they also might enable younger, more media-savvy audiences to better engage with the issue and rhetor's take on it, and in a more proairetic way. As my assignment sheet points out, our students are already using databases and their logic to create a number of social and professional texts, and this adaptation to my assignment could help prepare students for such work.

Bolter and Grusin explain that remediation can work both ways, as newer media and their uses are influenced by and refashioned through older media. Because my database assignment requires students to collect both extrinsic and intrinsic proofs, including some that they create or discover in language, it can perhaps help them view a database not just as a collection of menu choices predetermined by experts, but as tools that they can and should rhetorically contribute to and construct. When forming and selecting/compositing from a database becomes a self-conscious rhetorical exercise, the postindustrial logic of quick and efficient "production on demand" (applied in this case to crafting arguments that respond to rhetorical exigencies) can become more deliberative and even interactive, in contrast to what Manovich laments (36).

As I hope I have shown, electronic databases of rhetorical elements can provide students with a rich resource for a different kind of rhetorical invention, enable them to more deliberately craft informed arguments for specific rhetorical situations, and function as important types of arguments themselves. I plan to do additional assessment (including interviews with students) in future classes, but my evaluation of assignments four and five found that students' arguments were more thorough and better suited to their specific audiences than those of my previous students not working from databases. In conclusion, beyond remediating students' invention tools and processes in a manner that builds on their existing modes of composing, electronic databases can help us, as teachers of writing and rhetoric, rethink our pedagogical assumptions about what counts as an argument, how arguments can and should be formed, and how arguments ought to look and function.

Works Cited

Bolter, Jay David, and Richard Grusin. *Remediation: Understanding New Media*. Cambridge, MA: MIT P, 2000.

Brooke, Collin Gifford. *Lingua Fracta: Towards a Rhetoric of New Media*. Cresskill, NJ: Hampton P, 2009.

Darnton, Robert. "Extraordinary Commonplaces." *The New York Review of Books* 21 Dec. 2000. Web. 1 May 2010.

Enos, Richard Leo. *Greek Rhetoric before Aristotle*. Long Grove, IL: Waveland P, 1993.

Kennedy, George A. "The Earliest Rhetorical Handbooks." *On Rhetoric: A Theory of Civic Discourse*. New York: Oxford UP, 2007. 293–306.

Macintyre, Ben. "Last Word: There Should be Nothing Remotely Common in a Commonplace Book." *Times* Online 21 Apr. 2007. Web. 1 May 2010.

Manovich, Lev. *The Language of New Media*. Cambridge, MA: MIT P, 2001.

Ong, Walter J. *Orality and Literacy: The Technologizing of the Word*. London: Routledge, 2002.

Rice, Jeff. *The Rhetoric of Cool: Composition Studies and New Media*. Carbondale: Southern Illinois UP, 2007.

Appendix A
Argument-Building Assignment

TO: ENC 1102H Writers
FROM: Professor Blake Scott
SUBJECT: Argument-Building (Paper 3) Assignment Description

With its focus on argument building, this assignment will help prepare you for the final two papers in the course. In this assignment, you will get more practice investigating an issue, and you will develop a database of rhetorical reasons and proofs (i.e., available means of persuasion) to use in specific rhetorical situations. The assignment has four parts: (1) you will explain your plans for the assignment in a brief blog post; (2) in further researching the issue, you will create a Delicious tag that compiles your notes about relevant web sources, and you will also contribute and link to others' tags; (3) after determining your initial position on the issue, you will develop an electronic database (using Google Docs) of rhetorical proofs to support your claim (although this database can change if your position changes); and (4) you will then write a short paper (1–2 pages) that summarizes how you would select and merge items from the database to construct arguments for two specific rhetorical situations.

One of the assignment's purposes is to call attention to the ways contemporary rhetors construct texts through new media. Although ancient rhetors used conceptual systems (e.g., topoi) and handbooks as storehouses for possible arguments, new media have further facilitated the use of databases to construct texts and arguments through a menu-driven process of selection and compositing (i.e., assembling a number of elements into a single object; see Manovich 139). Think here about how you construct a Facebook page from a database of design options, pictures, and "friends," or how you construct an iTunes playlist from a database of songs. Many professional writers, too, use databases to construct verbal and multimedia texts; some technical writers, for example, construct different types of user documentation from a database of user instructions.

Part 1: Assignment Plan

In this brief blog post, you will briefly explain your issue, identify the types of sources you will consult to learn about the issue and locate possible reasons, warrants, and proofs, your plan for the database structure and categories, and the two rhetorical situations you will address in part 4.

Part 2: Delicious Tag and Bookmarks

We'll learn how to use multiple electronic research tools, and one of your tasks will be to use the social bookmarking site Delicious.com to create a tag (or set of tags) that bookmarks relevant web pages and your annotations about them. You will also, where appropriate, add to your classmates' sources/annotations and link to other people's tags about the issue.

Part 3: Developing an Electronic Database of Proofs

After you've determined your initial position through investigating the issue, you will then move to building a database of argument parts that could support your claim. The database should include a variety of intrinsic and extrinsic proofs and can include your major reasons, warrants, or assumptions, logical appeals, ethical appeals, pathetic appeals, commonplaces, and appeals to authorities and data. If appropriate, it should also include proofs to refute counterarguments, sources, and possible audiences for the various elements. In your search for extrinsic support, I encourage you to use the library's resource pages at http://libguides.lib.ucf.edu/content.php?pid=38311 and http://libguides.lib.ucf.edu/news-florida.

To make your database accessible for peer workshopping and my assessment, I'm asking you to create it using Google Docs, a free web-based program that allows you to create and store document and spreadsheet files and collaboratively work on them with others. If you don't have one already, you'll need to sign up for a free Google account. Within Google Docs, you can create your database as a spreadsheet file. We'll discuss different ways to organize your database (e.g., around major reasons or types of appeals). Much of the database design is up to you, but I expect you to experiment with different structures and categories, perhaps using multiple sheets in your spreadsheet file.

In conducting parts 2 and 3 of this assignment, you may find yourself qualifying or adjusting your position or claim (this is fine), which should prompt you to also adjust and/or add to the categories and specific elements of your database.

Part 4: Written Explanation of Argument Building

For this final part of the assignment, you will write a 1–2 page summary explanation of how you would select and assemble proofs from your database to construct arguments for two different rhetorical situations (including audiences, purposes, and forums through which you will reach your audience). Your paper should summarize *how* and *why* you would select and assemble a number of proofs for each situation.

Writing Workshop for Database

For this writing workshop, you will first create a document file (separate from your database file) titled "Writing Workshop for Database." Next, you will grant me and two of your classmates (I'll put you into groups based on common issues) access to your database and writing workshop file. You can do this by opening the files, clicking the Share (invite people/share with others) tab, entering the e-mail addresses of the others (make sure you allow them to edit/collaborate), and clicking Send. Then, you will make specific suggestions for and additions to the two classmates' databases using the comment tool within the spreadsheets themselves, and you will provide some overall comments in the writing workshop document file. Overall comments should include three specific suggestions for improving the database and could focus on the types and variety of proofs (including those for refuting counterarguments), the number of proofs, the sources for proofs, and the database categories and organization.

Evaluation

The assignment plan memo will count 10% of the assignment grade, the Delicious.com tag and bookmarks 10%, the database 70%, and the written explanation the remaining 10%. I'll assess the database primarily according to its thoroughness and the usefulness of its design and arrangement. I'll assess the paper according to its arrangement, style, and, above all, how well it explains your adaptation of arguments to the rhetorical situations.

Appendix B

Reasons	Logical Appeal	Situated Ethos	Pathetic Appeal	Example	Data/Source
Reason #1: A cap would promote competitive balance among MLB's 30 teams.	While Commissioner Selig states that competitive balance was present during the 2004–2008 seasons, the numbers seem to say otherwise. Of the 48 teams with a sub-$60 million payroll during that span, only 13 had a winning record and only 4 made the playoffs. On the other hand, of the 30 teams that spent at least $100 million, 26 had a winning record and 16 made the playoffs.		A new generation of young baseball fans who cheer for teams like the Pittsburgh Pirates will finally be exposed to the exciting atmosphere and feeling that comes with watching your favorite team battle its way through the playoffs. The Pirates have had an MLB record 17 losing seasons in a row and last reached the playoffs in 1992.	The New York Yankees were just crowned 2009 World Series champions after defeating the defending champions, the Phillies. Both teams rank among the highest in payrolls for all of MLB, with the Yankees at #1 with a staggering $201 million.	1. Joe Starkey—*Tribune Review* 2. Wikipedia—Pittsburgh Pirates 3. *USA Today*—Payrolls
Reason #2: Big market teams like the Yankees, Red Sox, and Cubs hold an oligopoly of the free-agent market.	Most teams do not have the money to compete against big market teams like the Yankees when chasing after a prime free agent because the Yankees can always offer a better deal since there is no limit to how much they are allowed to spend. Due to the lack of a salary cap, the Yankees had a ridiculous shopping spree during the 2008–2009 off-season and signed all 3 of the most sought after players: pitcher CC Sabathia for 7 years and $161 million, pitcher A. J. Burnett for 5 years and $82.5 million, and first baseman Mark Teixeira for 8 years and $180 million.	As a Marlins fan, I lost hope that the team can compete in the free agent market long ago. Year after year I have seen the Marlins make initial offers to prized free agents, and even moderately priced veterans, and come up short. Each time we are overmatched by big market teams with much more money available to throw around. This results with the Marlins only acquiring affordable players that no other team wants because of an injury-prone history or a poor performance record.	Although free agent signings don't always turn out as successful as planned, they can boost the morale of a team's players and fans. A big signing, like when the Dodgers acquired superstar Manny Ramirez, sends a message to the players and fans that the team's front office truly cares about the team and will do as much as possible to ensure that the team is successful. Fans of teams like the Marlins know it's hopeless when their team goes after big name free agents because in the end, the Marlins can't keep pace to offer a deal as lucrative as what the Yankees can offer.	The New York Yankees have been nicknamed the "evil empire" because of their huge team salaries and success in seemingly obtaining any player of their choice with lucrative contracts.	1. Wikipedia—2009 New York Yankees

Reason #3: The revenue sharing system currently in place has been unsuccessful in allowing small market teams to be more competitive due to its loose rules.	In place of a hard salary cap, MLB uses a luxury tax and revenue sharing to promote balance. This system is ineffective because all it does is transfer money from one owner to the pockets of another, while still allowing the richer owner to splurge on his team without a guarantee that the owner who received funds through revenue sharing will invest it in his team. Teams also receive a stipend of about $35 million from MLB that comes from revenue from licensing, properties, national TV, and advanced media. Despite this, the 2006 Marlins had a payroll of just $19 million, making it safe to assume that team owner Jeffrey Loria kept the rest of the revenue sharing money as income for himself. This defeats the purpose of revenue sharing, but there is no way to enforce it.	Regardless of how the Marlins are performing during the season, I typically enjoy going to a handful of games each year to support the team. However, most people don't feel the same way I do and complain on blogs and radio shows that they don't want to waste their money watching a mediocre team since the ownership doesn't want to spend money to field a more competitive ball club. I also personally feel that team owner Jeffrey Loria isn't actually contributing as much as he can to put together the most competitive team possible.	Many baseball fans, especially season ticket holders of the higher revenue teams, may feel as if they are receiving the short end of the stick. They may feel as if they're getting robbed because the money they spend on tickets or merchandise from their favorite team will simply fatten the pockets of a greedy owner who cares more about personal profit than reinvesting that money into his team in an attempt to put a winning product on the field.		1. Bill Madden—*NY Daily News* 2. *USA Today*—Payrolls 3. David Jacobson—Bnet 4. James Lincoln Ray—Suite101.com
Reason #4: Lack of competitive balance has a negative effect on the growth of the fan base and attendance at home games of some small market teams.	The payroll disparity can damage a small market team's ability to establish a solid fan base and result in poor attendance for a team's home games. Tampa Bay, for instance, is in the same division as the New York Yankees and the Boston Red Sox, two of MLB's biggest spenders with payrolls well over $100 million. Tampa, with an average payroll of $27 million, has no chance of keeping up with those two teams year after year and has only achieved one winning season in its entire existence. As a result of the team's poor performance, enhanced by the payroll disparity, Tampa Bay has consistently ranked near the bottom of all MLB in attendance year after year.	During the games that I attend, it's sad to often see an even amount of fans support the opposing team. It's also upsetting to see how many empty seats there are at each game. Big market teams like the Cubs and Mets seem to have found their way into Marlins territory. I sometimes wonder if this is the sixth borough of New York with so many Yankees and Mets fans at Land Shark Stadium. The Cubs and Mets spend so much money to build their teams that they are able to attract fans nationwide, damaging the Marlins' chances of establishing a fan base locally.	The huge disparity between payrolls may discourage fans from attending home games because they will feel as if their team has no chance against a division rival with a much larger payroll. They will lose hope in their team and as a result could stop following their hometown team altogether. Without fans who are confident in the team's ability to win, the organization will never be able to establish a good fan base.		1. *USA Today*—Payrolls 2. ESPN—Attendance report

Appendix C

	Reason 1	Reason 2	Reason 3	Reason 4	Reason 5	Reason 6	Counterargument 1	Counterargument 2
	The presence of oil rigs in hurricane prone waters only increases the possibility of oil spills occurring.	Building oil rigs in the Gulf will cause pollutants, not just from potential oil spills but also from the chemicals and processes oil companies utilize to extract the oil.	The pollutants and oil spills that are a likely result of oil rigs pose a major threat to both animal and wildlife.	There isn't much oil present to begin with.	In reality and in comparison to how much oil is there, the state won't get as much money as oil companies are claiming.	Offshore drilling will influence the tourist industry in a negative way.	Florida Energy Associates' Argument	Drilling for oil will decrease our dependence on foreign countries for oil.
Counterargument	Oil companies claim that they have new and improved technology that supposedly make oil drilling safe from spills and harmful effects to the environment.				Allowing oil to be drilled will not only give the state money but will also lower gas prices.		A similar oil company, Coastal Petroleum, attempted to find oil in 20 test wells and found nothing. Why does Florida Energy Associates think they'll hit oil?	
Refutation	(ALSO PATHOS) The recent oil spill in Australia greatly diminishes this counterargument as (LOOK UP INFO ON SPILL).			No matter who has the closest guess as to how much oil is truly there, there will only be 6–12 months worth (at most) of oil to be collected and consumed.	For eight years, under the Bush administration the number of oil leases on public lands almost tripled. It didn't help gas prices, which doubled in 2008.		"I'm not going to tell you what we think, but Coastal says they did not drill deep enough and did not drill in the right places," says Doug Daniels, oil consortium attorney.	The Bush administration almost tripled the number of oil leases on public lands in 8 years and it didn't make us energy independent.
Facts		Pollutants that leak into the water due to oil drilling include hydrocarbons, mercury, and toxic drilling muds.	The relatively shallow waters of the continental shelf allow greater penetration of sunlight, and rich deposits of sediment on the shelf floor provide nutrients not found in the deep ocean. This combination creates an incredibly productive ecosystem that is the nutrient base for ecologically and commercially important species from shrimp to fish to sea turtles and marine mammals.	National Petroleum Council estimates 5 billion barrels; Energy Information Association estimates 16 billion barrels; others estimate as much as 21 billion barrels.	It is estimated that the state would get about 2.3 billion dollars a year from offshore drilling in addition to an estimated 231,000 jobs that would open up to Florida residents.	The current tourist industry brings in about 50 billion dollars a year.	Florida Energy Associates has contributed \$55,000 to political parties—\$35,000 to Republicans and the rest to Democrats—since May. The group has sponsored legislative leadership dinners and recruited two of the most powerful state lawmakers to sponsor the oil drilling ban in 2010 (Sen. Mike Haridopolos and Rep. Dean Cannon).	
Audience	Government figures and adults in Florida.	Government leaders and Florida residents.	Florida residents.	Government leaders and Florida residents.	Government leaders and Florida residents.	Government leaders.	Florida residents.	Florida residents.

Ethos	"The technology has really changed. They can do it in a very safe way" says Dougher, senior economic adviser for American Petroleum Institute.					Senator Bob Graham: "The beaches of Florida are like the mountains of Colorado. They are somewhat our defining feature, and anything that threatens to jeopardize those raises great concern."	"We really do want to do for Florida what oil and gas has done for Texas," Lance Phillips, Texas oilman leading the case for offshore drilling.	"If we as a nation can bring our own resources into this mix, we would not see the prices we're seeing right now," says Rayola Dougher, senior economic adviser for the American Petroleum Institute.
Pathos	Oil spills and accidents that have occurred throughout history (http://home.versatel.nl/the_sims/rig/index.htm).	"Once you ruin those pristine beaches, they've been ruined forever."				"From her vantage point in Santa Barbara, CA, a city known for beautiful beaches and wealthy residents, Mayor Marty Blum recalls black: the color of more than 3 million gallons of oil that flowed from a drilling rig blowout in 1969 and covered 35 miles of coastline with a thick layer of goo."	Durell Peaden, a retired doctor who worked for Texaco before he went to medical school, described out-of-state oilmen as "shysters promoting a 'shell game' at the expense of Florida's tourism."	
Logos	"I don't want an oil spill between 3 or 10 miles off the coast of Florida, like they had off the coast of Australia," said McCollum. "I've got to be assured, before I support something like that, that modern technology would not permit that to happen off our coast."	Environmentalist group, Environment Florida, discusses safer and alternative ideas rather than offshore drilling such as increasing fuel economy, increasing funding for public transportation, and planning better transportation systems.	A steady stream of pollution from offshore rigs causes a wide range of health and reproductive problems for fish and other marine life.		In all reality there is not enough oil located off of Florida's coast to make a large impact, if one will happen at all, on the price of gas. The oil there will only last up to a year at most.			The US has less than 3% of the world's oil reserves. No matter how much we drill in the US we will never have enough to satisfy domestic demand for energy and we will not have enough to significantly impact prices on the world market.
Sources	http://www.washingtontimes.com/news/2009/feb/11/drilling-ban-revisited/	http://blogs.tampabay.com/buzz/2009/10/is-offshore-drilling-doomed-yet-again-in-the-senate.html and http://www.defenders.org/programs_and_policy/policy_and_legislation/energy/index.php	http://www.environmentflorida.org/issues/save-our-shores/stop-offshore-drilling and http://www.culturechange.org/caoe.html		http://www.wendmag.com/greenery/2009/10/oil-spill-off-australia-coast-points-to-dangers-of-offshore-drilling-in-us/	http://www.tampabay.com/news/environment/water/article634009.ece and http://www.usatoday.com/money/industries/energy/2008-07-13-offshore-drillingN.htm	http://www.miamiherald.com/news/florida/story/1242317.html	http://www.foxnews.com.story/0,2933,369121,00.html and http://www.defenders.org/programs_and_policy/policy_and_legislation/energy/index.php

8

Bringing Concord Out of Educational Discord by Teaching Political Controversy

Donald Lazere

My contribution to the 2010 conference session Restoring the Study of Political Rhetoric to the Humanities Curriculum consisted of a gloss on my then-recent column "A Core Curriculum for Civic Literacy" in the *Chronicle of Higher Education*, and I am elaborating on both here.[1] Relating this to the conference theme, it is all too clear that "discord" is the mode both of current American public discourse and of civic education at the K–12 and postsecondary levels, so I am envisioning ways of bringing a degree of concord through a coherent curriculum, or at least a sequence of general education requirements, that would foreground study of political controversy in the manner of Gerald Graff's "teaching the conflicts."

For me to make a case within the Rhetoric Society of America (RSA) for restoring the study of rhetoric, especially political rhetoric, to the center of the humanities is the ultimate in preaching to the choir, so I am seeking less to win converts than to find commiseration with my tale of woe or, more positively, to rally the troops toward concerted action. I am a convert to RSA in the last three years, although I have long been a rhetoric scholar within English, active in the Modern Language Association (MLA), National Council of Teachers of English, and Conference on College Composition and Communication (CCCC). I did subscribe to *Rhetoric Society Quarterly (RSQ)* for a while back in the days when it was a thin mimeographed publication edited by George Yoos, with a rather specialized scope. In the intervening years, I failed to track the rapid growth of RSA and *RSQ*, along with the increasing prominence there of modern political rhetoric, to the point of surpassing MLA or CCCC publications and conferences, which have become so vast and diffuse that occasional attention to political rhetoric gets eclipsed. Now if RSA only controlled the professional turf of MLA and CCCC, and if its subject matter was as established within liberal arts curricula. . . . (It was only in the past decade that the National Endowment for the Humanities categorized rhetoric as a humanistic discipline, which was at least a step in the right direction.)

My particular approach, first delineated in "Teaching the Political Conflicts" and developed mainly out of teaching second-term argumentative writing courses, incorporates elements of critical thinking and semantics in a model for analyzing argumentative rhetoric, combining the factual knowledge and critical skills that students need to make informed judgments about the partisan screaming matches and special-interest propaganda that permeate current political and economic controversies. (My approach owes much to the old International Society for General Semantics and its Institute for Propaganda Analysis.) Unfortunately, few high schools or colleges require courses devoted to this focus or to political and economic literacy in general. Civic education has been shamefully overlooked in both No Child Left Behind and the Obama administration's Race to the Top.

Before outlining my core curriculum here, I want to detour into some of the historical causes of the marginalization of the study of political rhetoric, which is the Humpty Dumpty of American secondary and collegiate education; it had a great fall in the twentieth century and its fragments are scattered throughout an over-departmentalized, over-specialized curriculum.

Political rhetoric was, of course, central for classical Greek and Roman authors, while in North America its study was at its peak in the late eighteenth century, serving a vital function in the Revolutionary era. That period has been studied by several fine American historians of rhetoric, perhaps most incisively by S. Michael Halloran. In his accounts, the eighteenth century secondary and college curriculum was not divided up into modern departments and disciplines. "Rhetoric and moral philosophy" was the broad rubric for humanistic studies, comprising of history, government, law, philosophy, religion, and literature. These subject areas were all based initially in the classics and studied largely in Greek and Latin, or translations thereof, although vernacular and modern studies gradually entered the curriculum. A letter from Thomas Jefferson to his nephew Peter Carr in 1785 recommended an undifferentiated mix of readings in all of these subjects, ancient and modern, through Swift and Pope, in order "to pursue the interests of your country . . . with the purest integrity, the most chaste honor" (814). Literature was not studied primarily in today's aesthetic, belletristic terms, but under the auspices of rhetoric; thus, Halloran notes that the student "literary societies" of the time were actually political debate clubs ("From Rhetoric" 159–60).

Nor were writing and speaking instruction split off from the subject areas, as in modern American education at all levels; they were an integral part of all humanistic fields, as is still widely the case in Europe. (In an interview with Gary Olson for *Journal of Advanced Composition*, Jacques Derrida expressed bewilderment over the American conception of composition as an autonomous discipline.) Writing was taught largely as the basis of texts for oratory, debate, and legal forensics, as well as for academic oral exams. Halloran notes that, "Examination for purposes comparable to what we call grading was done infrequently, usually in the form of oral disputation with the college president and perhaps the trustees judging the students' performance" ("From Rhetoric" 160–61). Most importantly, according to Halloran:

> In keeping with the emphasis of the current rhetorical theory on civic life, the topics on which students wrote tended to be political. Here is a list of some questions disputed at Harvard College commencements in the decades leading to the Revolution, illustrating the increasing focus on contemporary political affairs:
>
> > Is unlimited obedience to rulers taught by Christ and his apostles? (1729) . . .
> >
> > Is an absolute and arbitrary monarchy contrary to right reason? (1758) . . .
> >
> > Is a government tyrannical in which the rulers consult their own interest more than that of their subjects? (1770) . . .
> >
> > Is a government despotic in which the people have no check on the legislative power? (1770). (158–59)

We can easily imagine the Royalist conservatives of that time waging a campaign against tenured radical professors inflicting such politically correct biases on their students.

The central purposes of education, then, were civic leadership and critical citizenship. In a famous letter to John Adams in 1813, Jefferson discussed the model of public education he had proposed as governor of Virginia.

> To establish in every ward a free school for reading, writing and common arithmetic; to provide for the annual selection of the best subjects from these schools, who might receive, at the public expense, a higher degree of education at a district school, and from these district schools to select a certain number of the most promising subjects, to be completed at a university, where all the useful sciences [subjects of study in general] should be taught. Worth and genius would thus have been sought out from every condition of life, and completely prepared by education for defeating the competition of wealth and birth for public trusts. . . . This . . . would have raised the mass of the people to the high ground of moral respectability necessary to their own safety, and to orderly government; and would have completed the great object of qualifying them to select the veritable aristoi, for the trusts of government, to the exclusion of the pseudalists [the pseudo-aristocracy of inherited privilege]. (1308)

The integral role that the study of political rhetoric played in the early American republic is epitomized by the facts that John Quincy Adams, prior to his presidency, was the first Boylston Professor of Rhetoric and Oratory at Harvard and that his 1810 *Lectures on Rhetoric and Oratory* was a standard textbook. To be sure, the kind of education described in these sources was restricted mainly to a small portion of the population: upper-class white males preparing for the professions of law, government, the clergy, or teaching. There was no inevitable impediment to the extension of the same educational opportunities to all Americans; however, things did not play out this way historically, due to a variety of extra-academic forces that are fascinating to study but beyond my scope here. (Just one note: in today's class-structured American educational system, the segment that retains the most vestiges of the eighteenth-century model is the exclusive, private prep school and liberal arts colleges that still are the main habitus of those tracked for public leadership. It is one of those topics suppressed from our public discourse that liberal education is still considered valuable for the social elite, while business, professional, and vocational education are deemed sufficient for the masses.)

Halloran traces the gradual shift during the course of the nineteenth century of the primacy of rhetorical instruction in speaking over writing to the reverse. While instruction in public oratory and debate had always included a large component of political subject matter, that component eventually got dissipated in writing instruction, as a multitude of other purposes for written composition evolved, including expressive, creative, and critical writing, journalism, business and technical writing, and advertising and public relations. English departments became dominated by the belletristic study of literature. Composition, the other main division of contemporary English studies, is the poor-relation descendent of the long traditions of rhetorical study discussed above. The facts are all too well-known about the inferior status to which teachers and the teaching of composition are consigned by most undergraduate and graduate English departments, in perverse defiance of the reality that those departments derive most of their funding and allotment of required courses from composition studies. In recent decades, we scholars in composition have managed to upgrade our job description to "rhetcomp," establishing rhetoric divisions in many English departments, as well as some independent programs, and in MLA, studying political rhetoric under rubrics like cultural studies, critical pedagogy, Frankfurt school critical theory, feminist theory, and James Berlin's social-epistemic rhetoric: "The study and critique of signifying practices in their relation to subject formation within the framework of economic, social, and political conditions" (77). Unfortunately, little of this work in rhetcomp has trickled down (or up from freshman English?) to become a central component of English or other general education requirements. Some of us in English have also applied the study of critical thinking to political rhetoric, but philosophy won the curricular turf war for critical thinking when it was trendy in the 1980s. Even there, despite the survival of a professional society (Association for Informal Logic and Critical Thinking), specialists in critical thinking are marginal in the American Philosophical Association, and critical thinking courses incorporating argumentative rhetoric—which to my mind should be the master academic discipline—have withered away, whether in philosophy, English, or speech-communication departments.

In yet another historical bifurcation, the twentieth century saw the development of courses and departments in speech, which took over oral rhetoric from English departments, as well as maintaining vestiges of the declining field of classics. (I vaguely recall an amorphous course in junior high called oral English.) Considering the rich humanistic heritage of speech departments, one might suppose that they would have at least as prominent a position in the liberal arts curriculum as English. Such has never been the case, alas, as they have typically been relegated to being an orphan in undergraduate and graduate general education, regarded, justifiably or not, as having marginal academic substance. This low regard has resulted in part from the peculiarly eclectic nature of many speech departments (later to morph into communication or speech-communication), which might combine classical rhetoric, forensics and elocution (isolated from any specific liberal arts subject matter), audiology or speech therapy, empirical research and occupationally oriented courses in journalistic media, and advertising and public relations. Speech and communication departments carry a further stigma from the days when some were considered havens of "Mickey Mouse" or "jock" courses. These negative forces tend to overshadow the valuable scholarship in critical rhetorical studies that is done in many undergraduate and graduate speech-communication programs, as well as in the National Communication Association and in its affiliate journals like *The Review of Communication, Critical Studies in Media Communication, Communication and Critical/Cultural Studies*, and *Quarterly Journal of Speech*.

Of course, the most promising recent development for the study of rhetoric and political rhetoric has been the growth of undergraduate and graduate programs in rhetoric per se. Some of these are divisions within English or speech communication departments; a few are autonomous. The catch is that nearly all owe their existence to being granted the turf of writing programs at the basic and first-year levels, as well as some introductory public speaking courses, staffed mainly by adjuncts and grad students. Beyond that level, their resources for offering a full curriculum are often sparse and their tenure-track faculty's scholarly interests often remote from general education requirements. Some rhetoric programs, as well as speech-communication ones, do offer courses in political rhetoric or communication, as well as media criticism, but most are for upper-division majors or grad students. In short, political rhetoric is not the central focus of any such program I know of.[2] When scholars do focus on political rhetoric—as they do, admirably, in RSA or in journals like *Rhetoric & Public Affairs* or the biennial Public Address Conference—their aim is usually to address fellow specialists, not to contribute to undergraduate general education or to discourse in the public sphere. (The most praiseworthy recent exceptions have been in service learning/community literacy programs.)

Politics as a field of study in itself has been consigned to social studies in secondary schools and social science at the undergraduate and graduate levels. In neither of these realms is political rhetoric a central category of study. University social science scholarship is even more highly departmentalized, specialized, and dominated by quasi-scientific quantitative research. Scholars in several disparate social science disciplines have made contributions to the study of political rhetoric, but as in the humanities, the field itself is not well-defined or prestigious within or among these disciplines. Political rhetoric has been studied most prominently in the work of linguists and sociolinguists like Noam Chomsky, George Lakoff, Robin Lakoff, Basil Bernstein, Claus Mueller, Deborah Tannen, and Geoffrey Nunberg. In spite of their valuable work, most such scholars have a marginal role in their own disciplines, at least partly, and precisely, because of their interdisciplinary scope. As Stanley Fish once observed, being interdisciplinary is so very hard to do.

Isn't it sad that these wholly arbitrary dichotomies, like between the study of written and oral discourse, have led to scholars in the same general field being so isolated from one another professionally and in curricula? The publish-or-perish syndrome has driven the endless mitosis of disciplinary fields and the multiplication of specialized publications and conferences that make it impossible to "keep up" with scholarship outside of a narrow circle. (*Critical Studies in Media Communication* and *Communication and Critical/Cultural Studies* are both excellent journals, but who can afford the time or money to read both regularly, on top of the English-based *Cultural Studies*, *Cultural Critique*, and *Social Text*?) The reward system within each discipline prioritizes sticking squarely within it and penalizes straying outside of it. Even between English and speech-communication, it is rare for scholars who combine work in their own field with a secondary field to get a job teaching in that other field or to be able to place a journal article or a conference paper in a secondary professional organization. (One possible remedy here is for professional associations to offer discounted prices to members of other associations wanting to subscribe or attend conventions.)

As noted above, RSA has grown impressively in recent years and has increasingly provided a forum for studies in political rhetoric. Its virtue in drawing a membership from half a dozen disciplines is offset, however, by the paucity of rhetoric programs that control curricular turf on the scale of English and speech-communication programs. RSA's conferences are also unable to function as official events like single-discipline conferences where the business of the national profession and job exchanges are conducted. Thus, many of us participate in RSA out of enthusiasm rather than necessity, and, at least in English, it is far down the list for travel funds and for credit on one's vita. In short, if I were a higher education czar, I would just merge all the other disciplines back into rhetoric and moral philosophy, and make RSA their master organization.

To broaden this scope a bit more, study of political rhetoric in the liberal arts curriculum has been the ultimate casualty of the well-documented shift of academic priorities in the second half of the twentieth century from teaching undergraduates, especially in liberal education, to advanced research, specialized publication, and primary allegiance by faculties to fellow specialists nationally rather than to their undergraduate students. This shift took place primarily in the fields of science, technology, and social science, but the humanities were incidental beneficiaries of the boom in funding by corporations, government, and the military after World War II, when research grants became an increasingly dominant source of funding for institutions and individual scholars, whose numbers grew sharply. The share of the research grant pie may have been much smaller for humanities scholars, but our profession still bought into the ethos of specialized research and publish or perish, even when our subjects of research were relatively insignificant and redundant; after all, there is not an unlimited mine of research material, especially for an ever-growing number of researchers, in fields like literature, philosophy, or rhetoric. It is not as though every year brings vital discoveries and advancements, as in medicine, computer science, environmental studies, or even economics and political science, which actually warrant specialized publications and annual conferences. There may be a bitter justice in the financial crisis for the humanities precipitated by economic recession since 2008; they are paying the price for their growing dependency on the earlier boom in research funding, along with the resultant over-production of research faculties, for the current curtailed budgets by federal and local legislatures cannot make up the shortfall in subsidies from the private sector, especially in the humanities.

My point here has been that undergraduate and graduate course offerings in general have often been largely determined not by their foundational benefits for students, but by faculty members' specialized areas of research and publication. One consequence is the widespread deterioration of general education and the dilution of requirements into a cafeteria menu rather than a cogent sequence in a core curriculum. The general case I am making is hardly original, and the problems involved go beyond the disappearance of the study of political rhetoric. A restoration of such study might require removing the requirement of a research-centered PhD for undergraduate teaching in the liberal arts, and instead focus on an ABD graduate degree, in which study would center on the concerns of undergraduate learning and teaching.

Under such a paradigm shift, a reduced number of universities could remain oriented toward advanced research, including in the humanities, but for most, I believe this shift would be widely welcomed as a restoration of undergraduate liberal education to a central role in the university. It could also apply to the criteria used for the hiring of faculty, the granting of tenure, and promotion. Though we may not have wished for it, the current financial crunch on universities and research might end up producing similar results. (The down side here is that undergraduate liberal education has also been a victim of shrinking financial resources and declining student access.)

Discussion of a Political Curriculum

Imagine, then, that we could go back to the drawing board and envision an undergraduate curriculum that is not determined by departmental turf or the specialized scholarship of faculty members, but that would, as in Halloran's account of the eighteenth-century American model of rhetorical studies, "address students as political beings, as members of a body politic in which they have a responsibility to form judgments and influence the judgments of others on public issues" ("Rhetoric" 108). I propose something like the following sequence of courses, which would follow an English course in first-year writing, perhaps an introductory public speaking course, and one (either in English, speech-communication, rhetoric, or philosophy) in critical thinking and argumentative rhetoric. Each could incorporate argumentative writing and speaking, and they would, ideally, complement rather than replace basic courses in history, government, economics, and literature.[3] I devised most of this sequence for chapters in my textbook *Reading and Writing for Civic Literacy*, but my own and others' frustrating conclusion from teaching it was that no single book or course is anywhere near adequate to cover this subject matter as most students are so unfamiliar with or unprepared for the material that each chapter could easily become the basis for a course in itself.

Course One: Thinking Critically about Political and Economic Rhetoric

Survey of semantic issues in defining terms like left wing, right wing, liberal, conservative, radical, moderate, freedom, democracy, patriotism, capitalism, socialism, communism, Marxism, and fascism. Analysis of their denotative complexity and the ways in which they are oversimplified or connotatively slanted in public usage. Objectively defining ideological differences between the political left and right, along with the range of positions within both. Relativity of political viewpoints (e.g., the *New York Times* is to the left of Fox News but to the right of *The Nation*; the Democratic Party is to the left of the Republicans but to the right of European social-democratic parties). Contingency of political beliefs and biases on everyone's relative subject position on a spectrum from far left to far right, nationally and internationally. The need to identify one's own subjectivity in order to progress toward objectivity. Evaluating political and economic arguments. Application of principles of analyzing argumentative rhetoric to "reading the news" in a diversity of journalistic and scholarly sources and ideological viewpoints (newspapers, journals of opinion, books, web journals, etc.) on current political and economic controversies. Locating and evaluating partisan sources across the political spectrum. Predictable patterns of partisan rhetoric.

Course Two: Thinking Critically about Mass Society and Mass Communication

Survey of theoretical perspectives on and literary depictions of modern mass society and culture. Debates over elitism and populism. Academic versus popular discourse. Liberal and conservative theories of highbrow, lowbrow, and middlebrow culture and their modifications in recent cultural studies and postmodernist theory. Mass communication and social control. Cognitive effects of mass communication, especially on reading, writing, and political consciousness.

Do the media give people what they want or do people want what the media give them? Are news media objective, and should they be? The debate over political bias in media. Diverse influences in media: employees (editors, producers, writers, newscasters, performers), owners and advertisers, external pressure groups, and audiences. Levels of literacy in productions and audiences. Ideology in entertainment: images in media (present and past) of corporations, the rich, poor, and middle class, labor, professions, gender roles, minorities, gays, foreigners, other parts of the world, Americans' presence abroad, and war. How the Internet and the decline of print media have reshaped media issues. Possible alternatives to our present media, especially those in decline.

Course Three: Deception Detection: Propaganda Analysis

Study of problems in defining and evaluating propaganda. Possible biases in government, media, education, and research resulting from special interests, conflict of interest, and special pleading. Survey of varieties and sources of propaganda in contemporary society, including government and the military, corporate and other special-interest lobbying, advertising, public relations, and subsidized research. The anatomy of deception: patterns of propagandistic argument in public discourse and how to lie with economic statistics. Critical consumer education: reading the fine print in contracts such as those for student loans, credit cards, rental agreements, and mortgages; health and environmental issues in consumer products; the hidden facts of the production, marketing, and nutritional value of food.

Course Four: Civic Literacy and Service Learning

Connecting these academic studies with arenas of participatory research, public service, community or national activism, work in government or community organizations, journalism, and so on. (The challenge that I see here is overcoming the tendency for service learning to become isolated from, or even hostile toward, academic civic literacy through focusing exclusively on local community issues, diverse constituencies, and ideological pluralism at the expense of studying broader, common ideological and rhetorical issues. See Cushman for a good model of connecting the two realms.)

Obstacles to the Implementation of a Political Curriculum

My curriculum is, of course, a platonic ideal rather than a model that has much chance of being implemented anywhere in the near future. In that sense, though, it at least dramatizes the distance between any such concept of a cogent curriculum and the present realities; it implicitly indicates all the forces that stand in the way of implementing curricular reform, and it perhaps might help us envision avenues of action toward overcoming those forces. A prime obstacle, or challenge, would be the drastic shift in professional values needed toward rewarding faculty commitment to core-level course planning, teaching, and scholarship keyed to this level rather than specialized research and publication—a shift that might require a generation of re-gearing graduate studies.

Other obstacles include the fact that the very term "core curriculum" has sadly become a wedge in the culture war issues, with conservatives preempting it in the cause for Eurocentric tradition and American patriotism, thus provoking intransigent opposition from progressive champions of cultural pluralism and students' freedom to decide on their own studies. Surely, however, it is time for ideological adversaries to seek common ground in a curriculum that itself addresses issues of ideological partisanship and seeks to incorporate, if not overcome, them. Although my proposed curriculum leans to the left, I expect that conservatives would endorse parts of it and suggest reasonable modifications for others. In his recent *The Making of Americans*, E. D. Hirsch Jr. refines his notion of cultural literacy to champion a common national core of humanistic subject matter—"what every American needs to know"—in order to become an informed, critical citizen. He denies favoring rote memorization of dry facts, but argues that critical thinking or rhetorical instruction can only be effectively taught when applied to a base of essential factual knowledge. He opposes the kind of decontextualized standard tests imposed under No Child Left Behind but is for a standardized national core curriculum that would facilitate tests based directly on the factual content in courses all students have taken, incorporating critical analysis and argumentation, and determined with input from diverse educational constituencies.

I quite agree with Hirsch in relation to political literacy, and I admire his denial that he and his version of cultural literacy are politically conservative. In *Cultural Literacy*, he endorsed "radicalism in politics, but conservatism in literate knowledge" (22). In *The Making of Americans,* he adds, "Practical improvement of our public education will require intellectual clarity and a depolarization of this issue. Left and right must get together on the principle of common content" (177).

Any notion of national standards for curriculum or testing in secondary education, even if not required, sets off similar partisan hot buttons, with conservatives fearing the tyranny of the liberal elite and defending the Jeffersonian tradition of local control, and liberals become fearful of national conservative pressure groups imposing their own version of political correctness. For example, in 1994 a panel of distinguished historians, including Gary Nash and Joyce Appleby, produced an excellent set of national standards for high school history that applied critical thinking and argumentative skills to historical knowledge. These standards, in a depressing object lesson, became the victim of a Republican culture war offensive. They were bizarrely made the subject of a full Senate vote, which was railroaded through with almost no senators having read the proposed standards. They were overwhelmingly defeated (see Nash et al.). This fiasco set the cause of national standards back for over a decade, but bipartisan suggestions for its revival appear in the recent works of Hirsch, Diane Ravitch, Martha Nussbaum, Mike Rose, Gerald Graff and Cathy Birkenstein, and the National Governors' Association Common Core State Standards Initiative. In *Not for Profit: Why Democracy Needs the Humanities*, Nussbaum writes:

> If a nation wants to promote . . . democracy dedicated to "life, liberty and the pursuit of happiness" to each and every person, what abilities will it need to produce in its citizens? At least the following seem crucial: The ability to think well about political issues affecting the nation, to examine, reflect, argue, and debate, deferring to neither tradition nor authority. (25)

All the above obstacles and more have contributed to paralysis in both educational and political circles, obstructing even preliminary efforts toward a nationally coordinated movement for the upgrading of education toward a civic literacy that could include a component of rhetoric. Several organizations have recently been formed around the country, like the Campaign for the Civic Mission of Schools, the Carnegie Foundation for the Advancement of Teaching's Political Engagement Project, and the Center for Information and Research on Civic Learning and Engagement, along with programs such as Campus Compact and its Research University Civic Engagement Network and the Association of American Colleges and Universities' program Core Commitments: Fostering Personal and Social Responsibility on College and University Campuses. However, these organizations and programs lack coordination and none advocate a rhetoric-based curriculum. As surveyed in note 3, many local campuses have moved in this direction with single courses and some full programs, but again there is no national coordination. In *The Assault on Reason*, Al Gore praised the American Political Science Association for starting a Task Force on Civic Education. That should prompt similar task forces in MLA, National Council of Teachers of English (NCTE), National Communication

Association (NCA), and RSA, which could then, along with the other projects surveyed here, pool all their resources in an interdisciplinary National Council for Civic Education. Such a council could also serve to link civic education at the K–12 levels with college studies and to bring liberal and conservative educational theorists to the table to thrash out their differences. We could hope to find sponsorship for this effort by both conservative and liberal foundations, as well as support from the US Department of Education or National Endowment for the Humanities.

Michael Halloran was incisive as always in his paper at our session at the 2010 conference advocating linkage between K–12 and postsecondary rhetorical education. Recapitulating the history of classical rhetorical pedagogy, he observed,

> There's more than a bit of irony here: we devote scholarship to treatises from the past that were meant for students at what we would recognize as the elementary and secondary levels, but we give little if any attention to how the principles behind those treatises might be relevant in schooling at the elementary and secondary levels today. ("The Third C" 3)

He also recapitulated the schism in 1914 between NCTE and teachers of public speaking, who founded a series of organizations (eventuating in NCA) that regrettably did not include strong K–12 sections as NCTE has always done. He praised the recent Common Core State Standards Initiative of the National Governors' Association, which emphasized "college and career readiness standards," but he recommended adding a third C, "readiness for citizenship," in which study of political rhetoric would be central (5). He concluded by advocating that "the Rhetoric Society of America might strive in some official way to add citizenship to the agenda of education reform in our elementary and secondary schools" (7). His proposal coincided with a workshop presented by Ralph Cintron and David Joliffe at the conference that was part of their ongoing project for teaching rhetoric in secondary schools. Indeed, my entire curriculum by rights belongs in secondary education, and if anything like it were to be adopted there, it would relieve college teachers to pursue more advanced studies in good conscience.

As a novice in RSA, I will not presume to suggest to the officers what efforts they might make along these lines, beyond a nudge to initiate deliberations about what actions might be within our realm and to seek a place at the table in advancing the role of rhetoric in whatever national movement might shape up. So I hope here to prompt further discussion within RSA of these problems and possible strategies for overcoming them (perhaps as a topic for a summer institute or special issue of *RSQ*), and I welcome further information from members about local or national programs that you are involved in. I can be reached at dlazere@igc.org.

Notes

[1] I am deeply indebted to Michael Leff for his encouragement and suggestions in planning this session at a time when, unknown to most of us, he was fatally ill.

[2] Michael Leff brought to my attention "Citizens Speaking: Rhetorical Education and Civic Engagement," the excellent keynote address at the 2009 Brigance Colloquy on Public Speaking as a Liberal Art, in the Wabash College Rhetoric Department, by Denise M. Bostdorff, professor of communication at the College of Wooster. Bostdorff traced the decline of public speaking's status as a liberal art, expressed concerns about the quantity and quality of Americans' civic engagement, and suggested specific ways rhetoric scholars can revitalize connections between public speaking and democratic practices.

[3] My long-time mentor from Berkeley's graduate school, Charles Muscatine, was a champion of coherent liberal arts programs with a civic emphasis, even within large universities. Less than a year before his recent death at 89, he published *Fixing College Education*, whose viewpoint resembles mine here and which surveyed such curricula around the country, mainly at four-year liberal arts colleges. Similar surveys appear in collections edited by Colby et al. and Jacoby, although most of the programs studied in their and in Muscatine's work are not explicitly based in rhetoric. Rosa Eberly, a valued colleague who is professor of English and rhetoric and director of the Center for Public Speaking and Civic Engagement at Penn State, described her exemplary program in panels with me at the 2008 MLA and 2010 RSA conferences. Our other panelist at RSA was James Aune, a communication scholar whose work, in books like *Selling the Free Market*, is also exemplary in its study of the rhetoric of economic discourse, and whose paper at the conference ("Rethinking") argued for re-integrating such study in liberal arts curricula.

Works Cited

Adams, John Quincy. *Lectures on Rhetoric and Oratory.* Cambridge: Hilliard and Metcalf, 1810.

Aune, James Arnt. "Rethinking the Rhetoric of Economics." RSA Conference. Marriot City Center, Minneapolis. 30 May 2010. Address.

———. *Selling the Free Market: The Rhetoric of Economic Correctness*. New York: Guilford P, 2001.

Berlin, James. *Rhetorics, Poetics, and Cultures: Refiguring College English Studies.* Urbana, IL: NCTE, 1996.

Bostdorff, Denise M. "Citizens Speaking: Rhetorical Education and Civic Engagement." The Brigance Colloquy on Public Speaking as a Liberal Art. Wabash College, 26 Feb. 2009.

Colby, Anne, Elizabeth Beaumont, Thomas Ehrlich, and Josh Corngold. *Educating for Democracy: Preparing Undergraduates for Responsible Political Engagement.* San Francisco: Jossey-Bass, 2006.

Cushman, Ellen. "The Public Intellectual, Service Learning, and Activist Research." *College English* 61 (1999): 328–36.

Fish, Stanley. "Being Interdisciplinary Is So Very Hard to Do." *Profession* 89 (1989): 15–22.

Gore, Al. *The Assault on Reason*. New York: Penguin, 2007.

Graff, Gerald. *Beyond the Culture Wars: Revitalizing American Education by Teaching the Conflicts.* New York: Norton, 1992.

———, and Cathy Birkenstein. "A Progressive Case for Educational Standardization." *Academe Online* May–June 2008. Web. 7 Jan. 2010.

Halloran, S. Michael. "From Rhetoric to Composition: The Teaching of Writing in America to 1900." *A Short History of Writing Instruction: From Ancient Greece to Twentieth-Century America*. Ed. James J. Murphy. Davis, CA: Hermagoras, 1990. 151–82.

———. "Rhetoric in the American College Curriculum: The Decline of Public Discourse." *Pre/Text* 3 (1982): 93–109.

———. "The Third C of Education Reform: Citizenship." RSA Biennial Conference. Marriot City Center, Minneapolis. 30 May 2010.

Hirsch, E. D., Jr. *Cultural Literacy: What Every American Needs to Know*. New York: Houghton Mifflin, 1987.

———. *The Making of Americans: Democracy and Our Schools*. New Haven, CT: Yale UP, 2009.

Jacoby, Barbara. *Civic Engagement in Higher Education: Concepts and Practices*. San Francisco: Jossey-Bass, 2009.

Jefferson, Thomas. *Writings*. New York: Library of America, 1984.

Lazere, Donald. "A Core Curriculum for Civic Literacy." *Chronicle of Higher Education* 5 Feb. 2010: B4–5.

———. *Reading and Writing for Civic Literacy: The Critical Citizen's Guide to Argumentative Rhetoric*. Boulder: Paradigm, 2005. Brief Edition, 2009.

———. "Teaching the Political Conflicts: A Rhetorical Schema." *College Composition and Communication* 43 (1992): 194–213.

Muscatine, Charles. *Fixing College Education: A New Curriculum for the Twenty-First Century*. Charlottesville: U of Virginia P, 2009.

Nash, Gary B., Charlotte A. Crabtree, and Ross E. Dunn. *History on Trial: Culture Wars and the Teaching of the Past*. New York: Knopf, 1997.

Nussbaum, Martha C. *Not for Profit: Why Democracy Needs the Humanities*. Princeton: Princeton UP, 2010.

Olson, Gary A. "Jacques Derrida on Rhetoric and Composition: A Conversation." *(Inter)views: Cross-Disciplinary Perspectives on Rhetoric and Literacy*. Carbondale: U of Southern Illinois P, 1991.

Ravitch, Diane. *The Death and Life of the Great American School System*. New York: Basic Books, 2010.

Rose, Mike. *An Open Language: Selected Writings on Literacy, Learning, and Opportunity*. New York: Bedford/St. Martin's, 2006.

Section III

Freedom, Ethos, and the Rhetoric of Rights

The disjuncture that structures controversies over rights inheres between divergent registers of temporality: between historical contingencies and timeless principles, between chronological and anachronic time.

—Megan Foley

Concord—as also controversy—implies freedom. . . . The pages of all rhetorical theory are haunted by a usually unarticulated, but nonetheless consistent, notion of freedom. I have termed this "troubled freedom."

—Ira Allen

A feminist rhetorical theory of global citizenship sees metaphor as a key rhetorical strategy in building concord around social rights, despite the overall controversy as to whether or not social rights are privileged in the overall structure of the Universal Declaration of Human Rights.

—Rebecca A. Kuehl

The classical focus of rhetoric's ethics, on relations between subjects, ignores or, at a minimum, marginalizes the question of relating within the split subject.

—Lynn Clarke

We are not so different from any of the other social animals who engage in conspicuous displays of altruism in order to secure their goals. . . . Rhetoric is the natural act of a natural species.

—Alex C. Parrish

As feminist reformers imagined freedmen, black women, and voting citizens, they also constituted identities for themselves in their discourse that they sought to fit into their imagining of the ideal citizen. Similarity and difference, concord and controversy, are bound up in rhetoric's constitutive power, often inextricably so.

—Jennifer Keohane

9

Internal Discord and "the Signifying Process" in Ethico-Political Rhetoric

Lynn Clarke

Rhetorical theory has recently engaged the murky concept of affect (Chaput; Edbauer Rice; Lundberg).[1] What affect is and does, and where and how it does it, are live questions. But there is some general agreement on the concept. In *The Affect Theory Reader,* Seigworth and Gregg identify two main points of convergence. First, affect tends to influence in ways that are less than conscious. "Affect, at its most anthropomorphic, is the name we give to those forces—visceral forces beneath, alongside, or generally *other than* conscious knowing, vital forces insisting beyond emotion—that can serve to drive us toward movement, toward thought and extension," and more (1). Second, affect is thoroughly bound up in creative dynamics. "Perhaps one of the surest things that can be said of both affect and its theorization is that they will . . . always exceed the context[s] of their emergence, as the excess of ongoing process" (5).

Within the body of rhetorical theory interested in affect, one finds a small number of studies that introduce the concept to practical politics. There, affect is said to circulate between bodies, and link or articulate images, events, and representations, among other permeable entities (Chaput 8; Edbauer Rice 210). In addition, the forces or "energies" of affect are said to exist in a complex relationship with propositional statements and may, accordingly, not appear at the level of signification (Chaput 18; Edbauer Rice 211). Notably, some of these rhetoric studies retain an interest in ethical issues. Chaput and Greene are both concerned with human interaction in democratic spheres of talk; and Edbauer Rice expresses a desire for rhetorical scholars to "critically intervene" in public discourse on immigration in the name of "images and representations that are less oppressive" (210). With varying degrees of explicitness, then, Chaput, Greene, and Edbauer Rice are invested in questions of ethics. What's more, their studies appear to be premised upon a conception of ethics that one typically finds in neo-Aristotelian rhetoric. But the classical view can only take those of us interested in affect and human (inter)action so far. Why?

If affect operates on a level "other than conscious knowing," it must presuppose unconscious processes. Limiting ourselves to mental activity (versus, say, neurological processes), affect's operations are likely characterized by the two kinds of unconscious activity that Burke recognized in "Mind, Body, and the Unconscious." There, Burke distinguished the unconscious activity relevant to dramatism, which focuses on "symbolic action *in general*," from that of concern to psychoanalysis, which focuses on "'symptomatic action'" (63–64). Accordingly, the concept of affect seems to imply a split subject with a constitutive internal discord such that, when giving audience to credible, emotional-enthymematic appeals, this subject both *is* and *is not* motivated to form practical judgments. If so, the classical conception of ethics can only account for part of an interactive story weaved from affective threads. The classical focus of rhetoric's ethics, on relations *between* subjects, ignores or, at a minimum, marginalizes the question of relating *within* the split subject.

To help account for internal discord in an ethico-political theory of rhetoric, this essay suggests Julia Kristeva's concept of "the signifying process" as one place and movement to begin. To support this claim, I will flesh out my argument above by first discussing Greene's and Chaput's rhetorical theories, both of which take seriously the persuasive force of affect. The former considers affective labor as a mode of rhetorical agency; the latter conceptualizes rhetoric as the circulation of affective energy in a new model for rhetorical criticism. Next, I will show how the ethical investments of these studies are unwittingly undermined by their implicit reliance on conceptions of ethics that do not account for unself-conscious motives. Finally, I offer Kristeva's concept of "the signifying process" as a potential basis upon which the internal ethical issue may begin to be addressed.

Affect, Politics, and the Hope of Ethics

Traditionally, the relationship between rhetorical theory and ethics in politics was studied with regard to the potentials of language or speech. Today, efforts to theorize rhetoric in practical politics are no longer confined to verbal artifacts. Take, for example, the following recent studies by Ronald Greene and Catherine Chaput, both of which exemplify the relatively new and provocative affective turn in direction in pragmatically oriented rhetoric studies.

Aware of the threat that global capital poses to democratic life, Greene invites us to think about rhetoric as a form of "communicative labor" ("Rhetoric"). Concerned to move us beyond the "anxiety" that pervades debates on "rhetorical agency" (198), Greene places the ethical task of rhetorical criticism and theory squarely within the terms of a historical present discursively constituted by a globalizing bio-capitalism. A key characteristic of this stage of capitalism is its ability to deploy communication and rhetoric to create economic value and, thereby, subsume increasing types and numbers of products under the commodity form. Accordingly, Greene holds, a conception of "rhetorical agency as political communication" cannot but induce anxiety in the field, where rhetoric scholars draw lines between good and bad forms of political communication, only for capitalism to exploit those (fault) lines the moment they are drawn. In other words, for Greene, all communication practices are harnessed and channeled by capitalism.

Greene's solution to this widespread and ever-expanding corruption is to "remodel" "rhetorical agency . . . as communicative labor" ("Rhetoric" 201), where labor is defined as any activity that produces an identifiable entity—whether tangible, inferred, nonverbal, etc. To Greene, communicative labor operates along with, and "infuse[es] itself in," other forms of productive activity, including "affective labor" ("Orator" 90; "Rhetoric" 200, 202). From within this new model of persuasion, Greene argues, we can see once and for all how "rhetorical agency can be abstracted and captured" in capital's explicit name. In short, by taking "capitalism's need for communication" seriously, the concept of communicative labor "offers a starting point for how rhetorical studies might contribute to promoting the interests of living labor to outfox capitalism's logic of capture" ("Orator" 89–90). Such cunning is heavily influenced by Marx; and therein lies the ethical stakes for Greene. Deeply committed to "agency and social transformation," and working from "within a postmodern Marxist theory of value" that "ground[s] normative and epistemological judgments about exploitation and domination" (90–91), Greene puts his ethical stock in communist action: "The democratic future of rhetorical theory should be concerned with how the rhetoric-power of the orator-communist assembles the multitude" (94). Greene here imports Hardt and Negri's conception of "the multitude . . . *as an ensemble*, as a multiplicity of *subjectivities*, or rather *singularities*"; "as a *non*-working class social class" that engages in "immaterial" rather than "material labor"; and, finally, as "a *multiplicity* which is not reduced to that of mass, but which is *capable of autonomous*, independent, intellectual *development*" (Negri 101).

In the second contemporary case study, Chaput takes up Greene's call and investigates the potentials and limits of communicative labor in "neoliberalism" (4). Specifically, Chaput draws attention to the persuasive force of "affective energy" circulating in a network of different "events," "circumstances," "conditions," "currents," and "rationalities" (7–8). According to Chaput, these "moments" exist and unfold within the structures of neoliberal capitalism, and they are connected to each other by affects, which are forms of energy "sensed as intuitions, gut feelings, ideas, and beliefs that grip us regardless of precise facts" (14). Equally important, affects travel between and among bodies and, thereby, influence behavior; and communication is a prerequisite of this circulatory influence:

> Affect acts as an energy moving between human beings via communicative practices that inspire behavior instinctively. Affect . . . exerts pressure on our decision making and does not crumble under the deliberative weight of better arguments or more information. As a continuous process linking disparate actions, sensations, and events, affect operates within a transsituational and transhistorical structure and energizes our habituated movements as well as our commonsensical beliefs. (7–8)

Thus, by reconceptualizing rhetoric as a mode of "affective energy produced through communicative labor," Chaput invites us to set aside the idea of the single rhetorical artifact—as conceptualized in Bitzer's "rhetorical situation"—and the idea of several artifacts in a sequence of situations, and approach "rhetoric . . . as a circulation of exchanges" that coexist, are driven by persuasive affective energy, "govern our individual and collective decisions," and "operate on an entirely different level than rational deliberation" (8, 15).

Where lies the ethical dimension of rhetoric in this account? In Chaput's distinction between two kinds of affective energy: "Positive affective energies increase our potential openness to life and its possibilities; negative affective energies decrease our capacity for such openness" (15). Accordingly, Chaput sets forth a "new goal [that] is simply to increase communicative exchanges that circulate positive affects—to deliberate in such a way that we all become more open to the world's creative potential" (21). Chaput states that she does not want to replace the rhetorical situation with the rhetorical circulation model; instead, she envisions them working side by side.

Greene and Chaput each demonstrate rhetorical studies' expansion of what constitutes a legitimate object of study and, to a smaller or larger degree, express interest in thinking through rhetoric and affect without leaving ethico-politics behind. Yet the authors' concern for ethics may have been unwittingly undermined in these present accounts of affect's persuasive force. To see why, consider the unconscious mental processes that enable persuasion in each case.

Psychically Defensive Persuasion

The concepts of communicative and affective labor and affective energy presuppose unconscious psychic activity. As we saw with Burke, this activity includes the "ordinary" mental processes that enable (1) attention, perception, creativity, thought, judgment, reasoning, and action (mechanisms of interest to classical psychology and philosophy of mind) and (2) defensive psychic processes that prevent anxiety from reaching overwhelming levels and indicate varying degrees of psychopathology (mechanisms that facilitate and enact the repression with which psychoanalysis is chiefly concerned). To keep things concise, I shall refer to the first kind of unconscious activity as *cognitive-creative*, and the second kind as *defensive*.

Beginning with communicative labor, the rhetorical power this concept refers to is enabled by both cognitive-creative and defensive unconscious processes. Hinted at above,

> Communicative labor works transversally, infusing itself in all forms of labor, making all forms of labor more productive by activating networks of cooperation and social knowledge. You can find communicative labor at home, on the streets, in the firm, on the assembly line, in the sweatshop, on the unemployment line, in prison, in schools, and written on the walls. (Greene, "Orator" 90)

All of the referents of this quotation are probably more or less familiar to us, part of the everyday world of conscious activity. In terms of larger categories and based on Greene's above claim, one can also find communicative labor "infuse[ed]" in "intellectual" and "affective" activity, both of which, again, are exploited by capitalism in order to create economic value ("Rhetoric" 200). Arguably, these two forms of activity operate with the unconscious aid of cognitive-creative processes. But there are likely to be defensive processes at work here, too.

To take the more obvious example, Greene does not explicitly suggest that affective labor includes pathological variants, but psychoanalytic studies make clear that our frequent unawareness of affects in our own lives is not simply a product of affect's "yet-ness" (Seigworth and Gregg 3); it is also and often a sign that psychic defenses are in play (see, for example, Freud 177–78; Spezzano 40, 53, 65–66, 183). The defenses, which are themselves unconscious, are said to typically suppress painful affects, keeping them out of self-consciousness in the name of "psychological survival" (Spezzano 185); and when repeated frequently enough, the defenses become "unconscious affect-regulating structures" that systematically organize subjective experience to keep the painful affects at bay. Notably, Freud conceived of this pathological mechanism of control as part of normal mental life, even as it can escape the bounds of normality to reach clinical extremes. The conclusion I draw from all of this is that affective labor and its power may operate unconsciously in both cognitive-creative and defensive registers.

Similarly, the persuasion to which Chaput's concept of affective energy makes reference is probably enabled by both types of unconscious mental activity. Like Greene, Chaput does not make this argument; but recall her claim that affects "instinctively" guide "behavior" (versus action) and operate outside of rational frames. This clearly puts affects on the unconscious level; and if we take psychoanalysis into account, pathological variants of affect are just as likely to circulate along with their more healthy counterparts. Of course, this would mean that whether the energy is positive or negative is to some degree irrelevant. To be sure, Chaput claims that negative energies promote interpretive rigidity and thwart creative potentials (15); and as I mentioned, following Spezzano, psychic defenses calcify to terministically ward off intense anxiety-producing experiences. Still, positive affective energies can facilitate the closing off of experience. As Chaput says, capitalism is able to adapt to changing environments because it circulates positive energies that inspire us to be creative within the bounds of its "static modalities" (16). This adaptive circulation strongly suggests the potential for positive energy to sustain a particular defense structure, or what Burke termed "pattern of experience" ("Lexicon" 150), in the face of what might otherwise appear as oppositional facts. In a split word, this suggests false-consciousness, which can only be verified, ultimately, by those to whom it is attributed. At any rate, nothing that Chaput writes precludes the inference that affective energy may be enabled by cognitive-creative and defensive activity.

So what does all of this have to do with undermining ethics? As it stands generally, the normative relationship between rhetoric and ethics in (bio)politics is presumed to operate in the manifest world of ordinary psychic processes and corresponding symbolic action. But if modes of persuasion go beyond speech and into the affective realm, where unconscious drives play a key role, the conception of ethics must be brought up to speed. Otherwise, expressed commitments to normative claims and action are left to waver on shaky grounds.

To put the matter in Burkean terms, rhetorical theory is faced with a question of ethics that asks us to think the potential for motion to yield action, for humans' "animality" to yield persons' "symbolicity" ("Mind" 64, 63, 67). How might this potential be harnessed? This is no easy question. So, in the remaining pages, I offer one place where we might turn for a conceptual basis on which to fashion an ethics that is up to the contemporary rhetorical task set forth by Greene and Chaput. That place is Kristeva's theory of "the signifying process," which accounts for verbal and nonverbal modes of communication and the dynamic relationship between the two.

Between, Before, and Toward Self-Conscious Propositions

According to Kristeva, "the signifying process" has two "modalities," namely, "the symbolic" and "the semiotic" (*Revolution* 23–24). Comprising signs, propositions, and the syntax or structure that holds them together, the symbolic (*le symbolique*) facilitates acts of representation in language (40). It also presupposes a subject capable of definitional speech amidst objects she perceives as distinguishable from herself. Part of, but not reducible to, the symbolic order (*l'ordre symbolique*), which is the "code of linguistic and social communication," the symbolic posits identity and difference for the purpose of understanding (17, 24, 43–44, 54). The semiotic (*le sémiotique*), on the other hand, is the material other within signification. Defying generalization, it is the "distinctive mark, trace, index" or "imprint" of bodily drives as they irrupt into language to threaten its terms (25). In the context of spoken language, the irruption appears as "vocal play" that affords a connection between the body and the language (26). An affective representative of the drives, "voice," which Kristeva defines as the tones and rhythms of a person's speech, is a "material support" of signification that signals "connections" between parts of the body, and between the body, objects, and others (26, 29, 28).[2] An enactment of the "negativity," that is, the movement of heterogeneous drives, voice also reveals the contingent status of the terms of symbolic law and constitutes their transgression. Thus, for Kristeva, the semiotic articulates distinctive "phonic (and later phonemic)" marks that disturb identity and promote creativity (28, 62, 68–69).

Based on the semiotic and its generative relationship to referential speech, Kristeva argues that attention to "voice" is often warranted during analysis because, even though it does not have propositional content, it nevertheless has meaning or significance. On account of its status as an affective psychic representative, voice may index sensations of which the patient is not conscious—in part because the language he speaks does not (at the time) include terms that recognize or affirm the discharged instinctual need. Thus, if the analyst ignores voice, she risks giving short shrift to suppressed sensations and inadvertently limits the patient's opportunities to come to terms with his affective experiences. In short, Kristeva counsels, the analyst should take seriously the words, sounds, and rhythms (and behavior) of the patient as she reflects on the substance of any psychoanalytic interpretation she would offer to him.

Importantly, Jessica Benjamin has noted that during therapeutic sessions, analysts also fall under the influence of their defensive mental processes and often unconsciously ward off their own "bad" affects in deference to what they perceive to be the patient's needs (123–25). As this behavior constrains analysis in unproductive ways, Benjamin advocates that the analyst develop the habit of listening to the tones and rhythms of *his own* speech, interpreting and naming the affects voiced (such that the latter may become part of his self-consciousness), and expressing the names in words and ways that patients are likely to find respectful of their own affective experience. Benjamin's analyst is both observer and participant, "only able to help because she is inevitably implicated" (136).[3]

How might Kristeva's "signifying process," with Benjamin's addition, contribute to thinking ethics in political situations or networks where affective labor and energy unconsciously produce and motivate behavior? Simply and all too briefly, it provides a way to account for how the nonverbal yet meaningful elements of this energy or labor may be rendered productive of an always provisional self-conscious speech and, ultimately, action. The signifying process introduces the idea of "the subject in process/on trial" who is always becoming and only takes up the subject position in and through "enunciation" or referential speech (Kristeva, *Revolution* 17, 22, 54).

Conclusion

Let me end with a gesture to beginnings. Aristotle conceptualized rhetoric in close relation to his ethical theory (Farrell), which highlighted the moral and intellectual virtues and how they contribute to the good life—as much as this life could manifest itself in politics. Orators possessed practical wisdom and spoke a character that typified good sense, goodwill, and good moral judgment (see Aristotle, book 2). In select modern times and spaces, Hegel saw that Aristotle's conception of ethics was not up to the task of making choices in a world in which freedom and autonomy had come to matter. Hegel's response to this new situation was his concept of "ethical life," understood as the time, space, and relationship in which the other carries desirable weight for and against the self (and vice versa). As Robert Williams explains it, ethical life is present when an individual other, who is fundamentally different from yet equal to the self, is acknowledged and treated as such (86). "When the other comes to count for me, then the threshold of the ethical is crossed" (76–77). In Hegel's terms, "Self-consciousness attains its satisfaction only in another self-consciousness" (138).

But Freud's contribution to understanding consciousness (and its absence) reveals another kind of "other" that may come to count for the self in ways that outstrip Aristotelian and Hegelian ethics. This other, briefly stated, is defensive unconscious activity; and philosophy has begun to embrace it. Recently, for example, Jonathan Lear argued that Freud's fundamental insights raise important questions for philosophy:

> It is philosophers who have the task of exploring what matters to us most—What is freedom? What is it genuinely for us to be happy? What is worth valuing and why?—but it is psychoanalysis that teaches us how we regularly get in the way of our own freedom, systematically make ourselves unhappy and use values for covert and malign purposes. Philosophy cannot live up to its task unless it takes these psychoanalytic challenges seriously. (17)

While Lear's choice to reserve questions of freedom, happiness, and value for philosophers is debatable, his larger point is well taken: unconscious defensive activity is germane to human living. In the terms of one premise of my argument, internal discord is part and parcel of what it means to forever become a subject. The implication for us is clear: rhetorical studies that attend to affect in politics and proclaim ethical commitments to democratic (inter)action must go beyond classical and modern ethics and build their accounts on a normative relationship between unconscious defense structures, voice, speech, and action. Kristeva's "signifying process" is one place to begin this important conceptual work.

Notes

[1] I distinguish these studies from those that take up questions of affect and deliberation and use the former term as a synonym for emotion (e.g., Cloud; Hariman and Lucaites).

[2] Kristeva adds "colors" and "gesture" to the "material supports (*matériaux*) susceptible to semiotization." Insofar as she separates these from the relations of the semiotic to language, locating them instead in a relationship to visual forms of representation, I have chosen not to discuss these articulations in the present study. The choice is consistent with Kristeva's turn to "poetry" as the paradigm of transgressive signifying practice (*Revolution* 80–84).

[3] The valuable assumption is that "those who are part of the problem can also participate in the solution" (Benjamin 136); the important conceptual presupposition is twofold: (1) principles of the "energetic third" and "moral third" that represent respect, activity, and surrender to affective and dialogic interaction, and (2) the analyst must have these principles in mind-body if she is to cocreate with the patient two-way streets of reciprocal recognition. For a detailed discussion of the third and the space of "thirdness," see Benjamin.

Works Cited

Aristotle. *Rhetoric*. Trans. W. Rhys Roberts. New York: Modern Library, 1984.

Benjamin, Jessica. "Two-Way Streets: Recognition of Difference and the Intersubjective Third." *Differences: A Journal of Feminist Cultural Studies* 17.1 (2006): 116–46.

Burke, Kenneth. "Lexicon Rhetoricae." *Counter-Statement*. Berkeley: U of California P, 1968.

———. "Mind, Body, and the Unconscious." *Language and Symbolic Action: Essays on Life, Literature, and Method*. Berkeley: U of California P, 1966. 63–80.

Chaput, Catherine. "Rhetorical Circulation in Late Capitalism: Neoliberalism and the Overdetermination of Affective Energy." *Philosophy and Rhetoric* (2010): 1–25.

Cloud, Dana L. "Therapy, Silence, and War: Consolation and the End of Deliberation in the 'Affected' Public." *Poroi* 2.1 (2003): 125–42. Web.

Edbauer Rice, Jenny. "The New 'New': Making a Case for Critical Affect Studies." *Quarterly Journal of Speech* 94.2 (2008): 200–12.

Farrell, Thomas B. *Norms of Rhetorical Culture*. New Haven, CT: Yale UP, 1993.

Freud, Sigmund. "The Unconscious." 1915. *The Standard Edition of the Complete Psychological Works of Sigmund Freud. Volume XIV (1914–1916): On the History of the Psycho-Analytic Movement, Papers on Metapsychology and Other Works*. London: Hogarth P, 1963.

Greene, Ronald Walter. "Orator Communist." *Philosophy and Rhetoric* 39.1 (2006): 85–95.

———. "Rhetoric and Capitalism: Rhetorical Agency as Communicative Labor." *Philosophy and Rhetoric* 37.3 (2004): 188–206.

Hariman, Robert, and John Louis Lucaites. "Dissent and Emotional Management in a Liberal-Democratic Society: The Kent State Iconic Photograph." *Rhetoric Society Quarterly* 31 (2001): 4–31.

Hegel, G. W. F. *Hegel's Phenomenology of Spirit*. Trans. A. V. Millier. New York: Oxford UP, 1977.

Kristeva, Julia. *Black Sun: Depression and Melancholia*. Trans. Leon Roudiez. New York: Columbia UP, 1989.

———. *New Maladies of the Soul*. Trans. Ross Guberman. New York: Columbia UP, 1995.

———. *Revolution in Poetic Language*. New York: Columbia UP, 1984.

Lear, Jonathan. *Freud*. New York: Routledge, 2005.

Lundberg, Christian. "Enjoying God's Death: *The Passion of the Christ* and the Practices of an Evangelical Public." *Quarterly Journal of Speech* 95.4 (2009): 387–411.

Negri, Antonio. *Reflections on Empire*. Trans. Ed Emery. Cambridge, UK: Polity P, 2008.

Seigworth, Gregory J., and Melissa Gregg. "An Inventory of Shimmers." *The Affect Theory Reader*. Ed. Melissa Gregg and Gregory J. Seigworth. Durham, NC: Duke UP, 2010. 1–27.

Spezzano, Charles. *Affect in Psychoanalysis: A Clinical Synthesis*. Hillsdale, NJ: Analytic P, 1993.

Williams, Robert. *Hegel's Ethics of Recognition*. Berkeley: U of California P, 1997.

10

Troubled Freedom

The Grounds of Rhetoric and Psychoanalysis

Ira Allen

Concord—as also controversy—implies freedom. For the perfectly determined subject (the person considered as a Newtonian atom subjected to impersonal forces), "concord" (a temporary sort of desiring harmony, a state of agreement to be achieved and lost) is a term without meaning. Indeed, when used in the texts of classical physics or mathematics, it is at most figurative, a metaphor drawn from human experience.[1] Without some notion of freedom, discussion of *agreement* is pointless: say the tree branch agrees with its neighbor to bow before the wind, or that both agree with the wind. Equally, for its conceptual force controversy depends on a belief in freedom, for, (1) there reigns between contesting parties an unspoken agreement that the other, or some other other, may come to see matters differently or may be persuaded and (2) the idea of persuasion itself assumes a certain participatory capacity for change. The arguments of rhetoric, as Chaïm Perelman and Lucie Olbrechts-Tyteca put the matter in *The New Rhetoric*, address and are conducted by persons who would manage to be both "durable beings" and "free subjects," with the "possibility of submitting to or resisting persuasion" (295). This possibility, they argue, is central to the human experience and, in turn, "make[s] the social sciences disciplines that cannot merely copy faithfully the methodology of the natural sciences" (295). This, in a text that devotes hundreds of pages to cataloguing the modes of argument by which people happen regularly to be persuaded! Those pages, and the pages of all rhetorical theory, are haunted by a usually unarticulated, but nonetheless consistent, notion of freedom. I have termed this "troubled freedom."

Troubled freedom can come into clearer focus for rhetoricians through a comparison of our central tenets with those of psychoanalysis, in particular the version of it taught by Jacques Lacan. Of course, those who want to talk about freedom rarely begin with psychoanalysis, still less with Lacan, but any number of people have entered into analysis in search of freedom over the years. And now, ten years into a century inaugurated by Operation Enduring Freedom, an operation that very much still endures, it is not a bad time to check in with Lacan, to check up on ourselves, to check out what—precisely—we mean by "freedom." I am going to Lacan, however, for more than a checkup, and I am going not only on behalf of rhetorical theory, but also on behalf of a more general "we." I first argue that the vision of freedom that emerges in Lacan's *Seminar XI: The Four Fundamental Concepts of Psychoanalysis* is crucial to understanding the ground upon which rhetorical theory proceeds. In particular, his discussion of the aims of analysis helps clarify what is at stake in the Burkean concept of "pure persuasion," a concept that rhetorical theory has struggled to accept in the sort of grounding role Burke envisioned for it. But second, I want also to insist that the vision of freedom that emerges in rhetoric and psychoanalysis—*troubled freedom*—is more or less the signification proper to the word "freedom" itself. Troubled freedom, that is, may be taken as the ground on which rhetoric and psychoanalysis proceed; simultaneously, rhetoric and psychoanalysis can be understood as grounding (anchoring in meaning) "freedom" as such.

This push toward a unitary definition might seem counterintuitive or anachronistic. For one thing, the word "freedom" most often appears in an ordering role, organizing speech and activity without ever being quite pinned down. Also, prescriptive definitions are out of fashion; they are no longer commonsensical. This is surely in part because of the clarity with which we see today that *agon* inheres in all acts of defining, and that the exclusions implied by unified meanings or definitions are harmful. (I do not wish to do battle with this view, but rather to come to terms with the fact that, in holding it myself, I *can't not* subscribe to it—and thereby also to the metaconcept of conceptual unity or to-be-valued belief.) On one hand, although we may know *practically* what "freedom" means and act on that knowing, we ought not necessarily define it; should we set out to do so, the prevailing wisdom goes, we will at the very least find ourselves embroiled in controversy. One way of thinking of this doxa is offered by sociolinguist George Lakoff. He begins *Whose Freedom? The Battle over America's Most Important Idea* by explaining that "freedom" has an "uncontested core that we all agree on," our concord stemming from a meta-agreement not to really define the term at all (15). Such meta-agreement, he argues, is conversationally necessary precisely because freedom is simultaneously "an essentially contested concept" about which there will always be "radical disagreement" as to its particulars (15). Lakoff's own contribution to that controversy is to a large extent polemical. He believes, as he puts it, "that one version of freedom is traditional and important to keep for the deepest moral reasons," while another set of uses are "dangerous to our democratic ideals and to the moral system behind the founding of our nation" (16). I am engaged in a very different sort of endeavor here. Rather than arguing that one version of the term best fits the "moral system" of "our nation," I offer what I believe to be a covering definition. I argue, pace Lakoff, that "freedom as such" has a core that *can* be agreed on even when we do define it. As may be glimpsed through some attention to the grounds of rhetoric and psychoanalysis, "freedom" is troubled freedom; it is the negotiation of constraint.

The basic idea is this: rhetoric relies on audiences who are both circumscribed and capable of a kind of change that is to some extent intentional or desiring, audiences whose experience of doxa is the scene and agency of rhetorical invention. Rhetoric's audiences must be free enough to *participate in communication or persuasion*—to change from who or what they are to something other, as in the Burkean scene of identification and consubstantiality—while also being unfree enough to *be persuaded or communicated with*—to become other in ways that reflect rhetors' desires and not necessarily those of the audiences as they initially stand. Likewise, rhetors themselves must be constrained in both speech and desire by the circumstances of discourse, by the scene of doxa and the rhetorical situation, and yet unconstrained enough to use this scene's "available means" in inventing communicative or persuasive speech that may change that very scene. People must be free enough to have a role in their own changing, but unfree enough to change in accordance with desires not their own—if we don't believe both these things, there's little point in our studying rhetoric at all. The freedom of the rhetorical subject is thus troubled in much the way a conscience may be troubled: constitutively. To be at all, a conscience *must* be troubled. And, just as a conscience's trouble is the negotiation of constraints—what am I to do with who I have been, or who I imagine I have been?!—so, too, to be rhetorical is to negotiate constraint. All this speaks back to my uses of the word "free" in this paragraph itself. When I have spoken of people being free enough or unfree enough to be persuaded, I have meant—I could only mean—that they were more or less able to negotiate the constraints of their rhetorical situations.

Kenneth Burke places troubled freedom at the heart of rhetorical theory, suggesting in *A Rhetoric of Motives* that rhetoric as such must rest on a notion of "pure persuasion." Burke has been regularly misread on this matter, even in otherwise compelling and insightful pieces—James Zappen's recent "Kenneth Burke on Dialectical-Rhetorical Transcendence" comes to mind—and it seems to me that this is because readers have wanted "pure persuasion" to be a more or less concrete category, rather than a motivational element always present in rhetoric, something that Burke describes as bringing us "to the borders of metaphysics, or perhaps better 'meta-rhetoric'" (266). So, Zappen, for instance, sees pure persuasion as a "utopian ideal," and worries that rhetorical-dialectical transcendence here "seems almost to slip away into the realms of ritual, mysticism, and the poetic imagination" (293). But Burke is perfectly clear on this. He writes, "We are not offering this concept of 'pure' rhetoric as the highest ideal of human conduct. . . . We are suggesting that [the motive to persuade] is implicit in the 'transcendent' nature of symbolism itself" (271). Symbolic activity is a sort of movement beyond the being that it, too, is. Pure persuasion, that is, is part of the conceptual-motivational ground for symbolic—which is to say, rhetorical-dialectical—activity in general. I do not mean here to chide Zappen, but rather to point out the way in which otherwise insightful rhetoricians regularly misread Burke on this matter. I believe the difficulty—as much for Ross Wolin and Timothy Crusius and other readers of the *Rhetoric* as for Zappen, with Robert Wess being a notable exception—stems from rhetorical theory's more general difficulty in articulating its own foundations, and most especially its *psychological* foundations.[2] It is for help with such articulation that I will turn to Lacan in a moment.

But first, what does Burke say "pure persuasion," this ground of rhetoric, is? He writes that, though "biologically unfeasible," pure persuasion "would [nonetheless] be the state of intolerable indecision just preceding conversion to a new doctrine" (294). In this phrasing, Burke grapples with something that cannot quite be said, something at the limits of rhetoric, of persuasion, argument, conviction—something that is troubled freedom itself. Burke's description of pure persuasion as "preceding conversion" is thus particularly significant, since a conversion suggests not absolute novelty, but rather a meaningfully new organization of the old material of selfhood: a new constitution. And yet, this new constitution depends on the impossible, the "unfeasible." Pure persuasion is where the subject is prior to her new constitution, and being there is "intolerable." Pure persuasion appears here, then, not as an aim or utopia, but as a place of susceptibility. One occupies a state of indecision that one cannot, in fact, occupy (it is not just unfeasible, but *biologically* unfeasible), and it is in that state (or to escape it; it is intolerable) that one submits to discursive invention and becomes new to oneself. This would seem to accord with Perelman and Olbrechts-Tyteca's view of submission as characterizing rhetoric's subjects—both rhetor and audience—who are reinvented in the negotiation of arguments that have themselves been invented out of the material of tradition, of *endoxa* or common wisdom. . . .

I could continue in this vein, but am in truth still mostly talking *around* pure persuasion. I am not yet getting at the heart of it, at the notion of troubled freedom that this concept entails. Indeed, I cannot by definition—it is the ground on which my (rhetorical theoretical) activity proceeds. In order to better glimpse that ground, if only by analogy, I turn now to Lacan's articulation of the work of psychoanalysis, to the sort of freedom he sees emerging in the analytic situation. This, I will argue, is almost precisely that of the rhetorical situation as well, insofar as the rhetorical situation is undergirded by something like "pure persuasion."

Interpretation in psychoanalysis, Lacan says in Book XI, "is not open to all meanings" (250). To the contrary, its role is to help the analysand encounter "*le signifiant primordial*" (280, emphasis in original), the primordial signifier at the base of all experience of meaning or sense. This primordial or primary signifier occupies the same position relative to Lacanian analysis that pure persuasion occupies relative to Burkean rhetoric, and should thus help shed light on the latter. The primary signifier is irreducible; it cannot be referred to other signifiers along the chain—it grounds signification. It cannot represent a subject for other signifiers, it cannot pass its charge neatly on to the next signifier in order to produce some effect of meaning; since it is thus never available for the usual processes of signification, it cannot be interpreted. Instead, the primary signifier is "pure non-sense" (252), a simple and total absence of sense that nonetheless produces effects. It is not in itself the real, but is rather where being becomes meaning and is thereby eclipsed, where the real becomes symbolic and is thereby inaccessible.

Gilbert Chaitin captures the ambiguity of this point in *Rhetoric and Culture in Lacan*. He notes that the Lacanian real is "profoundly ambivalent: as that which escapes symbolization it is both the traumatic *par excellence*, the unassimilable kernel at the heart of human experience, and the contingent, the only haven for human subjectivity" (9). *Le signifiant primordial* is the place where being eludes meaning, the place where the real both serves as ground for and escapes symbolization. The primary signifier, like pure persuasion, is not in not being said, but in eluding being said. That eluding is marked by the primordial signifier that simultaneously inaugurates the possibility of meaning as a mode of being and itself disappears, making it possible for being to escape those words that would capture it, would thereby produce meaning. For Lacan, the work of interpretation in psychoanalysis is thus to "bring out irreducible, *non-sensical*—composed of non-meanings—signifying elements" (250): to bring to the table those primary signifiers that, to anchor the system of signifiers referring to other signifiers that is the realm of meaning properly so called, have been subjected to *urverdrängung*, primary or primordial repression. Lacanian analysis aims thus to bring these *signifiants primordials* out into the open in such a way that they may be encountered. The usual play of signifiers, the flow of meaning in commonsensical existence—that sort of being in the world *not* marked by "overthinking things"—entails precisely that primary signifiers *not* be encountered, not be met. The primary signifier is, quite literally, the limit of meaning; it is the edge where meaning ends or begins. And it is in developing ways of encountering primordial signifiers that Lacanian psychoanalysis becomes an orientation toward freedom, its operation as a negotiation of constraint helping us to understand pure persuasion and troubled freedom.

Lacan suggests that the primary signifier, the necessary condition of signification, be conceived as the denominator of a fraction: as a zero, to be precise, such that "the value of the fraction no longer has meaning, but assumes . . . what mathematicians call an infinite value" (252). If this is the basis of all signification, it might at first seem to suggest a freedom that would be the total absence of constraint, what is often thought of as "absolute" or "radical" freedom, or as "negative liberty." Instead, what this should make clear is the absolute unthinkability of such a notion of freedom—without, though, destroying the usability of the word. The primordial signifier lies at the root of meaning, but is not included in it; this is a space in being where the desire of the Other attaches to the field of symbols, of meaning, in a way that is parasitic on, that takes up, being without including it in meaning. To encounter this unthinkable place in oneself, in the primary signifiers of one's own unconscious, is thus to experience an anguishing abolition of meaning—and, if this were the end of the story, we should think only that Lacanian psychoanalysis must induce a sort of psychosis, where the entire chain of signifiers becomes a single, solid block.

But the story continues; analysis is, indeed, a continuation of storying by other means. Lacan writes, "This is why it is untrue to say that the signifier in the unconscious is open to all meanings. It constitutes the subject in his freedom in relation to all meanings, but this does not mean that it is not determined in it. For, in the numerator, in the place of the zero, the things that are inscribed are significations," beings-become-meaning, "and they give a particular value to the relation of the subject to the unconscious" (252). That is, while the primary signifier, the signifier in the unconscious, is without meaning, all the ways in which I or you have approached it thus far do have meaning and *cannot not* be negotiated. How our approaches are to be negotiated is a question at the heart of psychoanalysis.

In Lacanian terms, the aim of analysis is to provoke an encounter with the primary signifier, not because this in itself is of any value, but because doing so allows for a re-ordering of the relations of the subject to her unconscious, a conversion that is not a symptom.[3] As Bruce Fink puts it in *A Clinical Introduction to Lacanian Psychoanalysis: Theory and Technique*, "In psychoanalysis it is thus what the analysand actually says, not what he means that is important" (24). What an analysand means, or "intends to convey[,] is something that is consonant with his view of himself, with the kind of person he believes himself to be (or would like to believe himself to be, or is at least willing to believe himself to be)" (24); and it is only in surrendering one's constitution of self as having validity in the arbitration of meaning that one enters that space of intolerable indecision from whence the fullness of persuasion, of a new constitution, proceeds. Psychoanalysis, in this view, aims to facilitate or *provoke* (another) conversion. It does so by positing and engaging with a subject who is troubledly free.

An encounter with the bases of one's own meaning-being, one's own subjectivity, is always—even in analysis—just barely missed, but the basic thrust of Lacan's teaching is that the analytic situation can get you close enough to primary signifiers to make possible a renegotiation of your overall style of being. This is almost precisely the kind of freedom Burke associates with pure persuasion, which, like the irreducible signifier, is a mode of "self-interference" (269). Like the primary signifier, which is without meaning, and yet is at the base of the field of meaning, "Pure persuasion involves the saying of something, not for an extraverbal advantage to be got by the saying, but because of a satisfaction intrinsic to the saying" (269). It is, as Robert Wess notes, not an ideal to be instantiated but "a condition of rhetoricity" to be negotiated (213). Burke, significantly, argues that pure persuasion is crucial because it "permits us to include as elements of rhetoric both psychological and institutional motivations" (285). And what are such motivations if not, quite precisely, the enabling constraints of rhetorical activity? We want to include them in our discussion of rhetoric because—by coming to new terms with a dialectic between "pure" and "impure" persuasions—we ourselves become better able to negotiate our constraints as rhetorical theorists. So, too, the freedom of rhetor and audience, and the freedom of analysand and analyst, lies in the negotiation of constraints.

One thing this account of troubled freedom should make clear is that new ways of being become possible as new constraints—which may themselves become other to their original being—overlap, condensing with the old. Freedom, then, is *never* the unsayable absence of constraint, a fantasy place from which just anything might emerge, but rather *that which can't quite be said*. To recall my earlier point, freedom *is* not in *not* being said, but in *eluding* being said. There exists some *that which is* that *resists meaning* in its mode of being; this is troubled freedom, seen from one angle. From the complementary angle, freedom is *that which means* that somehow, impossibly, *promotes what will have been*. These two angles—freedom as that being which eludes meaning and freedom as that meaning which nominates being—offer a new perspective on the old standbys of negative and positive liberty.[4] As entangled aspects of troubled freedom, we may see these not as an absence of constraint and a power-to; rather, they are negotiation-oriented away from current constraints and negotiation-oriented toward new constraints. Concord and controversy demand both.

I want to close with a few relatively bald assertions: (1) There is no absence of constraint that could be at all meaningful (and hence could be the signification of "freedom"). (2) There is no freedom that would be well understood if reduced simply to effective activity. Likewise, (3) The negotiation of constraint does not "create" or "produce" freedom; it *is* freedom. Freedom is none other than such negotiation, which would seem to be all that is given to us as our lot. Troubled freedom thus implies an existential responsibility. An examination of this responsibility is a separate project, but it should be understood here at least that the responsibility attaches not to a moral ideal, but to an eminently practical consideration, a constraint: *we cannot not negotiate our constraints*. There is no action that we, symbol-using and mis-using animals, as Burke described us, can take that does not involve a negotiation of constraint. We knead being and meaning together from the very beginning of our subjectivity; we are constraint-negotiating animals. What has frequently gone unrecognized is that such negotiation of constraint—and here, symbol use presents itself as the readiest tool, though it is certainly not our only one—is the core of freedom itself. This is because freedom is, and must be if it is to be intelligible at all, troubled. The places where troubled freedom does not exist constitute the boundaries of what we can conceive of as personhood or subjectivity. To feel oneself within those boundaries is to be responsible to the troubled freedom that, at the core, one *is*. The troubled freedom that we all are.

Notes

[1] Though it would take me away from my argument to discuss it, the matter stands differently for quantum physics. For an excellent, posthumanist treatment of just such questions, see Karen Barad's *Meeting the Universe Halfway: Quantum Physics and the Entanglement of Matter and Meaning*, especially pages 106–21 and 175–79.

[2] I am, of course, far from the first rhetorical theorist to see important links between rhetoric and psychoanalysis. Without leaving my chair, the following come immediately to mind: Barbara Biesecker's "Rhetorical Studies and the 'New' Psychoanalysis," Victor Vitanza's *Negation, Subjectivity, and the History of Rhetoric*, Diane Davis's "Identification: Burke and Freud on Who You Are," David Metzger's *The Lost Cause of Rhetoric: The Relation of Rhetoric and Geometry in Aristotle and Lacan*, Marshall Alcorn's *Changing the Subject in English Class*, and Thomas Rickert's *Acts of Enjoyment: Rhetoric, Žižek, and the Return of the Subject*. And this is only a short list.

[3] The word "conversion" most frequently appears in psychoanalytic discourse as part of the duo "conversion symptom." Fink explains, "In the case of conversion symptoms—that is, symptoms expressed in the body (which run the gamut from minor aches and pains, tightness in the chest . . . paralysis, blindness, muteness, and deafness)—the medium the symptoms adopt is a body written with language, a body overwritten with signifiers" (114). The rhetorical constitution of selfhood here seems apparent, as does the need for a *new* conversion.

[4] The classic exposition of this is Isaiah Berlin's "Two Concepts of Liberty," collected (among other places) in *Liberty*, pages 166–217.

Works Cited

Alcorn, Marshall. *Changing the Subject in English Class: Discourse and the Constructions of Desire.* Carbondale: Southern Illinois UP, 2002.

Barad, Karen. *Meeting the Universe Halfway: Quantum Physics and the Entanglement of Matter and Meaning*. Durham, NC: Duke UP, 2007.

Berlin, Isaiah. *Liberty*. Ed. Henry Hardy. Oxford: Oxford UP, 2002.

Biesecker, Barbara. "Rhetorical Studies and the 'New' Psychoanalysis: What's the Real Problem? or Framing the Problem of the Real." *Quarterly Journal of Speech* 84 (1998): 222–59.

Burke, Kenneth. *A Rhetoric of Motives*. 1950. Berkeley: U of California P, 1969.

Chaitin, Gilbert. *Rhetoric and Culture in Lacan*. Cambridge: Cambridge UP, 1996.

Crusius, Timothy W. *Kenneth Burke and the Conversation after Philosophy*. Carbondale: Southern Illinois UP, 1999.

Davis, Diane. "Identification: Burke and Freud on Who You Are." *Rhetoric Society Quarterly* 6.3 (2008): 123–47.

Fink, Bruce. *A Clinical Introduction to Lacanian Psychoanalysis: Theory and Technique*. Cambridge, MA: Harvard UP, 1997.

Lacan, Jacques. *The Seminar of Jacques Lacan, Book XI: The Four Fundamental Concepts of Psychoanalysis*. Ed. Jacques-Alain Miller. Trans. Alan Sheridan. New York: W.W. Norton, 1998.

Lakoff, George. *Whose Freedom? The Battle over America's Most Important Idea*. New York: Picador/Farrar, Straus and Giroux, 2006.

Metzger, David. *The Lost Cause of Rhetoric: The Relation of Rhetoric and Geometry in Aristotle and Lacan*. Carbondale: Southern Illinois UP, 1995.

Perelman, Chaïm, and Lucie Olbrechts-Tyteca. *The New Rhetoric: A Treatise on Argumentation*. 1969. Trans. John Wilkinson and Purcell Weaver. Notre Dame, IN: U of Notre Dame P, 1971.

Rickert, Thomas. *Acts of Enjoyment: Rhetoric, Žižek, and the Return of the Subject*. Pittsburgh: U of Pittsburgh P, 2007.

Vitanza, Victor. *Negation, Subjectivity, and the History of Rhetoric*. Albany: State U of New York P, 1997.

Wess, Robert. *Kenneth Burke: Rhetoric, Subjectivity, Postmodernism*. Cambridge: Cambridge UP, 1996.

Wolin, Ross. *The Rhetorical Imagination of Kenneth Burke*. Columbia: U of South Carolina P, 2001.

Zappen, James P. "Kenneth Burke on Dialectical-Rhetorical Transcendence." *Philosophy and Rhetoric* 42.3 (2009): 279–301.

11

Adaptive Rhetoric

Ethos and Evolved Behavior in Cicero's *De Oratore*

Alex C. Parrish

In his 1966 article on the teaching of rhetoric, Robert Gorrell opens with a quote by the character Dogberry from *Much Ado about Nothing*: "To be a well-favored man is the gift of fortune; but to write and read comes by nature" (409). Gorrell interprets this as yet another instance of Dogberry getting things exactly wrong, rather than recognizing the occasional fits of genius the Bard loved to attribute to his fools and his madmen. In this case, Dogberry's comment is actually quite insightful: the genetic predispositions of each human allow them to acquire the skills of reading and writing, and these skills are natural. Culture then helps to shape how we read and write—in what contexts we assimilate and articulate texts—but we must not underestimate the necessity of certain genetic traits that allow humans to be the sole species on Earth capable of complex symbolic learning (Deacon 12).

Histories of rhetoric often neglect our genetic legacy in favor of discussing the equally complex network of cultural influences that shed light on rhetorical practices. Yet rhetoric comes to us by nature and reflects evolutionary pressures that might not, at first glance, be thought still to influence human behavioral patterns. Or perhaps the connections have become obscured by disciplinary thinking, whereas an interdisciplinary approach could reconnect the relationship between evolved behavior and rhetorical practice.

As the interdisciplinary work of evolutionary psychology and sociobiology have become more firmly established in the sciences, it is clear that animal behavior is both complex and often understandable through the observation of other, related animals. To explain human behavior, we need to study animal behavior, especially the behavior of those primates who are our closest genetic relatives. In *On the Origin of Stories,* evolutionary literary critic Brian Boyd explains that if animals and humans exist on a continuum of intelligence, their actions and motives can inform our studies of human actions and motives.

> From an evolutionary standpoint, explaining how *we* understand events and stories necessitates also discovering how *other* animals learn from events. Although we still have much to discover about advanced animal cognition, creatures of many species appear to infer meaning from events. At the simplest this involves, say, the recognition that food can be obtained through a certain procedure, as a pigeon pecks at . . . a lever in an experiment. Animals that observe others intently may acquire complex information about social opportunities and costs. Chimpanzees can find out not only the dangers of challenging a particular male or his coalition partners, but also, by observing over time how coalitions rise and fall, how to plan for their own strategic assault on the ruling alliance. (368)

To use a computer software analogy, if we want to understand Windows 7, it may be helpful to know how previous operating systems functioned. While there may not be direct translation of all cognitive activities among animals, many general features are shared among species. Just as knowledge of Windows 2000 will not guarantee your full understanding of Windows' newer operating systems, familiarity with the broad strokes eases the process of making connections between one system and the other. Biological systems are in many ways the same.

E. O. Wilson provides one particular example—our "experience in [analyzing] behavior such as incest avoidance has shown that the hard instincts of animals are translatable into epigenetic rules of human behavior" (195). This incest avoidance behavior in humans has been labeled the Westermarck effect. Contrary to Freud's belief that incestual desire is a norm of human psychology requiring societies to create taboos, Finnish anthropologist Edvard Westermarck found that human incest taboos arose naturally (352). Among the subjects he studied, those individuals who knew one another intimately before the age of 30 months had either no sexual feelings or feelings of revulsion toward the idea of sexual intimacy with one another when they reached sexual maturity. Likewise, this effect extended to any individual, genetically related or not, who shared the same domicile.

Insights like these reveal that rhetoric, as a field, is tarnished by human exceptionality. Incorporating studies of animal behavior will help situate the human animal in the larger world of communication studies. The consilient paradigm (consilience being William Whewell's term for a literal "jumping together" of knowledge) is essential to understanding the development of the art of persuasion over long evolutionary time, and relating that back to the efforts of individuals in specific cultural environments (Wilson 8). John Angus Campbell actually predicted this move to restore nature in rhetorical theory when he concluded that the evolutionary sciences have made a steady effort to absorb all human endeavors into their fold (369). This is not as startling as it sounds. While the move toward placing rhetoric back in the natural domain may feel to some like a paradigm shift, or even an incursion, it is little more than a minor course correction in an already productive field. The existing tools of rhetoric fit well with the new methods of evolutionary psychology and sociobiology.

Cicero's rhetorical and philosophical works are especially suited to a naturalistic analysis. The idea that biological and cultural forces are constantly cooperating and competing pervades his thought. In his first rhetorical treatise, he follows Isocrates in suggesting that persuasion was responsible for "the domestication of the human animal" *(De Inventione* I.i.2). Over forty years later, in *De Oratore,* Cicero has Crassus mouth the same sentiment, nearly word for word (I.30–5). Though Cicero's views on rhetoric changed over time we can find a naturalistic explanation for the origins of society throughout his body of rhetorical and philosophical work. His appeals to nature in *De Inventione* and *De Oratore* mirror those found in his best known philosophical exposition, *De Officiis.* In this text, Cicero uses his theory of the origins of civil society to justify his outline of natural reason, a concept tied intimately to his conception of persuasion (I.4). The civilized man would, through use of his highly developed mental abilities, seek society with his fellow men, develop love for his offspring, and nourish and support his family and those he is bound to protect. Natural reason allows society, formed on the basis of rhetoric, to thrive.

It is the aim of this essay, then, to connect two important modes of thought that are not commonly explored together. The first area of inquiry is into the utility of ethos in Cicero's *De Oratore,* a work that informs many speeches and philosophical treatises of the period Syme labeled The Roman Revolution, and whose importance extended into the modern period of rhetorical scholarship.[1] Work in this area has been taken up previously by a number of scholars, including James May, whose ideas about Ciceronian ethos inform this essay (see *Trials of Character: The Eloquence of Ciceronian Ethos*).

The second area of inquiry is into the practice of ethos-building in the natural world and how animals unaffected by complex cultural forces are still compelled by sexual selection pressures to perform altruistic, self-endangering, and sometimes absurd actions in order to prove themselves worthy to their mates. What lies between these two fairly mundane lines of inquiry is a world of unexamined connections among the art of animal displays that show their character and abilities in the best light and a parallel practice in oratory meant to accomplish a comparable goal for the patron-advocate's client. Furthering the work of George Kennedy, this essay could be considered one of the first exercises in evolutionary rhetorical theory, a perspective complementary to the emerging field of evolutionary literary criticism (also known as evocriticism or literary Darwinism), which attempts to explain the narratives humans create through reference to their adaptive function.[2] Some evolutionary benefits of constructing a positive ethos, then, will hopefully be apparent by the end of this discussion.

To Cicero the utility of ethos is the revelation of the client's good character in order to secure men's goodwill (*conciliari quam maxime ad benevolentiam*) (*De Oratore* II.182). As a rhetorical practice, securing goodwill through a display of admirable character is engrained deeply in human biology. As Brian Vickers insists, "In rhetoric, art not only imitates, it re-creates nature" (80). Ethos-building in nature is done through conspicuous displays of altruistic behavior, of proving one's fitness to procreate or one's ability to raise offspring. This is tied to emotional appeals—sometimes directly, and at other times through the construction of a pathetic narrative inside the audience's head. Appeals to logos are conceivably rare in nature, even though reason is not confined to homo sapiens; but it is ethos and pathos that drive people to action. For Cicero, use of *conciliare* connotes an active ethos. Whereas Aristotle meant merely representation of character, Cicero empowered ethos as an agent of persuasion in itself (May, *Trials* 5).

Likewise, ethos-building among some other animals demonstrates a natural capacity for survival and fitness as a potential mate. This can manifest itself through the ability to provide a steady stream of resources or the commitment to follow through with childrearing, postcoitus. If an animal has the same "gift of gab" (or squawk, etc.) then it can secure the goodwill of other animals.

My own approach to explaining the Ciceronian conception of ethos, then, is to treat it in the context of rhetorical practices that are evolutionarily adaptive. I explain the potential benefits of ethos-building in Cicero's *De Oratore* through the interpretive frame of animal behavior in the natural world. How such behavior adapted in other animals, and how it is common among many representatives of the animal kingdom, could shed light on important similarities in the development of human ethos construction as Cicero imagines it, and in conspicuous displays of altruism in other animals. Humans recognized the benefits of constructing an image of ourselves as *viri boni* before a modern evolutionary explanation existed. However, advances in the current study of animal behavior make possible fruitful comparisons between the complex behaviors of multiple species, provided we are aware of the limits of such an approach. No analogy should be taken too far, and no "ought" should be inferred from any "is" presented in this essay. That would turn this essay into an exercise in social Darwinism, which it certainly is not (and, I think, ought not to be). The goal is to connect Cicero's theory of ethos to its possible adaptive function in hopes that we may see a more complete view of the rhetorical function of this *pistis*.

Altruism

While Cicero may have thought that it was rhetoric that separated mankind from the rest of the animal kingdom, that we are "gathered together in one community" through eloquence and thus elevated above the "brutish beasts," it is through the concept of altruism that we see the similarities in the rhetorics of Animalia (Cicero, *De Oratore* I.33). Broadly, sociobiologists define animal altruism as any charitable action that costs the donor in some way, while in turn helping the recipient. An example of this is in bonobo (pygmy chimpanzee) food sharing among close relatives or mates. While it may seem intuitive for animals that are genetically related or emotionally bound to pool their resources, this is not to be taken for granted in nature—many species of animals are on their own from birth, and many more once they reach adulthood. An individual's willingness to give up precious resources in order to help another deserves explanation.

There are some special sorts of altruism, including kin altruism (above) and reciprocal altruism. The latter is especially germane, because it introduces the importance of ethos in the animal world (Trivers 35). It works like this: in a society of animals who live in close proximity to one another, it is sometimes necessary to request the aid of others. When one individual provides succor in the form of food, grooming, or any number of potential benefits, it is expected that this individual will receive similar treatment in its own hour of need from the fellow it had helped earlier. In an ideal world everyone would return favors in a timely manner, but in a world of limited resources, some animals decide it is more beneficial to refuse to help others at times. In a society built on reciprocal altruism there are various strategies for survival, including cooperation, defection, and any combination thereof. The animal that would get the most benefit from society would be the one who always reaps the benefit of its cooperating neighbors while being selfish with its own resources. However, others pick up on this antisocial behavior, and the defector soon loses out on the benefits of society.

This is where ethos becomes relevant, for persona-building in the animal world is how one assures others that their altruism will be returned. One wants one's fellows to reason: "Old Betty over there gave me a banana the last time I needed one, so it's probably safe to share my mangoes with her." Many species dedicate considerable time to cultivating positive public personae because the benefits of being thought a good neighbor could one day mean the difference between starvation and survival. This is not necessarily selfish or unselfish, but merely a behavior that has been encouraged through the success of animals that cultivate positive images of their character in others.

Kim Sterelny disagrees with this neutral stance, suspecting that all altruism could indeed be selfish, regardless of how benevolent an action may appear. In support of this, he cites Heinrich's study of reciprocal altruism in ravens (44–5). What Heinrich found was that when lone ravens were observed finding an animal carcass, rather than keeping the feast to themselves, they would call out to other scavengers, notifying them of the find. This seems counterintuitive in a competitive environment. One would think the individual would act for its benefit alone. The fact is, the lone raven might yet be acting selfishly, despite the apparent benevolence of its actions. What Heinrich finds is that juvenile ravens who do not hold territories of their own, and who are no match for an adult of their species, call out in order to alert other juveniles of the potential food source. The juvenile ravens then swarm the adult male's territory, leaving him to either join them in the shared feast or to futilely attempt to ward off a host of invaders. Thus the raven's call, while benefiting others, can be explained in terms of purely selfish motives.

This might do for ravens, but what of the more culturally complex human being? Reciprocal altruism occurs in human society as well, although we do not always identify it in such clinical terms. (How many little favors have you done for people today, with or without thought of reward?) It is the grease that keeps society's gears running smoothly, and scientists have written many articles on the subject. Yet, ironically enough, even this act of authoring scientific articles has come under scrutiny by skeptics of the idea that animals will at times act in purely altruistic ways. Warren Hagstrom makes the case that writing articles (and perhaps presenting papers at conferences?) can be equated to prehistoric gifting activities, in which the benefactor presents his or her offering fully expecting some sort of return gesture from others (12). In this case, ethos builds upon itself in the form of greater prestige.

If it is true that some complex human social behaviors can be related back to our prehistoric (or even prehuman) ancestors, that our motivations and responses are so similar to the animals we watch, then observing the less complex behaviors of other animals could inform our studies of human social interaction. Recognizing that the communicative structures of our counterparts in nature are less complex, and more closely related to emotional response, we can treat the responses and reactions of other animals as possibly analogous to the building blocks of our own modes of communication and behavior (Pinker 332–34).

Conspicuous Displays

Ethos, in *De Oratore,* is built through displaying tokens of good character, kindness, loyalty, and avoiding a mercenary image while listing one's good deeds in public. Rhetoric needs particular people, or it becomes an argument about principles, not ethos (Fott 1). These particular people must demonstrate *philanthropia* in order to sway a jury (Konstan 5). Through the use of conspicuous displays of altruism, the orator could build an ethos unassailable by the *mere facts* of the case. Evidence alone does not sway. Quoting James May:

> Because of the effectiveness of character as a source of proof, Roman orators, from early on, tended to list the facts of the case as reflections of the litigants' characters rather than as a basis for logical argument.

> Thus biographical description, an "ethical narrative" of sorts, often functioned as the speech's proof. (*Trials* 9)

This holds true in Batstone's discussion of Cicero's First Catilinarian. Cicero's strategy was to "construct an image of his passion and his concern, of his selflessness and his providence" (218). What he was not doing was providing evidence in order to build a reasoned argument; better to shape the situation so that Rome requires a man with the character traits Cicero emphasized. The goal of this dramatization

> was to win recognition for the speaker's own handling of the crisis, and in doing that to empower his voice as the voice of Rome, of her traditions and values, an empowerment that would effectively substitute the consul himself for the deliberative procedures of the republic. (219)

By portraying his own feats as having displayed the proper action at the proper time, Cicero was building ethos through displays of kairos. But were these acts on behalf of the state, no matter if they were exaggerated or not, altruistic? It must depend in part on whether *De Oratore* can represent the hybrid conceptualization of the expedient actions of the practical orator and the benevolent actions of the ideal orator. Michelle Zerba doubts Cicero's sincerity. Despite Cicero's claim that only a good man of wide learning can be an effective orator, Zerba suspects that "*De Oratore* extensively performs the varieties of duplicity it theoretically censures" (302). If this is the case, perhaps Cicero is pulling the wool over the reader's eyes with his own conspicuous displays.

Whether the conspicuous displays of the orator are truly altruistic or not, the immediate purpose is clear: ethos, as May writes, "is concerned with (painting an image of) all the orator's (positive) character traits," in order to secure "the goodwill of the audience on that basis" (*Brill's Companion* 386). The image of painting a picture is particularly apt, in that the artist who is best able to match his art to his audience will secure the highest praise for his product.

While displays of character are unavoidable in Roman rhetorical theory and practice, it remains to be seen just how important conspicuous displays of altruism are in building ethos among many of the social animals. The most obvious and recognizable case of ethos-building in the animal world comes from male displays of fitness to their prospective mates. One easily accessible example is what I call the "seductive rhetoric" of one of researcher Damian Elias's jumping spiders. The male spider constructs a positive image through a ritualized mating dance. One video of a male spider performing his dance, which any layperson can access via websites like YouTube, shows a suitor making "thump," "scrape," and "buzz" signals, which sound to the observer much like a small Harley Davidson running circles around the living room, while simultaneously "saluting" the female with violent motions of his front legs. The devotion it takes to perfect and then execute an extended performance like this, rather than using this time hunting for food or another mate, shows that the suitor not only has the means to support such activities, but also has the physical and intellectual prowess to make his mating dance the best show in town.

Beyond mating practices, ethical displays are also used in the complex web of associations social animals make when sorting the honest individuals in their tribe from the cheats lurking among them. George Kennedy reports that "an inveterate liar, or even a well-intentioned individual whose judgment has proved wrong, soon loses authority in the hierarchical world of social animals" (17). Moreover, reciprocal altruism will only work if enough animals are providing benefits in return for those they receive. Kulakowski was able to demonstrate a justifiable cooperation model based not on reward alone (as most models attempt), but on the reputation of the other player involved. This indicates that selfish desire may have less to do with outcomes than the evolved psychological mechanism that rewards positive traits in others; and it is this reward system that ethos builders rely on, according to Boyd:

> Primates such as baboons and chimpanzees discriminate among individuals on the basis of character and adjust their behavior accordingly—even to the point of female baboons' accepting males as partners according to their demonstrated social sensitivity. (*On the Origin* 139)

Knowledge of this preference might even lead to the cultivation of a "nice guy" persona, since the female primates seem to prefer a baboon that is "in touch with his emotions."

X. T. Wang's study of rational and emotional decision making in humans contributes to this conversation as well. His research shows that emotional decision making tends toward risk taking more often than rational decision making (1146). If securing good will translates logos into ethos or pathos, then this conversion rate is in the favor of the speaker, for the audience can be manipulated into making risky decisions. Likewise, Steven Katz notes that while logos considers the means to reach one's deliberative goal, "it is *pathos* and *ethos* that provide the impetus to act" (259). As the old salesman's maxim goes, "Facts tell; stories sell." Convincing a female that he will stick around and care for her children requires the seductive rhetor to create an emotional narrative by constructing the proper series of logical pillars to support that species' romantic ethos.

The most notorious example of such a construction project (literally and metaphorically) is the bowerbird male's assembly of a complex bower made of sticks and weeds, decorated with as many shiny or brightly colored objects as he can collect. He does this in order to attract females. If he can build such a fine structure, the reasoning goes, he has high-quality genes that help provide him with the excess resources and leisure time this display requires. The bower is a representation of the male bowerbird's ethos, which convinces the female to accept the male's sexual advances.[3]

Conclusions

Cicero, a *novus homo* who worked his way through the *cursus honorum* to an eventual consulship, made his career through rhetoric. It was only by means of his conspicuous displays of altruistic behavior—such as saving Rome from the villainous Cataline (whose villainy Cicero might have exaggerated)—that he could construct an ethos that assured the *optimates* of Rome that he was not a threat to the existing order (Taylor 124). *De Oratore* itself is a "dramatized social performance" indicating the ways in which Roman aristocrats in the late republic maintained their ethical standings (Zerba 302).

We are not so different from any of the other social animals who engage in conspicuous displays of altruism in order to secure their goals. We have the advantage of collective memory and culture to enhance our understanding of what is and is not effective in these endeavors. We have become cleverer than the other primates, but we still play the same games. As Brian Boyd tells us, "naturalistic criticism assumes continuity between human action and that of other animals" ("Art and Evolution" 53). Being able to examine our motivations from an evolutionary standpoint allows us to cut through the haze of anthropocentrism, putting us on a plane with the other animals whose behaviors are explicable from an adaptationist viewpoint. It is important for us to recognize the similarities in our behavioral tendencies to those of other animals because of the insight it can lend us into our subject of study. Rhetoric is the natural act of a natural species. If we attempt to dissociate ourselves from nature and the behaviors our evolutionary environment prompts, we will neglect some of the most important motivations for our actions.

Consilient studies of rhetoric open the doors to collaborations with ethologists, primatologists, and sociobiologists who are already working on projects that could benefit from rhetorical theory, and whose own methods could enhance our traditions. Treating communication as something shared among all intelligent animals, rather than something specifically human, allows for archaeologies of rhetoric that will inform the histories we want to reconstruct. Stronger inferences about the bases of rhetorical acts will come from close analysis of the simpler forms of communication that underlie humanity's complex symbolic languages. In the end, consilience will expand the scope of rhetoric considerably, and could strengthen its place as a vibrant and necessary discipline in the modern university.

Notes

[1] That is, the turbulent final years of the republic that led to the beginning of Augustus's empire; this began with Ti. Gracchus's tribunate in 133 BCE and lasted until the battle of Actium in 31 BCE.

[2] Inspired by E. O. Wilson's *Consilience*, recent works exploring the utility of this approach to literature are Gottschall's *Literature, Science, and a New Humanities* and Carroll's *Literary Darwinism: Evolution, Human Nature, and Literature*.

[3] Yet, male bowerbirds devote no additional time to their offspring. Rather than demonstrating parental investment potential, they are demonstrating the quality of their genes.

Works Cited

Batstone, William W. "Cicero's Construction of Consular Ethos in the First Catilinarian." *Transactions of the American Philological Association* 124 (1994): 211–66.

Boyd, Brian. "Art and Evolution: Spiegelman's *The Narrative Corpse*." *Philosophy and Literature* 32.1 (2008): 31–57.

———. *On the Origin of Stories: Evolution, Cognition, and Fiction*. Cambridge, MA: Belknap, 2009.

Campbell, John Angus. "Scientific Revolution and the Grammar of Culture: The Case of Darwin's Origin." *Quarterly Journal of Speech* 72.4 (1986): 351–76.

Carroll, Joseph. *Literary Darwinism: Evolution, Human Nature, and Literature*. London: Routledge, 2004.

Cicero, Marcus Tullius. *De Officiis*. Trans. Walter Miller. London: Heinemann, 1913. xvi, 423.

———. *De Inventione*. Trans. Harry Mortimer Hubbell. Cambridge: Harvard UP, 1949.

———. *De Oratore*. Rev. ed. London: Heinemann, 1948.

Deacon, Terrence William. *The Symbolic Species: The Co-Evolution of Language and the Brain*. New York: W.W. Norton, 1997.

Fott, David. "Cicero on the Relation between Philosophy and Rhetoric." *Proceedings of the 104th Annual Meeting of the American Political Science Association, August 28–31, 2008: Categories and the Politics of Global Inequalities*.

Gorrell, Robert. "Not by Nature: Approaches to Rhetoric." *The English Journal* 55.4 (1966): 409–49.

Gottschall, Jonathan. *Literature, Science, and a New Humanities*. Basingstoke: Palgrave Macmillan, 2008.

Hagstrom, Warren O. *The Scientific Community*. New York: Basic Books, 1965.

Katz, Steven B. "The Ethic of Expediency: Classical Rhetoric, Technology, and the Holocaust." *College English* 54.3 (1992): 255–75.

Kennedy, George Alexander. *Comparative Rhetoric: An Historical and Cross-Cultural Introduction*. New York: Oxford UP, 1998.

Konstan, David. "Altruism." *Transactions of the American Philological Association* 130 (2000): 1–17.

Kulakowski, Krzysztof. "To Cooperate or to Deflect? Altruism and Reputation." *Physica A* 388.17 (2009): 3581–84.

May, James M. *Brill's Companion to Cicero: Oratory and Rhetoric*. Leiden: Brill, 2002.

———. *Trials of Character: The Eloquence of Ciceronian Ethos*. Chapel Hill: U of North Carolina P, 1988.

Pinker, Steven. *The Language Instinct*. New York: W. Morrow, 1994.

Sterelny, Kim. *Dawkins vs. Gould: Survival of the Fittest*. Cambridge, UK: Icon Books, 2001.

Taylor, Lily Ross. *Party Politics in the Age of Caesar*. Berkeley: U of California P, 1961.

Trivers, Robert L. "The Evolution of Reciprocal Altruism." *Quarterly Review of Biology* 46.1 (1971): 35–57.

Vickers, Brian. *In Defense of Rhetoric*. Oxford: Clarendon P, 2002.

Wang, X. T. "Emotions within Reason: Resolving Conflicts in Risk Preference." *Cognition & Emotion* 20.8 (2006): 1132–52.

Westermarck, Edvard. *The History of Human Marriage*. London: Macmillan, 1891.

Wilson, Edward O. *Consilience: The Unity of Knowledge*. New York: Knopf, 1998.

Zerba, Michelle. "Love, Envy, and Pantomimic Morality in Cicero's *De Oratore*." *Classical Philology* 97.4 (2002): 299–321.

12

"In the Bonds of Woman and the Slave"

Analogy and Collective Identity in Woman's Rights Discourse, 1860–1869

Jennifer Keohane

The organized movement for woman's rights was closely linked with the abolition movement from its birth (Hersh 7). Accordingly, as nineteenth-century women reformers argued for suffrage and the woman's rights cause, the rhetoric of antislavery was prominent in their discourse. After the Civil War, national attention focused on black male suffrage instead of woman suffrage, and women activists began to question the "junior status and dependent position" that they held in the reform coalition (55). This led to tension between the two movements because members disagreed about the appropriate sequence of pursuing their reform goals. Nonetheless, leaders tried to keep their movements together by creating the American Equal Rights Association (AERA) in 1866. They struggled to remain unified until 1869, when the AERA dissolved, to be replaced by two rival feminist organizations (DuBois 163–64). The changing relationship between woman's rights and African American civil rights in the post-Civil War period could be seen as leaders debated timing for both woman and freedman suffrage at national conventions.

Frequently, women reformers argued that the plight of all women was similar to the plight of slaves because wives often felt bonded to their husbands in marriage. In fact, because women lost legal status upon marriage, they often were effectively tied to husbands just as slaves were to masters. Thus, women reformers repeatedly articulated analogies comparing all women to slaves.[1] Close rhetorical attention to the ways reformers used the woman/slave analogy highlights problems with creating a reform coalition based on exclusive subjectivities. This study offers rhetorical insight into how women reformers used analogies to consolidate a collective identity for their reform coalition and how their understandings of the coalition's priorities and their own claims to citizenship were colored by this analogy. Ultimately, this article concludes, the woman/slave analogy promoted exclusionary visions of who could be considered both a US citizen and a member of the AERA.

This case study also provides a unique opportunity to consider the themes of concord and controversy, specifically in light of rhetoric's constitutive powers. The usage of the woman/slave analogy in convention discourse calls attention to the coincidence of similarity and difference in constitutive rhetoric. As white women claimed to share the experiences of male and female slaves, they simultaneously perpetuated hierarchies that saw educated, white women as better citizens than freedmen and women. Because they claimed to speak on behalf of the freed slave, such arguments furthered common perceptions of the moral superiority of white women, demonstrating they were acting in a benevolent manner suitable to their gender and class. Moreover, as Susan Zaeske notes in her exploration of women's antebellum antislavery petitions, such rhetoric created identities for abolitionist women and slave women that intersected along the lines of gender, but diverged along the line of race, which tended toward exploitation because white women used these differences to elevate themselves from dependents to representatives of those who lacked autonomy. White women reappropriated the political power arrangements that subordinated all women to white men and perpetuated this rationale in their imagined relationship with black women, endowing those with wealth and education the power to represent dependents (Zaeske 65). Female reformers rejected the identity of enslavement for themselves by re-placing it on the black women for whom they claimed to speak. Such claims also solidified the exclusion of black women from the AERA by not allowing them to speak for themselves and denying their capacity for action. This essay demonstrates how rhetoric's constitutive power works alongside its exclusionary potential. Concord, i.e., the drawing together of two reformist coalitions, sowed controversy when reformers silenced the voices of former slaves and ultimately disbanded their organization. The possibility to divide and the power to bridge difference exist together in tension as rhetoric constitutes collective identities.

Women reformers were certainly not unique in making claims that they were like slaves. This comparison has been a common theme throughout eighteenth-, nineteenth-, and twentieth-century discourse.[2] Nonetheless, how analogy and claims of identity served to bridge the antislavery and woman's rights movements remains relatively unstudied.[3] As this essay will show, in 1860, white women argued that they were bonded to their husbands like slaves to their masters. However, by 1869, as the African American civil rights movement and woman's rights movement experienced growing tension over the priorities of the reform coalition, women began to argue in conventions that ignorant men acted as slavemasters. This essay argues that the woman/slave analogy first brought the two movements together by attempting to create a collective identity for the women in the coalition, and then it divided them along male-female and black-white lines. I examine the usage of the analogy in national convention rhetoric including the 1860 Tenth National Woman's Rights Convention, the 1866 Eleventh National Woman's Rights Convention, the 1867 First Anniversary of the American Equal Right Association, and the 1869 Anniversary Convention of the American Equal Rights Association.[4]

Analogy, Evidence, and Identity

Reasoning by analogy functions as more than a rhetorical device; it is a form of evidence (Campbell and Huxman 78). Analogy was appropriate for women reformers because the strength of analogy lies in pointing out resemblances of relationship (Perelman and Olbrechts-Tyteca 372). Moreover, analogy is influential because it allows rhetors to go from what is known and familiar to their audiences to what is unfamiliar (Campbell and Huxman 79; Zarefsky 406). In this way, analogy facilitates the development and extension of argument. The analogies utilized by the rhetors in the national convention debates most frequently took the form of literal analogies, or simple comparisons.[5] And women could make a strong case that they were like slaves (Nadelhaft 407).

In addition to serving as a type of evidence for claims that white, educated women deserved the right to vote, I suggest that this analogy provided the "seeds of collectivization" for women reformers to coalesce around a shared identity (McGee 242). James R. Wilcox and H. L. Ewbank note that reliance on a single analogy can lead to the identification of the analogy with its subject (17). The analogy's frequent use in postbellum conventions suggests that for these female reformers, the characteristics it highlighted were real, powerful, and important to their collective sense of identity and mission.[6] The analogy served to, in Louis Althusser's terms, "hail" or "interpellate" reformers (44–48) (Enstad 748). As the woman/slave analogy underwent a fundamental shift in 1867–1868, so too did the understanding of the work of the AERA and who its members should be.

"A Gold Band Is More Efficacious Than an Iron Law"

During the 1860 National Woman's Rights Convention held at the Cooper Institute in New York City, the woman/slave analogy often took the form of an explicit comparison between all women and slaves or an implicit reference to being bonded. The use of the analogy at the 1860 convention suggests that tensions between the movements had yet to intensify as women saw themselves as like slaves and with the same goals as abolitionists. Nonetheless, the analogy as a claim of identity asserted the powerlessness of women and had exclusionary potential for the reform coalition, as all political subjectivities do.

The analogy functioned as a claim of identity that women reformers adopted and used to bind themselves to the African American civil rights coalition in an attempt to overcome their powerlessness. For example,

Elizabeth Cady Stanton explicitly used the analogy as evidence for her argument. She stated:

> Allow me just here to call the attention of that party now so much interested in the slave of the Carolinas, to the similarity in his condition and that of the mothers, wives and daughters of the Empire State. The negro has no name. He is Cuffy Douglas or Cuffy Brooks, just whose Cuffy he may chance to be. The woman has no name. She is Mrs. Richard Roe or Mrs. John Doe, just whose Mrs. she may chance to be. ("Proceedings of the Tenth" 37)

By pointing to evidence like the similarities between their lack of individual names, Stanton strengthened her analogy. Moreover, binding her analogy to the fundamental attribute of a name, Stanton invited women reformers to identify with those enslaved.

However, it is important to note that despite the fact that women reformers took up the collective identity of slaves to justify their reform actions, they most often did not invite slaves to share in their struggle for rights. That is, while white women were hailed as slaves, slaves were not hailed to be active in this collective. Instead, reformers spoke on their behalf. Despite their powerlessness, white women still asserted their right to speak on behalf of slaves and describe their conditions.

"We Shall Be Known as the American Equal Rights Association"

Six years passed before woman's rights advocates and their supporters gathered again at a national convention. After the Civil War, the explicit comparison between all women and slaves greatly diminished in frequency and was replaced by new arguments that suggested that women were like former slaves because they too sought the ballot. The common identity constructed was no longer that women were like slaves, but that the disenfranchised were all human, and thus, deserved suffrage.

Legislators proposed the Fourteenth Amendment in December 1865 and the supporters of African American civil rights saw their political goals within reach. The amendment introduced the word "male" into the Constitution for the first time, making many woman's rights activists fear that the amendment would bar women from voting (Hersh 68). Most feminist-abolitionists wanted the word "male" deleted from the amendment, but many male supporters of African American civil rights (along with some women) were unwilling to jeopardize freedman suffrage by tying it permanently to woman's rights (69). Thus, feminists found themselves in a political dilemma: should they support suffrage for African American men in hopes that it would pave the way for woman suffrage later, or should they insist that both reforms happen at the same time? These important divisions were, for the most part, swept under the rug at the Eleventh National Woman's Rights Convention in lieu of hopeful rhetoric about the collective humanity of the disenfranchised.

The 1866 Eleventh National Woman's Rights Convention rhetoric reflects the initial antebellum strategy of the woman's rights movement: to make black suffrage and woman suffrage equal and inseparable demands (DuBois 55). For example, Susan B. Anthony claimed,

> The only tenable ground of representation is Universal Suffrage, as it is only through Universal Suffrage that the principle of "Equal Rights to All" can be realized. All prohibitions based on race, color, sex, property, or education, are violations of the republican idea; and the various qualifications now proposed are but so many plausible pretexts to deter new classes from the ballot box. . . . Neither time nor statutes can make a black white, or woman man! ("Proceedings of the Eleventh" 35)

Anthony's speeches did not use the woman/slave analogy, but instead appealed to a republican ideal of the humanity of all.

Anthony also presented a resolution that enshrined the principles that most speakers had supported during their speeches. She assimilated the freed slave and the woman and argued,

> Whereas, by the set of Emancipation and the Civil Rights bill, the negro and woman now hold the same civil and political status, alike needing only the ballot; and whereas the same arguments apply equally to both classes, proving all partial legislation fatal to republican institutions, therefore Resolved, That the time has come for an organization that shall demand Universal Suffrage, and that hereafter we shall be known as the "American Equal Rights Association." (35)

Thus, Anthony used a new form of the woman/slave analogy to show that all women and former slaves were seen as similar under the law because they were disenfranchised. The actual creation of the American Equal Rights Association is particularly significant because it represented the formation of a concrete link between the African American civil rights and the woman suffrage movements. The convention unanimously adopted Anthony's resolution.

The group then put in place a constitution and a set of officers for the newly formed organization. Stanton, the AERA's new president, called the meeting to order and abolitionist Stephen Foster delivered a brief address to the convention. He expressed his belief that "the human family are so linked together, that no one man can ever enjoy life, liberty or happiness, so long as the humblest being is crippled in a single right" (55). He concluded, "Therefore, our demand for this hour is equal suffrage to all disfranchised classes, for the one and the same reason—they are all human beings" (55). The convention was also filled with a hopeful tone that the new strategy of banding together would succeed in achieving suffrage for both disenfranchised groups.

The question becomes, if the woman/slave analogy united the movement in 1860 because women identified with the plight of slaves, why did the analogy disappear in 1866, at a moment when the abolition and feminist movements should have been closer than ever? Perhaps women felt that the analogy that they were actually enslaved lacked the power it once had since chattel slavery had officially been abolished. Perhaps women no longer felt that they needed to graphically express their displeasure with their situation. However, it seems that because the analogy of white women as slaves was exclusionary, as we saw in our analysis of the 1860 convention, the appeal to republican humanity was more appropriate. Women reformers ultimately abandoned comparing women to slaves and instead used phrases like "universal suffrage" and "equal rights for all" to claim that their movements were similar in goals and objectives.

"If She Remain a Slave, She Will Debase You and Your Sons"

By 1867, rhetoric at the national convention grew tense, and hopeful calls for equal rights greatly diminished in frequency. In March 1867, Kansas proposed two referenda, black suffrage and woman suffrage, for its November election. The campaign to drum up support for these efforts consumed and divided the AERA (DuBois 80). The woman/slave analogy reappeared in the AERA's 1867 convention as reformers argued again that they were victims of enslavement. Women began to argue that their husbands were like slavemasters. The analogy resolidified a claim of identity: women were slaves.

In February 1869, Congress passed the Fifteenth Amendment, which enfranchised former male slaves, but not women. Some factions of the feminist coalition supported the Fifteenth Amendment, but the more radical reformers, including Stanton and Anthony, refused to support the amendment unless it was accompanied by a Sixteenth Amendment that would enfranchise women (DuBois 172). In 1869, Stanton and Anthony fervently hoped to reunite the AERA around advocating a Sixteenth Amendment. The splits in the association and its priorities, however, were far too deep to be remedied by this campaign. Speakers at the 1867 convention used rhetoric that is remarkably similar to those in 1869, so for the purpose of space and clarity, this essay focuses on the 1869 convention.[7]

Some reformers, such as Stephen Foster, continued to advocate universal suffrage, but these calls were rare and drowned out by partisan bickering. Frederick Douglass also addressed the convention and argued that rampant lynching made freedman suffrage much more urgent than white woman suffrage, certainly a controversial claim (Stanton et al. 382).

Lucy Stone spoke next and argued that the equal rights movement was lost if it divided into two separate coalitions. She adopted a critical and forceful tone and deplored educated suffrage. Stone also refused to let Douglass's comments about the urgency of suffrage for freed slaves stand. She replied,

> Woman suffrage is more imperative than [Douglass's] own; and I want to remind the audience that when he says what the Ku-Kluxes did all

> over the South, the Ku-Kluxes here in the North in the shape of men, take away the children from the mother, and separate them as completely as if done on the block of the auctioneer. (Stanton et al. 384)

Not only did Stone utilize the woman/slave analogy by suggesting that divorce regulations were like the splitting of families on the auctioneer's block, she compared men to slavemasters and to racist extremists in the form of KKK members. She even suggested that northern men, not just southern men who had condoned or advocated chattel slavery, gave in to pressures to act as masters over their wives.

The arguments during the 1869 convention increasingly showed women directing their anger toward men in the form of the male/slavemaster analogy. For example, white law student Phoebe Couzins spoke at the evening session and argued that black men learned lessons of tyranny during slavery. Couzins then applied her argument to white men as well:

> And what is said of the ignorant black man can as truthfully be said of the ignorant white man; they all regard woman as an inferior being. She is their helpless, household slave. He is her ruler, her law-giver, her conscience, her judge and jury, and the prisoner at the bar has no appeal. The XVth Amendment thrusts all women still further down in the scale of degradation and I consider it neither praiseworthy nor magnanimous for women to assert that they are willing to hold their claims in abeyance, until all shades and types of men have the franchise. (Stanton et al. 384)

Thus, to Couzins, white women were also enslaved to men who were as ignorant and tyrannical as the freed male slave. This analogy illustrated Couzins's vision of the appropriate priorities of the reform coalition and showed how alliances had shifted. However, given the paucity of black women in the reform coalition, it is difficult to know how they would feel about Couzins's summary of their feelings and being ushered into an alliance with white women. The definite shift from woman as slave to man as slavemaster is reflective of a different collective identity construction. By this analogy women were still implicitly slaves, but this hailing did not focus on helplessness, but instead on the act of being wronged by vicious men. In this way, it seems that although the identity seemed to imply victimage, it also encouraged action on the part of those being hailed because they could no longer rely on men to help them.

French philosopher and feminist Madame Jenny P. De Hericourt delivered a scathing address representative of the threatening and ominous discourse at the 1869 convention. She argued,

> Up to the present day, man has usurped what belongs to woman. That is the reason why we have injustice, corruption, international hatred, cruelty, war, shameful laws—man assuming, in regard to woman, the sinful relation of slaveholder. Such relation must and will change, because we women have decided that it shall not exist. (Stanton et al. 395)

De Hericourt used the man/slavemaster analogy in a biting and critical manner and encouraged action instead of helplessness. Moreover, she turned around the common argument that chattel slavery caused the country's moral vice and argued that instead male domination over women was to blame. De Hericourt continued to condemn men directly:

> You are, indeed, very absurd or very silly. Your judgment is so weak that you reproach woman with the faults of a slave, when it is you who have made and who keep her a slave, and who know, moreover, that no true and virtuous soul can accept slavery. (395)

De Hericourt continued with a threatening message for the future:

> If she remain a slave, she will debase you and your sons; and your country will come under the rule of tyranny. Insane men cannot understand that where there is one slave there are always two—he who wears the chains and he who rivets it. (395)

Thus, she used the analogy of women as slaves and turned around the man/slavemaster analogy to claim men would end up enslaved as well, similarly flipping common arguments about republican citizenship and its relation to independence on their head.

De Hericourt's speech represented a marked departure from the hopeful rhetoric of 1866. Women felt betrayed and angry and were not afraid to let that be known. The 1869 convention put forth a call for action by rejecting an identity that implied victimage and embraced righteous anger. In addition, De Hericourt's speech demonstrated that the analogy of both woman/slave and man/slavemaster could be used to tap into larger circulating discourses about who could and could not be a citizen. Finally, her usage of the analogy denied abolitionist men the chance to join the imagined coalition because they were the perpetrators of wrong.

Ultimately, 1869 was the last time the AERA would meet. The organization disbanded, and the woman's rights advocates split into two rival factions largely based on whether or not they supported the Fifteenth Amendment. *History of Woman Suffrage* says little about this formal split, leaving the convention rhetoric to be one of the most important sources through which to study the existence of deep tensions among reformers. In their history, Stanton, Anthony, and Gage did note:

> Out of these broad differences of opinion on the amendments, as shown in the debates, divisions grew up between Republicans and Abolitionists on the one side, and the leaders of the Woman Suffrage movement on the other. The constant conflict on the Equal Rights platform proved the futility of any attempt to discuss the wrongs of different classes in one association. (400)

The Boston-based American Woman Suffrage Association, whose members supported the Fifteenth Amendment and accepted male leadership, was organized in the same year (Ray and Richards 379–80). Stanton and

Anthony and other more radical suffragists directed their energies toward cutting ties with the male-dominated African American civil rights movement and made this break clear by turning to a rhetoric that assimilated men, particularly black men, with slavemasters.

Conclusion

Delving into how analogic argument worked to both hold together and fragment a diverse reform coalition illuminates the tensions and assumptions underlying who could be a citizen in the postbellum United States. As this case study illustrates, it is useful to contemplate the implications of analogy as a rhetorical tool for collective identity construction. All identity constructions are inherently exclusionary and condition possibilities for those deemed to belong to the group. By claiming the identity of slaves, women were capitulating to feelings of powerlessness and reproducing the argument that they lacked the independence and rationality to be voting citizens. However, when they turned to comparing men to slavemasters, the identity compelled action, not powerlessness. The analogy suggested that women needed to act without the protection of men, who would undoubtedly continue their tyrannical ways.

The analogy was also one-sided. A truly universal reform coalition could not exist while white, female reformers continued to grant themselves the power to define the slave experience and speak on behalf of formerly enslaved men and women. Even as the analogy stood in for the breaking down of the coalition along the lines of sex, and white women claimed to share more of the experiences of black women than freed male slaves or white men, black women only rarely had the opportunity to share their stories with the reform collective. As other rhetorical scholars have noted, the danger with reform rhetoric is that often in speaking for the oppressed, dominant reformers speak instead of the oppressed (Alcoff 6). By silencing freed slaves and black women, feminist reformers and abolitionists could control the meaning and reception of slavery. However, perhaps the most problematic aspect of the feminist reformers' arguments is that they had to insist upon the silence of former slave women in order for their claims to power to be legible in the context of republican citizenship. They *benefited* from the exclusion of African American women.

In this particular instance, then, concord and controversy operated simultaneously. Rhetoric's power to represent and to misrepresent is always bound up in its constitutive possibilities. Analogy provided the means for reformers to imagine, include, and exclude potential members from their group. As feminist reformers imagined freedmen, black women, and voting citizens, they also constituted identities for themselves in their discourse that they sought to fit into their imagining of the ideal citizen. Similarity and difference, concord and controversy, are bound up in rhetoric's constitutive power, often inextricably so.

Despite the instability of the AERA, historian DuBois suggests its importance in the history of the struggle for woman suffrage:

> The Equal Rights Association period . . . was both the fullest and finest expression of the politics that feminists had developed through their alliance with abolitionists, and a revelation of the limitations that being dependent on other reformers' political initiatives placed on them. (77)

After the AERA dissolved, the National Woman Suffrage Association (headed by Stanton and Anthony, who were committed to a Sixteenth Amendment for woman suffrage) and the American Woman Suffrage Association (headed by Stone and Antoinette Brown Blackwell, who were in support of the Fifteenth Amendment) existed as rivals in strategy, priorities, and goals until 1890 (DuBois 200). Even after reunification of the two associations, it would be a long road to the passage of the Nineteenth Amendment, granting suffrage to women. Nonetheless, as this essay has argued, the woman/slave analogy, prominent in discourse produced by the short-lived AERA, was a powerful way for feminist reformers to express frustration and create a collective identity as they argued for change both before and after the Civil War.

Notes

[1] I use the phrase "all women to slaves" despite its somewhat awkward construction because often in their use of the woman/slave analogy, white women reformers were claiming themselves to be similar to black women, who in the antebellum United States predominantly were slaves. I find this phrase to most accurately convey the argument and advocacy of the reformers.

[2] American rhetors have been making analogies that certain conditions were akin to slavery or servitude since the colonial era. For example, the revolutionaries often described their condition in relation to the British crown as one of slavery. John Dickinson, in his well-known 1768 pamphlet "Letters from a Farmer in Pennsylvania to the Inhabitants of the British Colonies," argued that taxation without consent of the governed rendered the governed in a state of slavery (see Reid and Klumpp 92). Comparisons to slavery did not end with the Revolution. The woman's rights movement picked up this strain of argument as well, but its usage also continued in the rhetoric of labor agitation. In 1880, Terence Powderly, leader of the Order of the Knights of Labor (the first successful labor union), argued that laborers were like slaves. In a speech to the Knights, he claimed, "Without organization we cannot hope to accomplish anything; through it we hope to forever banish that curse of modern civilization—wage slavery" (605). Additionally, Eugene V. Debs, founder of the Socialist Party of America, argued in 1910 that workers must unite and organize because leaders' control over them was possible when they were "craft-divided wage-slaves" (617). Many other examples can be found.

[3] Scholars have, however, devoted much attention to nineteenth-century reform rhetoric. This exploration of the woman/slave analogy enters into primary conversation with studies of nineteenth-century women's reform rhetoric, a well-analyzed tradition that includes, for example, Zaeske, *Signatures of Citizenship;* Browne, *Angelina Grimké;* Mattingly, *Appropriate[ing] Dress*; Ray, "What Hath She Wrought?"; and Campbell and Ray, "No Longer by Your Leave." Others could be included, but I have selected scholarship that focuses on how women negotiated claims of identity in their activism. Many of these scholars have explored how advocacy for woman's rights intersected other areas of reform rhetoric, such

as antislavery or temperance. I also aim to add to a historiography of women's activism and the organized woman's rights movement around the time of the Civil War. Contributors to this dialogue include, for example, Hersh, *The Slavery of Sex*; DuBois, *Feminism and Suffrage*; Riegel, "The Split of the Feminist Movement in 1869"; Clark, "Matrimonial Bonds: Slavery and Divorce in Nineteenth-Century America"; Conrad, "Transformation of the Old Feminist Movement"; and Kraditor, *The Ideas of the Woman Suffrage Movement.*

[4] The texts for the debates occurring in 1860, 1866, and 1867 are located in the microfilmed set *The Papers of Elizabeth Cady Stanton and Susan B. Anthony.* The complete meeting proceedings for the 1868 American Equal Rights Association convention could not be found, although the meeting is briefly described in Stanton et al., *History of Woman Suffrage, Vol. 2, 1861–1876.* The text of the 1869 debates is found in the same volume.

[5] While this was often the case, I do not wish to oversimplify the way the analogies operated in convention discourse. The work of rhetorical criticism of these debates is complicated by the fact that the analogy appears in different forms throughout the texts and with varying degrees of specificity. Some speakers only make implicit references to bondage, some explicitly argue that all women are like slaves, and some argue that women are slaves. I took into account these varying ways that the analogies appeared by classifying them. The first type of analogy I noticed was an explicit comparison: a woman is/is like a slave in X way. This often took the form of a simple simile. Second, some speakers made more implicit allusions to living in bondage. While not as explicit as the first type of classification, this argument still argued that women and slaves were subject to similar conditions. Third, I noticed arguments that called for equal rights for all people, frequently appearing when speakers asserted that the woman question and the slave question were one and the same. This argument often did not suggest that all women lived in conditions that were similar to the conditions of slavery, but it assimilated the plights of people of concern to the two movements. Fourth, speakers, especially Susan B. Anthony and Elizabeth Cady Stanton, argued that educated white women were superior to former male slaves. This comparison argued that women were in fact not like slaves and ought to be preferred over former slaves as voting members of the polity. Finally, women reformers argued not that women were slaves but that men were like slavemasters. Since the types of these arguments were altered with the passage of time, this classification scheme is important to demonstrate how the analogy developed and changed. Because I aim to understand the rhetorical culture and, as McGee introduces, myths that underlie this social movement, merely counting how many times each type of analogy appeared would not provide a successful rhetorical picture of how the analogy created political subjectivity. Instead, I closely read the debates in an attempt to understand the context, tone, and persona of the speaker so I could better analyze how the analogy worked in relation to the speaker's understanding of self and the mission of the AERA.

[6] Most rhetorical scholars who study collective identity formation have tended to focus on national identity and narrative as a tool for facilitating such ends. See, for example, McGee, "In Search of 'The People'"; and Charland, "Constitutive Rhetoric." Nonetheless, I find their insights valuable for understanding how rhetorical appeals might constitute a collective group of reformers.

[7] The AERA held a convention in 1868, but I could only find a very abridged version of the proceedings in my archival research. As a result, I focus my analysis here on the 1869 convention.

Works Cited

Alcoff, Linda. "The Problem of Speaking for Others." *Cultural Critique* 20 (1991–92): 5–32.

Althusser, Louis. "Ideology and Ideological State Apparatuses (Notes toward an Investigation)." *Essays on Ideology.* London: Verso, 1976.

Browne, Stephen H. *Angelina Grimké: Rhetoric, Identity, and the Radical Imagination.* East Lansing: Michigan State UP, 1999.

Campbell, Karlyn Kohrs, and Susan Schultz Huxman. *The Rhetorical Act: Thinking, Speaking, and Writing Critically.* 3rd ed. Belmont, CA: Thomson Wadsworth, 2003.

Campbell, Karlyn Kohrs, and Angela G. Ray. "'No Longer by Your Leave': The Impact of the Civil War and Reconstruction Amendments on Women's Rhetoric." *A Rhetorical History of the United States. Vol. 4: Public Debate in the Civil War Era.* Ed. David Zarefsky and Michael C. Leff. East Lansing: Michigan State UP. N.d. MS, pp. 1–27.

Charland, Maurice. "Constitutive Rhetoric: The Case of the *Peuple Québécois.*" *Quarterly Journal of Speech* 73.2 (1987): 133–50.

Clark, Elizabeth B. "Matrimonial Bonds: Slavery and Divorce in Nineteenth-Century America." *Law and History Review* 8.1 (1990): 25–54.

Conrad, Charles. "Transformation of the Old Feminist Movement." *Quarterly Journal of Speech* 67 (1981): 285–97.

DuBois, Ellen Carol. *Feminism and Suffrage: Emergence of an Independent Women's Movement in America, 1848–1869.* Ithaca, NY: Cornell UP, 1999.

Enstad, Nan. "Fashioning Political Identities: Cultural Studies and the Historical Construction of Political Subjects." *American Quarterly* 50.4 (1998): 745–82.

Hersh, Blanche Glassman. *The Slavery of Sex: Feminist-Abolitionists in America.* Champaign: U of Illinois P, 1978.

Kraditor, Aileen S. *The Ideas of the Woman Suffrage Movement, 1890–1920.* New York: Columbia UP, 1965.

Mattingly, Carol. *Appropriate[ing] Dress: Women's Rhetorical Style in Nineteenth-Century America.* Carbondale: Southern Illinois UP, 2002.

McGee, Michael C. "In Search of 'The People': A Rhetorical Alternative." *Quarterly Journal of Speech* 61.3 (Oct. 1975): 235–49.

Nadelhaft, Jerome. "Review: Subjects and/or Objects: Abolitionist and 'Utopian' Women." *Reviews in American History* 21.3 (Sept. 1993): 407–14.

Perelman, Chaïm, and Lucie Olbrechts-Tyteca. *The New Rhetoric: A Treatise on Argumentation.* 1958. Trans. John Wilkinson and Purcell Weaver. Notre Dame: U of Notre Dame P, 1969.

"Proceedings of the Eleventh National Woman's Rights Convention." *The Papers of Elizabeth Cady Stanton and Susan B. Anthony.* Ed. Patricia G. Holland and Ann D. Gordon. Wilmington, DE: Scholarly Resources, 1991. Microfilm. Reel 11, frames 474–504.

"Proceedings of the First Anniversary of the American Equal Rights Association." *The Papers of Elizabeth Cady Stanton and Susan B. Anthony.* Ed. Patricia G. Holland and Ann D. Gordon. Wilmington, DE: Scholarly Resources, 1991. Microfilm. Reel 12, frames 154–90.

"Proceedings of the Tenth National Woman's Rights Convention." *The Papers of Elizabeth Cady Stanton and Susan B. Anthony.* Ed. Patricia G. Holland and Ann D. Gordon. Wilmington, DE: Scholarly Resources, 1991. Microfilm. Reel 9, frames 612–59.

Ray, Angela G. "What Hath She Wrought? Woman's Rights and the Nineteenth-Century Lyceum." *Rhetoric and Public Affairs* 9 (Summer 2006): 183–214.

Ray, Angela G., and Cindy Koenig Richards. "Inventing Citizens, Imagining Gender Justice: The Suffrage Rhetoric of Virginia and Francis Minor." *Quarterly Journal of Speech* 93.4 (Nov. 2007): 375–402.

Reid, Ronald F., and James F. Klumpp. *American Rhetorical Discourse.* 3rd ed. Long Grove, IL: Waveland P, 2005.

Riegel, Robert E. "The Split of the Feminist Movement in 1869." *Mississippi Valley Historical Review* 49.3 (1962): 485–96.

Stanton, Elizabeth Cady, Susan B. Anthony, and Matilda Joslyn Gage, eds. *History of Woman Suffrage. Vol. 2, 1861–1876.* Rochester, NY: Susan B. Anthony, 1881.

Wilcox, James R., and H. L. Ewbank. "Analogy for Rhetors." *Philosophy and Rhetoric* 12.1 (Winter 1979): 1–21.

Zaeske, Susan. *Signatures of Citizenship: Petitioning, Antislavery, and Women's Political Identity.* Chapel Hill: U of North Carolina P, 2003.

Zarefsky, David. "Strategic Maneuvering through Persuasive Definition: Implications for Dialectic and Rhetoric." *Argumentation* 20 (2006): 399–416.

13

When Are Human Rights?

Democratic Anachronism and Obama's Rhetoric of Reproductive Posterity

Megan Foley

When are human rights? Initially, this may seem like an odd question. In the American democratic vernacular, human rights are considered inalienable—inviolable, untransferrable, and indefeasible. Human rights without permanence seem like no rights at all. It is much more common to spatialize the question of right, to ask *where* human rights are, or more precisely, to ask which bodies are bearers of right. But staking rights on the terrain of the body already begs the question of temporality. Bodies themselves are impermanent, limited by lifetimes, marked by birth and death. Although democratic rhetorics imagine rights in timeless perpetuity, they enshrine those rights in bodies that are themselves temporally bound.

The contemporary democratic tropology of right thus hinges on an anachronism. Generically, anachronism refers to a historical disjuncture—in this case, a disjuncture between the timelessness of human rights and the time-boundedness of human bodies. In a stricter etymological sense, anachronism refers to a time both adjacent to and in opposition to chronological, historical temporality: *ana-*, or against, the linear progression of *chronos*. An anachronism emerges contemporaneous with a situated historical moment to which it does not belong. Because the immortality of right has an anachronic relationship to the mortality of rights-holders, the structure of right is vexed by a temporal aporia that manifests itself most clearly at life's beginnings and ends. Although the American political imagination tends to view rights as everlasting, these liminal thresholds of life expose the historical contingency and bodily precarity on which rights hang.

Bearing on the thresholds of life's emergence, the question "When are human rights?" has become increasingly pressing in the ongoing controversy over American reproductive policies. For example, a widely circulated 2008 interview with presidential hopeful Barack Obama raised the issue of human rights in precisely this temporal register, asking: "At what point does a baby get human rights?" (Boyer 24). Over the course of his campaign and continuing into his presidency, Obama articulated a political rationality that dramatically shifted the temporal frame that figures reproductive rights—and the notion of right in general.

By expanding the temporal horizon of reproduction from individual gestations to future generations, Obama's rhetoric projects immutable rights onto the collective future of the American body politic. By extending citizens' mortally bound bodies into a boundless regenerative future, Obama's rhetoric sutures the long-standing political anachronism between rights and the bodies that bear them. By closing that temporal fissure, Obama aims to resolve the abortion controversy and find common ground between pro-life and pro-choice advocates. In this way, Obama's rhetoric of reproductive posterity offers an exemplary illustration of the temporal disjunctures and conjunctures that undergird controversies over human rights.

Such temporal realignments are the very stuff of controversy. Following Thomas Goodnight's landmark keynote address on the controversial, rhetorical theorists and critics have emphasized how "controversy elicits temporal displacements that tangle up notions of historical events" (2). As Kendall Phillips has compellingly shown, controversies often hinge upon competing historical accounts, which belie grand narratives that tell "a unified linear History" ("Rhetoric" 490). While these critiques of a single, unified history reveal how controversies may emerge from a plurality of rhetorical histories, such critiques contain an even more radical kernel.

By calling the grand narratives of linear history into question, Goodnight and Phillips do more than theorize the temporality of controversy as a clash between rival retellings of the past. They open the way toward considering how history itself may be only one possible rhetorical rendering of time. Controversies not only pivot around opposing histories, but also around oppositions between historical and ahistorical temporalities. As the debate over abortion rights indicates, the temporal displacement that structures controversy may be more than a dispute between divergent historical accounts. Rather, the disjuncture that structures controversies over rights inheres between divergent registers of temporality: between historical contingencies and timeless principles, between chronological and anachronic time.

The Anachronic Structure of Right: From Eternity to Posterity

Today's disjunctive conjuncture between mortal bodies and immortal rights remains a secularized vestige of the premodern, monarchal conception of right as divine sovereignty. The modern, democratic concept of popular sovereignty had its precursor in what Ernst Kantorowicz calls "the king's two bodies" (9). The king's physical body moved in chronological time, a lifespan begun and ended by birth and death. Yet in medieval political thought, the monarch was also invested with an eternal, divine body that lived on when the king died. This duplication of the monarch's natural body in a supernatural authority secured the imperishable seat of sovereign right.

Anachronism structures the temporality of this undying sovereign authority. The divine authority that grounds sovereign right sat outside secular chronology, in a temporal register that J. G. A. Pocock describes as "the *nunc-stans* or eternal now" (39). *Nunc-stans* denotes a static position outside history, simultaneous with but not immanent to the succession of mortal political events. As Pocock explains, this *nunc-stans* was a "standpoint in eternity from which God saw every moment in time as simultaneously created and present" (7). From the vantage of this static time of the infinite present, the unfolding of political contingencies acquired the authority of divine providence, imagined as manifestations of God's sovereign will.

The advent of democracy reconfigured the temporality of sovereign rights with respect to political bodies. In the shift from monarchal to popular sovereignty, the embodied locus of right shifted from the individual corpus of the king to the body politic. Claude Lefort explains that at the end of the eighteenth century, the democratic revolutions in France and the United States produced a "disincorporation" of sovereignty: "Just as the figure of power in its materiality and substantiality disappears, . . . the exercise of power proves to be bound up with the temporality of its reproduction and to be subordinated to the conflict of collective wills" (18). As the place of sovereignty changed, so did its time. No longer vested in the transcendental body of the monarch as the incarnation of divinity, the notion of right was laicized in the collective body of citizens. No longer located in the celestial *nunc-stans*, sovereign right became subject to history.

Yet in this historicization of sovereign right, the notion of immortality was not completely erased. Rather, the immortality of the sovereign body politic became disarticulated from divine eternity. Hannah Arendt introduces this distinction between eternity and immortality: unlike the eternal "standing now" of the *nunc-stans*, "Immortality means endurance in time, deathless life on this earth and in the world as it is given" (*Human* 18). The immortal time of right thus remained despite its secularization, albeit relocated from the celestial body of God to the earthly body of the citizenry.

Like the king's two bodies, citizens came to embody both mortal and immortal forms of life. Arendt explains: "Men are 'the mortals,' the only mortal things in existence, because unlike animals they do not exist only as members of a species whose immortal life is guaranteed through procreation" (*Human* 19). The individual life of the human body is mortal, but the collective, reproductive life of the human species is immortal. The mortal life of the individual has a "recognizable life-story from birth to death" that "move[s] along a rectilinear line" (19). This individual lifespan "rises out of" and "cuts through the circular movement of biological life," the immortal life that Arendt describes as the "species' ever-recurring life cycle" (7).

Normatively, Arendt criticizes this modern conception of immortality for reducing political singularities to "endlessly reproducible repetitions" (*Human* 8). However, she indicates that the worldly permanence of posterity was the hallmark of the secularization of political theology brought about by the modern democratic turn:

> Nothing perhaps indicates more clearly that the revolutions brought to light the new, secular, and worldly yearnings of the modern age than this all-pervasive preoccupation with permanence, with a "perpetual state" which, as the colonists never tired of repeating, should be secure for their "posterity." (*On Revolution* 232)

Building on Arendt's distinction between eternity and mortality, Lefort explains that the theologico-political concept of sovereignty's immortality has survived democratic secularization by being refigured as posterity. The notion of posterity historicizes immortality, enabling democratic subjects of right "to hand on to future generations the torch borne by the living" (Arendt, *On Revolution* 273). Generational posterity enables sovereign right to withstand the transient time of mortal individuals' births and deaths. Rather than being split into the two bodies of the monarch, the doubled time of sovereignty lives on in one democratic body. Mortal and immortal time crystallize in the rights-bearing body politic, imagined as an enduring generational relay of perishable lives that keeps the torch of sovereignty burning.

Through this rhetorical condensation, the temporal structure of sovereign right is reposed from a logic of transcendence to a logic of immanence. Rather than locating immortality outside the historical time of the body, immortality becomes internalized within the body politic. Yet this containment of immortality within historical time does not resolve sovereignty's anachronic disjuncture between immortality and mortality. Instead, it restages that split within the life of the body politic. No longer divided into two bodies, the modern notion of right is incarnated in a single body still riven by two temporalities: the infinitely recursive regeneration of the population and the finite lifespan of each individual member.

The democratization of sovereign right thus corresponds with the rise of biopower as a mode of governance that targets the lives of populations. As Michel Foucault has chronicled, in the eighteenth century the state's control over the life of its subjects shifted from the divine fiat of a sovereign decision—"to take life or let live"—toward strategies of biopolitical faciliation—"to make live or let die" (241). When the immortality of right became contingent upon the fragility of mortal bodies, the preservation and perpetuation of the body politic's life became a duty for the state. As immutable sovereign right was vested in the bodies of citizens rather than the head of state, the normative role of the state turned toward securing the enduring future of those rights for and through posterity.

Suturing the Anachronism of Right: Rescaling Posterity

In a temporal political logic that wagers the permanence of popular sovereignty on posterity, it should come as no surprise that one of the most persistent controversies in which American democratic rights are negotiated surrounds the moment of birth, when the rights of one generation of citizens are passed on to the next. Today, the question "When are human rights?" continues to be framed by the trope of posterity, pinpointing the moment in time when a body acquires rights, the moment where sovereignty's torch is passed. In his interview of Obama, Pastor Rick Warren put the question in exactly this way: "*At what point* does a baby get human rights?" Initially, the subtlety of Obama's answer was overshadowed by the notorious "above my pay grade" sound byte extracted from it (Boyer 24). However, Obama's answer that day—and throughout his candidacy and early presidency—markedly refigured the temporal logic underwriting that question. Rather than imagining the temporality of rights as the miraculating instant of a body's inclusion in the rights-bearing body politic, Obama's rhetoric figured the time of rights as the collective American body's recursive and perfectible endurance.

From stump speeches to policy statements, Obama has emphasized the political stasis between right-to-life and right-to-choose advocates. In his first week in office, Obama released a public statement calling the abortion question: "a political wedge issue, the subject of a back-and-forth debate that has served only to divide us. I have no desire to continue this stale and fruitless debate" (Baker 13). Against the image of this unproductive back-and-forth stalemate, Obama then called for a more united future. He continued: "It is time that we end the politicization of this issue. In the coming weeks, my administration will initiate a fresh conversation on family planning, working to find areas of common ground." Linking the division of the American political body with the past and its unity with the future, Obama calls for a new start. But rather than ending the politicization of abortion rights, his administration reconfigures the political logic that frames the public controversy over reproductive policy.

While the metaphor that Obama marshals—"common ground"—is decidedly spatialized, his speeches link the common ground of a united political body to the collective future of America. Envisioning a more productive future for reproductive policy, the call for "common ground" between pro-life and pro-choice advocates is an exhortation to move ahead, past old arguments. In an early campaign speech, Obama said: "We're at a crossroads right now in America, and we have to move this country forward. . . . It's not just about defending what is, it's about creating what might be in this country. And that's what we've got to work together on" (Planned). Obama identifies two paths at this national crossroads: a conservative present—"defending what is"—and a creative future—"creating what might be." For Obama, this road toward our national future is the road toward common ground: "We have an opportunity to move forward and agree" (Planned). In his repeated calls for common ground, Obama has painted America's future as a unified political body.

To craft common ground between pro-life and pro-choice positions, Obama expands the temporal scale of posterity to restage the abortion question as a matter of future collective welfare that surpasses present individual rights. In his controversial commencement speech at the University of Notre Dame, Obama acknowledged, "at some level, the views of the two camps are irreconcilable." Certainly, the pro-life protests outside the auditorium attested to that incommensurability. But while pro-life and pro-choice views are irreconcilable *at some level,* Obama pointed to another level at which pro-life and pro-choice advocates can work toward common goals: "Let's work together to reduce the number of women seeking abortions by reducing unintended pregnancies, and making adoption more available, and providing care and support for women who do carry their child to term" (University). Taking up Bill Clinton's call to make abortion "safe, legal, and rare," Obama places the reduction of unintended pregnancies at the center of his reproductive policy initiative.

And indeed, this "common ground" objective of reducing the abortion rate does mark a change in level. Traditionally, the American controversy over abortion has been framed by liberal rhetorics that stage the debate at the level of immediate individual rights (Condit 59–78); instead, Obama's rhetoric relocates his administration's abortion policy at the level of long-term public health. Obama highlights this change in scale as the key to finding common ground in the abortion debate. During his presidential run, he explained that reframing the scale of the abortion debate could operate as a rhetorical strategy of division or unity:

> There are those who want us to believe . . . that there's nothing that unites us as Americans, there's only what divides us. They'll seek out the narrowest and most divisive ground. That is the strategy: to always argue small instead of looking at the big picture. (Planned)

Linking the narrow view with division, and the "big picture" with national unity, Obama declared: "When we argue big, we win" (Planned). Rather than focusing narrowly on individual bodies, Obama appeals to the reproducing population of the body politic. Acknowledging disagreement on the abortion question, Obama urges both pro-life and pro-choice advocates to target the social circumstances that raise that question in the first place: "Nobody wishes to be placed in a circumstance where they are even confronted with the choice of abortion. How we determine what's right at that moment, I think, people of good will can differ" (Democratic). These words bracket this divisive moment of individual right, the hotly debated question of when the torch of rights is passed to posterity, the moment when the rights of maternal and prenatal bodies split and confront one another. Obama went on: "And if we can acknowledge that much, then we can certainly agree on the fact that we should be doing everything we can to avoid unwanted pregnancies that might even lead somebody to consider having an abortion." Obama presents abortion as a problem at the level of the population's collective circumstances rather than at the level of a person's individual choice. In Burkean terms, Obama reconceives abortion at the level of the scene rather than the level of the agent (*Grammar* 7). Reframing abortion as an outcome of tragic circumstances, Obama offers a solution that preempts the politically and ethically controversial moment in which individuals may choose to abort.

Reducing the abortion rate has become the policy mantra in Obama's "common ground" rhetoric. This policy agenda was set in the 2008 Democratic National Committee Platform, which Obama helped to craft during his presidential campaign. The platform endorses policies that "help reduce the number of unintended pregnancies and thereby also reduce the need for abortions" (50). Based on this platform, pro-life Democrat Tim Ryan and pro-choice Democrat Rosa DeLauro have cosponsored the Preventing Unintended Pregnancies, Reducing the Need for Abortion and Supporting Parents Act. The bill includes Medicaid coverage of contraception and maternity care for low-income women, tax credits and information campaigns to promote adoption, grants to prevent unplanned pregnancies and provide child care for teen and college-aged women, and grants to establish programs to prevent domestic violence and sexual assault (Eggen and Stein). Rather than legislation that directly addresses a woman's individual, legal right to choose an abortion, these initiatives all aim to cultivate the social and institutional conditions under which fewer women overall would face that choice. This shift in focus from individual rights to the population's abortion rate is the political cornerstone of Obama's rhetorical attempts to build common ground.

As the Obama administration has increasingly embraced population-centered legislation on abortion, they have suspended their earlier initiative to shore up the reproductive rights of individual women. During his presidential campaign, Obama promised to support the Freedom of Choice Act, which aimed to make the freedom to choose an abortion a fundamental right. However, the Obama administration has put this legislation on hold. At a press conference on the 100th day of his presidency, Obama explained his administration's shift in focus:

> Now, the Freedom of Choice Act is not my highest legislative priority. I believe that women should have the right to choose, but I think that the most important thing we can do to tamp down some of the anger surrounding this issue is to focus on those areas that we can agree on.

Obama then reiterated that the reduction of unwanted pregnancies was a shared goal that could allow pro-life and pro-choice advocates to "arrive at some consensus." To some extent, then, population-focused policies have displaced individually focused rights legislation in the Democratic agenda. However, the individual right to choose still plays a role in this reconfigured political logic.

Securing the individual right to choose is no longer deemed a political objective in itself; instead, it becomes a way of achieving an expanded political end-goal. In 2008 the Democratic National Convention Committee's national platform provides the key to this new rhetoric of choice. Under the heading "Renewing the American Community" and the subheading "Choice," the abortion policy statement begins with an affirmation of a woman's right to choose an abortion. It declares: "The Democratic Party strongly and unequivocally supports *Roe v. Wade* and a woman's right to choose a safe and legal abortion" (50). In the next paragraph, the platform begins to recommend policies that use choice to promote life: "The Democratic Party also strongly supports access to comprehensive affordable family planning services and age-appropriate sex education which empower people to make informed choices and live healthy lives." According to this policy statement, "healthy lives" are a result of "informed choices." That is, the statement positions informed choices as an instrument for living healthy lives. Here, the right to choose becomes a biopolitical technology; its political objective is to improve public health. It is through this biopolitical logic that "Choice" becomes a part of—even a tool for—"Renewing the American Community."

In his early campaign speech to Planned Parenthood, Obama developed this articulation of individual choice to collective life: "What's at stake is more than whether or not a woman can choose an abortion. Choice is about how we lead our lives. It's about our families and about our communities." Here, whether or not a woman chooses an abortion is not an end in itself. Rather, it is the means to achieving a broader political goal: building the life of the American community. The speech expands the scale of life in our political imagination, moving from individual life choices, to family life, to community life. In this way, the speech positions individual choice as a device for directing collective life—"*how we lead* our lives." In Obama's formulation, individual choice promotes healthy family life, which in turn promotes the healthy life of our political community.

In the search for common ground between pro-life and pro-choice advocates, "arguing big" entails rhetorically expanding the scale of life, recoding it as the ongoing collective life of the American public. Rather than an atomizing view of individual bodies as discrete sites of life, the speech links individual, family, and national bodies by crafting a generational vision of life. In his Planned Parenthood speech, Obama narrates his own life story as a matrilineal arc:

> I'm here as a candidate for the Presidency of the United States of America because I had a grandmother . . . I'm here because of a mother . . . I'm here because of my wife. . . . But most of all I'm here as a candidate because there are these two little girls . . . whose futures depend upon us creating a more equal society. I want my daughters to

grow up in an America where they have the exact same opportunities as America's sons.

Framing individual lives in generations rather than in isolation, this family genealogy settles on young girls—daughters—as the embodiment of America's future. Positioned as the next generation in this matrilineal relay, the figure of the citizen-daughter condenses individual, family, and national life. According to this political rationality, daughters and their individual futures promise the next birth of the American family and the renewal of the American community. The speech imagines "an America that might be, an America of equality and opportunity for our daughters." The citizen-daughter serves as a site of future political possibility.

Furthermore, the daughter serves as a bridge figure, the site of common ground, between life and choice rhetoric. The daughter is *both* the child whose life generates America's future *and* the woman whose right to choose must be protected. Moreover, in this formulation, the daughter's right to choose functions as the primary biopolitical instrument through which our healthiest national future can be secured. This rhetoric of common ground calls Americans to support the equal rights of their daughters in order to (re)produce the healthiest possible political body. By linking individual choice, family life, and the body politic, the citizen-daughter becomes the rhetorical linchpin of Obama's call for common ground in the abortion debate.

The figure of the daughter—and more specifically *our daughters*—reappears again and again in Obama's "common ground" rhetoric on abortion. "Too often," he argues, "our daughters don't have the same opportunities as our sons. But that's not who we are. That's not the America we want for our children" (Planned). Figuring rights-claiming citizens as "our daughters," "our sons," and "our children," Obama addresses and constitutes his audience as parents. "Who we are" is an America where parents pass on equal opportunities to their daughters. "We're the country," Obama declares, "that's fought generation after generation to extend that equality." Individual reproducing bodies become metonymically linked into generations and then synechdochally substituted for the American political body. The American political body becomes coextensive with the reproducing American family, the generative and generational site where parents extend equal rights to and through their daughters.

The Teleological Horizon of Perpetual Posterity

Juxtaposed with this image of the national body as a fecund childbearing and rights-bearing family, the stagnant back-and-forth rights dispute between pro-life and pro-choice advocates becomes "stale and fruitless" by comparison (Baker 13). In Obama's "common ground" rhetoric, the abortion controversy appears as a divisive and infertile threat to the future of our "fruitful" nation. It is in the name of this fertile future that

Obama makes the call for common ground on abortion. His rhetoric of common ground rescales posterity to the level of the population in order to move forward, beyond the stalemate in US reproductive politics. Obama advances this procreative biopolitical agenda to challenge what he calls "a politics of cynicism and fear—fear, above all, of the future" (Planned).

By redirecting American political vision toward an expansive future horizon, Obama resolves the anachronic structure of right by rhetorically extrapolating the regenerating body of the national population to make it temporally coextensive with the immortality of right. Obama's rhetoric scales the mortal body of the American people out to the never-ending time of perpetual posterity. In this new biopolitical rationality, the American population's future extends as long as rights are permanent. This national body, whose life promises to chain out into endless generations, remains healthy and fertile through the citizen-daughter's right to choose the next generation of the national family.

But instead of positioning the American political body as the vehicle through which the immortality of right may be achieved, Obama's rhetoric transforms right into an instrument for achieving an undying political body. In Obama's public statements on abortion, rights are no longer a sacralized end in themselves, but rather a means toward the prospective telos of the biopolitically optimal American population. This rhetorical maneuver resolves the anachronic double structure of rights by reconfiguring its temporal aporia as an entelechy. Rather than an undecidable gap between the mortality of the body politic and the immortality of rights, the persistence of rights becomes the instrument by which the perpetuity of the body politic is secured.

Using this "purposive or teleological metaphor," the rhetoric of reproductive posterity crafts common ground through what Kenneth Burke calls "metabiology" (*Permanence* 261). Obama's rhetoric of reproductive posterity appeals to the perfectible potential of the body politic in order to move beyond the impasse of present controversy. Through this teleological temporality, the rhetoric of reproductive posterity crafts a unified national body around a common good, a common purpose, and a common future. Considered alongside Obama's response to the abortion controversy, Phillips' claim that consensus has long functioned as a telos for the study of rhetoric ("Spaces" 232) appears particularly prescient. Obama's rhetoric indicates that this insight can be heuristically extended beyond an internal critique of the discipline: perhaps entelechy is the characteristic time signature of rhetorical consensus itself.

Still, Phillips is right to caution rhetorical critics against the telos of consensus, especially when it comes to the question of human rights. Resolving the question of rights' temporality, the rhetoric of reproductive posterity raises the specter of rights' instrumentality. Michael Dillon and Julian Reid argue when "human existence begins to be drawn too tightly around utilitarian and instrumental measures of what it means to be human, more generally also what it means to be a living thing, when species life is taken to be the referent object of politics" (147), the liberal democratic logic of human rights begins to undermine itself. Rather than asserting the singular value of a life that cuts through the ever-recurring cycle of species being—what Arendt calls "natality" (*Human* 9)—this instrumentalization of reproductive rights makes the value of a life depend on its worth to the population.

In this teleological rhetoric of reproductive posterity, it matters not whether this singular life is the life of a pregnant woman or the life of a fetus, for the value of both is determined by their value to the collective regenerative future of the American national body. Trading one quandary for another, this utilitarian instrumentalization of rights poses a problem that may prove even more vexing for the democratic logic of popular sovereignty. Instead of asking, "When are human rights?" this new reproductive rhetoric begins to ask: "What are rights for?"

Works Cited

Arendt, Hannah. *The Human Condition.* Chicago: U of Chicago P, 1958.

———. *On Revolution.* London: Faber & Faber, 1963.

Baker, Peter. "Obama Reverses Rule on U.S. Abortion Aid." *New York Times* 24 Jan. 2009: A13.

Boyer, Peter. "Party Faithful: Can the Democrats Get a Foothold on the Religious Vote?" *New Yorker* 8 Sept. 2008: 24.

Burke, Kenneth. *A Grammar of Motives.* Berkeley: U of California P, 1969.

———. *Permanence and Change: An Anatomy of Purpose.* Berkeley: U of California P, 1954.

Clinton, William. "Nomination Acceptance Speech." Democratic National Convention. Madison Square Garden, New York. 23 July 1992.

Condit, Celeste. *Decoding Abortion Rhetoric: Communicating Social Change.* Champaign: U of Illinois P, 1994.

Democratic National Convention Committee. *2008 Democratic National Platform: Renewing America's Promise.* Denver, CO. 25 Aug. 2008.

Dillon, Michael, and Julian Reid. *The Liberal Way of War: Killing to Make Life Live.* London: Routledge, 2009.

Eggen, Dan, and Rob Stein. "Abortion Opponents Criticize Health Reform Bills." *Washington Post* 23 July 2009: A5.

Foucault, Michel. *"Society Must Be Defended": Lectures at the College de France, 1975–76.* Trans. David Macey. New York: Macmillan, 2003.

Goodnight, G. Thomas. "Controversy." *Proceedings of the Seventh AFA/SCA Conference on Argumentation: Argument in Controversy.* Ed. Donn Parson. Annandale, VA: Speech Communication Association. 1–13.

Kantorowicz, Ernst. *The King's Two Bodies: A Study in Mediaeval Political Theology.* Princeton, NJ: Princeton UP, 1957.

Lefort, Claude. *Democracy and Political Theory.* Trans. David Macey. Oxford: Polity P, 1988.

Obama, Barack. Democratic Compassion Forum. Messiah College, Grantham, PA. 13 Apr. 2008.

———. Planned Parenthood Action Fund. Washington, DC. 17 July 2007.

———. Press Conference. Washington, DC. 29 Apr. 2009.

———. University of Notre Dame 164th Commencement Ceremony. Notre Dame, IN. 17 May 2009.

Phillips, Kendall. "A Rhetoric of Controversy." *Western Journal of Communication* 63 (1999): 488–510.

———. "The Spaces of Public Dissension: Reconsidering the Public Sphere." *Western Journal of Communication* 63 (1999): 488–510.

Pocock, J. G. A. *The Machiavellian Moment: Florentine Political Thought and the Atlantic Republican Tradition.* Princeton, NJ: Princeton UP, 1975.

14

Toward a Feminist Theory of Global Citizenship

(Re)contextualizing Social Rights in the Universal Declaration of Human Rights

Rebecca A. Kuehl

Characterized by genocide, torture, discrimination, and the suppression of basic freedoms, the first half of the twentieth century had been perilous for many people in the world (Korey 1). In response to such atrocities, the Universal Declaration of Human Rights (UDHR) was "unanimously" adopted by the United Nations (UN) on December 10, 1948 (Normand and Zaidi 193).[1] "Never Again!" became the slogan associated with the declaration in an attempt to prevent future human rights abuses (Korey 2). The Commission on Human Rights (CHR) was responsible for drafting the declaration for the General Assembly's vote, and the document largely passed because of the dedication of CHR President Eleanor Roosevelt. Roosevelt faced numerous difficulties in directing the creation of the UDHR, including challenging negotiations with other nations and receiving instructions from US government officials to limit the scope of the document through "focus[ing] only on a declaration of principles of human rights" that could not be enforced by any institution (Gordon Lauren 223). Despite these difficulties, the declaration was drafted and voted on within a span of only two years, from February 1947–December 1948 (Normand and Zaidi 178).

More than 60 years after the international community adopted the UDHR, it remains central to a debate concerning what human rights should be valued, as well as how to enforce such rights (Hauser 446–47, 460; "Universal Declaration"). Amid controversy over what rights should be included and whether such rights would be legally protected, CHR members came together and crafted a human rights document that has become a centerpiece of many NGOs' work—often through mission statements and operating principles—and has served as the standard by which to measure the progress or deterioration of human rights (Korey 1–2). Indeed, "the establishment of the UN and the adoption of the Universal Declaration of Human Rights . . . laid the foundations for contemporary WHR [women's human rights] movements" (Reilly 19). The document has become a foundational text of global citizenship and human rights for activists, scholars, and numerous human rights organizations.

When the UDHR was approved by the General Assembly, some nations that abstained from voting criticized the document for a lack of emphasis on social rights, including rights to education and welfare. Indeed, a common critique of the UDHR continues to be its lack of focus on social rights, as well as economic and cultural rights (Joppke 36; Normand and Zaidi 188–89; Wellman 20–21). These rights were given less space in the UDHR in favor of civil and political rights. Socialist nations, especially the Soviet bloc countries, did not support the declaration, in part because of a failure to emphasize social rights (Normand and Zaidi 193). However, at the time it passed in 1948, people were more concerned with civil and political rights and had not yet realized the potential of social rights, which were just beginning to materialize in citizenship scholarship written at the time, especially in work by the well-known British sociologist and citizenship theorist T. H. Marshall.

This essay (re)contextualizes the UDHR, arguing that social rights have more importance in the text than most global citizenship scholarship has recognized. I suggest that the apparent limitation of the UDHR's lack of attention to social rights makes more sense when analyzing the text in its historical and institutional context. After (re)contextualizing the UDHR, I suggest that it *does* privilege social rights through its language, which relies on procreation metaphors to build global citizens through human relationships that warrant the recognition of human rights, suggesting a move toward a feminist rhetorical theory of global citizenship. Such a move posits that spaces of controversy, including the controversy over whether to adopt the UDHR, involve rhetorical strategies that unite people to find agreement among differing values of human rights. A feminist rhetorical theory of global citizenship sees metaphor as a key rhetorical strategy in building concord around social rights, despite the overall controversy as to whether or not social rights are privileged in the overall structure of the UDHR.

Most theorists of global citizenship see the UDHR as one of the first institutional documents to argue for global human rights (Carter 144; Glendon xvi–xvii; Hayden 55; Schattle 33–34). Ratna Ghosh explains that in addition to the Nuremberg Trials and historical genocide, the UDHR is one of three major precedents in a "change toward recognition of human rights as inalienable rights of any citizen" (82). Norberto Bobbio explains:

> I do not know whether people are aware of just how much the Universal Declaration [of Human Rights] represents an unprecedented historical event, given that for the first time in history, a system of

> fundamental principles for human behaviour has been freely and expressly accepted by the majority of the people living on this planet through their governments. (14)

Although theorists of global citizenship regard the UDHR as a major document, rhetorical scholars have not yet analyzed the text in-depth. How does this founding text of global citizenship and human rights rhetorically construct global citizenship and human rights in the context of 1948, in the present, and in the future?

Rhetorical scholars have studied human rights as a presidential rhetorical strategy to garner support for an administration's policies (Howell 391; Neier 29; Stuckey and Ritter 647), analyzed human rights talk in conversational cases (Englund 527) as well as more general rhetoric of human rights organizations (Hauser 443), and argued for additional human rights such as the right to information (Nilsen 203) and health and identity rights (Shafir and Brysk 280). However, scholars have distanced themselves from an institutional view of the document's importance. Reading the UDHR within its institutional and historical context focuses attention on how the text was structured. An analysis of the metaphors used in the UDHR has implications for how we conceptualize global citizenship and human rights, especially since the text is a critical document for many human rights organizations' visions and principles. A rhetorical analysis of this foundational text helps us understand how global citizenship persuades people that human rights are possible.

(Re)Contextualizing Citizenship Rights in the UDHR

In *Rhetorical Power,* Steven Mailloux argues that a rhetorical hermeneutics relies on contextual arguments to make rhetorical claims about a specific text. Mailloux explains: "Like any other reading, claims about a text's 'undecidability' and 'indeterminacy' are simply interpretations to argue for or against in particular historical (primarily academic) contexts" (149). Just as he argues that the context of "bad boy" literature influenced the reading of Mark Twain's *Huckleberry Finn,* I suggest that the context of T. H. Marshall's influential writing on citizenship and the importance of civil, political, and social rights in the 1940s and 1950s influenced the reading of the UDHR in global citizenship scholarship. Unlike other scholarship on global citizenship, my essay posits that the importance of civil and political rights in the UDHR makes sense in light of Marshall's writings during this historical period.

T. H. Marshall lectured and wrote about citizenship primarily during the late 1940s and early 1950s in Great Britain. He is most well-known for arguing for a hierarchy of citizenship along with an evolution of citizenship rights: civil rights were primarily accepted in the eighteenth century, political rights were entrenched in the nineteenth century, and social rights were accepted in the twentieth century (Stevenson 6). Political theorist April Carter explains: "Marshall had in mind a historical progression from basic civil liberties to a widening franchise and evolving social welfare" (6). Marshall saw social citizenship as the means to reduce social class inequalities: "the preservation of economic inequalities has been made more difficult by the enrichment of the status of citizenship" (77). Marshall is credited as the first theorist of citizenship to argue for social rights; he saw social rights as newly accepted in the twentieth century. Since Marshall was an important citizenship theorist writing during the 1940s, it makes sense that the UDHR would focus mostly on civil and political rights in this context.

Marshall's conceptions of civil, political, and social rights laid important groundwork for global citizenship scholars. Darren J. O'Byrne articulates the importance and meaning of the three sets of rights laid out by Marshall: (1) civil rights as "those rights necessary for individual freedom . . . provided for . . . by the legal system"; (2) political rights as "the right to participate in the exercising of power as a member of a governing body . . . allowed for by the nature of the democratic system"; and (3) social rights as "the rights to welfare, education, security, and well-being . . . allowed for by the Welfare State" (7). Although critics of global citizenship argue that Marshall was theorizing citizenship primarily through the nation-state (and specifically in Great Britain), his analysis is still an important starting point for almost all global citizenship scholarship.

Marshall's theory of citizenship has been critiqued by most theorists of global citizenship, who tend to dismiss his conceptions when analyzing the development of the UDHR. Nick Stevenson's critique of Marshall serves as one example of this trend: "Marshall's analysis—while still influential—fails to locate the state within a complex web of international flows and relations, while assuming that the 'political' works within stable national cultures" (6–7). While Stevenson criticizes Marshall for assuming stable national cultures, it might be pertinent to consider that Marshall published his writings soon after the end of World War II, when the UN was in its infancy. Perhaps for Marshall, theorizing rights in the context of "stable national cultures" was one of the only ways to consider universal citizenship rights during this turbulent historical period, when supranational entities such as the UN, International Monetary Fund, and World Bank had yet to achieve global dominance.

As nation-states were being formed and re-formed after the war, Marshall may have decided to focus on civil and political rights as accepted in the past because these were rights that people were familiar with and could identify with in a changing landscape of national boundaries. Derek Heater offers evidence as to why Marshall might have theorized "stable national cultures" during this time period. Heater explains the historical situation that allowed for the possibility of the UDHR in 1948:

> The scale and intensity of the First World War came as a shock. The Second World War was even more horrifying. . . . Consequently, when

> war ended, the belief that the statesmen of 1919 had failed and that this was a "second chance" to create a peaceful, stable world order was held with conviction by many politicians, intellectuals and the general public in most regions of the world. (139)

T. H. Marshall was one such intellectual who argued that social rights would be the newest rights accepted by all of humanity in the twentieth century, but he argued for the primacy of civil and political rights due to the tumultuous time period in which he was writing. As an institution in 1948, the UN was primarily seen as an *international* entity that maintained the legitimacy of individual nation-states, as opposed to a *global* supranational institution. This institutional context helps explain why Marshall would theorize citizenship rights primarily through civil and political rights and the legitimacy of nation-states, as opposed to social, cultural, and economic rights and the concept of global citizenship.

An additional critique of Marshall's conception of citizenship comes from feminist scholars, who assert that Marshall and others have theorized citizenship in primarily white and male terms (Pateman 14). For instance, Nancy Fraser and Linda Gordon argue that Marshall took for granted distinctions between civil, political, and social rights rather than appropriately theorizing those distinctions to account for gender and racial hierarchies (49–50). Their biggest point of concern is Marshall's "optimism about the ease with which social citizenship could be built upon a foundation laid in terms of civil citizenship" (50). Although I agree that Marshall did not fully account for gender and race, I disagree with the criticism that social citizenship cannot be built upon civil citizenship. The text of the UDHR shows that although its authors might not have articulated social rights in the most explicit way, they did make certain social rights primary in the text through the use of rhetorical metaphors. In this way, the text uses social rights as the primary means for recognizing larger human rights and global citizenship.

Embedded Social Rights through Rhetorical Metaphors

The UDHR is a document that, on its surface, appears to be a straightforward, bureaucratic text that follows the genre of declarations from the eighteenth century. The genre of declaration is important to the formation of the UDHR, as a contributor was the French political official Rene Cassin (James 127). The influence of French writers in the history of declarations is notable; ideas such as fraternity and brotherhood come from this French tradition (Normand and Zaidi 187). Instead of analyzing the UDHR from this genre perspective, however, I analyze how an overarching metaphor of procreation frames the document.

The declaration sought to create a new world of cosmological implication; after the atrocities of World War II, citizens could not go back to thinking of themselves only as citizens of individual nations, but must instead become global citizens who primarily relate to one another through human relationships. The procreation metaphor frames the UDHR through emphasizing the importance of social relationships and social rights, including civic education, security and development of one's personality, and social well-being. The rhetoric of the UDHR orients people who follow the document toward a future yet to happen—a future we can all actively shape in such a way that human rights are promoted in the present. By using metaphors that emphasize procreation through the human family, the UDHR argues for the existence of general human rights *through* the importance of social rights such as well-being and education.

Before I provide evidence for how the metaphor of procreation shapes the UDHR, I first need to explain how Black, as well as Lakoff and Johnson, define metaphor through an interaction view. Black explains that in an interaction view of metaphor, two terms interact to create meaning (286). In this view of metaphor, metaphors act as a filter in that they evoke a "system of related commonplaces" (288). Lakoff and Johnson also see the filtering capacity of metaphors as important. They write that "the metaphor highlights certain features while suppressing others" (141). Metaphors serve as filters. For instance, Black uses the metaphor of "man is a wolf" to explain his system of related commonplaces. In this example, the metaphor of man as wolf organizes our characteristics about men to fit the system of wolf-related commonplaces; we suppress some of our ideas of man that are *not* wolf-like in favor of those qualities that *are* wolf-like, such as aggressive, animalistic, or savage. In this way, metaphors bound a potentially endless set of meanings.

In the UDHR, the metaphor of procreation can be seen through this interaction view of metaphor that filters out some meanings from others. For example, the phrase "the advent of a world" is the most explicit metaphor of procreation in the UDHR and is found in the second stanza of the preamble. Here is the stanza in full to give an idea of the context of its place in the declaration and its poignancy:

> Whereas disregard and contempt for human rights have resulted in barbarous acts which have outraged the conscience of mankind, and the advent of a world in which human beings shall enjoy freedom of speech and belief and freedom from fear and want has been proclaimed as the highest aspiration of the common people.

The system of related commonplaces associated with this metaphor, especially the key term of "advent," could include meanings such as innovation, birth, or rejuvenation. The emphasis on creating a new world, free of "barbarous acts," has primacy because of its early location within the context of the entire declaration. This metaphor also limits our meaning through its comparison to the past atrocities from World War II. Procreation has a specific meaning here in this context of previous world wars.

"The advent of a world" helps us to envision a future that not only promotes but *protects* human rights in light of a past that has, in fact, denigrated or, in some cases, eliminated such rights. The text of the UDHR is not able to enforce the protection of human rights due to the United States and the United Kingdom not wanting to enforce human rights in their own nations; however, the procreation metaphor embraces the possibility of creating a world where human rights can in fact be protected through the recognition of global citizenship. The connection to World War II is partially about a return to the past, but in many parts of the world in 1948, this text is also about a proposal of human rights that is entirely new. This means the declaration is not so much about a return to a pre-World War II world, but instead about an attempt to "give birth" to a world that has never existed before.

In addition to "the advent of a world," this overarching metaphor of procreation can also be found in an extension to the procreation of individuals; this is another way in which the procreation metaphor filters meaning, and in so doing, emphasizes the relationship of individuals to one another through social relationships. This, in turn, bolsters social rights such as well-being, security, and education. Procreation is specifically in the hands of individuals and their personal development and in the social relationships they develop with other human beings. There seems to be an emphasis on the productive evolution of humans. One especially poignant example of this focus on the individual can be found in article 26 through the metaphor of the "full development of the human personality." This metaphor is used in the context of education, which is a primary social right:

> Education shall be directed to the full development of the human personality and to the strengthening of respect for human rights and fundamental freedoms. It shall promote understanding, tolerance and friendship among all nations, racial or religious groups, and shall further the activities of the United Nations for the maintenance of peace.

Through offering education to all human beings, everyone can achieve the "full development of the human personality." The development of a world that respects human rights and fundamental freedoms is only possible through educating all citizens to achieve their full potential. Human rights writ large become possible *through the social right* of education. Individuals can be "re-created" through education.

In addition to thinking about the procreation metaphor at this individual level, the UDHR also emphasizes procreation in terms of a larger "social and international order," which is one way to articulate collectivity. This metaphor can be found in article 28: "Everyone is entitled to a social and international order in which the rights and freedoms set forth in this Declaration can be fully realized." The previous argument about the extension of the procreation metaphor to individuals plays a role in this extension of the metaphor to a larger "social and international order." Only through the full development of individuals, which is a social right of security, can a larger society that upholds human rights be fully realized.

Through the interaction of the individual metaphor with the collective metaphor, we obtain a better understanding of *how* "the advent of a world" that promotes and protects human rights is possible. We must first develop our full potential as individual human beings, but we must also communicate with other citizens in the world to create a social and international order that sustains and privileges human rights around the globe.

This division of individual versus collective might indicate a tension among the individuals who drafted this declaration. The interests of the United States would be served by more of an emphasis on individual education and development rather than too much emphasis on collective, social, or corporate forms of development that might someday rise up to challenge the United States in areas where the nation does not want to be challenged. However, the procreation metaphors used to structure the declaration—ranging from "advent of a world" to "full development of the human personality"—are in fact imbued with social rights, including education, security, and well-being, as the means to attain human rights more generally.

The declaration closes with the metaphor of "destruction," which seems to complement and complete the overarching procreation metaphor. This metaphor is found in the last article of the UDHR:

> Nothing in this Declaration may be interpreted as implying for any State, group or person any right to engage in any activity or to perform any act aimed at the destruction of any of the rights and freedoms set forth herein.

While the rest of the declaration establishes the role of both individuals and society in the creation of a future that protects human rights around the world, this last article focuses on the importance of recognizing destruction as a possibility. The UDHR explicitly states that the declaration should not be interpreted in any way that would allow for the destruction of rights and freedoms. In the context of the rest of the document, this last metaphor of destruction offers a counterpart to the procreation metaphor. We often fail to realize the meaning of a term without its opposite. The destruction metaphor limits and filters the meaning of procreation by bounding it through its relationship to oppositional meanings such as death, finality, and ruin, just a few of the meanings in the "system of related commonplaces" associated with destruction. If social rights are embedded through procreation metaphors to undergird human rights, the final destruction metaphor shows that citizens must be vigilant in protecting such social rights, or in the process of losing social rights will lose the grounding of overall human rights.

A Subordinate Metaphor: The "Human Family"

With this understanding of the overarching metaphor of procreation, I now turn to one subordinate metaphor that becomes an implication for the primary procreation metaphor in the UDHR. Black argues for the importance of both primary and subordinate metaphors in constructing meaning and shaping our reality: "In any case, primary and subordinate metaphors will normally belong to the same field of discourse, so that they mutually reinforce one and the same system of implications" (290). In the rhetoric of the UDHR, the primary metaphor of procreation is reinforced through the subordinate metaphor of the "human family."

"Human family" is a subordinating metaphor that in and of itself has a variety of other metaphors attached to it. This metaphor is found in the UDHR in the first stanza of the preamble:

> Whereas recognition of the inherent dignity and of the equal and inalienable rights of all members of the human family is the foundation of freedom, justice and peace in the world. . . .

This metaphor's placement in the first stanza of the declaration gives it importance in bolstering the overall procreation metaphor. The "human family" is a vital component to the procreation metaphor; it is only through the "human family" that the creation of a future where human rights are protected is possible. Notice that the "human family" implies tight-knit social relationships regardless of reason. People do not belong to a family because of rational thought, but instead, because of ethnic ties, blood relations, or perhaps the most audacious of reasons, love.

There are a variety of different iterations of this metaphor of "human family" in the UDHR. All of these metaphors support the view of the family as crucial to procreating and furthering a cohesive community and society, in which social rights such as education and well-being are protected and promoted to ensure human rights in general. As I noted earlier, the community and society metaphors are important to fostering the creation of a future world that values larger human rights and freedoms. Social rights, such as security and education, are attached to these collective ways to promote human rights. Security is a right that can only be enforced through social cooperation, and education is a social right that is necessary in order to cultivate global citizenship and the full development of citizens, thereby promoting human rights. Metaphors such as "organ of society," "spirit of brotherhood," and "duties to the community" all get at this meaning of the importance of community and duty to one another, which are the grounding for social rights to come into being. The "organ of society" metaphor is located in the final stanza of the preamble, the "spirit of brotherhood" metaphor is located in the first article of the declaration, and the "duties to the community" metaphor is located toward the end of the declaration in article 29.

First, the "organ of society" metaphor reinforces the importance of human family in the UDHR; the human family is one of the key units (or "organs") of society in advancing a future that enforces human rights for all. Here is the metaphor in the final stanza of the preamble:

> **Now, Therefore THE GENERAL ASSEMBLY proclaims THIS UNIVERSAL DECLARATION OF HUMAN RIGHTS** as a common standard of achievement for all peoples and all nations, to the end that every individual and every organ of society, keeping this Declaration constantly in mind, shall strive by teaching and education to promote respect for these rights and freedoms and by progressive measures, national and international, to secure their universal and effective recognition and observance, both among the peoples of Member States themselves and among the peoples of territories under their jurisdiction.

By using the metaphor of "organ," the rhetoric of the UDHR implies that the family unit is vital to the health of society as a whole; the body of society cannot live without the organ of the human family to sustain it.

In addition to the "organ of society" metaphor, the "human family" metaphor is also represented in the "spirit of brotherhood" in the UDHR: "All human beings are born free and equal in dignity and rights. They are endowed with reason and conscience and should act towards one another in a spirit of brotherhood." The "spirit of brotherhood" directly relates to the metaphor of "human family" through the relationship of brother. This metaphor explains how members of a family should relate to one another as siblings and relates to an overarching emphasis on procreation as well. This means that although we may at times become angry with our fellow citizens, we should never sever our social relationship with them, nor our sense of belonging to the larger human family. Without these social relationships and sense of belonging to one another as global citizens, social rights would be less likely to come to fruition. Since social rights are embedded in the procreation metaphor as the means for promoting more general human rights, this demonstrates the importance of the "human family" metaphor in the UDHR.

The "spirit of brotherhood" metaphor is another example of how some groups are not represented in the UDHR, however. Choosing "brotherhood" rather than "humankind" clearly has gender implications in describing the human family's relationships with one another as masculine. Perhaps the text is sexist; however, one explanation for the masculine language is that the concepts of fraternity and brotherhood were common themes found in prior French declarations, which were an influence on some CHR members. The "brotherhood" aspect of the metaphor does provide meaning into the closeness of this relationship between members of the "human family." We must treat one another as if we were "brothers," which implies a close relationship to everyone in our human family. This type of social relationship exists not because of reason alone, but because of other feelings that we experience and share with those in our family.

Finally, the "duties to the community" metaphor is important in establishing the actions of the "human family" and how that family plays a role in the procreation of a future that defends and protects human rights around the globe. Here is the context for the "duties to the community" metaphor: "Everyone has duties to the community in which alone the free and full development of his personality is possible. . . ." This metaphor connects to the earlier description of the procreation metaphor and its role in bolstering the "full development of the human personality." It is only through the establishment of a strong community that individuals can develop to their fullest potential. We can only fully develop our personality and potential as individuals through social rights, such as well-being and security, which in turn are made possible through social relationships with one another.

Importantly, being a part of the "human family" entails certain duties to the community, including helping others develop as citizens, primarily through the social right of education. Maximizing individuals' potential as citizens in the present through social rights, such as education, security, and well-being, makes possible a future that supports more general human rights. The rhetoric within the text, through the primary procreation metaphor and the subordinate human family metaphor, emphasizes social rights (such as education) *through* social relationships (such as the family) as the *means* toward recognizing larger human rights. The "duties to the community" metaphor shows how citizens are imbued with political agency in the present and must take an active role in participating and legitimating social rights. If we do not uphold ourselves to duties toward the human family through communities and a sense of belonging, we lose the ability to shape the future of our world.

Conclusion: Implications of Metaphor in the UDHR

The procreation metaphor structures the rhetoric of the UDHR in such a way that it orients people toward the future, instilling audiences with political agency in the present. If people believe they can influence the future of our world through thinking of themselves as members of the "human family," this can have important policy implications for people's actions in the present and the future.

In contrast to much of the global citizenship scholarship that critiques the text for its lack of attention toward social, economic, and cultural rights, this essay shows how the CHR successfully embraced social rights rhetorically, and how they made these rights the linchpin to recognizing all human rights. Indeed, the procreation metaphor constructs citizens not through nation-states, but through global citizenship in the context of human relationships and cultivating a sense of belonging, which suggests shifting toward a feminist rhetorical theory of global citizenship. By utilizing the procreation metaphor as the overarching framing metaphor of the UDHR, members of the CHR were able to leave the future of human rights open to—and also dependent upon—citizens of the present.

Note

[1] Although the text was "unanimously" accepted with the General Assembly's vote on December 10, 1948, three groups of nations declared their opposition through abstentions. South Africa defended its apartheid regime, Saudi Arabia was against the secular Eurocentric focus on human rights, and the Soviet bloc found the UDHR biased toward Western individual rights.

Works Cited

Black, Max. "Metaphor." *Proceedings of the Aristotelian Society.* N.p., 1954–1955. 273–94.

Bobbio, Norberto. *The Age of Rights*. Cambridge, UK: Polity P, 1996.

Carter, April. *The Political Theory of Global Citizenship*. New York: Routledge, 2001.

Englund, Harri. "Towards a Critique of Rights Talk in New Democracies: The Case of Legal Aid in Malawi." *Discourse & Society* 15.5 (2004): 527–51.

Fraser, Nancy, and Linda Gordon. "Contract Versus Charity: Why Is There No Social Citizenship in the United States?" *Socialist Review* 22.3 (1992): 45–67.

Ghosh, Ratna. "The Short History of Women." *Educating for Human Rights and Global Citizenship*. Ed. Ali A. Abdi and Lynette Schultz. Albany: State U of New York P, 2008. 81–95.

Glendon, Mary Ann. *A World Made New: Eleanor Roosevelt and the Universal Declaration of Human Rights*. New York: Random House, 2001.

Gordon Lauren, Paul. *The Evolution of International Human Rights: Visions Seen.* 2nd ed. Philadelphia: U of Pennsylvania P, 2003.

Hardt, Michael, and Antonio Negri. *Empire*. Cambridge: Harvard UP, 2000.

———. *Multitude: War and Democracy in the Age of Empire*. New York: Penguin Press, 2004.

Hauser, Gerard A. "The Moral Vernacular of Human Rights Discourse." *Philosophy and Rhetoric* 41.4 (2008): 440–66.

Hayden, Patrick. *Cosmopolitan Global Politics*. Burlington, VT: Ashgate, 2005.

Heater, Derek Benjamin. *World Citizenship and Government: Cosmopolitan Ideas in the History of Western Political Thought*. New York: St. Martin's P, 1996.

Howell, B. Wayne. "Reagan and Reykjavík: Arms Control, SDI, and the Argument from Human Rights." *Rhetoric and Public Affairs* 11.3 (2008): 389–416.

James, Stephen. *Universal Human Rights: Origins and Development*. New York: LFB Scholarly Publishing, 2007.

Joppke, Christian. "The Evolution of Alien Rights in the United States, Germany, and the European Union." *Citizenship Today: Global Perspectives and Practices.* Ed. T. Alexander Aleinikoff and Douglas Klusmeyer. Washington, DC: Carnegie Endowment for International Peace, 2001. 36–62.

Korey, William. *NGOs and the Universal Declaration of Human Rights: "A Curious Grapevine."* New York: St. Martin's P, 1998.

Lakoff, George, and Mark Johnson. *Metaphors We Live By.* Chicago: U of Chicago P, 1980.

Mailloux, Steven. *Rhetorical Power.* Ithaca, NY: Cornell UP, 1989.

Marshall, T. H. *Citizenship and Social Class, and Other Essays*. Cambridge: Cambridge UP, 1950.

Neier, Aryeh. "Rights and Wrongs." *Columbia Journalism Review* 46.4 (2007): 29–31.

Nilsen, Thomas R. "Persuasion and Human Rights." *Western Speech* 24.4 (1960): 201–05.

Normand, Roger, and Sarah Zaidi. *Human Rights at the UN: The Political History of Universal Justice*. Ed. Louis Emmerij, Richard Jolly, and Thomas G. Weiss. Bloomington and Indianapolis: Indiana UP, 2008.

O'Byrne, Darren J. *The Dimensions of Global Citizenship: Political Identity Beyond the Nation-State*. London: Frank Cass, 2003.

Pateman, Carole. *The Disorder of Women: Democracy, Feminism, and Political Theory*. Stanford: Stanford UP, 1989.

Reilly, Niamh. *Women's Human Rights: Seeking Gender Justice in a Globalizing Age*. Malden, MA: Polity, 2009.

Schattle, Hans. *The Practices of Global Citizenship*. Lanham, MD: Rowman & Littlefield, 2008.

Shafir, Gershon, and Alison Brysk. "The Globalization of Rights: From Citizenship to Human Rights." *Citizenship Studies* 10.3 (2006): 275–87.

Stevenson, Nick. *Cultural Citizenship: Cosmopolitan Questions*. Maidenhead, Berkshire: Open UP, 2003.

Stuckey, Mary E., and Joshua R. Ritter. "George Bush, <Human Rights>, and American Democracy." *Presidential Studies Quarterly* 37.4 (2007): 646–66.

"The Universal Declaration of Human Rights." General Assembly of the United Nations, 1948. Web. 15 May 2010. <http://www.un.org>.

Wellman, Carl. *The Proliferation of Rights: Moral Progress or Empty Rhetoric?* Boulder, CO: Westview P, 1999.

Section IV

Invention, Ambiguity, and Rhetorical Constraint

A rhetorical understanding of translation gives shape to the space between languages by considering what is invented in this space and how that invention occurs.

—Rebecca Lorimer

A reasonably polarized analogy rearranges pieces of a puzzle that need not be quite so puzzling and in the process raises or renews controversies. . . .

—Kyle Schlett

Communicating bold ideas need not be equated with "fearless speech" that disregards social consequences and ignites controversy. Likewise, a "rhetoric for avoiding offense" need not be one of advancing tepid arguments and pandering to one's audience.

—Claudia Carlos

Andreia, then, could be called a key term for rhetoric, with characters of both women and men oriented to it . . . a dominant element of aretê and a category used, transformed, ironized, and negotiated in the ethical practices of varying contexts.

—Ellen Quandahl

We gathered together to ask, among other things, how rhetoric divides and unites; how diversity and homogeneity "meet on the tongue"; how community is gained and how dissent is expressed. . . . An examination of the early literature from the Anglophone Caribbean offers a fresh take on this ambiguous in-betweenness.

—Timothy Henningsen

Cicero chose circulation in the *domus* instead of direct delivery in the Senate or Forum because he knew that women were involved in these political discussions. With women involved, he could count on the political dynamics of the *domus* as interchange between public and private and as exchange between male and female.

—Nancy Myers

15

Rhetoric for Avoiding Offense

Insinuatio in French Rhetorical Manuals of the Renaissance

Claudia Carlos

As we consider our theme this year—rhetoric's potential for unifying or dividing us (or perhaps for both unifying *and* dividing us)—what comes to mind is a contrast between, on the one hand, rhetoric that appeals to common values (e.g., when a politician says we're not divided between red states and blue states but that we're the *United* States) and, on the other, rhetoric that reminds us of our differences (e.g., when a politician says he represents the *real* Americans who live in small towns). But another opposition that also comes to mind is the one between rhetors who speak prudently, attempting to state their views in a non-offensive way that maximizes concord, and those who speak bluntly and (to borrow Foucault's term) "fearlessly" regardless of the social consequences. This second tension is what will interest me as I consider three French Renaissance treatments of *insinuatio*, a strategy in which the rhetor hints at his arguments without explaining them overtly.

In Roman rhetoric, most notably in *De Inventione* and *Rhetorica ad Herennium*, *insinuatio* offers the rhetor an oblique approach for introducing his case, an approach that becomes necessary whenever he faces a hostile or a difficult audience. While we often associate this sort of deviousness with the most manipulative rhetorical practices (e.g., the kind we see in Mark Antony's speech against Brutus in Act 3 of *Julius Caesar*), we should not assume that it always functions to stir up dissension and discourages meaningful exchange. In fact, in sixteenth-century France, where brutal wars between Catholics and Protestants plagued the entire country during the last half of the century, *insinuation*—or "dissimulation" as it was often called—provided a means for writers, such as Montaigne, to denounce fanaticism and religious violence without seeming to do so overtly—an important rhetorical achievement not only with respect to insuring that the Catholic aristocracy would keep reading but also with respect to passing the examination of the church's censors.[1]

Other scholars, most notably Margaret McGowan and Jean-Paul Sermain,[2] have already shown the influence of *insinuatio* on both the content and the style of Montaigne's essays. My goal is a much more limited one: (1) to explore the appropriation of classical *insinuatio* by three French manuals: Pierre Fabri's *Le grand et vrai art de pleine rhétorique* (1521), Pierre de Courcelles's *Rhétorique* (1557), and Peter Ramus's *Dialectique* (1555); and then (2) to briefly see how these techniques are put into practice by Montaigne in one of the boldest of his essays, "On Freedom of Conscience."

My argument will not be that Montaigne necessarily read these particular manuals and had them by his side as he wrote the essays, but that both the manuals and the essays suggest the prominence of these ideas in sixteenth-century French culture and, more significantly, their important role in presenting Renaissance rhetors with a "safe" means of expressing controversial views.

Insinuatio in Three French Treatises

In *De Inventione*, Cicero notes that rhetors must have recourse to *insinuatio* in the exordium "when the spirit of the audience is hostile" (1.17.23). According to Cicero,

> This hostility arises principally from three causes: if there is something scandalous in the case, or if those who have spoken first seem to have convinced the auditor on some point, or if the chance to speak comes at a time when those who ought to listen have been wearied by listening. (1.17.23)

For the purposes of this essay, it is especially the techniques relating to the first two causes that will be of interest. If your opponents have already won favor, then the advice is simple: you should begin by addressing whatever they think is their strongest argument (1.17.25). On the other hand, when there is a scandal involved, you can try techniques such as the following: (1) shifting the audience's attention away from what makes them angry to an object they favor, (2) hiding your intention to defend the position your audience expects you to defend, (3) working up to your defense in a gradual way, (4) showing that you are displeased by the same objects that displease the audience, and most importantly, (5) being careful never to openly attack your opponents (1.17.24).

Both Fabri and Courcelles recommend *insinuatio* as an approach under circumstances similar to the ones Cicero gives. For Fabri, insinuation, or proceeding covertly (*couvertement*) (43), is an option that the rhetor has when composing his exordium. If the cause is an honorable one, there is no need for insinuation; we can simply begin by narrating the facts or by setting forth the law or a strong argument (43). However, in a case where the rhetor may need to defend a scandalous case or person, Fabri suggests the following:

> If the case is vile, then we construct our exordium by insinuating the case simply and in brief, and declaring the simplicity of the person, complaining that the case was made worse [than it really is], or the person speaks falsely. . . . And [through these techniques] doubt is shown.[3] (43–44)

Thus, the idea behind insinuation in this instance (e.g., downplaying what is scandalous, insinuating that our opponent is lying) is not necessarily to win our skeptical audience over on the spot but to plant the seeds of doubt in their minds, so that we will have a better chance of convincing them later on.

A few paragraphs later, Fabri further describes insinuation as a sinewy process by which the rhetor leads his audience where he wants to take them, but then pretends not to be making any argument at all:

> By dissimulation we will also defend [only] what we can defend, and, whatever displeases our adversary we will say displeases us, and we will mount our [secret] defense immediately, and when we have softened him, we will say that the matter is not worth talking about or [we will say] other [similar] things, etc.[4] (44)

In the passage above, we detect two of the techniques recommended by Cicero: showing that we are displeased by the same objects that displease our adversaries and hiding our intention to defend the position our audience expects us to defend. Another appears when Fabri discusses cases in which the rhetor must treat a topic that he knows will displease his hearers. In these situations, according to Fabri, "we must disguise our exordium by keeping silent about the unpleasant thing and [instead] mention something else that is pleasant to the hearers . . ."[5] (45).

Contrasting somewhat with Fabri, Courcelles seems to view insinuation as an alternative to an exordium rather than as a kind of exordium itself:

> There is this difference between the exordium and the insinuation, in that the exordium and beginning should be [written] in such a way so that immediately the reasons . . . are clearly and manifestly stated. . . . But insinuation, in contrast, is [done] in such a way that everything we do and say be [done] secretly and by dissimulation to the end of more easily arriving at this work of perfection of speaking well and with grace.[6] (18)

Thus, the use of insinuation provides not only an alternative strategy to the exordium, but is connected with the goal of overall eloquence that the rhetor strives to achieve in the speech. He adds, however, that we should never seem as though we are engaging in dissimulation, lest it become apparent to the hearers that we are trying to deceive them. The speech should never seem "too prepared, dressed up, ornate, & studied"[7] (19), but should seem natural and spontaneous.

There are three specific occasions on which it is fitting to use insinuation, and they closely echo those found in *De Inventione*:

> Either when we have a dishonorable case, that is when this thing we are defending alienates the mind of the hearers; removing any good will or friendship they might have for us. Or when the mind of the hearers or judges seems to have been persuaded by those who spoke before us and who oppose us. Or, when the hearers and judges are worn out by listening to those who, a little before us, gave an embellished speech. (Courcelles 16)

With respect to the first situation—defending something dishonorable—Courcelles gives the same sorts of recommendations that we saw in Fabri with respect to de-emphasizing the person or the thing, depending on which is more disreputable. If it is the cause itself that is dishonorable, then the rhetor should begin the speech with such techniques as "saying to the hearers or judges that they should consider the man, rather than the thing [he did] . . ." (16). On the other hand, if the problem is with the man himself, as in cases involving "pimps, tyrants, rapists, thieves, and brigands" (16), then the rhetor should emphasize "the good and honorable thing, rather than the evil and detestable man" (16).

Unlike Fabri and Courcelles, Ramus is not writing primarily about rhetoric but about the "*art de bien disputer*" (the art of arguing well; I.1). This art is presented in two books—one focusing on the invention of dialectical arguments and the other on their expression. It is in the second book that Ramus discusses how to arrange syllogisms either by a logical, what he terms "natural," method (*méthode par nature*) or an unscientific, prudent method (*méthode par prudence*), which requires the dialectician to draw not on precepts but on his own cleverness for how to proceed. He adds:

> But how often has this method [of prudence] been the subject of observation by philosophers, poets and orators, for here we can refer to what Aristotle calls *cripsis*, that is, hidden and deceiving insinuation . . . [which techniques include:] beginning in the middle and not declaring at all in the introduction what the intent is, nor providing its parts; seeking from far away the means and antecedents of our end and doing this mainly by similitude and parable, and presenting them immediately if our person is imprudent, because such [imprudent] minds are easily surprised. If the person is cunning and clever, we do not have to present our points right away one after the other, but [should] change them, mix them up, argue over trifles, pretend the opposite, criticize ourselves, not give any inkling that we are thinking about the matter, say that this is a common and ordinary matter, speak quickly, become angry, debate, proceed with great audacity, and in the end reveal and put into play the ambush so that our stunned adversary says: "Where is [all] this going?"[8] (150)

So the idea here—one not derived from Cicero but from Aristotle's *Sophistical Refutations* and *Topics*—is that of throwing one's opponent off guard. Ramus tells us that Aristotle learned this practice from Plato, who in his dialogues has Socrates use these tactics against the sophists (150); however, as Ramus shows us two pages later, these same techniques can be found in Cicero's "Second Agrarian" (152).

We see a parallel with Fabri and Courcelles when Ramus notes that orators have often advocated such techniques in situations where the rhetor must defend a dishonorable cause. But unlike these other two writers, Ramus highlights the role of figures and delivery in effectively putting this method into practice:

> All the tropes and figures of style, all the graces of delivery, which is the whole of rhetoric, . . . have no other purpose than guiding the stubborn hearer which this method envisions, and they have only been used because of the intractability and perversity of this [hearer].[9] (152)

In concluding his treatment of insinuation, Ramus highlights its importance for dialecticians by reminding his readers that the best examples of this strategy come from their everyday lives:

> So we see how this method of prudence has been taught and practiced by philosophers, poets and orators, and we know by their precepts and examples how great this prudence is, but we will recognize it much better by the daily business activities of men whose clever practice of insinuation, if they must persuade somebody who does not want to listen, will have the upper hand. For this reason, the dialectician, if entry to the artificial and true path is closed, will construct another track by the force of his mind and his prudence, and will seek everywhere all the aids of custom because he is without the help of art; and because he cannot stay on a straight course, he will change sails and, by whatever winds he can, he will steer the ship, safe and in one piece, into the port.[10] (152–53)

Insinuatio in Practice: Montaigne's "On Freedom of Conscience" (1580)

I now want to look briefly at some of the techniques I have just described as they appear in Montaigne's "On Freedom of Conscience" (II.19). Much of recent scholarship on Montaigne has insisted that any serious reading of the essays needs to take into account that the recurrent themes of war, torture, barbarism, intolerance, and cruelty have immediate and concrete implications for Montaigne's readers, and so as one scholar has noted, we can read the essays in large part "as a response to the horror of the French civil wars" (Quint xiii). The phrase that dominates the essay's title, "Liberté de conscience" (Freedom of worship), refers directly to the royal proclamation of 1576, which allowed freedom of worship for Protestants, but only in regions outside Paris, where they could not be vanquished. Hence, by the title, the readers would have immediately understood that Montaigne was alluding to recent French politics. However, when we look at the first sentences of the text, we do not yet see any direct mention of this theme:

> It is quite normal to see good intentions, when not carried out with moderation, urging men to actions which are truly vicious. In the present quarrel which is driving France to distraction with its civil wars, the better and more wholesome party is certainly the one upholding the religion and constitution of our country. Now among the men of honour who support it (for I am not talking about people who use it as a pretext for settling private scores, satisfying their greed or courting the favour of princes but about those who support it out of true zeal for their religion and a sacred desire to defend the peace and good estate of their homeland) even among such men as these you can find many who, once passion drives them beyond the bounds of reason, take decisions which are unjust, violent and rash.[11] (759)

The first sentence is an aphorism suggesting the dangers of passion: lack of moderation can lead men of good intentions to do vicious things, hardly an opinion that would have been controversial for the readers. In the second sentence, which introduces the topic of the civil wars, Montaigne explicitly states the side he is on: "the one upholding the religion and constitution of our country"; in other words, that of the Catholic monarchy. We know from other sources that Montaigne was not pleased with the Valois kings, especially Henry III, who reigned during the time when Montaigne published the essays. Yet, by taking the Catholic side, the one a majority of his readers would take, he has let his audience know that what displeases them displeases him. Yet, despite the early reassurance of loyalty to the Catholic cause, the final sentence tells the readers that many of the "men of honour" who belong to their side have been driven by passion and consequently have made decisions that are unjust. So, even though Montaigne has explicitly taken the Catholic side, he also expresses criticism of the "men of honour" who support it; what further adds to this criticism is the parenthesis that explains what he is *not* supposedly talking about, and yet of course is still mentioning: all of the dishonorable people who support this cause. Even from these first few sentences, then, the readers have the sense of being caught off guard—on the one hand Montaigne takes their side, but on the other, he reminds them of Catholics who have committed unjust acts: what are Montaigne's intentions and where is he leading us?

Further complicating our ability to pin down the author's position is that after this opening, Montaigne spends most of the rest of the essay discussing how early Christians (i.e., Catholics) unjustly vilified the Emperor Julian, who, despite renouncing his Christian faith and being dubbed "the Apostate," was in Montaigne's view "a truly great and outstanding person" (760). While Montaigne expresses no sympathy for Julian's heretical act ("In matters of religion he was altogether vicious" [761]), he concentrates on Julian's chaste lifestyle, his nonviolence toward those of his subjects who dared to criticize him, and his valiant performance on the battlefield. Hence, Montaigne downplays the act that Catholics would perceive as dishonorable and instead focuses on all his other acts, which suggest those of a noble and enlightened leader.

It is only at the very end of the essay that Montaigne returns to the main theme—freedom of worship—and this is through a surprising comparison between Julian the Apostate and Henry, the *roi très chrétien:* "It is worth considering that, in order to stir up the flames of civil strife, the Emperor Julian exploited the self-same remedy of freedom of conscience which our kings now employ to stifle them"[12] (763). He then lists reasons that voice two opposing rationales about the wisdom of this decision: (1) that allowing Protestants "*liberté de conscience*" could amount to giving free rein to chaos and (2) on the other hand, "slackening the reins" and allowing the Protestants to keep their beliefs without a struggle could "soften and weaken" them by laxity (763). While not appearing to take one side or the other, Montaigne simply ends with this point: "Yet for the honour and piety of our kings I prefer to believe that, since they could not do what they wished, they pretended to wish to do what they could"[13] (763). That is, Montaigne prefers to believe that Henry was forced by circumstances to allow the Protestants to worship freely. And yet, the implications of this last thought are hardly comforting to the Catholics who must choose between an impious king and an ineffective one. Montaigne has, in other words, insinuated a strong critique of the monarchy he professes to support.

While Montaigne is famous for denouncing rhetoric and the artifice of well-arranged words, as Jean-Paul Sermain has pointed out, he is not unfamiliar with practicing something quite similar to *insinuatio* in certain social situations. For instance, in "On Diversion" (III.4), Montaigne explains what he believes to be the best approach in helping women overcome by extreme grief at the death of a husband:

> From the outset you must encourage women's lamentations and show that they are justified and have your approval. This understanding between you will earn you the trust needed to proceed further, then you can glide down an easy and imperceptible slope to the more steadfast arguments appropriate for curing them. (935–36)

In describing this surreptitious method of persuasion, Montaigne makes no reference to Cicero. However, by advocating these techniques—saying that what pleases the woman in question pleases him, concealing his intentions, delaying his arguments until he has won the woman's trust—Montaigne is advocating precisely the sorts of techniques recommended by Fabri, Courcelles, and Ramus.

To conclude, the survival of Ciceronian *insinuatio* in French Renaissance treatises suggests that this strategy still had use in the context of a sixteenth-century monarchy. While certain of its techniques (especially in the Ramian version) would seem to risk inflaming an adversary (e.g., speaking with boldness or anger), the example of Montaigne suggests, on the contrary, that *insinuatio* could function as a means of communicating truth to power covertly—a useful skill for avoiding the divisive, and potentially dangerous, results of its overt counterpart.

What this analysis illustrates, then, is that communicating bold ideas need not be equated with "fearless speech" that disregards social consequences and ignites controversy. Likewise, a "rhetoric for avoiding offense" need not be one of advancing tepid arguments and pandering to one's audience. Rather, in the opposition of prudent and fearless speech, we have two different methods by which rhetors can deliver potentially offensive ideas: the first, a covert means that attempts to promote concord, which has the advantage of insuring both the rhetor's own self-preservation[14] and that even a hostile audience will keep listening or reading, while the second method invites controversy and places the audience in a position of having to directly confront ideas that seem threatening. Thus, considering the concord-controversy tension in this way can offer us a more nuanced understanding of what it means to speak boldly to those who hold power over us: for in addition to clashing directly with the people he will offend, the truthteller always has the equally important—and still greatly understudied—option of a more prudent boldness.

Notes

[1] In order to obtain the *privilège royal*, authorizing publication.

[2] See McGowan and Sermain, pp. 123–39.

[3] All of the French passages were taken from Montaigne, *Les Essais.* Se le cas est vilain, et adonc l'en faict son exorde par insinuation du cas simplement en brief, et declarant la simplesse de la personne remonstrant que le cas est plus aggravé, ou la personne parle mauvais langaige et faulce invention des gens, . . . Et doubt estre faict brief ou point.

[4] Par dissimulation aussi nous deffendrons ce que nous pourrons deffendre, et, ce qui desplaist a l'adversaire, nous dirons qu'il nous desplaist, et mettrons nostre deffence incontinent, et quant nous l'auron adoulcy, nous diron que la matiere ne vault pas le parler ou aultre choses, etc.

[5] "il fault couvrir son exorde en taisant la chose desplaisante et nommer aultre chose plaisante aux auditeurs. . . ."

[6] Il y a difference entre L'Eorde & l'insinuation, d'autant que l'Eorde & commencment doit estre de telle maniere, que tout incontinant les raisons . . . soyent clerement & manifestement declarees. . . . Mais l'insinuation au contraire est de telle façon que tout ce que faisons & disons soit secretement & par disimulation a celle fin de plus commodement & aysement parvenir à cest oeuvre de perfection de bien & ornement parler.

[7] "trop preparee, appareillee, ornee, & instruite"

[8] Combien toutesfois que ceste méthode ayt quelque observation ès philosophes, poëtes et orateurs car nous pouvons icy rapporter ce qu'Aristote appelle *crypse*, c'est-à dire cachée et trompeuse insinuation . . . par plusieurs advertissemens qui sont en somme: commencer au milieu et ne poinct déclairer au commencement son entreprise, ny déduire les parties d'icelle; chercher de bien loing les moyens et antécédentz de nostre attente et ce, principallement, par similitude et parabole, et les pousuyvre incontinent si nostre partie est imprudente car telz espritz se laissent incontinent surprendre. Si c'est homme cault et fin, il ne fault pas incontinent manifester noz pieces l'une après l'autre, mais changer, entremesler, frivoler, feindre le contraire, se reprendre, ne monstrer aucun semblant d'y penser, dire que c'est chose vulgaire et accoustumée, se haster, courroucer, débatre, procéder par grande hardiesse, et en fin finalle descouvrir et exécuter l'embusche tellement que l'adversaire estonné dye: "A quelle fin tend cecy?"

[9] Tous les tropes et figures d'élocution, toutes les grâces d'action, qui est la Rhétorique entière . . . ne servent d'autre chose sinon pour conduire ce fascheux et rétif auditeur qui nous est proposé en ceste méthode, et n'ont esté pour autre fin observées que pour la contumace et perversité d'icelluy.

[10] Ainsi donques nous voyons comme ceste méthode de prudence a esté enseignée et practiquée par les philosophes, poëtes et orateurs, et cognoissons par leurs préceptes et exemples combien est grande ceste prudence, mais nous le cognoistrons beaucoup plus par les affaires journelles et négoces des homme ésquelz ceste caulte insinuation, s'il fault persuader quelque chose à celuy qui n'y veult entendre, obtiendra facillement le premier lieu. A ceste cause le dialecticien, si l'entrée de l'artificiel et vray chemin est fermé, se fera autre voye par force d'esprit et prudence, et cerchera de toues pars toutes aydes de coustume et usage pour ce qu'il est destitué du secours de doctrine; et pour ce qu'il ne peult tenir la droicte course, il changera voiles et conduira par telz ventz qu'il pourra, la nef saulve et entière à port.

[11] Il est ordinaire, de voir les bonnes intentions, si elles sont conduites sans moderation, pousser les hommes à des effects très-vitieux. En ce debat, par lequel la France est à present agitée de guerres civiles, le meilleur et le plus sain party, est sans doubte celuy, qui maintient et la religion et la police ancienne du pays. Etre les gens de bien toutesfois, qui le souvennt (car je ne parle point de ceux, qui s'en servent de pretexte, pour, ou exercer leurs vengeances particulieres, ou fournir à leur avarice, ou suivre la faveur des Princes: mais de ceux qui le font par vray zele envers leur religion, saincte affection, à maintenir la paix et l'estat de leur patrie) de ceux-cy dis-je, il s'en voit plusieurs, que la passion pousse hors les bornes de la raison, et leur faict par fois prendre des conseils injustes, violents, et encore temeraires.

[12] En quoy cela est digne de consideration, que l'Empereur Julien se sert pour attiser le trouble de la dissension civile, de cette mesme recepte de liberté de conscience, que noz Roys viennent d'employer pour l'estaindre.

[13] Et si croy mieux, pour l'honneur de la devotion de noz Roys; c'est, que d'ayans peu ce qu'ils vouloient, ils ont fait semblant de vouloir ce qu'ils pouvoient.

[14] That is, his preservation from the consequences of having violated restrictions against free speech, whether legal ones or simply societal ones. For more on the advantages of a covert approach for advancing bold ideas, see Leo Strauss's introduction to *Persecution and the Art of Writing*.

Works Cited

Cicero. *De inventione. De optimo genere oratorum, Topica*. Trans. H. M. Hubbell. Cambridge, MA: Harvard UP, 1968.

Courcelles, Pierre de. *Rhétorique*. Paris: G. le Noir, 1557.

Fabri, Pierre. *Le grand et vrai art de pleine rhétorique de Pierre Fabri*. 1521. Ed. A Héron. Rouen: Cagniard, 1889.

McGowan, Margaret. *Montaigne's Deceits. The Art of Persuasion in the* Essais. Philadelphia: Temple UP, 1974.

Montaigne, Michel de. *The Complete Essays*. Trans. M. A. Screech. London: Penguin, 2003.

———. *Les Essais*. Ed. Jean Balsamo, Michel Magnien, Catherine Magnien-Simonin. Paris: Gallimard, 2007.

Quint, David. *Montaigne and the Quality of Mercy: Ethical and Political Themes in the Essays*. Princeton: Princeton UP, 1998.

Ramus, Peter. *Dialectique*. 1555. Ed. M. Dassonville. Genève: Droz, 1964.

Sermain, Jean-Paul. "*Insinuatio*, *circumstantia*, *visio* et *actio*. L'itinéraire rhétorique du chapitre III, 4: 'De la Diversion.'" *Rhétorique de Montaigne. Actes du Colloque de la Société des amis de Montaigne, 14 et 15 décembre 1984*. Ed. Frank Lestringant. Paris: Champion, 1985. 123–39.

Strauss, Leo. *Persecution and the Art of Writing*. Glencoe, IL: Free P, 1952.

16

Working for Concord amidst the Controversy

The Role of the *Domus* in the Circulation of Cicero's "Second Philippic"

Nancy Myers

Cicero knowingly stepped into controversy with his return to Rome in August 44 BCE. Looking to the glory of the past, he, as an elder statesman, was working to overthrow the dictatorship of the assassinated C. Julius Caesar and those who might follow after him with his bid for a return to the Republic. For Cicero, the Republic was concord, but to others who wanted sole control, such as Mark Antony (Marcus Antonius), who had military, political, and rhetorical influence, the conflict was pivotal. Cicero's debate with Antony during fall and spring 44–43 BCE illustrates the classic tension between pen and sword and is the last, and perhaps most important, political debate of Cicero's life (Wooten). This debate highlights his rhetorical attempts to establish concord in the midst of Roman social and political chaos following Caesar's assassination. Known as the *Philippics*, Cicero wrote fourteen speeches to counter Antony and to argue for the return of the Republic, but the second one is unique.

The second of Cicero's *Philippics* was not delivered in the Roman Senate, the male-dominated governmental sphere, but was intended to be circulated as a pamphlet in the *domus*, the social and more private sphere of the senators' households, a location from which women had great influence (Cape; Millar). In the 25 October 44 BCE letter to Atticus, his close friend as well as copier and distributor of his writings, Cicero's intention to circulate the "Second Philippic" as a polished pamphlet rather than to deliver it as a public speech is evident: "I am sending you the speech, to be kept back and put out at your discretion. But when will we see the day when you will think proper to publish it?" (*Letters* 341). Although the actual circulation of the pamphlet is in question, I argue that Cicero's decision to circulate it in the *domus*, rather than orating it as a Senate speech, allowed him to control the reception of the "Second Philippic," thus increasing the probability of gaining the adherence of his audience for a return to the Republic. This approach, which allows women equal access to the text and those discussions about it, highlights, first, the interreliance of the political and the social spheres and, second, the influence of women in decisions (and votes) made in both spheres.[1]

If Cicero had delivered the speech in the Senate, its vitriolic tone and approach might inflame the senators, and the image of Cicero as the *paterfamilias*, as head of the household, of both *domus*, where friends and clients came daily to seek favor with a powerful *paterfamilias*, and the state might meet with resistance, completely undermining Cicero's purpose of rallying support against Antony. However, with circulation in the *domus*, men and women simultaneously heard or read the speech in controlled environments chosen by Cicero. He could construct his text slowly and carefully and release it when he felt the timing was right. At the start, Cicero would expect to receive a response to the "Second Philippic" from those who were sympathetic to his idea; then he would discuss it with those who were persuaded by him; and finally it would be released to more antagonistic audiences. According to Raymond Starr, the sharing of print matter went first to a close friend who it was assumed "would not show it to anyone else" (213). Both Atticus and Sextus read and responded to the "Second Philippic" in late October and early November 44 BCE. After revisions and modifications, several friends received copies, or they were invited to a recitation at the home of the orator. The chosen audiences for these first two rounds were expected to praise and discuss style. The next round moved beyond this closed sphere. Copies of the speech were made by the author and, sometimes, close friends, who then circulated them to their friends (213–15). This strategy, which was played out by Atticus and Cicero on several previous occasions, allowed Cicero to use the conversations and discussions surrounding the readings to support the positive reception of the document. The image of Cicero as the *paterfamilias* had not only a receptive audience but also a compatible site, the *domus,* for its influence and success.

Cicero chose circulation in the *domus* instead of direct delivery in the Senate or Forum because he knew that women were involved in these political discussions. With women involved, he could count on the political dynamics of the *domus* as interchange between public and private and as exchange between male and female. According to Suzanne Dixon, "He [Cicero] never considered them [women] unimportant in the political-social milieu in which he lived. His assumption is, clearly, that wives and close female relations can, if they wish, alter the political actions of leading men at Rome" (96–97). Without the dynamics of the *domus*—its relationships between men and women working together to sustain the family name through children, to manage the estate through wise investments, and to engage in the social relationships among patrons, clients, and friends—the public sphere would not have senators, a public Forum, or a chance for a renewal of the Republic. The politics of government and law mingled with the politics of property and commerce in the *domus*: "A senator's house functioned as his political base, both in the sense that large numbers of people were received there, and in that he proceeded ceremonially from there, escorted by followers, to go down to the Forum and Curia" (Millar 239). The *paterfamilias* met daily in his home with friends and clients, those needing his support. In exchange, the friends and clients voted with the *paterfamilias*. Besides being the site for discussion of governmental and legal issues and decisions, the *domus* also served as the headquarters for the social and financial negotiations of the *paterfamilias*' property and commerce. This included marriage agreements, the buying and selling of property, and the daily organizational and financial dealings with farms and businesses. The *domus* was a site where the politics of government and law and the politics of commerce and property met, and women of the privileged classes were well versed in both domestic and public affairs (Cape 118). Thus, in this ongoing political battle between dictatorship and Republic, Cicero counted on the circulation of the "Second Philippic" via the *domus* to work to his rhetorical and political advantage.

Composed during October 44 BCE, the "Second Philippic" was Cicero's calculated political and rhetorical strategy to foster agreement for a return to the Republic outside of the conflicted and volatile political arena. It countered Antony's rebuttal to the "First Philippic," which had marked Cicero's return to political life after years of absence due to Caesar's bid for and achievement of his dictatorship during the 50s and 40s BCE. With Caesar's death in March 44 BCE, Cicero actively reentered the political scene with the goal of restoring the Republic and of countering Antony's attempt to replace Caesar. Amidst this political upheaval, Cicero composed the fourteen speeches of the *Philippics* between September 44 and April 43 BCE. Antony had already attacked Cicero's actions before his delivery of the "First Philippic," and the protocol of public accusation was to reply "with moderation," and appeal to "the public interest whenever possible" (Konstan 126). Cicero's "First Philippic" appears to do that with its restrained tone and conciliatory manner, but it is filled with covert references of Antony's misconduct and was met with little if any support in the Senate (Frisch 131–32; Kennedy, *Art* 269–70; Mitchell 301–02). However, its delivery so infuriated and insulted Antony that he engaged his tutor Sextus Clodius to help him compose the reply, which was delivered 19 September 44 BCE, then circulated, and probably summarized in *acta diurnal*, a document comparable to a newspaper (Frisch 132–33).

After Antony's speech, Cicero was faced with the dilemma of reply. How could he vilify Antony, exonerate himself, and rally support? Antony, having been close to Caesar, had committed followers and others who would easily shift their loyalties to support his bid for sole control (Wooten 162). With the lack of success of the "First Philippic," Cicero chose circulation in the *domus* for the pamphlet of the "Second Philippic." As he knew, the written form circulated and communicated in the civic as well as the private spheres.[2] The difference with the distribution practices of written genres as compared to governmental oral discourse was that the pamphlet circulated first in the *domus* then moved to the civic sites. That reversal of political circulation and exposure—from private to public instead of public to private—allowed for the documents to be read, listened to, and discussed first with the family and a circle of close friends and clients (the like-minded) instead of in the more antagonistic civic spaces. As an undelivered circulated speech, the pamphlet included among its first readers and hearers women in the houses of Cicero's friends and clients. Jerzy Axer points out that a "published oration is supposed to be primarily a contribution to political disputes of the time," so Cicero's published pseudo-oration added to the political discussion in the more stable and safer environment of the *domus* (58).

The pamphlet's style belies Cicero's purpose of circulation in the domestic sphere, for it gives the impression that it was an immediate and spontaneous oral reply to Antony's charges in the Senate on 19 September—a seemingly calculated and regular feature of Cicero's circulated texts. As a crafted print text giving the impression of an oral Senate speech, the "Second Philippic" carries the characteristics of a literary work, a play within a play. The woman reader or hearer of the pamphlet envisions the spectacle of honorable Cicero illustrating Antony's infamy before the senators and male citizens. As Axer explains about Roman pamphlets' effects, "the orator himself, as well as his audience, are a part of that presented world" (60). The words of the text become images of Antony's humiliation, of Cicero's courage, of the senators' affirmation, and of the citizens' approval, even though the words were never uttered. This layered fiction of Antony and Cicero operates within the conventions of a literary text while offering the style of an oral rhetorical one. Using the Senate as a backdrop, Cicero blurs the lines between the state and the *domus* to appeal to women's concerns tied to financial and familial stability. With women in agreement, he could count on their influence to "transmit large bodies of *clientes* [clients] and *amici* [friends] to further far-reaching political ambitions" (Dixon 94). Across the text, Cicero generates images and allusions that render him the *paterfamilias*, the respected and powerful head of the family, working toward concord in both the political and domestic spheres while portraying Antony as unrestrained with and disrespectful of the men of the Senate and the women of the *domus*.[3] As speaker and narrator, he systematically uses feminine allusions and other expected defamatory topoi to evoke the emotional states of distress and disbelief when responding to accusations. For example, in his rendition of the love letter scene, Antony in disguise delivers a letter to Fulvia declaring his love: "Straightaway he is conducted to the lady on whose account he had come and hands her the letter" (*Philippics* 2.77).[4] Cicero's portrayal starts with Antony in the third person, but ends by directly charging Antony with abandoning his military duties: "Well, indoors you had a lover's reason; out of doors your reason was still more discreditable" (2.78). The shifting pronoun use between "he" and "you" provides the effect of direct address to two audiences, neither of which is the reader: the "he" implies that Cicero is talking to the senators, offering evidence about Antony's desertion and immorality, and the "you" indicates Cicero as addressing Antony. This scenic convention of literary style is an impossible reality, as Cicero did not attend the Senate that day, most likely fearing for his life. Even though Antony called on him to appear, Cicero claimed fatigue upon arriving in Rome (Frisch 132).[5] Both in the portrayals in the text and in the distinction between oral and written discourse genres, Cicero promotes himself as the leader capable of orchestrating the return of the Republic.

Not only did Cicero understand the importance of creating a society in text—a presented event, which played on beliefs and suspicions—but he also knew the possible effects of text in society, which were discussed in both public and private venues. With this print circulation route, the multilayered effects of the "Second Philippic" would be passed from one *domus* to another with an introductory statement or follow-up discussion offered by the presenters. Aware that women were in those discussions, Cicero did not discount the influence of their response, maybe even counted on it. Since his practice was to appeal to women when he needed assistance with their male family members, Cicero wanted them to hear or read the speech in order to actively promote and recruit senators for his coalition against Antony. Women had the opportunity to hear, discuss, and act on the speech because the *domus* was a space where public and private overlapped. Not only were they able to converse about the documents that entered the household, but many women of the upper classes were literate and could read them. Moreover, most senators' households included literate private clerks, either slaves or freedmen, who read aloud to and took dictation from family members; as a result, women had other means of learning the contents of a document aside from their own literacy abilities.

Cicero's rendition of himself as *paterfamilias*, as protector of both state and home, rhetorically operated to reassure women, whose control over their own property depended on maintaining the legal status quo, and to sway them to influence others for a return to the Republic. They needed reassurance because dowries and inheritance were women's property and stayed with them in a divorce, so they controlled and managed their own financial affairs through male representatives, which might be their fathers, brothers, uncles, or husbands. Usually, a woman's political ties were, first, to her *paterfamilias* (since that is where her dowry and inheritance came from) and, second, to her husband. To rally support for the Republic and against Antony, Cicero needed women's influence with others. Women could use marriage as a means to garner political power and control, since they were able to divorce almost as easily as men and since they took their property with them. When husbands were away on military campaigns or governing territories, their wives often were in charge of their estates and financial affairs. Because of the Roman patronage system, with its clients and friends offering support in return for gifts and favors, the realms of finance and commerce provided women with power to negotiate and barter for the political aims they supported. In "A Family Business," Dixon persuasively argues, "The subtle business of alliance, obligations, favours, friendship, intervention, reconciliation and offence was one in which the socially competent Roman matron from a distinguished family would naturally play an active part" (109). Thus, the "Second Philippic's" constructed conflict between Cicero, representing the traditions and stability of the Republic politically and socially, and Antony, supposedly disregarding both, appeals to a woman's concern to maintain her legal rights over her dowry and inheritance.

Cicero's intention to circulate the "Second Philippic" as a pamphlet provided the means for a regulated reception by both men and women of the time period. His decision included his awareness of women in the private sphere as having access to documents and influential males, as managing domestic affairs and people from all social levels, and as participating in the politics of commerce and property and indirectly in the politics of government and law. This knowledge was particularly important given that the first defense he makes in reply to Antony is about his supposed breach of friendship, for "personal friendship was always important to Cicero, and personal relationships in Rome often played a stronger role than ideology" (Kennedy, *New* 140). Both men and women would recognize and understand the political and personal ramifications of Cicero's portrayal of Antony's accusation of violated friendship (Cicero, *Philippics* 2.3–10). Moreover, Cicero's claim that Antony read aloud his personal letter in the Senate (2.7–9) not only showed a breach of conduct on Antony's part, but also was proof that Cicero considered Antony *amici* (friend), a welcome guest in his household. Because of what he understands of the *domus* and women's powers within it, Cicero employs the examples he does to argue Antony's lack of discipline, restraint, and courtesy in both the public and domestic spheres, and he depicts himself as the *paterfamilias*, an image that speaks to both men and women.

While the "Second Philippic" champions patriarchal supremacy, it highlights the reciprocity between the state and the *domus* and women's engagement and influence in that exchange. Cicero's intention to circulate the speech in pamphlet form reinforces this intermingling of spheres and sexes in that, as a pamphlet, women had the opportunity to hear or read the speech at the same time as the men, not after the fact, as in the standard practice of circulating public oratory in written form after the speech had been given. To garner both support against Antony and a harmonious return to the Republic, Cicero intended the circulation of the "Second Philippic" to be a rhetorical means of achieving concord in the face of political controversy. Ultimately, Cicero, losing his hands and head, failed in his attempt for a return to the concord of the Republic. While not reaching the accord he sought in his fourteen speeches, he did demonstrate that in controversy the pen is as important as the sword for both men and women.

Notes

[1] Whether the pamphlet was circulated during late 44 BCE is less important for my argument than is Cicero's intent to publish it privately and disseminate it as a written text rather than give it as an oral civic performance (Frisch; Kennedy, *Art*; Shackleton Bailey; Wooten). Often the speech is explained as being undelivered, while others speculate that it was not circulated at all (Fuhrmann; Mitchell), and still others believe it probably was.

[2] Cicero's letters to his fellow senators located outside of Rome because of military appointments and public offices support the content of the "Second Philippic," as they argue against Antony and for Cicero's fight for the Republic. These letters followed the same circulation routes as the "Second Philippic," even though they were not intended for circulation (Fuhrmann 180, 203). For a detailed account of pamphlet circulation, see Starr's "The Circulation of Literary Texts in the Roman World"; for the public and private use of letters, see Fernandes' "The Public Letters of Cicero"; and for Atticus' exchanges and accounts of the circulation of Cicero's writings, see Phillips' "Atticus and the Publication of Cicero's Works."

[3] For a demonstration of Cicero's use of feminine allusions and female representations as an argumentative strategy to portray himself as *paterfamilias* and to defame Antony's character, see Myers' "Cicero's (S)trumpet: Roman Women and the 'Second Philippic.'"

[4] All quotations and citations from the *Philippics* are from Shackleton Bailey's 1986 translation.

[5] In fact, the "Second Philippic" does not add to the history of the political scene and some of the accusations and information are inaccurate (Frisch 139; Kennedy, *Art* 271–72). Using Cicero's letters as proof against his claims about Fulvia in the "Second Philippic," Delia argues that Cicero was contradictory and inconsistent, thus unreliable, when making public claims about political enemies (200).

Works Cited

Axer, Jerzy. "Cicero's Court Speeches: The Spoken Text Versus the Published Text. Some Remarks from the Point of View of the Communication Theory of Text." *Rhetoric and Pedagogy: Its History, Philosophy, and Practice*. Ed. Winifred Bryan Horner and Michael Leff. Mahwah: Lawrence Erlbaum, 1995. 57–63.

Cape, Robert W., Jr. "Roman Women in the History of Rhetoric and Oratory." *Listening to Their Voices: The Rhetorical Activities of Historical Women*. Ed. Molly Meijer Wertheimer. Columbia: U of South Carolina P, 1997. 112–32.

Cicero. *Letters to Atticus*. Ed. and trans. D. R. Shackleton Bailey. Vol. 4. Cambridge: Harvard UP, 1999.

———. *Philippics*. Ed. and trans. D. R. Shackleton Bailey. Chapel Hill: U of North Carolina P, 1986.

Delia, Diana. "Fulvia Reconsidered." *Women's History and Ancient History*. Ed. Sarah B. Pomeroy. Chapel Hill: U of North Carolina P, 1991. 197–217.

Dixon, Suzanne. "A Family Business: Women's Role in Patronage and Politics at Rome 80–44 B.C." *Classica et Mediaevalia* 34 (1983): 91–112.

Fernandes, James J. "The Public Letters of Cicero." *Communication Quarterly* 26.1 (1978): 21–26.

Frisch, Hartvig. *Cicero's Fight for the Republic: The Historical Background of Cicero's* Philippics. Trans. Niels Haislund. Copenhagen: Gyldendalske Boghandel, 1946.

Fuhrmann, Manfred. *Cicero and the Roman Republic*. Trans. W. E. Yuill. Oxford: Blackwell, 1992.

Kennedy, George A. *The Art of Rhetoric in the Roman World 300 B.C.–A.D. 300*. Princeton: Princeton UP, 1972.

———. *A New History of Classical Rhetoric*. Princeton: Princeton UP, 1994.

Konstan, David. *Friendship in the Classical World*. Cambridge: Cambridge UP, 1997.

Millar, Fergus. "The Last Century of the Republic. Whose History?" *Journal of Roman Studies* 85 (1995): 236–43.

Mitchell, Thomas N. *Cicero: The Senior Statesman*. New Haven: Yale UP, 1991.

Myers, Nancy. "Cicero's (S)trumpet: Roman Women and the 'Second Philippic.'" *Rhetoric Review* 22.4 (2003): 337–52.

Phillips, John J. "Atticus and the Publication of Cicero's Works." *Classical World* 79.4 (1986): 227–37.

Shackleton Bailey, D. R. *Cicero: Classical Life and Letters*. New York: Scribner's, 1972.

Starr, Raymond J. "The Circulation of Literary Texts in the Roman World." *Classical Quarterly* 37.1 (1987): 213–23.

Wooten, Cecil W. *Cicero's* Philippics *and Their Demosthenic Model: The Rhetoric of Crisis*. Chapel Hill: U of North Carolina P, 1983.

17

Andreia in the Nunnery

Rhetorical Learnedness in Twelfth-Century Byzantium

Ellen Quandahl

Recent scholarship in gender studies has witnessed a shift from reclaiming women's voices to examining how the female and feminine are constructed in language, and also, more recently, the male and manly (Martin 12–13). Investigations of the Greek term *andreia* (manly spirit or courage) have revealed the extent to which advice to rhetors and the history of rhetoric are entangled in manliness and manly courage. As Joy Connolly suggests, the binary opposites of gender are often deployed not only where virtue and vice are in question but also the legitimacy of rhetoric itself ("Virile" 84). The semantic reach of manliness extends well beyond deeds of war to questions of education, including, for example, in Plato's *Laches*; to Greek and Roman treatises on habits of propriety and speech; sophistic defenses of *paideia* and its teachers as manly, despite their distance from physical deeds of manliness (Connolly, "Like"); all the way to the emergence of modern composition studies and its shaping of students' character (Brody). Early Christian struggles to claim Greek *paideia* as legitimate and even necessary to Christian philosophy include strands of argument through manliness. Discourses of ascetic practices also reveal, as Brent Shaw has argued, the transformation of manliness to include traditionally female virtues (280). The manliness of holy women and female transvestite monastics as "honorary men of god" is now well-documented (Burrus 144–46; Delierneux; Miller 88).

Andreia, then, could be called a key term for rhetoric, with characters of both women and men oriented to it. In the discourses I have mentioned, it is a dominant element of *aretê* and a category used, transformed, ironized, and negotiated in the ethical practices of varying contexts. Thus, one finds varieties of manly men and women—strong and stupid, cunning and tactical, rash and enduring, naturally gifted and trained. There are, then, manliness topoi, appearing frequently, as one might expect, in epideictic discourse. As Menander Rhetor claims in his treatise on imperial oration, for example, "courage [*andreia*] reveals an emperor more than do other virtues" (qtd. in Russell and Wilson 85).

Building on this scholarship, the present essay considers rhetorical learnedness and its relation to manliness in the logos on the death of a Byzantine woman, the historian and polymath Anna Comnena, composed by a sophist-bishop, Georgios Tornikes, in about the year 1155. The work combines features of the funeral speech, imperial praise, and scientific hymn as described by Menander Rhetor. Thus, it illustrates in its very genre a simultaneous concord and controversy, the tradition of the Christian elegy that adapts pagan Greek forms of very long standing. I show, moreover, that attention to manliness within that already paradoxical form reveals that the terms enabling and constraining what Tornikes can say about a learned woman are a rich site for rhetorical investigation. We can see in them a merger and division of spaces inside and outside, activities and genders, recalling Burke's well-known work on the realms or "orders" to which words refer—natural, verbal, sociopolitical, supernatural ("What Are" 374).

Burke shows that social attitudes are created and maintained in the ways that names for one order are carried into another. For example, references to God as "Lord" or "Father" take words from the sociopolitical to name the beyond-the-political or "supernatural," which, in reverse, lends the awesomeness of God to political kingship (*Rhetoric of Religion* 7–8, 15). Something like this happens where manliness is concerned, using gender words to name the nonbiological. Terms for physical bodies and their actions name the spiritual, familial, political, and educational, and back again, *inspiriting*, to use Burke's word, the nonphysical with gender and gender, in reverse, with values and hierarchy. While Burke rarely concerned himself with gender, these namings, I suggest, are so potent and frequent as to be paradigmatic of rhetorical convertability (*Rhetoric of Motives* 232) and its ordering effects. These are especially evident, as we will see, where questions of power, religion, and education intersect.

As readers may know, Anna Comnena is the author of the *Alexiad*, an encomiastic history of Emperor Alexius I, her father. Tornikes was a member of the clergy of Hagia Sophia, who, according to Darrouzès (editor of Tornikes' speeches and letters), preferred teaching, but perhaps because of his feeble voice or the burdens of family, pressed for advancement (29).[1] He may have been a part of the circle of scholars who, according to this speech, were engaged in study with her and would have worked in the imperial apartments housed within the monastery Kecharitomene, where Anna lived after the death of her father. A letter to Anna's daughter, written from the period of his position as Bishop of Ephesus and deploring the conditions of the crumbling church in such a rural outpost—a refuge for birds and hedgehogs—suggests to me that he had the patronage of the family (157–58).

To begin the analysis, consider this passage from the prooemium of Tornikes' speech. He has just expressed surprise that logographers and rhetors have not taken for themselves this astonishing topic for speech, this woman. He writes:

> Here is a woman, by nature of the tender and soft race, and skilled only for weaving and distaff and spindle, . . . raised with softness and caressed of royal luxury; . . . having entered youthful prime, she put round her head the crown of marriage at the same time as the imperial crown, and imperial marks of distinction, garments empearled and set with precious stones, . . . [she had] crowds of eunuchs [and], servants, . . . one after another reporting or carrying such things that make fast the desire of girls in general, [novelties] for beauty . . . [that] a woman among all these things shows manly virtue and drives to the height of wisdom, as much human and outside the door, as divine and ours, what wonder is more incredible? (229–31)

The periodic movement of the passage offers a capsule biography and prepares the hearers for the excellences that the author will most amplify. But it has what may have been a surprise ending for Tornikes' audience, not only in not rounding out the story they knew (that Anna did not marry the fiancé with whom she was co-crowned in girlhood), and not only in the detail that alerts us, tuned as we are to gender, that he calls her *virile* (for this, as we will see, was conventional), but rather in the accomplishments through which she *displays* her virile character, her learning.

Much of Tornikes' speech is devoted to Anna's learning, and even the sections on family, upbringing, and so on praise her learnedness, contributing to and confirming the historiographic persona of Anna that emerges in the *Alexiad*. In one sense, however, I would argue that Tornikes' representation of Anna's learning is radically different from her demonstration of it in her history. For he takes pains to represent her as highly skilled in profane literature or Greek *paideia*—what is "outside the door"—and in Christian philosophy—what is "divine and ours"—claiming in many passages that she used the former always in the service of the latter. Anna, on the other hand, though careful to depict her parents as defenders of orthodoxy, offers no apologia for her own expansive use of the "profane" tradition in what is in most ways a very self-conscious work. So, in the experience of reading the two texts (even allowing for their different genres) there is this intriguing difference concerning the tensions of theology and *paideia*.

The difference, in one sense, can be accounted for by considering the rhetorical situation of the two writers. Greekness, as every writer on the period points out, was the language of the cultivated, and critical to any man of letters who sought a position of consequence (Kennedy 170). Whether Greekness and Greek rhetoric were integral to Christianity, as the Cappadocchian Fathers Basil the Great and Gregory of Nanzianzus, among others, had made it, was a question that had to be reargued repeatedly. "What Christian Byzantium inherited from Hellenic antiquity," as Anthony Kaldellis has said, "was a set of tensions rather than a resolution" (*Hellenism* 165). Thus, as he crafts Anna's intellectual biography and describes the work that she commissioned in her scholarly circle, Tornikes takes pains to lay out, for example, the points of her Christian disagreement with Aristotle and what she takes and rejects from Plato concerning the engendering of the universe and soul. Robert Browning, who brought the speech to light in 1962, avers that, on his reading of this material, neither Anna nor Tornikes were strong philosophers (8). But I would suggest, rather, that the *rhetorical* work of this strand of the speech might be called an *epideixis philosophias*, a demonstration of Christian philosophy as it stands in relation to *thurathen paideia.* As Averil Cameron has said about an earlier context, "Christianity implied a structured system of explanation, covering everything from the natural world and the nature of history to anthropology and the nature of man" (199), and thus the style of this section of the speech bears resemblance to what Menander calls scientific hymns *(physiologikoi)* (qtd. in Russell and Wilson 13–15).

What we have of Anna's writing, on the other hand, is *Alexiad.* She writes it from within the space of Kecharitomene. She has not taken the veil, and her role as hereditary *ephor* of the convent is to preserve the instructions laid out in its *typikon* by her mother for its regimens and self-governance. Interestingly, the dedicatory prayer of the *typikon*, like documents for other monasteries, asks the mother of God to preserve the sisters and convert their nature to manly virtue (Galatariotou 288; Gautier 24–25).[2] From within this space, both apart from and a part of imperial and monastic culture, Anna demonstrates *paideia* in an untroubled way. She embeds in the history and praise of her father a display of a historian's use of Greek culture, placing herself in the tradition of Thucydides, Polybius, and Psellos. In a digression on the neglect of general education, she claims without qualification, "When I was released from . . . childish teaching and betook myself to the study of rhetoric and touched on philosophy and in between these sciences turned to the poets and historians, by means of these I polished the roughness of my speech" (Dawes 411). This strand of her work could be called an *epideixis paideias*, a demonstration of Greek learning. If Tornikes is connected with Anna by patronage and/or study of the Greek philosophical texts (whose use was always a delicate matter in Christian Byzantium), surely it would have been prudent, for audiences in any way linked to church, imperial family, or state, as well as himself and his subject, to make this defense for the Christian orthodoxy.

If these are the exigencies of the discourse, out of what available means can Tornikes praise Anna and make his case?

It would have been traditional in both Greek and Christian literature to praise a woman for accomplishments and actions showing temperance, modesty, care for husband and family, and generosity. For example, in the fourth century, Julian (who was to become emperor) praises the empress Eusebia (wife of Constantius) for these qualities. He uses Homer's praise of Penelope as his guide, and specifically contrasts the blessings of those virtues with the calamities arising from the qualities of women who acted like men (*gunaikôn andrizomenôn*), about whom speakers can amaze their audiences (338). Likewise, Tornikes, acknowledging his learned audience toward the end of his discourse, asks them not to cite from among the Greeks virile women whose virility is negative, when there are women (e.g., Anna and her daughter) who keep their nature and yet surpass men in virtue (317).

Resources for what I am calling the *epideixis philosophias* are also ample, going back at least to the fourth century and Basil's "Address to Young Men on the Right Use of Greek Literature," and include arguments from *manliness*, manly struggle, and topoi of battle. It would not require a lengthy detour to show that Basil draws upon a line of arguments that make rhetorical *paideia* itself a manly activity, preparatory to spiritual understanding as military exercise is to battle (sec. 2). But to perform its praise of a woman whose accomplishments and actions show not only the character and virtues of imperial and pious wives and mothers, but also *her* right use of Greek literature, the text draws on other conventions.

If we look at our opening passage alongside speeches in praise of other women, we can see at once that it is topos-laden. Consider, for example, the "life and encomium" of another imperial woman, the empress and saint Theodora, a restorer of image veneration in the ninth century. The author attributes these words to Theodora addressing her daughters:

> Even if you . . . have enjoyed the pleasures of imperial life [and] were resplendent with gold and decked out with precious jewels . . . and slaves have been given to you for your personal use, know that this present life comes to an end for every individual, but that the everlasting pleasures of the angels are promised to us if only we carry out God's ordinances. (Talbot 380)

What might be called the "virtue over jewels and beauty" topos, used to praise women since antiquity,[3] is evidently taken over for the praise of saintly women. This case shows Theodora arguing for giving wealth to the poor in order to gain wealth in heaven. For an example more nearly contemporaneous with Tornikes, we could look at Michael Psellos' encomium for his mother, in a passage of lament that makes explicit the opposition of feminine beauty products to masculine virtue:

> O, the painted lines and eye-liners unknown to my mother alone; O, the deceitful bloom and counterfeit whiteness, which paled in her presence and retreated from her. . . . O, for one who knew nothing feminine, except what was decreed by nature, but was in all other respects strong and manly in soul and even showed herself to be more resilient than the other portion of our species, prevailing over all men and women. (qtd. in Kaldellis, *Mothers* 64)

Yet another example, most likely a source text for both Psellos and Tornikes, is Gregory of Nanzianzus' Funeral Oration for his sister Gorgonia, using a version of the same topos. Gregory depicts his sister as modestly disdaining rich clothes, jewels, and makeup and, like Psellos, claims that she surpasses men in her spiritual practices (McCauley 107–10). The surpassing virtue of holy women is itself a topos and, as Elizabeth Clark has shown, there is even a rhetoric of shame, whereby Christian men are rebuked and exhorted to virtue through the surpassing manly conduct of women martyrs and saints (221–22).

These comparison passages were likely known to Tornikes. All three deploy values carried in the virtue over jewels and beauty products topos and in all three the virtue is spiritual. Two include the manliness of that virtue (as indeed Basil had done in his advice to young men) and the surpassing of men by women. But only in Tornikes' speech does the woman show masculine virtue by driving to the height of wisdom, both "human and outside the door" and "divine and ours," and *this* is the subject of wonder.

From antiquity, there are a few models of praising women for learnedness;[4] under the subject of nurture education was among Menander's headings for the praise of men, and it was standard in the curriculum of progymnasmatic exercises. But in Byzantium, where the education of women and Greek literature are concerned, another topos emerges. Tornikes asserts that Anna's parents were wary of *thurathen paideia* because of its polytheism and indecent erotica. But Anna "stole learning from the side from not unlettered servant eunuchs. Just as a maiden, seeing the bridegroom through some openings with secret eyes, so she secretly conversed with letters, when she was not with her mother" (243–45).

We find the same parental worry over the erotic dimension of Greek poetry in Gregory of Nyssa's *The Life of Macrina*, and according to Psellos, since his mother was not a man, education was forbidden her:

> Regarding the working of the loom . . . not a single woman could have competed with her, not even the one who is attested by Solomon in these matters. . . . The fact that she happened not to be a man by nature and that she was not allowed to study literature freely caused her anguish. Evading the attention of her mother whenever she could, she picked up the basic principles of letters from someone and soon began through her own efforts to join them together and form syllables and sentences. (qtd. in Kaldellis, *Mothers* 55)

In all three passages, we see that girls were forbidden to study literature; in two of them girls study on the sly. Of these, Anna is said to study Greek literature—in this instance on her own, and in a later passage in Tornikes' encomium, both with the consent of her mother and in accordance with the taste of her husband (263), whom God had chosen for her, overriding through events her childhood betrothal to a more handsome, but less intellectually compatible, mate (253). At the moment of the emperor's death, Anna and her husband are said to forget the imperial title (269), and Anna, not in order to escape from God but to find God, launches herself into profane wisdom (281). It cannot go without saying that this passage differs markedly from the later representation of Anna by historian Niketas Choniates. This is a brief mention, but one amplified in the secondary literature into our own time, of Anna conspiring to take the throne at this juncture and blaming nature for not making her a man

(Magoulias 8).[5] By contrast, Tornikes makes little of the moment of succession and represents Anna as an ideal woman and a virile scholar. That is, in the recollections of history and eulogy, the full range of rhetorical headings—power, virtue, character, achievements—come in for praise and blame through equivalences with biological and learned manliness.

But our last example from Psellos includes a reference to women's particular suitedness to weaving, which we saw in our first passage from Tornikes and which in my research appears as the most-used of topoi for praising Christian women—the allusion to Solomon and the biblical book of Proverbs. This is the passage variously translated from Hebrew into English as the virtuous (or excellent) or good wife (or good woman). In the Septuagint (Proverbs 31:10) she is *andreian*, manly, and this must be a significant source text for the praise of pious women as manly. All of her qualities in Proverbs—skill in weaving, wise household management, deference to husband—are much-quoted, and to praise a woman by saying that she surpasses the one praised by Solomon is conventional. Thus, Gregory of Nanzianzus in regard to Gorgonia says that to praise his sister on the points praised by Solomon would be to praise a statue for its shadow (McCauley 106).

Tornikes, too, uses this allusion. Toward the end of the speech, in a passage of lament similar to the one by Psellos, we find:

> O what a mouth is closed! What a mind is hidden! . . . A woman more virile than the most virile men both in wisdom and prudence! Soul firm and worthy of a man, enclosed in a body feminine and delicate. . . . O hands, instead of wool and distaff, taking in hand tablet and reed, and working at the loom, skillfully wove a beautiful web of words after the manner of the manly [*andreian*] woman who, according to Solomon, wove tunics for her husband [tunics] radiant for the mind, the garments [*peribolaia*] of speech. (315)

In this extraordinary passage, which comes after Tornikes has described Anna's history and letters, Anna is said to surpass men and women, and she excels in the spiritual and rhetorical work that cultural tradition has made manly. But Tornikes, using the Proverbs reference, figures writing through the womanly work of weaving. The figure represents a woman who engaged with *thurathen paideia,* or what is metaphorically outside the door, with what was literally outside the door, or the events of empire represented in the *Alexiad,* as the most traditional work inside the women's quarters. This is done with a sophistic touch: the woven garments are *peribolaia,* a rhetorical term, forms of which are used by Hermogenes and by Anna herself to denote amplitude (Dawes V.8.6.6; Kustas 12). This recalls the cluster of common Greek expressions for composing or textual work as clothing, weaving, and embroidery: *plekon* (weaving); *poikilos* (intricate or embroidered); and the noun and verb forms of this passage, *hufainô* (to weave or ply the loom) (Goldhill 161).

The merger here of literal and figural insides and outsides, activities, and genders recalls for me the point already made by Connolly. While gender is conventionally used to valorize or legitimate rhetorical activity, the texts do not permit a neat mapping of male and female where either words or deeds are concerned ("Virile" 84). Such thinking highlights the relation of manliness to issues of power and the conundrum of Tornikes speech. He can, as I have suggested, make his *epideixis philosophias* out of available arguments for the service of rhetoric for the spiritual struggle. More problematic is to praise a woman who lives "inside the door," in the private women's quarters in the nunnery, where women are required to overcome nature and be manly in private spiritual practice, but who excels in a male domain, what is outside the door, *thurathen paideia*. Calling attention to this paradoxical situation, he says that the voice of Anna's history seeks a Panhellenic theater, but is confined in too narrow a space (305, 307).

This speech, alongside an admittedly small sampling of praises of other women, shows the system of cultural materials through which Tornikes can praise a learned woman. Tornikes praises Anna by doing what Byzantine sophists did best—many things at once. He writes a speech that deploys traditional Greek forms, yet verges on something new, an intellectual biography of an orthodox woman; and he constructs a woman who preferred study—but in balance with the traditional womanly virtues—to political power. The well-documented rhetorical practices of this "third Sophistic," to use Kaldellis' phrase (*Hellenism* 225), are all in evidence in the speech: the performance of classical Greek from elements of diction to allusion and genre (Kennedy 169), the negotiation of Hellenism and matters of faith (Magdalino 366), and the habit of indirection or figured speech (Quandahl and Jarratt 317–19; Walker 62–64). To these practices could be added one more, stated as an addendum to the logological analogies of Burke's *Rhetoric of Religion*. It might run like this: in Byzantium, words about men in the biological realm are said about women's and men's bodies, actions, words, and relationships to the extra-worldly. More than any other borrowings, these simultaneous identifications and divisions make clear Burke's view of the classifying feature of language itself as emblematic of the human scene—a scene of infractions and achievements (Quandahl 13). In the texts we have seen, *andreia* is assigned to Burke's nature (biology) and also to a realm that hovers between nature and the sociopolitical (something like temperament—as in girls' susceptibility to the passions of the poets). Manliness is assigned to Burke's sociopolitical, both as scene of actions and actions themselves (grooming, weaving, governing, running a convent), and, clearly, to the supernatural. Manliness is linked to the verbal realm, both rhetorical and theological, where words about words and words about God shift among the analogous, complementary, and "polar" (Burke's "moralized" opposites [*Rhetoric of Religion* 23]). Most intriguing is the realm of training and study, actions further distant from biology than temperament and more linked with trained habit or character, where Anna, in Tornikes' eulogy, surpasses men and women. *Andreia*, it seems, infiltrates, authorizes, and disciplines all of the terministic orders. To track these gendered equivalences—asking Burke's productive question *what equals what?*—in the genre of praise and blame can offer much to the current revival of interest in epideictic rhetoric.[6]

Notes

[1] All Tornikes references are to the edition by Darrouzès. Translations are mine.

[2] An English translation of the *typikon* is available in Thomas and Hero. I cite Gautier, whose Greek text and French translation of this passage show the sense of making the feminine masculine.

[3] For example, see Lucian's praise of Panthea in "Essays in Portraiture" (279).

[4] Lucian, for example, praises Panthea's eloquence and knowledge (283–85).

[5] For a reading of receptions of Anna's history and biography, see Quandahl and Jarratt (304–10).

[6] Evident in this year's RSA seminar topic.

Works Cited

Basil of Caesarea. "Address to Young Men on the Right Use of Greek Literature." *Essays on the Study and Use of Poetry by Plutarch and Basil the Great.* Ed. Frederick Morgan Padelford. *Yale Studies in English* 15 (1902): 99–120.

Brody, Miriam. *Many Writing: Gender, Rhetoric and the Rise of Composition*. Carbondale: Southern Illinois UP, 1993.

Browning, Robert. "An Unpublished Funeral Oration on Anna Comnena." *Studies on Byzantine History, Literature and Education*. London: Variorum Reprints, 1977. 1–12.

Burke, Kenneth. *A Rhetoric of Motives*. Berkeley: U of California P, 1969.

———. *The Rhetoric of Religion*. Berkeley: U of California P, 1970.

———. "What Are the Signs of What?" *Language as Symbolic Action*. Berkeley: U of California P, 1966. 359–79.

Burrus, Virginia. *The Sex Lives of Saints: An Erotics of Ancient Hagiography.* Philadelphia: U of Pennsylvania P, 2004.

Cameron, Averil. "How to Read Heresiology." Martin and Miller 193–212.

Clark, Elizabeth. "Sex, Shame and Rhetoric: En-Gendering Early Christian Ethics." *Journal of the American Academy of Religion* 59.2 (1991): 221–45. *JSTOR*. Web. 11 Jan. 2009.

Connolly, Joy. "Like the Labors of Heracles: *Andreia* in Greek Culture under Rome." *Andreia: Studies in Classical Antiquity.* Ed. Ralph M. Rosen and Ineke Sluiter. Boston: Brill, 2003. 287–317.

———. "Virile Tongues: Rhetoric and Masculinity." *A Companion to Roman Rhetoric*. Ed. William Dominik and John Hall. Malden: Blackwell, 2007. 83–97.

Darrouzès, Jean. *George et Dèmètrios Tronikès: Lettres et Discours.* Paris: Èditions du Centre National de la Recherche Scientifique, 1970.

Dawes, Elizabeth A. *The* Alexiad *of Anna Comnena*. London: Kegan Paul, 2003.

Delierneux, Nathalie. "Virilité et Sainté Féminine Dans L'Hagiographie Orientale Du IVe au VIIe Siècle." *Byzantion: Revue Internationale des Études Byzantines* 67 (1977): 179–243.

Galatariotou, Catia. "Byzantine Women's Monastic Communities: The Evidence of the *Typika*." *Jahrbuch der österreichischen byzantinistik* 38 (1988): 263–90.

Gautier, Paul. "Le Typikon de la Théotokos Kécharitôménè." *Revue des Études Byzantines* 43 (1985): 5–165.

Goldhill, Simon. *The Poet's Voice: Essays on Poetics and Greek Literature*. Cambridge: Cambridge UP, 1991.

Gregory of Nyssa. *The Life of Macrina*. Trans. W. K. Lowther Clark. London: SPCK, 1916. *Medieval Sourcebook*. Web. 1 Apr. 2010.

Julian. "Panegyric in Honour of Eusebia." *The Works of the Emperor Julian*. Ed. and trans. Wilmer Cave France Wright. Cambridge: Harvard UP, 1954. 273–345.

Kaldellis, Anthony. *Hellenism in Byzantium*. Cambridge: Cambridge UP, 2007.

———. *Mothers and Sons, Fathers and Daughters: The Byzantine Family of Michael Psellos*. Notre Dame: U of Notre Dame P, 2006.

Kennedy, George. *Classical Rhetoric and Its Christian and Secular Tradition from Ancient to Modern Times*. Chapel Hill: U of North Carolina P, 1980.

Kustas, George. *Studies in Byzantine Rhetoric*. Thessalonike: Patriarchal Institute for Patristic Studies, 1973.

Lucian. "Essays in Portraiture." Trans. Austin Morris Harmon. *Lucian in Eight Volumes*. Cambridge: Harvard UP, 1969. 257–95.

Magdalino, Paul. *The Empire of Manuel I Komnenos, 1143–1180*. Cambridge: Cambridge UP, 1993.

Magoulias, Henry J. *O City of Byzantium, Annals of Niketas Choniates*. Detroit: Wayne State UP, 1984.

Martin, Dale B. Introduction. Martin and Miller 3–21.

Martin, Dale B., and Patricia Cox Miller. *The Cultural Turn in Late Ancient Studies*. Durham, NC: Duke UP, 2005.

McCauley, Leo P., SJ. "On His Sister, St. Gorgonia." Trans. Leo P. McCauley, SJ, John J. Sullivan, CSSp, Martin R. P. McGuire, and Roy J. Deferrari. *Funeral Orations by Saint Gregory Nazianzen and Saint Ambrose*. Washington: Catholic U of America P, 1953. 101–18.

Miller, Patricia Cox. "Is There a Harlot in This Text? Hagiography and the Grotesque." Martin and Miller 87–102.

Quandahl, Ellen. "'It's Essentially as Though This Were Killing Us': Kenneth Burke on Mortification and Pedagogy." *Rhetoric Society Quarterly* 27.1 (Winter 1997): 5–22.

Quandahl, Ellen, and Susan Jarratt. "'To Recall Him . . . Will be a Subject of Lamentation': Anna Comnena as Rhetorical Historiographer." *Rhetorica* 26.3 (2008): 301–35.

Russell, D. A., and N. G. Wilson. *Menander Rhetor.* Oxford: Clarendon Press, 1981.

Septuagint. Prov. 31. *Internet Sacred Text Archive*. N.d. Web. 22 Feb. 2010.

Shaw, Brent. "Body/Power/Identity: Passions of the Martyrs." *Journal of Early Christian Studies* 4.3 (1996): 269–312.

Talbot, Alice-Mary, ed. "Life of St. Theodora the Empress." Trans. Martha P. Vinson. *Byzantine Defenders of Images*. Washington: Dumbarton Oaks Research Library Collection, 1998. 353–82.

Thomas, John, and Angela Constantinides Hero, eds. "Kecharitomene: Typikon of Empress Irene Doukaina Komnene for the Convent of the Mother of God Kecharitomene in Constantinople." Trans. Robert Jordan. *Byzantine Monastic Foundation Documents: A Complete Translation of the Surviving Founders' Typika and Testaments*. Washington: Dumbarton Oaks Research Library and Collection, 2004. 649–724.

Walker, Jeffrey. "These Things I Have Not Betrayed: Michael Psellos' Encomium of His Mother as a Defense of Rhetoric." *Rhetorica* 22.1 (Winter 2004): 49–101.

18

Rhetorical Translation and the Space between Languages

Rebecca Lorimer

The act of translation, between languages, texts, or people, is not typically considered to be rhetorical. Many translators consider their practice to be one of poetic choice—choosing among multiple meanings, or choosing appropriate and beautiful words and figures to best bring the original text to a new language. In one exception, translator Suzanne Jill Levine understands translation more rhetorically, claiming that "a good translation, as with all rhetoric, aims to (re)produce an effect, to persuade a reader" (4). But translation itself, as an entirely unique literate act, is also rhetorical beyond the reproduction of persuasive effects. This is not to exclude persuasion from rhetoric's purview, but to highlight the possibility that translation can function rhetorically as a kind of engagement with consequences beyond poetic or persuasive effect.

Translation traffics in linguistic difference. By its very nature, it makes use of linguistic similarity to distinguish an "us" from a "them," finding commonalities across languages and cultures in order to create further separation: a shared dialect designates familiar language-speakers from linguistic outsiders; a translated text in a new language is separated and made distinct from its original. In the movement between languages, identification and division appear together, and the simultaneity of these contradictory impulses is Burke's "characteristic invitation to rhetoric" (25). In other words, the slippage between linguistic concord and controversy is pronounced in translation, highlighting just how rhetorical the activity may be.

Translation is rhetorical because it is an activity of linguistic conflict. In *A Rhetoric of Motives,* Burke asks "who is to say, once and for all, just where 'cooperation' ends and one partner's 'exploitation' of the other begins" when rhetors "collaborate in an enterprise to which they contribute different kinds of services and from which they derive different amounts and kinds of profit" (25). Burke's inquiry is an apt description of rhetorical translation in which language-users bring their linguistic "services" to the collaborative enterprise of meaning making. And because languages are rarely situated as equals—each carries historically and geographically contingent levels of power—translation is often a collaboration of uneven contributions. In this way, "cooperation" and "exploitation" overlap in the scene of translation, as language-users barter for power and influence in the movement between languages. Therefore, a more rhetorical understanding of translation highlights the movement between, the ambiguous in-between space where multiple languages dwell, moving beyond conventional understandings of translation as a bridge and instead bringing into view the full architecture and exigency of multilingual rhetorical situations.

A Bridge

Often, translation is understood as a bridging of cultures through language, a textual hand off of sorts from an original language writer to a "target-language" reader, with the translator doing the passing. If taken literally, one could imagine two lingual representatives meeting in the middle of a bridge that spans the gap between two cultural landmasses, the translator waiting in the middle to hand the text from one to the other. This understanding of translation as a cultural crossing is supported by a long tradition. For example, in an 1813 lecture, "On the Different Methods of Translation," often cited as one of the most foundational in translation studies, author Friedrich Schleiermacher speaks of "moving" the text along a continuum between a writer from one language and the reader from another (233). This continuum acts as a bridge between the two, a well-suited image for ensuring the writer and reader do not "miss each other" as they travel from one side to the other. Schleiermacher adds, "The source-language author and the target-language reader must either meet at a middle-point, which is always that of the translator, or the one must cross over to the camp of the other" (229).

In this way, much translation scholarship works from an assumption that translation's potential is realized in the cultural bridge. As Walter Benjamin notes in his essay "The Task of the Translator":

> The traditional concepts in any discussion of translations are fidelity and license—the freedom of faithful reproduction and, in its service, fidelity to the word. These ideas seem to be no longer serviceable to a theory that looks for other things in a translation than reproduction of meaning. (78)

In other words, to look for "other things" in translation than fidelity, accuracy, or "reproduction of meaning," one must theorize around—below and above—traditional talk of moving a text across a cultural or linguistic reader/writer continuum. To realize the rhetorical function of translation then, translation must be situated more dynamically.

The Space Between

This more dynamic situation is constituted in the bridge's surroundings. What might happen if, when meeting each other in the middle of the cultural bridge, the writer, reader, and translator looked down? What might they see? And what might happen if they fell, leaped, or heaved the text-to-be-passed into the space below? Benjamin says that in the act of translation "meaning plunges from abyss to abyss until it threatens to become lost in the bottomless depths of language" (82). Gayatri Spivak calls translation the place "where meaning hops into the spacey emptiness between two named historical languages" (178). A rhetorical view of translation might take these spaces, the abysses of meaning, as the focus of engagement, allowing meanings to spring forth from the space created between the texts. In other words, translation is constituted not only in movement from one language to another, but in the generative site that movement creates.

This site is the in-between, a gap that actually prevents simple horizontal shifts of syntax from one text to another. It is a space cleared for the potential of translation to do more. For, as Benjamin notes, "any translation which intends to perform a transmitting function cannot transmit anything but information—hence, something inessential" (69). He calls this "transmitting function" the "hallmark of bad translations," marking this function as one that rhetorically framed translation would avoid. Therefore, a rhetorical understanding of translation gives shape to the space between languages by considering what is invented in this space and how that invention occurs.

Examples from widely different moments in history show rhetoricians understanding translation as an exercise in invention. In classical Roman rhetoric, both Quintilian and Cicero take up translation as a generative pedagogical method. Cicero recommends translation exercises for the inventive potential of rewriting a foreign text in one's own language. Cicero's Crassus explains, "when rendering in Latin what [he] had read in Greek, [he] could use the finest words that were nevertheless common, but also that, by imitating Greek words, [he] could coin certain others that were new to our language" (92). Here, for Cicero's Crassus, translation is an exercise in both eloquence and invention, searching in another language for fine words and creating new ones in the process. Quintilian echoes Cicero almost exactly, explaining that translating the Greek would help Latin speakers "use the very best words," and "inventing a great number and variety of [figures]" would necessarily follow "because the Roman tongue differs greatly from that of the Greeks" (408). The invention, Quintilian says, is necessarily forced upon the writer, as he attempts to transfer words from one text to another. But while Cicero and Quintilian's exercises in translation acknowledge the ability to invent between difference, they still, in a way, rest on the assumption that translation's rhetorical potential is realized by moving text or content across the bridge from Greek to Latin.

Much more recently, Damián Baca explores how speaking from multiple rhetorical traditions and histories is a process of invention. Using Gloria Anzaldua's theory of mestiza consciousness, he considers what is created between multiple languages and worldviews: "Contemporary Mestiz@ rhetorics . . . enact a strategy of invention between different ways of knowing. Crossing between comparative and conflicting elements creates a symbolic space beyond the mere coming together of two halves" (5). Baca acknowledges a symbolic space between languages and also suggests that this space offers more than a simple completion of previously unfinished halves. For him, in this space "collective expressions merge" or become hybrid. Thus, what is "beyond the mere coming together of two halves" is the potential for "inventing between." Certainly Baca points to the rhetorical potential in the spaces between, but he seems to keep translation in a lateral realm—two sides meeting, meshing, and coming together—leaving us the question of how, exactly, that invention occurs.

A rhetorical understanding of translation might emphasize the agency of this in-between space itself, or how the space acts on the translator and translation. Both Thomas Rickert and Debra Hawhee offer theories of kairos that, when used to build a framework around the space between languages, show how this invention might take place. In his chapter "Invention in the Wild," Thomas Rickert foregrounds invention's "spatial quality and [shows] its necessity for understanding invention as an ambient and not a subjective activity" (72). Here Rickert focuses on the space itself as the source of inventive activity, shifting agency out of the hands of the subject and into the hands of the situation or setting in which the subject may find him or herself. Thus the space, not the subject, produces or creates. Applied to an analysis of translation, then, Rickert's notion of kairos shifts the agency of translation away from the subject translator and into the translation space itself. Rickert explains that this shift of agency is not "an impediment for a rational, willing subject to take decisive advantage of the kairotic moment, [but] is actually generative, a catalyst" (78). Thus, the site where the translator collides with multiple cultures and languages is in and of itself generative. In this way, the abyss of meaning below the cultural bridge, as a space between languages, text, and translating subject, produces rhetorical possibilities. This "middle place" is described by Rickert as "not a stable realm between poles, but an always on the move, temporally unstable, and emergent moment" (76). This description is certainly appropriate for the visual conception of translation built so far—if the "poles" designate the far reaches of the cultural bridge, then the space in the middle is a "temporally unstable," "emergent moment" "always on the move."

It is the movement necessitated by multiplicity that enlivens the space between languages. Debra Hawhee suggests that kairos "enables a consideration of 'invention-in-the-middle,' a space-time which marks the emergence of a pro-visional subject, one that works on—and is worked on by—

the situation." Here she is drawing on the notion of the middle voice—neither passive nor active—to understand the interaction between the subject, which in this case we might consider the translator, and the kairotic situation, in this case the space between languages. Hawhee continues, saying, "*kairos* offers a tool through which to articulate invention away from notions of rhetorical beginnings, with specific 'ends' in sight (persuasion for example), and towards notions of discursive movement, the inbetweeness of rhetoric" (18). In other words, for her, kairos can expand rhetoric beyond one-way persuasion from subject to audience, and instead highlight the dynamic interaction between the subject and the situation. It is in this way that kairos is both helpful and, according to Hawhee, "critical" to understanding what is produced by kairotic spaces since "invention-in-the-middle" "marks the opportunity for a subject to produce discourse" even as one is being produced by it (18). In other words, translation is rhetorical *because* it encapsulates and necessitates a kairotic moment—the middle space, the in-between—which allows for production of certain outcomes.

The abyss of meaning, then—shaped by a spatial understanding of kairos and enlivened by the reality of movement between languages—is a site of rhetorical engagement. This gap under the bridge and between multiple languages, created by translation, clears space to make or do something more than move a text from one language to another. Instead, the space of the abyss is itself ever-moving with an energy that is constituted by its environment in tandem with the subject or translator who has created it.

What Is Produced

There is little limit to what might be produced in translation. The energy of this space might produce textual fragments, shards of languages and narratives flying high above the conventional bridge of translation, reforming into new permutations of languages and ideas previously unimagined. These theoretical possibilities foreground a more material outcome as translation scholars such as Lawrence Venuti propose translation's ability to bring exposure to new languages and literatures or produce new literary or linguistic products.

This is not to say that what is rhetorically produced in translation is made always for cooperation and understanding. In fact, it is important to push against the notion that all cultural collisions produce heightened acceptance or insight. One might look to colonial spaces, for example, to see translation creating outcomes both productive and destructive. Consider the historical narrative around the translator Malintzin, a Mayan woman educated at an Aztec *calmecac*, who served as interpreter and translator for conquistador Hernando Cortez, eventually becoming his mistress and giving birth to a son that Mexican myth says was the first child of *mestizaje* (Baca). Malintzin stood between the Aztecs and the ominous overtures of Cortez as she translated among Spanish, Maya, and Nahuatl, "inventing between the historical memories engrained in each language" (111). Malintzin, as translator, facilitated communication across the colonizers and soon-to-be-colonized even as she may have facilitated the destruction of many indigenous cultures and the eventual creation of a new mestizo culture.

Burke calls war the "most tragically ironic of all divisions, or conflicts, wherein millions of cooperative acts go into the preparation for one single destructive act" (22). The "disease of cooperation" that was Malintzin's movement between languages shows translation at its most rhetorical, not because Malintzin used persuasion as she translated, but because the situation produced, simultaneously, harmonious and destructive outcomes (22). In small ideological steps or through outright mass murder, Cortez and the Spanish conquistadors were able to colonize Mesoamerica through Malintzin's help, which, centuries later, produced the nation of Mexico.

Baca notes that Malintzin is both cursed as a symbolic betrayer in Mexican history, but regarded by some who have attempted to "vindicate [her] from her negative mythology" as a woman in a potentially impossible position (110). Thinking about her acts of translation in a rhetorical sense allows us to consider Malintzin's agency as she made choices in the movement between languages, and we can equally consider the agency of the space itself, as the kairos of translation produced unimagined outcomes that shaped both the memories of the translating subject Malintzin as well as the historical record of colonization. So while it is true that Malintzin certainly acted as a persuasive rhetor in this case, she used, and was used by, rhetoric to create and destroy, influence outcomes and invent possibilities inside the space between languages.

A rhetorical understanding of translation allows us to consider both the agency of translators as they make choices between languages, as well as the ways in which these translators are acted on by historical space and time. Even as kairotic situations that are simultaneously productive and destructive, these multilingual spaces generate meaning, effects, and outcomes. Rhetorical translation, as a making, starkly contradicts commonplace notions of language and meaning "lost in translation." From a rhetorical point of view, language and meaning are not only found in translation, they are created.

Works Cited

Baca, Damián. *Mestiz@ Scripts, Digital Migration, and the Territories of Writing*. New York: Palgrave Macmillan, 2008.

Benjamin, Walter. "The Task of the Translator." *Illuminations*. Ed. Hannah Arendt. Trans. Harry Zohn. New York: Schocken, 1969.

Burke, Kenneth. *A Rhetoric of Motives*. Berkeley: U of California P, 1969.

Cicero, Marcus Tullius. *On the Ideal Orator*. Ed. James M. May and Jakob Wisse. New York: Oxford UP, 2001.

Hawhee, Debra. "Kairotic Encounters." *Perspectives on Rhetorical Invention*. Ed. Janet M. Atwill and Janice M. Lauer. Knoxville: U of Tennessee P, 2002. 16–35.

Levine, Suzanne J. *The Subversive Scribe: Translating Latin American Fiction*. St. Paul, MN: Graywolf P, 1991.

Quintilian. "Institutes of Oratory." *The Rhetorical Tradition: Readings from Classical Times to the Present*. Ed. Patricia Bizzell and Bruce Herzberg. Boston: Bedford/ St. Martin's, 2001. 364–428.

Rickert, Thomas. "Invention in the Wild: On Locating *Kairos* in Space-Time." *The Locations of Composition*. Ed. Christopher J. Keller and Christian R. Weisser. Albany: State U of New York P, 2007. 71–89.

Schleiermacher, Friedrich. "On the Different Methods of Translation." Ed. Doug Robinson. *Western Translation Theory From Herodotus to Nietzche*. Manchester, UK: St. Jerome Publishing, 1997. 225–38.

Spivak, Gayatri Chakravorty. "The Politics of Translation." *Destabilizing Theory: Contemporary Feminist Debates*. Ed. Michéle Barrett and Anne Phillips. Palo Alto: Stanford UP, 1992. 177–200.

Venuti, Lawrence. "Translation, Community, Utopia." *The Translation Studies Reader*. Ed. Lawrence Venuti. New York: Routledge, 2000. 99–147.

19

Eiromenē and *Katestrammenē*

Styles in Opposition

Kyle Schlett

To a typical speaker of modern American English, the word *opposition* often bespeaks of willful, polarized conflict: two parties representing not only different views, but antithetical perspectives vying for supremacy at the expense—if not elimination—of the opposing other. Boxers in the ring, candidates at the debate, estranged spouses in the courtroom, all reflect and reinforce a perspective of opposition as conflict. In fact, it is an exaggerated manifestation of such opposition that the October 30, 2010 Rally to Restore Sanity and/or Fear satirized, where many picket signs illustrated the absurdity of polarized discourse with modest demands like, "I want more tortillas when I order fajitas at a restaurant." Even the ambiguous use of conjunctions in the rally's title parodied the kind of exaggerated perspective of opposition that currently dominates American political discourse.

Since its apocryphal introduction over 2,500 years ago, the word *dialectic* has, like many useful terms, gotten rather broadly applied, reinterpreted, and adapted to various philosophical perspectives. Not all casting of opposites is, classically speaking, dialectic. When Aristotle opposes two rhetorical styles against each other in book 3, chapter 9 of his *Rhetoric*, it is not as *dialektos*, but as *endoxos*; that is, the opposed items (as Aristotle would have his audience believe) are not up for exploration through debate, but are accepted. By using the particle *mén* and not leaving the work entirely up to the verb construction, Aristotle takes pains to reinforce that the terms are not in doubt: there are but two ways to connect lexical units in speech and prose, one of which is clearly to be preferred. One might reasonably consider his summary definition of terms premature and disingenuous; after all, if the categories are so clearly understood, why must he explain them, in which case, even more is at stake in his representation of the terms of opposition. Regardless, one is obligated to recognize his intention to polarize, and when that aim is expressed by a mind as broadly respected as Aristotle's, an apparent incongruity in the terms of opposition warrants reconsideration. It is a key assumption of this essay that just such an incongruity has been repeatedly carried from transitional (from *Attic* to *Koiné*) classical Greek into English. It is the aim of this essay to provide that reexamination. Naturally, all translation involves loss and compromise, but one must constantly interrogate the terms of that compromise according to his or her own values and goals.

It is in the context of those competing values that consistently constructed oppositions in a passage, such as the one presently under consideration, reveal their most pressing significance: the vitality of communication and cooperation across disciplines. To assess the bases for previous scholars' translational decisions is neither productive nor within my scope of clairvoyance, but the mastery of an archaic foreign language requires focus and dedication, virtues that can obscure or de-emphasize the valuation of literary concerns, especially among translators who work primarily with what might be regarded as nonpoetic texts. In weighing various concerns, such translators may easily (and quite understandably) discount the so-called practical for the poetic. Ultimately, however, human experience and the writing that is supposed to reflect it are not so easily compartmentalized. Poets may calculate practical concerns into their poetry, just as philosophers may enhance their speculation by the manipulation of formal elements. As long as the creators of texts write eclectically (e.g., without regard for supposed rules of their forms), scholars who study those texts will need to approach them humbly, ever conscious that another scholarly perspective may clarify the seemingly obscure.

To contextualize the relevant opposition from Aristotle's *Rhetoric*, I will quote Kennedy's translation (214) of an entire (but short) section (3.9.1, 1409a29):

> The *lexis* [of formal speech and artistic prose] is necessarily either strung-on [*eiromenē*] and given unity by connection, like the preludes in dithyrambs, or turned-down [*katestrammenē*] and like the antistrophes of the ancient poets.

One of this translator's strengths throughout the text—namely, his tendency to calque confusing or idiomatic passages at least as often as he tries to conduct them into a modern English idiom—also serves as a kind of red flag in this passage to alert the reader to the fact that something unusual is happening; for the observant reader will tend to wonder what makes a particular word or phrase so hard to adapt, especially in the case of such central terms. That reader might even think that he or she can deduce what a "strung-on" style looks like, but the phrase "turned-down" (in reference to rhetorical style) would be entirely cryptic if not set in contrast to the first, and even with the opposition offers several tantalizing possibilities.

Earlier attempts often abandoned the metaphorical nature of "*eiromenen kai toi sundesmoi mian*" altogether, exchanging it for such bland phrasing as "continuous and united by connecting particles" (Freese 387), "free-running, with its parts united by nothing except the connecting words" (Roberts 132), or "running, the whole made one only by a connecting word between part and part" (Cooper 202). One may credit Roberts and Cooper for at least retaining some figurative sense to the passage, albeit an inappropriately dynamic one (in the sense that they suggest significant physical motion where no such connotation exists in the original metaphor). Their compensating is certainly understandable, since "running" has long served to communicate a kind of necessary continuity in an English-speaking context, often with a negative connotation (e.g., "running one's mouth" or "my nose didn't stop running"—in both cases suggesting something that has trouble stopping). The normally reliable Freese wandered farthest off the beaten path on this one, distilling the metaphor to the much more abstract "continuous."

By contrast, John Gillies most closely approximates Kennedy's "strung-on" with his "linked in a long, extended chain" (Gillies 393). In some ways, one might even find the imaginative perspicuity of Gillies' translation preferable for at least providing an image of a tangible object. While Cope taps into the same image of items that are linked (to do a little metaphor-mixing of my own), the word "concatenated" tends much more toward the concept of *connection* and hardly suggests any additional images, other than a translator with a large vocabulary and perhaps a pipe (Cope 92).

There is plenty of support from other texts to suggest "linked on a chain" as a reasonable translation: Eurymachus' gift to Penelope, the *êlektroisin eermenos*, or necklace *strung* with pieces of amber (Homer, *Odyssey* 18.296), but the question is not whether the translation is merely reasonable, but whether there might not be alternatives of equal potential validity within the context. A word-by-word investigation of the original Greek suggests that the search for just such an alternative for *eiromenen* as "fastened together in rows" might prove beneficial. One can easily understand why those translating this phrase into English might happily avoid the mention of rows. For one thing, it lacks a substantial cultural analogy. While a modern audience can quickly get a feel for how beads strung along a chain can resemble certain kinds of phonemes, words, or phrases "strung" together in close, tight fashion—an image that probably retains its currency from craft day at summer camp—the idea of bound-together rows lacks a familiar analog.

Notice the use of the word *rows* in the definition. Certainly one may refer to the alignment of beads on a chain as a row, although the use of its plural form may strike one as odd in regard to the act of stringing a single chain. Even more intriguing—and potentially telling—is the choice of verb *to fasten* in this definition. We may think of stringing a chain strictly as an act of dropping some bored-through item onto the chain, but what if one wants to affix the bead or gem at some point on the necklace? Certainly one could call a means of making them stationary—whether through melding, tying knots, or some other method—a kind of fastening. Perhaps this is what Gillies and Kennedy had in mind when they stopped, respectively, at "linked" or "strung-on," but the combination of these two terms might well prompt, first, a workable countertheory and, second, research to confirm or debunk that theory.

That theory, in brief, suggests that Aristotle's intended metaphor may have been designed to picture something much more complex than simply stringing together beads on a line, wherein the individual units conjoin to create a system with both "horizontal" and "vertical" elements. The details of how the elements of that system might interact will unfold later.

One complicating factor in such investigation of this rather unusual term is its similarity to a conjugation of the common Attic Greek verb *eromai* (to ask or inquire), which can also resemble some forms of *eramai* (to love). However, the labor can still produce some fruitful possibilities. A parenthetical note to Cope's elusive "concatenated" hints at one of these: "the sentences loosely strung together, connected solely by connecting particles, as *de* and *kai*, like onions on a string" (92). While onions are generally tied on a single line, the method by which they are tied is one of overlapping and interweaving, suggesting something more complicated than a single, threaded straight line. Even the bundled appearance of tied onions suggests a complex image not reflected by any of the translations, even Cope's. To improve the validity of this image, it would not be entirely inaccurate to describe the layout as bound together in rows. Furthermore, communication with one scholar clarified the definition of the word in question as, "strung or woven together like a necklace or garland," suggesting at least an even footing for the image of something wound and bound (Fenno). Perhaps he was thinking of a phrase from Pindar's Nemean Ode Number 7: "*eirein stephanous elaphron anaboleo*" ("it is easy to weave garlands") (7.112).

Of course, garlands are not the only things that get woven. Reeds get intertwined to make baskets, hats, and other goods. Methods of net-making could definitely be described as weaving. Even precious metals were often interlaced for decorative effects. But the most common intertwining (and perhaps least obvious to a postindustrial mind) would involve articles of clothing, whose means of manufacture would be a much more common aspect of daily life to Aristotle and his predecessors. Dr. Jonathan Fenno's responses to my query speculated that an etymological chain (if you will) may have linked back to such weaving, "which was once a common metaphor for certain kinds of poetry." What does that "once" mean, though? It is certainly conceivable that an idiom that was common when Aeschylus or Pindar were writing, about one hundred years before Aristotle was teaching, could have fallen out of usage by the time the philosopher penned his *Rhetoric*. As it turns out in this case, *once* may not be so far removed as "once upon a time." Apollonius Rhodius was likely writing his *Argonautica* at some point in the late third century BCE. A passage within it describing a charm of Medea's may shed some light: "*to rh'eg eksanelousa thuodei katheto mitre, / hete hoi ambrosioisi peri stethessin* ***eerto***," translated by R. C. Seaton as, "And she brought the charm forth and placed it in the fragrant band which ***engirdled*** her, just beneath her bosom, divinely fair" (3.867–68, 252–53). The "fragrant band" to which he is referring is alluded to earlier in the passage, "She donned a beautiful robe, fitted with well-bent clasps." Nowhere else in the passage is she described as donning any other accessories, other than the veil on her head, so the most reasonable conclusion is that the participle refers to the garment itself, which, incidentally, is not described as anything resembling a rope or garland arrangement. I assert that it is the robe whose threads themselves represent the things fastened together in rows.

In drawing a link from rhetorical style to something as intricately woven as cloth, one should not lose sight of the references that Aristotle himself makes, even as we remain mindful of weaving's usefulness as a metaphor of poetry. Even though he is concerned primarily with the lexis of rhetoricians, he deliberately illustrates the stylistic poles via dithyramb and antistrophe. As Egbert Bakker points out, Aristotle's inclusion of the iambic lines suggests a more direct link between the meter of the poet and the period of the rhetorician (37). Even the parallel structure by which he contrasts periodic and "strung-on" styles only intensifies this connection to poetic forms. Is this mere coincidence, or is he engaged, as seems more likely, in a layered pun? If the latter, one must also confront the possibility that it could be directed and purposeful in illustrating a larger point. Perhaps an assessment of the opposing term will shed some light.

If *eiromenē* is difficult to approach due to its deceptively simple meaning and resemblance to forms of other verbs, *katestrammenē* is elusive for its rarity (not even eight occurrences for every hundred thousand words of non-Aristotelian text, according to Tufts University's Perseus Project) and complete lack of analogy to current English idiom. What is one to make of Kennedy's source-language faithfulness that renders the problematic English phrase "turned down"? I say "problematic" because it can be difficult to move beyond very familiar, but very misleading, English meanings. Clearly, it would be difficult to refer to a rhetorical style as "refused," in the manner in which Aristotle describes it. If we try to think of the term as a metaphor, it might summon images of turned-down bedsheets (maybe even a mint on the pillow), or the tail of a "bad dog." As one might imagine, Aristotle had something quite different in mind, but what it is can be difficult to determine from other well-known English translations.

In order to cope with this unfamiliar term, many translators employ a strategy of turning it into a compound phrase, and there is a remarkable amount of similarity among them (leading one to question the degree to which later translators, having no idea what to do with it, fell back on precedent). The first half of Gillies' rendering of the phrase, "collected in itself and periodic," understandably attracts no followers, although Cooper's "returning upon itself" also sounds as if "*lexin katestrammenen*" might have some psychological issues or is trying to find its way out of a fun house. For a modern, English-speaking audience, these vaguely self-destructive sounding phrases are nearly as indecipherable as if they had remained in Greek characters. By contrast, Freese and—in the form of a parenthetical note—Cope both embrace the adjective *periodic*. It is easily enough understood, as something broken down into manageable chunks. The problem is that Aristotle himself introduces a form of the word *periodos* (which originally held implications of a path around for flanking purposes) in the beginning of section 3, in a sentence that—with this translation—would sound something like, "the periodic style is something that occurs in periods." This clearly does not work unless one retreats to a more figurative interpretation of *periodos*. For obvious reasons, this one died with Freese, who was one of the few who did not even offer a second half of a compound phrase on which to fall back.

Even more popular (attracting Cope, Cooper, and Roberts) was the use of the word "compact," which communicates a spatially self-contained unit but, once again, sacrifices figurative depth to do so. Aristotle may eventually be heading into a discussion of the efficiency of this style, but the term itself does not really carry any such thought with it up front.

The problem with trying to express something more closely resembling the cultural baggage of the term is that, first, that baggage is generally negative in connotation and, second, it is grounded, in an almost literal sense, in a physical aspect of Greek culture. The first of these points is evidenced in the Greek etymology of our own English word, *catastrophe*. In his third hymn, Homer uses a phrase containing the same root: "*possi **katastrepsas** ôsêi halos en pelagessin*" ("***overturn me*** and thrust me down with his feet in the depths of the sea")—a passage intended to express Delos' fear of the scorn of Apollo and the disastrous effects that could accompany that scorn (3.70–75). The threat here is a kind of one-two punch of getting plowed over and then getting plowed under. If Homer sounds as if he is suggesting an agricultural metaphor, a passage from Xenophon's *Works on Socrates* defines such terms more clearly still. The eponymous philosopher's debater *du jour*, Ischomachus, is challenging his opponent on a point about planting seed: "If after putting in the seed you plough it in [*katastrepsêis*] again . . ." (17.10). One need not be a professional farmer to catch the image of land turned over again upon the planted seed. One can see the term somewhat abstracted in a scene from Aristophanes' *The Knights*, in which the leader of the chorus complains that Cleon is "upsetting" (*katastrephei*) the city (274).

That so many reliable scholars overlook an alternative that addresses the depth of the term can, itself, be rather upsetting. How does one get from "overturned" or "trampled on" to "compact and antithetical" (Roberts)? While a simple answer can be elusive, it seems that most of them work from what they see as the "big picture"; namely, that if Aristotle's ultimate point is to praise this form, then they must use terms that an audience contemporary to the translator would perceive as positive, thus eradicating its potentially violent—but what I consider essential—overtones.

Admittedly, the big problem for such an approach is either justifying or re-casting that perceived violence in a way that does no violence of its own to the broader context of the passage. To cast that problem as a question, how is "trampled-down" the opposite of "bound together in rows" in such a way that the former is preferable to the latter? On one level, the question is Aristotle's first and his translators' second. Connoting negatively from the plain definition of *eiromenen* may not be easily done, and reading *katestrammenen* as a positive would be difficult in many contexts—nearly impossible with "free-running" as your antithesis. But to leave the argument there would eliminate the opportunity for possible countertheories.

Recall for a moment the weaving imagery used in the earlier discussion of *eiromenen*. We tend to think of woven-together things always as products of artisans, deliberately plying their craft. In fact, all of the items I cited as evidence—baskets, metalwork, nets, and clothing—are exactly that, but not every tightly woven thing is the product of intentional art. Just ask anyone who has developed knots in long, straight hair. We might call the word *tangled*, but that term does not apply to deliberately—but errantly—woven things. I do not knit, but I have often seen friends who do look down with a sudden disgust, sigh, and begin the slow, arduous, and seemingly unproductive activity of taking it all apart.

It does appear to remain difficult, however, to cast "turned-down" or "trampled-on" in opposition to this kind of unweaving, until one turns to the world of Greek drama. The English word *catastrophe* comes from *katastrepho* (*katestrammenen*'s root), but it also has, since before Aristotle, been used to describe the resolution of a play, particularly a tragic one. In fact, in his *Poetics*, Aristotle himself demonstrates a conceptual familiarity with the idea of an "unraveling" plot, which often gets translated via the French *denouement*, but for which he uses the equally problematic verb *luô* ("to loose") (1454a). Many English translations even prefer *unraveled* to its more popularized French counterpart.

For clarity's sake, at this point I would like to suggest a summary alternate translation, substituting what I believe to be more appropriate terms of opposition into Kennedy's otherwise excellent translation (with emphasis added to illustrate the changes):

> The lexis [of formal speech and artistic prose] is necessarily either *tangled up into a single mass by connectives*, like the preludes in dithyrambs, or *untangled* like the antistrophes of the ancient poets.

In a world in which physical labor was frowned upon and in which inappropriately asking someone to perform it would not only potentially inconvenience them but embarrass the asker, analogizing tangled speech to, for instance, tangled nets would carry an implicit, but unmistakably clear, warning. For a speaker and audience who are engaged in the heady business of discourse, the latter is being required to perform the equivalent of physical labor before being able to evaluate concepts. That victimized audience may make it all the way through the mess, but will emerge both worn out and humiliated for the process and will clearly not remain allied with the speaker for long.

A reasonably polarized analogy rearranges pieces of a puzzle that need not be quite so puzzling and in the process raises or renews controversies, such as Aristotle's view of the state of prespoken language or the role of the audience in the rhetorical event, but all the while doing so through the lens of a reasonable, colorful linguistic opposition.

Works Cited

Apollonius Rhodius. *Argonautica.* Trans. R. C. Seaton. London: Heinemann, 1921.

Aristophanes. *The Knights*. Perseus Digital Library Vers. 4.0. Ed. Gregory Cane. Tufts University, n.d. Web. 8 Oct. 2008.

Aristotle. *Poetics*. Perseus Digital Library Vers. 4.0. Ed. Gregory Cane. Tufts University, n.d. Web. 8 Oct. 2008.

Bakker, Egbert. *Poetry in Speech: Orality in Homeric Discourse*. Ithaca, NY: Cornell UP, 1997.

Buckley, Theodore A., trans. *Aristotle's Treatise on Rhetoric*. By Aristotle. London: Henry G. Bohn, 1820.

Cooper, Lane, ed. and trans. *The Rhetoric of Aristotle*. New York: Appleton-Century-Crofts, 1932.

Cope, Edward Meredith. *The Rhetoric of Aristotle with a Commentary.* 3 vols. Rev. John Edwin Sandys. Cambridge: Cambridge UP, 1877.

Fenno, Jonathan. "A Bit of Help with Aristotle?" Messages to the author. 6, 10 Oct. 2008. E-mail.

Freese, John Henry, trans. *The "Art" of Rhetoric*. By Aristotle. London: Heinemann, 1926.

Gillies, John, trans. *A New Translation of Aristotle's Rhetoric*. By Aristotle. London: T. Cadell, 1823.

Homer. "Hymn 3 to Apollo." *Homeric Hymns*. Perseus Digital Library Vers. 4.0. Ed. Gregory Cane. Tufts University, n.d. Web. 6 Oct. 2008.

———. *Odyssey.* Perseus Digital Library Vers. 4.0. Ed. Gregory Cane. Tufts University, n.d. Web. 6 Oct. 2008.

Kennedy, George, trans. and ed. *On Rhetoric: A Theory of Civic Discourse*. By Aristotle. Oxford: Oxford UP, 1991.

Pindar. *Nemean Odes*. Nemean 7: For Sogenes of Aegina Boys' Pentathlon. Perseus Digital Library Vers. 4.0. Ed. Gregory Cane. Tufts University, n.d. Web. 8 Oct. 2008.

Roberts, W. Rhys, trans. *Rhetoric*. By Aristotle. Mineola, NY: Dover Thrift Editions, 2004.

Xenophon. *Works on Socrates*. Perseus Digital Library Vers. 4.0. Ed. Gregory Cane. Tufts University, n.d. Web. 8 Oct. 2008.

20

The Caribbean Conundrum

The Restrictive Liberation of Language, Rhetoric, and Idiom in Anglophone Caribbean Literature

Timothy Henningsen

In Earl Lovelace's short story "Joebell and America," the self-titled Trinidadian antagonist is bent on emigrating to the United States, for it is a place he claims to know well:

> I grow up on John Wayne and Gary Cooper . . . I know the Dodgers and Phillies, the Redskins and the Dallas Cowboys . . . I know Walt Frazier and Doctor J, and Bill Russell and Wilt Chamberlain. Really, in truth, I know America so much, I feel American. Is just that I ain't born there. (123)

Of course, readers interpret this declaration as Lovelace's playful tongue-in-cheek jab at Joebell's naïve understanding of America and its concomitant pop culture. America is a country, Joebell lavishly adds, "where everybody have a motor car and where . . . it have seventy-five channels of colour television that never sign off and you could sit down and watch . . . all the boxing and wrestling and basketball, right there as it happening" (111). Despite the humorous poking-fun that Lovelace wields throughout this story—of Trinidadian stereotypes and of America's television-obsessed culture—the undercurrent here emits curious rhetorical and transnational associations. Joebell, a Trinidadian, can claim to be American because he *feels* it. As Lovelace writes, "he grow up in America right there in Trinidad" (121).

This seemingly absurd notion certainly has qualities of in-betweenness, one of the concepts that provided the premise for the 2010 RSA meeting. Thanks to the composite considerations of Cicero and Burke, we gathered together to ask, among other things, how rhetoric divides and unites; how diversity and homogeneity "meet on the tongue"; how community is gained and how dissent is expressed. If Burke's contention is right, that the answers to these questions most often reside, rhetorically, in the in-between spaces, then it seems to me worth considering this outlandish notion that Joebell grew up in America, *in Trinidad*. An examination of the early literature from the Anglophone Caribbean offers a fresh take on this ambiguous in-betweenness.

The English-speaking Caribbean, it might be said, is a region historically castigated as an in-between space. I need not provide a complete summation of the turbulent colonial past that constitutes the region, but for the contexts of this essay it is worth noting that since the conquest of Columbus, the Caribbean islands have served, for lack of a better term, much like a truck stop for Europe and the United States. The West Indies (now generally referred to as the Anglophone Caribbean) has been left in a continuous state of flux, the residue of which is deposited, perhaps most explicitly, in the English language.

The notion of language as constitutive of reality is, of course, nothing new to the scholar of rhetoric. However, the colonial Caribbean of the early- to mid-twentieth century provides a curious case of this. In what has now become an oft-told tale that reveals the sheer absurdity of colonial pedagogies, students in the British West Indies were often asked on their composition exams to articulate England's winter season. Renowned Barbadian poet Edward Kamau Brathwaite underscores the tragedy in this when he writes:

> we are more conscious . . . of the falling snow . . . than of the force of the hurricane which takes place [here] every year. In other words, we haven't got the syllables . . . to describe the hurricane, which is our experience, whereas we can describe the imported alien experience of the snowfall. (8–9)

The colonial pupils of Brathwaite's generation were thus stuck in-between colonial pedagogies and their cultural realities; torn between the search for ways to rhetorically describe the hurricane while taught how to describe the falling snow. If language does, in fact, constitute reality, this reality left scores of Caribbean students in a seeming never-never land.

By mid-century, however, in the midst of the growing national independence movements throughout the Caribbean region, writers like Brathwaite, among others, looked to change this perplexing situation. In the hopes of establishing their own literary canon, which could replace the dominant texts in the British-centered pedagogy, dozens upon dozens of now-seminal novels were published in the 1950s and 1960s by Caribbean-born writers with the very onus of discovering a rhetoric that would, say, describe the hurricane (prior to this period, literature produced within the region was scant, to say the least). As Barbadian George Lamming would write, these home-based texts offered a "genuine, organic report of experience of a specific social reality" ("Western Education" 17). His *The Pleasures of Exile*, a memoir that has become among the most respected and widely read ruminations on the Caribbean colonial situation, seeks to negotiate this in-betweenness by, in citing Herman Melville's legendary whaling ship, "build[ing] our own Pequod" (153).

Curiously, Lamming is but one among a handful of Anglophone Caribbean writers who summon the American novelists and poets of the nineteenth century in an effort to confront this colonial separation with England. Writers like C. L. R. James, Sylvia Wynter, and Nobel laureate V. S. Naipaul, among others, engage with the likes of Melville, Mark Twain, and Walt Whitman in negotiating this in-between state. Yet, despite the high critical profiles that many of these American and Caribbean writers currently inhabit, rarely are they considered in tandem. Given the so-called transnational turn, this is curious. And given the historical fact that American literature held absolutely no place in colonial syllabi, it is even more curious. The presence of Twain and Melville in the works of those like Lamming raises the question: *why?*

If we can return briefly to Lovelace's Joebell, readers find that the high-rolling bravado is convinced that his linguistic fortitude will allow him to dupe the immigration officials that block his path to the United States. Wielding a fake American passport, a new brown suit topped off with a cowboy hat, and a fabricated story involving his participation in the American army, Joebell thinks he only needs to "talk Yankee" to the border officials, and he's through:

> Joebell smile, because if is one gift he have it is to talk languages, not Spanish and French and Italian and such, but he could talk English and American and Grenadian and Jamaican; and of all of them the one he love best is American. If that is the only problem, well, Joebell in America already. (112)

Once again the humor supplied by Joebell's ignorance veils the rhetorical topoi at play here. What might it mean for Joebell to "speak Yankee"? In a superficial sense, it is easy to imagine Joebell tweaking his dialect to sound relatively convincing as a Mr. James Armstrong Brady, a southern US veteran of the Vietnam War. But it seems Lovelace is implying that there is more than just accent adjustment at work here. He invites readers to unpack this transnational lingo.

Lamming offers a viable start to an understanding of this American-based "language" and its relevance to the Caribbean. In a rather unequivocal way, Lamming argues throughout *The Pleasures of Exile* that when considering the novels of himself and his Caribbean contemporaries, the geographical gap with America is bridged by none other than *idiom*. He writes, "the West Indian novel, particularly in the aspect of idiom, cannot be understood unless you take a good look at the American nineteenth century, a good look at Melville, Whitman, and Mark Twain" (29). Unfortunately, on the fiftieth anniversary of Lamming's seminal text, this thesis has been all but ignored. It is, after all, a curious phrase—and "idiom" a more curious choice of word. Lamming's eighth chapter in *Pleasures*, called "Ishmael at Home," considers America and its unique relation to the Caribbean, and it is here where readers receive his pledge of allegiance through idiom. The chapter essentially operates as a manifesto that damns the repressive power of language, and how, for centuries, Shakespeare's Prospero, as the emblematic European colonial master, has maintained control of the Anglophone Caribbean and its island subjects ("Calibans") through the constitutive potential of word. Throughout, Lamming borrows from *The Tempest*, playing upon Caliban's well-known damnation of Prospero, which goes:

> You taught me language, and my profit on't
> Is, I know how to curse. The red plague rid you
> For learning me your language! (26–27)

Lamming argues that Prospero used "that weapon of language" in an effort to shape *Law*, which, as always, is so much more than a collection of rules dictating social and cultural conduct. Adding that law is "the expression of a particular spirit in a particular historic time and circumstance," Lamming suggests that throughout colonial history it is *language*, in this constitutive sense, that allowed Prospero to "climb to his throne" and dictate the day-to-day lives of its subjects (156–57). However, writing throughout the 1950s, on the heels of what would become the Caribbean literary renaissance and on the cusp of national independence for many Caribbean islands, Lamming can insist that the times have changed. He writes: "For the language of modern politics is no longer Prospero's exclusive vocabulary. It is Caliban's as well; and [he] is at liberty to choose the meaning of this moment" (158). It is through language as such—a constitutive tool of redemptive postcolonial power—by which we can come to an understanding of how early Anglophone Caribbean novelists like Lamming used it. But how might "idiom," then, bridge the West Indian novel with those of the American nineteenth century? And why is this relation notable?

As I see it, there are two reasons. In making one of the earliest cases for "idiomaticity" as a legitimate aspect of linguistics, Logan Pearsall Smith notes that idiom is sometimes employed "to describe the *form* of speech peculiar to a people or nation" (67, emphasis added). In this sense, Lamming cites idiom for the colloquial nature—the spoken, dialectical *form*—in which many of the early Anglophone Caribbean texts are written. Lamming argues throughout *The Pleasures of Exile* that the West Indian novel is concerned with the life and language of West Indian common folk, a subject matter that puts its writers in the same realm as Mark Twain, a master of American dialects.

But this tactic is nothing new to the reader of postcolonial writing. As has been argued by postcolonial theorists for decades, language appropriation acts as a way of "seizing" language and "re-placing it in a discourse fully adapted to the colonized place" (Ashcroft et al. 37). We see Lamming suggest this in his post-Prospero anointment of Caliban. However, despite Lamming's suggestion that his Caribbean contingent of writers share an "aspect of idiom" with the likes of Twain, this certainly is not to suggest that they are alone in sharing a proclivity to use regional dialects in literature. Manifold writers from Dante to Dickens also toy with written versions of colloquial lingo; which is merely another way of saying that Lamming's use of "idiom" as a bridge with America goes deeper than a desire to explore colloquial vernacular and regional dialects.

Pearsall Smith offers a supplemental explanation of "idiom," stating that it can also be considered one of those forms of expression peculiar to a language, and approved by its usage, but whose meanings are often different from their grammatical or logical signification (67). We have heard hundreds if not thousands of these odd expressions in our lifetime. We tell someone to "break a leg," per se, and of course we do not mean it literally. The same can be said for other quirky yet common idioms like "knock 'em dead," "spill the beans," "beat around the bush," or, "pardon my French": "shoot the shit." All of these idioms have meanings far different than their literal string of words convey.

Idioms provide us with an interesting, yet tricky, cultural snafu. Take the saying "break a leg," for example. A relatively short time ago, had you been on the outside of theater culture, you likely would not have known that to say "good luck" to someone before taking the stage was, in fact, bad luck (like a jinx); hence, the seemingly oxymoronic employment of a negative blessing was creatively used and appropriated to mean something quite the opposite. "Break a leg" was thus a particular phraseology unique to the culture of the theater, their own sort of language that revealed (were you keen enough to know its nonliteral meaning) insight into the dynamic that constituted that cultural world. Language scholar Murat H. Roberts succinctly writes that idiom is "the attitude of mind common to all members of a linguistic community" (291). Thus, merging the work of Pearsall Smith with Roberts, it can be said that idioms belie logic (logos), but convey characteristics or the character (ethos) of a community. To understand how the phrase "break a leg" works is no doubt a logical challenge to cultural outsiders; simultaneously, it is a tie that binds the members already accepted into that linguistic group. To know the idiom is thus to know something about that particular community.

Considering this particular "aspect of idiom" brings us back to Lamming, and of course raises a variety of questions. First, it makes one consider the cultural characteristics emanated by certain nineteenth-century American writers—through this code of idiom—and how it is that Lamming, a Barbadian by birth and a British colonial by education, might find allegiance to this American-based idiomatic club. Additionally, if idiom is a cultural marker (sometimes revealed through regional dialects), how is it that, in order to understand the Anglophone Caribbean novel you must first take a good look at the works of Melville, Twain, and Whitman? Since these distinct American and Caribbean groups of writers are separated by manifold variables (culture, class, countries, dialects, and a near century), how does this notion of American idiom trickle down through time and space to Lamming's Barbados? Or to James' Trinidad? Or to Wynter's Jamaica? Might Joebell's seemingly silly ability to "talk Yankee" provide some insight here? Could it be possible that Lamming grew up in America? in Barbados? Are the answers to all of these questions finally found in that curious "aspect of idiom"?

Idiom is, after all, the central premise for Lamming's identification with his literary forebearers of the American nineteenth century. That he, a non-American, chooses to align with certain American idiom—that distinct cultural code—opens the Burkean in-between area delineated by that oft-quoted passage from *A Rhetoric of Motives*:

> A is not identical with his colleague, B. But insofar as their interests are joined, A is *identified* with B. Or he may *identify himself* with B even when their interests are not joined. . . . In being identified with B, A is "substantially one" with a person other than himself. Yet at the same time he remains unique, an individual locus of motives. Thus he is both joined and separate, at once a distinct substance and consubstantial with another. (20–21)

On the surface of things, the identification Lamming made with America is different than that which enticed Joebell. Joebell constructs an idealistic version of America based around star athletes, Hollywood stars, and the presumption that "everybody have a motor car" (Lovelace 111). Lamming, on the other hand, wishes to explore an America that was launched "as an alternative to the old and privileged Prospero"; he admits identifying with "that expectation upon which America was launched" (*Pleasures* 152). Contextually speaking, Lamming and his fellow contingent of writers emerge under the promises of the Caribbean independence movements, and it would seem their acknowledgement of the American writers of the previous century admits a desire to construct their own literary renaissance. While the so-called American renaissance (of which Melville and Whitman play a significant part) has been rightly targeted by contemporary critics as a misleading ideology—the long-time "preserve of white male views," writes Toni Morrison (5)—what it can justly contend is that a distinct literature, written by Americans, emerged within this era under the shadow of European literary superiority. While it would be nefarious to cite any one particular writer or group of writers as heralding a meta-American literature, what Caribbean writers like Lamming, James, and Wynter see in the likes of Twain and Melville, thanks to that cultural signifier of idiom, is *distinctly* American (which, as it turns out, is not all that different from Joebell's reception of those distinctly American figures like John Wayne or Dr. J). As such, it would seem that the notion of "America" carries an ideological and rhetorical currency that Caribbean writers would like to adopt and develop *in their own right*. In shaping a unique idiom to describe the hurricane, they identify with, but hope to become distinct from, "America."

Evidence of this idiomatic alignment and appropriation appears when Édouard Glissant, of Martinique, dubs his home region the "Other America" (4), or when poet and publisher John Anthony La Rose, of Trinidad, lyrically proclaims he is simultaneously José Martí and Walt Whitman (23). Glissant and La Rose are, in a strange way, not so different from Joebell, who can call himself an American despite not having been born there (nonetheless ever having visited). For Joebell has received an idiomatic version of America that, as bloated and ridiculous as his sports and television-saturated rendition may be, reveals the rhetorical topoi of "America," and how it operates as a distinct, yet highly shapeable, idea. For example, C. L. R. James receives and enacts a different version of America than Lamming does, who receives and enacts a different version than Sylvia Wynter, who receives and enacts a different version than Joebell, and so on. What seems needed, then, is a theoretical practice that accounts for the pseudo-anthropological exchange across time and space; a theory that can explain how and why Lamming's contingent of writers would align with American idiom, and how they might divert it for their own literary, and thus communal, purposes.

As a student of literature, this is the reason I am drawn to the RSA, because these curiosities seem best explained not in the field of literary theory, but rather through rhetoric. As the 2010 conference announcement noted, Burke suggests that when identification and division are boxed together, "you have the characteristic invitation to rhetoric" (25). Lamming's nods to the idiom of his American predecessors inhabits this seemingly paradoxical, yet revealing, in-between area. It is, quite frankly, a conundrum. Because, despite the linguistic promise of aligning with American idiom as an alternative to old Prospero, the Anglophone Caribbean is still—and forever will be—haunted by the language of that Shakespearean figurehead. Though Caliban is "at liberty to choose the meaning of [his] moment," he is still rhetorically constituted by the words of his conqueror. While this colonial history—embedded in language—forever remains an "inhibiting menace," it is the duty of the Caribbean novelist, writes Lamming, to "incorporate it into our collective sense of the future" ("Western Education" 25). Perhaps this is the idiom emanated by the literature of the so-called American renaissance. After all, the negotiation of historical trauma, social reality, and future potential is the crux of texts like *Huckleberry Finn*, *Moby-Dick*, and *Leaves of Grass*. Lamming surely identifies with these texts ("we don't mind worshipping in that kind of cathedral" [*Pleasures* 154–55]); and yet, he simultaneously desires difference ("but we would like to build our own Pequod" [153]). If, as Burke suggests, rhetoric can "lead us through the Scramble" (23), literary critics might begin by approaching such texts from the position of this Burkean in-between space where sameness and difference ambiguously embrace. In doing so, they might find that the early Anglophone Caribbean writers have already been there for a long time, wrangled together and "talking Yankee" in an attempt to negotiate this restrictive liberation of language and idiom.

Works Cited

Ashcroft, Bill, Gareth Griffiths, and Helen Tiffin. *The Empire Writes Back: Theory and Practice in Post-Colonial Literatures*. London: Routledge, 1989.

Brathwaite, Edward Kamau. *History of the Voice: The Development of Nation Language in Anglophone Caribbean Poetry.* London: New Beacon, 1984.

Burke, Kenneth. *A Rhetoric of Motives*. Berkeley: U of California P, 1969.

Glissant, Édouard. *Caribbean Discourse: Selected Essays*. Charlottesville: UP of Virginia, 1989.

Lamming, George. *The Pleasures of Exile*. Ann Arbor: U of Michigan P, 1992.

———. "Western Education and the Caribbean Intellectual." *Coming Home: Conversations II*. St. Martin: House of Nershi, 2000.

La Rose, John Anthony. *Foundations: A Book of Poems*. London: New Beacon, 1966.

Lovelace, Earl. "Joebell and America." *A Brief Conversion and Other Stories*. Oxford: Heinemann, 1988.

Morrison, Toni. *Playing in the Dark: Whiteness and the Literary Imagination*. Cambridge: Harvard UP, 1992.

Pearsall Smith, Logan. *Words and Idioms: Studies in the English Language*. London: Constable & Company, 1948.

Roberts, Murat H. "The Science of Idiom: A Method of Inquiry into the Cognitive Design." *PMLA* 59.1 (Mar. 1944): 291–306.

Shakespeare, William. *The Tempest: A Case Study in Critical Controversy.* Ed. Gerald Graff and James Phelan. Boston: Bedford/St. Martin's, 2000.

Section V

Interdependence, Identity, and the Rhetoric of Dissent

Rhetorical discourse is unique in the way it can simultaneously divide and unify people. A message can promote harmony between groups of people who were not previously in concord, but it can also contribute to tension, disagreement, and controversy.

—Heather A. Roy

Sites of memory should be actively marked and designated as sites of struggle and tension.

—Kelly M. Young and William Trapani

Through such apocalyptic rhetoric, Malcolm X simultaneously separates African Americans from whiteness, bonds them together, and hands them a dazzling jewel of immediate and certain hope.

—Keith Miller

What about rhetors who not only assume that persuasion will fail, but seem to hope that it will? . . . Rhetoricians need language for describing the "good-faith apostasy."

—Paul Lynch

The language we use to talk about concord and controversy reveals a spatial dimension: when we find ourselves in agreement, we are "on the same page" or "with" someone, we "come together." When we disagree, we often represent others as "outsiders."

—Rosalyn Collings Eves

21

The Rhetoric of Apostasy

Christopher Hitchens at War with the Left

Paul Lynch

> He says it's axiomatically reactionary to change: I would warn him that it can be very conservative to remain the same.
>
> —Christopher Hitchens ("Hitchens Responds" 250)

> What kind of contrarian leaves a column—called "Minority Report," no less—because too many of the readers disagree with him?
>
> —Katha Pollitt (Hitchens and Pollitt)

In his recent *Rhetorical Refusals: Defying Audiences' Expectations*, John Schilb defines a rhetorical refusal as "an act of writing or speaking in which the rhetor pointedly refuses to do what the audience considers rhetorically normal" (3). For Schilb, "rhetorically normal" refers to expectations about the occasion. Defying those expectations, he suggests, offers another available means of persuasion. "By rejecting a procedure that the audience expects, the rhetor seeks the audience's assent to another principle, cast as a higher priority" (3). A theatre critic, for example, refuses to see a play on the grounds that she rejects the particular genre she has been asked to review. Her refusal may confound one audience, but it becomes a call-to-arms for another (1–2). Those audience members inclined to agree with the critic may be persuaded less effectively by arguments and more effectively by the rhetor's refusal to engage in argument at all. Frederick Douglass's infamous 1852 Fourth of July speech offers another example of a rhetorical refusal (82–83). By turning an epideictic occasion into a deliberative one, Douglass defies his audience's expectations and demands more from them rhetorically than they might otherwise have been prepared to give. Though the refusal may initially bewilder the audience, its purpose is to push them toward deeper reflection.

Kenneth Burke would surely remind us that identification is a product of disidentification, and disidentification a product of identification. To refuse an audience's friendship is to invite a different sort of friendship, or perhaps different sorts of friends. Yet whatever the paradoxes of concord and controversy, there is a difference, I think, when the rhetor seeks disidentification first. Schilb argues that the question "Who's with me?" is "every rhetor's cri-de-coeur" (55–56). Douglass may defy the audience's expectations, but he still hopes that they will finally live up to his. But what about rhetors who not only assume that persuasion will fail, but seem to hope that it will? What about rhetors who seek to sow discord? We have thought a lot about audiences addressed and invoked, less about audiences alienated and insulted. How should we understand a rhetorical refusal in which the writer's primary purpose seems to be his own rejection?

In my attempt to answer these questions, my case study will be Christopher Hitchens, erstwhile "designated hitter" of the Left (Raz), who shocked many of his former allies with his support of the Bush administration's foreign policy in general and the Iraq War in particular. The question has been asked many times over, but Ian Parker articulates it most succinctly:[1]

> How did a longtime columnist at *The Nation* become a contributor to the *Weekly Standard*, a supporter of President Bush in the 2004 election, and an invited speaker at the conservative activist David Horowitz's forthcoming Restoration Weekend, along with Ann Coulter and Rush Limbaugh? (152)

Some have suggested that the answer lies in Hitchens' contrarian nature, a surmise supported by Hitchens' own writings, including *Letters to a Young Contrarian*. Others, less kindly, suggest that Hitchens' prodigious drinking is the cause of his decline (see Cole; Corn; McCarthy). The phraseology of George Galloway, a notable Hitchens antagonist, offers perhaps the most memorable description of Hitchens in this vein. He is, argues Galloway, "a drink-soaked former Trotskyite popinjay" ("Galloway"). Among Hitchens' opponents, the latter theory is more popular than the former. To attribute Hitchens' reversal to contrarianism is to blame him for what he was once praised; alcoholism, on the other hand, offers an explanation as to why those who once revered him may now reject him.

Among the various theories, however, *apostasy* stands out as the most rhetorically interesting. Norman Finkelstein makes this suggestion in his "'Fraternally Yours': Hitchens as Model Apostate." Finkelstein shares the general assumptions of other Hitchens detractors—that is, the assumption that his stance on the Iraq War means that he is out of the tribe and no longer worth talking to. Yet, Finkelstein also dismisses Hitchens' apostasy on the grounds it was "accompanied by fanfare and fireworks" and therefore was "truly repellent" (243). One might have good reasons for losing one's political faith, writes Finkelstein, but "the impetus behind political apostasy is—pardon my cynicism—a fairly straightforward, uncomplicated affair: to cash in, or keep cashing in" (243). In the case of Hitchens, Finkelstein thinks the motivation for this capitulation is obvious: "It's not exactly a martyr's fate defecting from *The Nation*, a frills-free liberal magazine, to *Atlantic Monthly*, the well-heeled house organ of Zionist crazies"

(250). For Finkelstein, then, a public apostasy must almost always be regarded as a cynical and hypocritical attempt to gain fame and fortune. The only genuine apostates are those whom we know nothing about.

Though one's opinion of Finkelstein's arguments may depend on one's opinions of Finkelstein himself, there is no doubt that he articulates a widely held view: Hitchens had once been a reliable colleague/public intellectual, but his opinion on the Bush doctrine demands repudiation, not only of argument but also of arguer. Hitchens himself is to be blamed for inviting an *ad hominem* rebuke. Rhetoricians, however, should quarrel with this notion of apostasy, not only because it relies on what Wayne Booth would identify as crude motivism, but also because it precludes the possibility of recognizing an authentic change of mind. In *Deliberate Conflict*, Patricia Roberts-Miller reminds us of one use of the Enlightenment ideal of the autonomous individual:

> We have, at times, felt ourselves in conflict with a group whom we considered ourselves to be a member; we have all had dark moments of the soul when we had to decide whether to voice a strongly held position we knew to be unpopular. There are aspects of our tradition we reject, there are cultures we have chosen to leave. (63)

Hitchens' apostasy is only the latest in a recent string of such acts, including the (ir)religious apostasies of Ayaan Hirsi Ali, Dan Barker, and Bart Ehrman and the political apostasies of David Brock and Kevin Philips. Consider, too, conservative education scholar Diane Ravitch's shifting position on the usefulness of charter schools and standardized testing.[2] If Finkelstein were to have the last word, all these people would have to be dismissed as hucksters. Rhetoricians need language for describing the "good-faith apostasy."

This seems like an oxymoronic idea: an apostasy is, by definition, an act of *bad* faith. Yet, this assumption presumes that there is only one audience for an apostasy—the group or organization that has been rejected. If, however, an apostasy is public, then it also assumes another audience of judges whose pieties—whether religious, political, or intellectual—are not directly at stake. One does not need to be a member of a rejected group in order to take an interest in a given controversy. Perelman and Olbrechts-Tyteca's complex notion of the universal audience offers important insight here. Though the apostate rejects a particular audience, he or she does so in ways that may appeal to a universal audience, a "universality and unanimity imagined by the speaker" (31). As Walter Ong might observe, such an appeal can invoke an audience willing to play that role. Hitchens' arguments may not be designed to convince the Left, but rather those who are judging this dispute as a whole. The reverse is not necessarily true. While it is unlikely that Hitchens' opponents believed that they could win him over in the end, it is unclear that they were trying to convince a wider public. Either way, it should be the task of rhetoricians to discover the available means of understanding the difference.

If nothing else, the term *apostasy* should attract our notice because its root is *stasis*. The most basic etymology of apostasy means "a stand apart," which suggests an utter rejection of stasis. However, as we have already seen, the act of apostasy invites continuing stasis, if we define it as both "stand" and "strife." Indeed the term stasis itself already suggests contradiction in that the word means not only "position" or "place," but also "strife" or "discord." Other definitions include "party," "company," and "band," along with "faction," "sect," and "sedition." In its most ancient usage, then, stasis itself suggested both stand and strife with a group. The notion of apostasy already contains paradoxically competing pieties. The apostate establishes one's independence through the rejection, and one's implied identification, of a group. The group maintains itself through the rejection, and implied (dis)identification, of the apostate. The apostate and the group both reject and need each other, suggesting that apo + stasis rests squarely within stasis rather than outside it.

In common discourse, however, apostasy has referred to revolt or defection, as evidenced by the word's use in Herodotus, Thucydides, and Josephus (Wilson 14). Though the word was sometimes used synonymously with *heresy*, in both Jewish and Christian rhetoric, apostasy came to mean something much stronger. In early Christian sources, the word meant "a serious act of rebellion, something more than mere dissent or disagreement" (16). In Jewish sources, "apostates in general were judged to have abandoned the covenant community, while heretics, however troublesome, remained with it" (18–19). Note the distinction between heretics and apostates. One disagrees within the family; the other rejects the family altogether.

We might then begin to analyze Hitchens' actions according to whether he remained within his "family." That question seems easy to answer. Hitchens publicly resigned from *The Nation* in an essay titled "Taking Sides." A week later, he added "So Long, Fellow Travelers" in the *Washington Post*. These titles say it all, but the essays drive the point home further. In "Taking Sides," he writes,

> When I began work for the *Nation* over two decades ago, Victor Navasky described the magazine as a debating ground between liberals and radicals. . . . In the past few weeks, though, I have come to realize that the magazine itself takes a side in this argument [about the US response to 9/11], and is becoming the voice and the echo chamber of those who truly believe that John Ashcroft is a greater menace than Osama bin Laden. (104)

In "So Long, Fellow Travelers," he adds, "I can only hint at how much I despise a Left that thinks of Osama bin Laden as a slightly misguided imperialist" (108). These do not seem to be the words of one who wants to remain allied with his former colleagues. If we follow the distinction between a heretic and an apostate, Hitchens seems to qualify as the latter.

The feeling was mutual. In *Counterpunch*, Tariq Ali suggested, "If Hitchens carries on in this vein, he'll soon find himself addressing the same gatherings as his sparring partner, Henry Kissinger." Because Hitchens' *The Trial of Henry Kissinger* argues that the former secretary of state is a war criminal, Ali's are truly fighting words. "Sparring partner" further suggests a relationship of dependence; the sparring partner, after all, is a member of the boxer's own team. In "Memo to Hitchens," Noam Chomsky dismissed Hitchens in even stronger terms:

> Since Hitchens evidently does not take what he is writing seriously, there is no reason for anyone else to do so. The fair and sensible reaction is to treat all this as some aberration, and to await the return of the author to the important work he has often done in the past.

Chomsky also accused Hitchens of racism. In reference to the US bombing of a pharmaceutical plant in Sudan, Chomsky writes, "[Hitchens] must be unaware that he is expressing such racist contempt for African victims of a terrorist crime, and cannot intend what his words imply." Later that same month, Edward S. Herman made a similar accusation of racism in his "For Rationalization—Of Imperial Violence." "We on the left," he writes, "must sadly kiss Christopher Hitchens goodbye. He has joined the Swiss guards, is now a U.S. and NATO cheerleader, and is on his way up the mainstream media ladder."

Certainly some readers will object to these writers appearing to represent the Left. In *The Left at War*, for example, Michael Bérubé laments the rise of what he calls the "Manichean left," a group of leftists who hold two and only two premises: anything the United States does is bad; anything anyone does in opposition to the United States is good. Rather than mounting a serious critique of Bush–Cheney foreign policy, these critics have

> stepped forward with a form of critique which holds that the United States is responsible for the emergence of al-Qaeda, that the war in Afghanistan is one of the most grotesque acts of modern history, and that anyone who demurs from these judgments is either an apologist for imperialism or a moral imbecile. (11)

Some might wonder whether this herd of independent minds really warrants analysis. But my reason for doing so is also borrowed from Bérubé. The Manichean habit of thought is itself worth resisting, whether in Hitchens or his opponents. (The recent question of "epistemic closure" on the Right offers another example of the Manichean tendency, and it should be no more welcome there than it should be on the Left.) Speaking of the invasion of Afghanistan, Bérubé writes, "it is critical, therefore, even now, to distinguish between plausible and implausible—or if you prefer, credible and incredible—rationales" (*The Left* 100). The same holds true for the war in Iraq. Moreover, a rhetoric of apostasy should be able to invent language for distinguishing between dissent and apostasy—the former of which demands that we consider the criticism, the latter of which allows us to ignore the critic. The resulting precision of language may discredit the herd rather than the lost sheep.

Dana Anderson's *Identity's Strategy* offers a distinction worth remembering. Anderson argues that rhetoricians must distinguish between ethos and identity. While the former may be appropriate (or inappropriate) for a given rhetorical situation, the latter tends to signify a perception that is "trans-situational" (98). He continues, "You may enact antitheses of character in different rhetorical situations, wrathfully indignant in one yet patiently forgiving in another; but antitheses of identity are not so amicably received by one's audiences" (98). Using Anderson's distinction, we might say that apostasy engages identity rather than character. Anderson does not deny that identity is strategic, but he does seem to say that it involves a different tactic. "When ethos fails to meet the expectations that underlie its persuasiveness, it is appropriate. When identity fails, it is a lie" (98). This is an important point, and it can help us to distinguish between dissent and apostasy. In Anderson's language, the apostate undergoes a change in identity. By this reasoning, the dissenter does not, even if he or she adapts his or her ethos to changing situations.

Scholars of apostasy in sociology also recognize similar distinctions, even if they do not use the language of rhetoric per se. Stuart A. Wright, for example, draws a basic distinction between the *leavetaker,* who exits an organization quietly, and the *apostate*, who exits an organization publicly.

> The leavetaker may be defined as one who decides to terminate his or her commitment and disaffliate in a non-public act of personal reflection and deed. The decision to leave may involve different levels of anguish, equivocation, or strategy but the leavetaker does not assume a public role of hostile recrimination in the wake of departure. (96)

The lapsed Catholic, then, does not necessarily qualify as an apostate, even if that Catholic no longer accepts the tenets of the creed. First and foremost, this means that apostasy *must* be public, and that criticizing it for being public makes no sense. More importantly, Wright's understanding of apostasy suggests what Anderson might call a change in identity. "The apostate, on the other hand, is defined as a defector who is aligned with an oppositional coalition in an effort to broaden a dispute, and embraces a posture of confrontation through public claimsmaking activities" (97). This definition seems to fit Hitchens perfectly. He has embraced a confrontational posture, and there can be little doubt that he sought to broaden the dispute. Moreover, he appears never to have shied from a debate on the invasion of Iraq.

But whether Hitchens has aligned himself with an oppositional coalition might remain open to debate. Again, as Ian Parker noted, Hitchens contributed to the *Weekly Standard*, endorsed President Bush in the 2004 election, and was invited to David Horowitz's Restoration Weekend. It may seem, then, that he has joined the other team. One might argue that these are the activities of a public intellectual, and it is the job of the public intellectual to resist the habit of speaking to those with whom he or she already agrees (or speaking only in "approved" venues). Edward Said, for example, insists that

> the intellectual . . . is neither a pacifier nor a consensus-builder, but someone whose whole being is staked on a critical sense, a sense of being unwilling to accept easy formulas or ready-made clichés, or the smooth, ever-so-accommodating confirmations of what the powerful or conventional have to say, and what they do. (23)

It may be hard to imagine the Left after 9/11 as powerful, but certainly one can argue some leftist thought was conventional, if only because of the sense that there was/is a group called "the Left."

This is an important point for understanding whether Hitchens' behavior qualifies as an apostasy. To be an apostate, one has to belong to a group. But as Perelman and Olbrechts-Tyteca observe,

> Argumentation concerning a group and its members is far more complex than that concerning a person and his acts . . . because the notion of a group is vaguer than the notion of a person. There may be doubt not only as to the limits of the group, but as to its very existence. (322)

Ede and Lunsford's notion of "audience invoked" suggests at the very least that a group can be invoked simply within a rhetorical situation. Thus, we may be able to identify a group not by a constitution or membership role but by the way people argue with each other. If enough rhetors quarrel over who is "out," then we know that there is an "in." Certainly, this observation is complicated by the fact that we are talking about an argument between people who would see themselves as intellectuals—beholden, ostensibly, to no one but themselves. It may seem implausible to consider Hitchens and his opponents a "group." Nevertheless, all the writers I have quoted—including Hitchens—presumed (a) that there is a "Left," (b) that they themselves are a part of it, (c) that Hitchens once was a part of it, and (d) that his pro-war position meant that he could no longer be a part of it.

Beyond establishing the existence of a group, we must understand the sort of group to which the apostate once belonged. David G. Bromley describes three typical organizations from which people exit: allegiant, contestant, and subversive. The first of these, *allegiant,* includes organizations "whose interests coincide to a high degree with other organizations in their environments," groups such as "therapeutic/medical organizations, mainline churches, colleges, professional organizations, and various voluntary associations" (21). These are seen as generally politically uncontroversial and uncompetitive with other similar organizations. *Contestant organizations* include "the plethora of profit-making economic organizations" (22). Unlike allegiant organizations, contestant organizations openly compete with each other, and "the social expectation is that normal competition and conflict will involve these organizations in an ongoing pattern of claimsmaking" (22). Finally, there are *subversive organizations*, which have an "extremely low coincidence of interests with other organizations in the environment" (23). These would include "alternative religious movements, radical rightist and leftist political movements, and various forms of underground economies" (23). Such organizations have the least public legitimacy of the three groups Bromley describes. Indeed, allegiant organizations are often interested in suppressing subversive groups, which are perceived as threats.

As one might expect, the differences between the groups also manifest themselves in the differences among the means of exit. Bromley uses the term "defector" to describe those who leave allegiant organizations and "whistle-blowers" to describe those who leave contestant organizations. "Apostates" are those who leave subversive organizations, the organizations that find themselves in the deepest tension with their surrounding environments.

> The apostate role is thus defined as one that occurs in a highly polarized situation in which an organization member undertakes a total change of loyalties by allying with one or more elements of an oppositional coalition without the consent or control of the organization. (36)

Again, this description seems to fit Hitchens: the time after 9/11 was certainly highly polarized, and the apostate appeared to undertake a total change of loyalties.

But that "total change of loyalties" does not stand up under close scrutiny. Hitchens continually argued that his foreign policy beliefs had not changed. His leftist credentials, he insisted, were in good order. He describes himself "as someone who has done a good deal of marching and public speaking about Vietnam, Chile, South Africa, Palestine, and East Timor in his time (and would do it all again)" ("So Long" 108). His loyalties to the victims of Saddam Hussein, he argued, ran deeper than his loyalties to the Left.[3]

> Sooner or later . . . the Iraqi and Kurdish peoples will be free of Saddam Hussein. When that day comes, I am booked to have a reunion in Baghdad with several old comrades who have been through hell. We shall not be inviting anyone who spent this precious time urging democratic countries to give Saddam another chance. (108)

Whether these arguments are persuasive on the question of the war is beside the point. I offer them as evidence that Hitchens' loyalties—and, Anderson might point out, identity—have not undergone the massive change that his critics have claimed. As he puts it, "I have never disowned, in the *auto da fe* sense, any of my past on the left" ("Hitchens Responds" 253). Some might dispute Hitchens' characterization of himself, but what is beyond dispute is that Hitchens has never repudiated his past.

This is a crucial point; indeed, the entire question hinges on it. Apostasy narratives are often constructed as captivity narratives. According to Bromley,

> there is considerable pressure on individuals exiting subversive organizations to negotiate a narrative with the oppositional coalition that offers an acceptable explanation for participation in the organization and for now once again reversing loyalties. (37)

In other words, apostates from subversive groups usually tell a story in which they themselves are the victims of their own naiveté and the subversive group's manipulation; thus, they can explain how they were once apparently so foolish to belong to the subversive group in the first place (37). In Anderson's terms, the apostate has to explain a change in identity. Bromley goes on to insist that "the personal ordeal of the apostate" is "the testimonial centerpiece" of the narrative (38). Rhetorically, this story casts the apostate's ethos as that of a victim rather than a traitor. To be sure, this ritualistic humiliation can increase the apostate's profile, and the allegiant organization can benefit from such publicity.

But Hitchens has never told the usual story. He has not disavowed (an apt word) the beliefs that have fueled his politics. Again, we may not find his arguments persuasive, but it becomes harder to argue that Hitchens professes them merely for nefarious purposes of self-interest. Ultimately, what I am arguing is that rhetoricians who would analyze apostasies must reject Finkelstein's clumsy use of the term. He wields it like an axe; we should wield it like a scalpel. Bérubé would likely suggest that this imprecision is trademark of the Manichean left. What we need, however, is precision. Like all serious rhetorical needs, this particular one is not "merely rhetorical." Again I turn to Bérubé to articulate why:

> Don't let the language of "discourse" and "argument" fool you: when we decide that someone is "a figure outside the conversation," we might, in fact, be providing grounds for imprisoning or killing him, on the ground that he advocates—or is actually conducting—genocide. There is nothing flabby about this. Liberals, even liberals friendly to some of the theses of postmodernism, can kill you. But they are duty-bound to exhaust every other rational remedy first, and then to determine that the incommensurability facing them is not merely non-negotiable but deadly. (*What's Liberal* 238–39)

Bérubé's admonition reminds us of what is at stake when any group decides that someone is not worth talking to anymore. But the situation becomes even more complex when the dissenter has been a prominent member of the community. The "subversive community," to use Bromley's word, has to then explain how their champion has become their enemy. Apostasy—or a simplistic understanding of apostasy—becomes a convenient explanation, as it puts the moral burden on the apostate rather than the community. But as Bromley suggests, the tendency to cry apostasy may reflect not the apostate's action, but rather the nature of the accusing community—alienated from and hostile to similar communities. Unfortunately, a self-critical attitude seemed beyond the reach of the Manichean left, which never entertained the possibility that Hitchens might have a case. But such self-reflection must be a basic part of rhetorical analysis. Some breaks are irreparable, but others may simply stave off self-criticism. As rhetoricians, our job demands that we discern the difference, along with the paradoxical nature of the "good-faith apostasy."

Notes

[1] These questions have occasioned at least two books: Cottee and Cushman's *Christopher Hitchens and His Critics: Terror, Iraq, and the Left,* which takes a generally pro-Hitchens stand, and Scott Lucas's *The Betrayal of Dissent: Beyond Orwell, Hitchens, and the New American Century,* which attacks Orwell and Hitchens as faux-leftists who were actually company men. There is also a website dedicated to monitoring Hitchens: "Christopher Hitchens Watch" (http://christopherhitchenswatch.blogspot.com/).

[2] See Richard Bernstein's "A Change of Heart on Education."

[3] Hitchens has made much of his connections to the Iraqi community, both in Iraq and in exile. In *A Long Short War,* he recounts a 2003 trip he took to Dearborn, Michigan, the center of the largest Arab-American community in the United States. "Several people in the audience were known to me personally and I was known to some others from having defended the regime-change viewpoint on television" (1). Not only has he visited Arab-American communities, but also Arab communities: "In front of me is a copy of the *Arab Times,* published in Kuwait City and picked up during my recent trip to the region" (86). He describes Halabja after the 1991 war, where "women, in a region celebrated for modesty, could roll up their heavy skirts to show horrifying burns. People were blind. Children were in semi-autistic states" (37). He describes his guide and interpreter from a trip he took in the 1970s, a man who, because of his English, went on to become Hussein's interpreter. "I wondered," Hitchens writes, "how long he'd survive. (Not all that long: He was tortured to death on a whim and then denounced for being a queer.)" (92). These images make not only arresting appeals to pathos, they also invoke values that the Left would hold—intellectualism and cosmopolitanism. Thus, we see Hitchens attempting to argue for the war on what he sees as leftist grounds. Again, these arguments may not be persuasive, but they do suggest that he has not experienced a massive "de-conversion."

Works Cited

Ali, Tariq. "Hitchens at War." *Counterpunch* 26 Sept. 2001. Web. 4 Apr. 2007.

Anderson, Dana. *Identity's Strategy: Rhetorical Selves in Conversion*. Columbia: U of South Carolina P, 2007.

Bernstein, Richard. "A Change of Heart on Education." *New York Times* 5 May 2010. Web. 17 May 2010.

Bérubé, Michael. *The Left at War.* New York: New York UP, 2009.

———. *What's Liberal about the Liberal Arts?: Classroom Politics and "Bias" in Higher Education.* New York: Norton, 2006.

Bromley, David G., ed. "The Social Construction of Contested Exit Roles: Defectors, Whistleblowers, and Apostates." *The Politics of Religious Apostasy: The Role of Apostates in the Transformation of Religious Movements*. Westport, CT: Praeger, 1998. 19–48.

Chomsky, Noam. "Memo to Hitchens." *Counterpunch* 1 Oct. 2001. Web. 31 Aug. 2007.

Cole, Juan. "Hitchens the Hacker; And, Hitchens the Orientalist; And, 'We Don't Want Your Stinking War!'" *Informed Comment* 3 May 2006. Web. 23 Jan. 2007.

Corn, David. "Sorry Hitch, You're Wrong about Niger." *Slate* 26 Sept. 2006. Web. 26 Jan. 2007.

Cottee, Simon, and Thomas Cushman, eds. *Christopher Hitchens and His Critics: Terror, Iraq, and the Left*. New York: New York UP, 2008.

Ede, Lisa, and Andrea Lunsford. "Audience Addressed/Audience Invoked: The Role of Audience in Composition Theory and Pedagogy." *CCC* 35.2 (1984): 155–71.

Finkelstein, Norman. "'Fraternally Yours': Hitchens as Model Apostate." Cottee and Cushman 242–50.

"Galloway and the Mother of All Invective." *The Guardian* 18 May 2005. Web. 10 Oct. 2010.

Herman, Edward S. "For Rationalization—Of Imperial Violence." *Outlook India* 25 Oct. 2001. Web. 18 July 2008.

Hitchens, Christopher. "Hitchens Responds." Cottee and Cushman 250–56.

———. *Letters to a Young Contrarian*. New York: Basic Books, 2001.

———. *A Long Short War: The Postponed Liberation of Iraq*. New York: Plume, 2003.

———. "So Long, Fellow Travelers." Cottee and Cushman 104–08.

———. "Taking Sides." Cottee and Cushman 101–03.

———. *The Trial of Henry Kissinger.* New York: Verso, 2001.

Hitchens, Christopher, and Katha Pollitt. "The Hitchens–Pollitt Papers." *The Nation* 26 Nov. 2002. Web. 5 May 2010.

Lucas, Scott. *The Betrayal of Dissent: Beyond Orwell, Hitchens, and the New American Century.* London: Pluto P, 2004.

McCarthy, Jack. "I'll Drink to That: Another Ad Hominem Attack on Christopher Hitchens." *Counterpunch* 21 Feb. 2003. Web. 27 Mar. 2007.

Ong, Walter, SJ. "The Writer's Audience Is Always a Fiction." *PMLA* 90.1 (1975): 9–21.

Parker, Ian. "He Knew He Was Right." *The New Yorker* 16 Oct. 2006: 150–61.

Perelman, Chaïm, and Lucie Olbrechts-Tyteca. *The New Rhetoric: A Treatise of Argumentation*. Trans. John Wilkinson and Purcell Weaver. Notre Dame, IN: U of Notre Dame P, 1971.

Raz, Guy. "Christopher Hitchens, Literary Agent Provocateur." National Public Radio. 21 June 2006. Web. 9 Apr. 2007.

Roberts-Miller, Patricia. *Deliberate Conflict: Argument, Political Theory, and Composition Classes.* Carbondale: Southern Illinois UP, 2004.

Said, Edward W. *Representations of the Intellectual*. New York: Pantheon Books, 1994.

Schilb, John. *Rhetorical Refusals: Defying Audiences' Expectations.* Carbondale: Southern Illinois UP, 2007.

Wilson, Stephen G. *Leaving the Fold: Apostates and Defectors in Antiquity.* Minneapolis: Fortress P, 2004.

Wright, Stuart A. "Exploring the Factors That Shape the Apostate Role." *The Politics of Religious Apostasy: The Role of Apostates in the Transformation of Religious Movements*. Ed. David G. Bromley. Westport, CT: Praeger, 1998. 95–114.

22

Harleys and Angels' Wings

Nonverbal Rhetorical Response to the Westboro Baptist Church

Heather A. Roy

Rhetorical discourse is unique in the way it can simultaneously divide and unify people. A message can promote harmony between groups of people who were not previously in concord, but it can also contribute to tension, disagreement, and controversy. This essay examines the simultaneous action of concord and controversy by looking at the protests of the Westboro Baptist Church in relation to the counterprotests of the Patriot Guard Riders and Angel Action.

Reverend Fred Phelps of Topeka, Kansas, formed the Westboro Baptist Church (WBC) in 1955. The seventy-member church congregation is mainly comprised of Phelps' family members: thirteen of his children and fifty-two grandchildren (Leon 130). Phelps originally started out alone as a street preacher in 1952, railing against "dirty jokes and sexual petting." But his primary focus currently, along with the rest of the WBC, is on spreading the message that "every tragedy in the world is linked to homosexuality—specifically society's increasing tolerance and acceptance of what he [Phelps] calls the Homosexual Agenda" (131). One of the many websites hosted by the WBC explains that the "WBC engages in daily peaceful sidewalk demonstrations opposing the homosexual lifestyle of soul-damning, nation-destroying filth" (Westboro). The church claims to have conducted over 44,377 protests since June 1991, and to have done so all over the United States and internationally. Members proclaim their "gospel message to be this world's last hope" (Westboro).

WBC protests have become particularly noteworthy because they often happen at the funerals of American soldiers. Phelps and his congregation believe that soldiers have been brainwashed by homosexual propaganda and "with full knowledge of what they were doing, they voluntarily joined a fag-infested army to fight for a fag-run country" (Westboro). Because the WBC is focused on condemning homosexuality, members center their protests and sermons on how it has infiltrated all aspects of life, including war. Phelps was quoted in an article from the *National Post* saying soldiers "turned America over to fags; now they're coming home in body bags" and that "God Himself has now become America's terrorist, killing Americans in strange lands for *Brokeback Mountain* fag sins" (Vallis, "Funeral" A3).

Though small, the group has gained international attention for its tactics and language. Consider: "God Hates Fags," "Pope In Hell," "2 Gay Rights: AIDS & Hell," "Your Pastor Is A Whore," "God Hates America," "Thank God For 9/11," or a sign bearing a crude stick figure representation of two men having anal sex. These are just a few of the incendiary posters carried by WBC protestors (Leon 129, 137).

In response, countermovements have formed against the WBC. People who disagree with the WBC have unified in dissent. As WBC acts attract negative media attention, they give rise to opposition groups who themselves become rhetorically united. For instance, Angel Action and the Patriot Guard Riders are two groups that have formed. They enact different rhetorical strategies, but work toward similar ends. Angel Action uses visual rhetoric by spreading large angels' wings in front of WBC protestors. The Patriot Guard Riders use aural rhetoric by using their loud motorcycle engines to drown out WBC voices. These innovative acts of dissent seek to counter the WBC with a corresponding form of nonstandard rhetorical power.

WBC protests create what DeLuca calls "image events" (14). The vulgar words and visual images combine to evoke intense emotion from observers, forestall reasoned discourse, and make deliberation impossible. Attempts to engage WBC protestors, moreover, risk giving them what they seem to want: a reaction, and preferably a violent reaction that will guarantee additional media coverage. Because WBC's members employ unusual rhetorical strategies, knowing how to respond to such acts without adding to the church's media attention creates a rhetorical dilemma for counterprotestors, an exigency shaped by the violent, visual, and religious rhetoric they seek to undermine.

Indeed, countermovement groups have realized that traditional discourse, such as a debate, is not an effective response to the WBC. As a result, these groups employ other tactics such as visually and aurally blocking the WBC protestors. Angel Action and the Patriot Guard Riders are moved to an immediate response because of the rhetorical situation's demand for timeliness. These groups' nonviolent strategies, with their use of strong aural and visual rhetoric, appropriate image events once reserved by and for the WBC.

According to DeLuca, an image event uses visual rhetoric and does not require words for a rhetorical response. Groups use image events to "deconstruct and articulate identities, ideologies, consciousnesses, communities, publics, and cultures" (17). An image event goes against conventional means of discourse by using bodily and nonverbal rhetoric that can create a media spectacle. Image events are "designed to flag media attention and generate publicity." However, DeLuca cautions that image events "are more than just means of getting on television. They are crystallized philosophical fragments, mind bombs, that work to expand the 'universe of thinkable thoughts'" (6). DeLuca points out how "image events are the central mode of public discourse both for conventional electoral politics and for alternative grassroots politics in an era dominated by a commercial televisual electronic public sphere" (17).

The WBC creates image events when protesting at funerals, desecrating American flags, and parading extreme posters. However, Angel Action and the Patriot Guard Riders counter the WBC's with image events of their own, which alter the media response. I label this rhetorical act an *appropriation of image events* because these two countermovement groups are responding to the rhetorical problem by shifting the focus and attention away from the WBC and onto their groups with the use of nonviolent image events.

The first of the two countermovements, Angel Action, was started in the late 1990s by activist Romaine Patterson. Patterson formed Angel Action in response to Phelps' protest at the funeral of Matthew Shepard, a gay student at the University of Wyoming beaten to death in an act of homophobia.

Patterson has described the purpose of Angel Action in terms that stress the group's use of nonverbal, nonviolent rhetoric:

> So often we find that people are willing to make a lot of noise about what they believe to be true. We don't believe that we have to say anything at all. . . . Our actions will speak for themselves. Just one look and the truth is plainly clear. Our focus is to bring forth a message of peace and love. (Hinds)

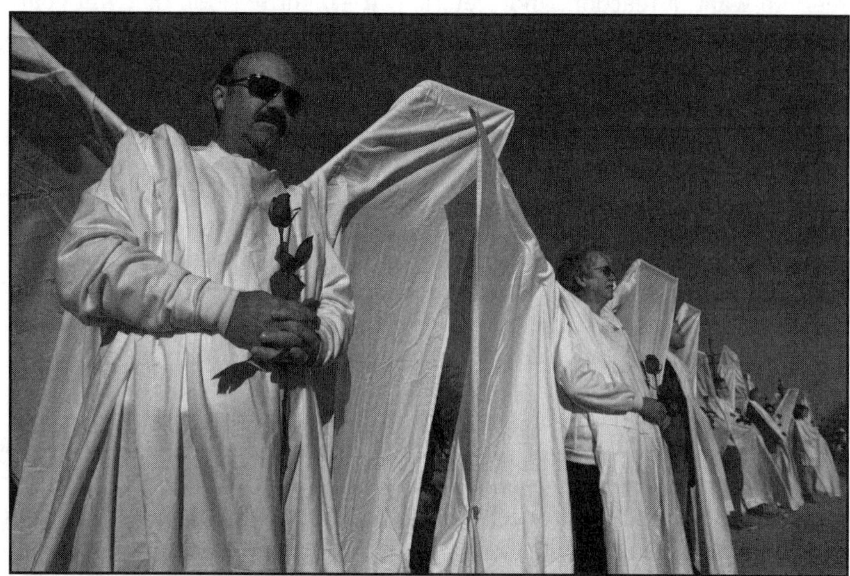

Angel Action counterprotest. AP photo/Chris Carlson.

Smiling, standing quietly in angel costumes in front of loud, obscene WBC protestors, Angel Action's silent, peaceful protest is more captivating than the hateful signs and tattered US flags used by the WBC protestors. No words need to be exchanged between the two groups because the visual rhetoric of large angel wings and coordinating costumes blocking hateful protestors says what words cannot. It is clear, from DeLuca's definitions of an image event, that the rhetorical strategies used by members of Angel Action shape an image event as well. Patterson and members build angel costumes that are seven feet tall and have ten-foot wingspans. They silently line up in front of the WBC protestors, blocking their signs and actions so grieving families can pass by in peace.

In a similar vein, Platoni has reported on the Patriot Guard Riders, a countermovement group that formed in November 2005 and consists of more than 30,000 bikers from all around the United States. Comprised mostly of war veterans who follow the families of dead soldiers from funeral services to cemeteries on their Harleys and Hondas, Patriot Guard Riders' members attempt to block and drown out the protests from the WBC. This "spontaneous mass movement" was formed "as a response to the Rev. Fred Phelps" and now "attend[s] every single military funeral for which the family gives permission" (Biema). The rhetorical response of the Patriot Guard Riders is significant, not only because they visually block the protestors with their motorcycles, but also because their engines drown out the numbing chants from the WBC.

Each of the countermovements constructs its image event differently, but each is targeting the same problem and striving for the same overall result, which includes influencing how the church's message becomes mediated more broadly. For example, a search for the "Westboro Baptist Church" on search engines like Google or LexisNexis returns results that list Angel Action and the Patriot Guard Riders right along with the WBC. By contrast, when Phelps founded the church, media coverage was quite different.

Harmon Leon interviewed Shirley Phelps, Fred's daughter, about a protest she attended at the funeral for a gay journalist, Randy Shilts, in San Francisco in 1994. The WBC received a great deal of attention from gay activists at Shilts' funeral. "Hon, those fags were twenty rows deep. They were beating on our van. It was awesome . . . we were jumping, we were so happy. We were the top story on the news! Hon, that event exploded our group on the radar!" (133–34). The WBC was happy to receive attention, even if that meant angry protestors throwing bags of eggs, bricks, and urine at the church members (134). The violent reaction created a media spectacle and put the WBC on the map for the world to see. Now that groups have formed to respond to Phelps, however, focus has shifted and media reports center on Angel Action and the Patriot Guard Riders as well.

On August 8, 2003, Teri Thomson Randall, from the *Santa Fe New Mexican*, gave a report about the WBC and Angel Action. Romaine Patterson, founder of Angel Action, stated: "I decided that someone needed to stand toe to toe with this guy [Phelps]. Someone needs to show that there is a better way of dealing with that kind of hatred" (55). For her, counter-protesting the WBC had a specific rhetorical goal, one that was itself about rhetoric: for others to understand that we need to "silence and overcome hate. These individuals remind us that it takes more than just an 'ain't-it-awful' attitude to prevail over hatred" (55). Previously, Mary C. Schneidau, of the *University Wire*, reported on a event held on November 11, 2002, where Phelps protested at the University of Maryland because its theater department was presenting "The Laramie Project," an account of the aftermath of Shepard's murder. Approximately ten members from Angel Action were at the protest, outnumbering the protestors from the WBC. The spotlight was on Angel Action, as illustrated by "the flood of donations" that came to the group to provide services for people living with HIV and AIDS. This is just one example of how Angel Action appropriated the image event, grabbed media attention, and gained support from the community.

Another newspaper article highlighted the activism of Angel Action. In the *Austin American-Statesman*, on April 6, 1999, Gwen Florio recounted events outside the Shepard murder trial. Phelps protested in front of the courthouse with signs that read "Matt in Hell." The WBC was blocked from the public's view, however, as angel wings from members of Angel Action masked the image of the anti-gay posters and Phelps, curtailing the ability of WBC protestors to dominate media attention.

In the May 1, 2006, issue of *Time* magazine, Patriot Guard Rider Cheryl Egan explained that her reason for attending soldiers' funerals was originally "because of Fred Phelps, but now the whole focus is off Fred Phelps . . . it's more about the troop who just gave his or her life" (Biema). Nonverbal rhetorical responses from the engines of motorcycles silence the WBC protestors, but the Patriot Guard Riders are also known for visually blocking the protestors. Lizette Alvarez from the *New York Times* reported how the group comes together to "form a human shield in front of the protestors so that mourners cannot see them" (81). The thunderous motorcycles cover up the protestors' words visually and aurally. The image of a chain of Harleys draped with American flags creates a media spectacle that journalists and observers can hardly ignore. The Patriot Guard Riders have, like Angel Action, invented an unconventional way to protest an unconventional group.

As James Kirchick explained in the May 2009 issue of the *Advocate*, Fred "Phelps makes a living by seeking publicity . . . treating Phelps as a genuine security threat along the lines of a terrorist gives him the attention he so desperately seeks" (50). Indeed, the September 14, 2006, issue of *USA Today* highlights the pride Phelps himself feels in his ability to garner attention: "How in the world did we get this humble message from this humble little old nothing of a church to shake the whole country up?" (Keen 5A). The WBC is not looking for debate. They want free publicity. Angel Action's and the Patriot Guard Riders' responses create an opening for a broader public debate, however, and in the process have helped to hinder WBC's ability to create further image events.

Due to the countermovements' efforts, not only have families been able to grieve more privately, but laws have been enacted for limiting protests at funerals in several states. I am not arguing that there is a direct causal relationship between this legislation and the actions of the countermovements. There is no way of measuring such a relationship. However, I do believe that groups like Angel Action and the Patriot Guard Riders have helped to at least encourage such laws. The *National Post* issued an article on November 2, 2007, listing a host of legislative changes. Mary Vallis reported how "the actions of the Westboro Baptist Church members have prompted more than 20 states, including Maryland, and the federal government to pass laws banning protests within a certain distance of funerals" ("Church's" A3).

Many of the members of Angel Action and the Patriot Guard Riders do not consider themselves activists. As quoted by Kara Platoni in the July/August 2006 issue of *Mother Jones*, motorcycle rider Glenn Palmer said, "Our mission statement is strictly in support of the troops and their families. That's all we do" (17). The Patriot Guard Riders would rather focus their attention on the lost soldiers and the grieving families than to label themselves politically. Nevertheless, like Angel Action, they have developed strategies that reveal how rhetoric's creativity can emerge in response to the dilemmas of controversy.

Works Cited

Alvarez, Lizette. "Outrage at Funeral Protests Pushes Lawmakers to Act." *New York Times* 17 Apr. 2006: A1.

Biema, David V. "The Harley Honor Guard." *Time* May 2006. Web. 16 Sept. 2009.

DeLuca, Kevin M. *Image Politics: The New Rhetoric of Environmental Activism*. New York: Guilford, 1996.

Florio, Gwen. "Man Pleads Guilty to Beating Death of Gay Student." *Austin American-Statesman* 6 Apr. 1999: A2.

Hinds, Patrick. "The Whole World was Watching: Living in the Light of Matthew Shepard." *Romaine Patterson* 2005. Web. 9 Dec. 2009.

Keen, Judy. "Funeral Protestors Say Laws Can't Silence Them; Their Belief: Troops Dying because USA Tolerates Gays." *USA Today* 14 Sept. 2006: 5A.

Kirchick, James. "God Hates Censorship." *Advocate* May 2009: 50–51.

Leon, Harmon. *The American Dream: Walking in the Shoes of Carnies, Arms Dealers, Immigrant Dreamers, Pot Farmers, and Christian Believers*. New York: Nation Books, 2008.

Platoni, Kara. "The Hogs of War." *Mother Jones* July/Aug. 2006: 16–17.

Randall, Teri Thomson. "Where Angels Tread." *Santa Fe New Mexican* 8 Aug. 2003: 55.

Schneidau, Mary C. "Phelps Protests Spark Little Clamor, Only 1 Arrest." *University Wire* 11 Nov. 2002.

Vallis, Mary. "Church's Judgment Day; U.S. Sect Ordered to Pay Father $11M for Picketing Marine's Funeral." *National Post* 2 Nov. 2007: A3.

———. "Funeral Protesters Say God is Punishing United States: Military Casualties Blamed on Gay Rights Advances." *National Post* 28 Apr. 2006: A3.

Westboro Baptist Church. "About Us." *God Hates Fags*. Web. 23 Oct. 2010.

23

Controversy under Erasure

Memory, Museum Practice, and the Politics of Magnitude

Kelly M. Young and William Trapani

Long gone are the days in which collectivizing memory might be considered an inevitable and placid force operating cryptically and without agent as it fashions the public and their affairs. Indeed, although it may (still) be experienced otherwise, scholars across the humanities have labored in recent decades to demonstrate that what turn of the twentieth-century writer Hugo von Hofmannstahl once called the "dammed up force of our mysterious ancestors within us" is, instead, an interested, tumultuous, and often acrimonious affair (Olick and Robbins 106). In its broadest sense, of course, public memory aims toward a symbolic consubstantiality—those "mystic chords of memory," as Lincoln called them—that might forge a group's identity and history (Bodnar; Kammen). Yet, the sense and sentiment such a force provides is necessarily "partial, partisan, and thus frequently contested" (Blair, Dickinson, and Ott 9). Indeed, because no representation can include everything we know about commemorated people, events, or places, public memory is inherently selective, foregrounding certain elements or events at the expense of others (Zelizer).

As a specific material expression of public memory, museums and similar display institutions have complex and conflicting goals due to demands made on them by a range of different parties and their relationship to other institutions and sites of memory. As a result,

> the range of museum roles, definitions, and cross-institutional relations entails conjunctions of disparate constituencies, interests, goals, and perspectives. These conjunctions produce debates, tensions, collaborations, contests, and conflicts of many sorts, at many levels. (Kratz and Karp 2)

Due to this partiality, public memory is frequently contested. As Bernard Armada explains,

> By privileging certain narratives and artifacts over others, museums implicitly communicate who/what is central and who/what is peripheral; who/what we must remember and who/what it is okay to forget. Because exhibits are inescapably selective, history museums become public sites of dialectical tension when underrepresented groups question the cultural authority and validity of curators and designers. (236)

In recent years, rhetorical scholars have increasingly engaged in analyses of museums, commemoration, and other sites as a way of accessing these moments of concord and controversy (Armada; Balthrop; Biesecker; Blair, Jeppeson, and Pucci; Blair and Michel; Dickinson, Ott, and Aoki; Gallagher; Taylor). Yet, despite our contemporary understanding that public memory and commemorative discourses are inherently partisan, partial, and operate to articulate a harmonious collective identity, despite the antagonisms that are rife within this kind of rhetorical practice, our places of public memory all too often operate as though there is little controversy, discord, or politics intrinsic within their operation and, more to our interests, that what controversy exists is imminently manageable (Armada; Blair, Dickinson, and Ott; Blight; Bodnar; Zelizer). Indeed, in our view, both through their processes and their effect, these sites too often seek to quash or negotiate disagreement by modifying displays and/or their (re)presentations of history.

In this essay, we examine the controversy surrounding one such revision: the removal, at the beginning of 2010, of a nearly fifty-year-old installation of dioramas representing eight indigenous cultures at the University of Michigan's Exhibit Museum of Natural History. Our motivation for engaging this debate comes less from an interest with the verisimilitude of the dioramas as it does from our concern with the rhetoric of emancipation shot through the discourse of all of the players in the controversy. That is not to suggest that the specific contours of the controversy at the University of Michigan—principally, that the mute, inert, and diminutive diorama figures, sealed as they were in glass cases and frozen in their various narratives of tribal life denied vitality or agency to living indigenous peoples, a concern all the more enhanced given that the collection was housed in a museum space otherwise dedicated not to the ethnological, but to the biological—do not deserve their own attention. Indeed, arrayed against the backdrop of dinosaur bones, various rock and mineral formations, and an extensive collection of Great Lakes wildlife, the dioramas may all too easily reify the long-damaging narrative of Native primitivism and savagery—a thing of nature long since passed over that we are to exercise our dominion.

It is, however, the particularities of the Exhibit Museum's solution to these difficulties that most draws our attention. Seeming to follow the wishful logic of several recent Hollywood films such as *The Indian in the Cupboard* (1995) and *Night at the Museum* (2006) (in which, through some miracultating agency, indigenous figurines are brought to life and in their escape from a modern cabinet of curiosity establish mutually beneficial and rewarding relationships with their Euro-American owners), the museum ultimately felt obliged to respond to the concern of local indigenous communities by shuttering the exhibit altogether, removing it to storage where it is only accessible to faculty with special permission (Harris et al.). As Raymond Silverman, director of museum studies, argued, the dioramas were highly significant sites for representation—analogous in their caricature and pervasive impact to sports mascots—and, hence, needed to be removed and, we would note, treated as a dangerous, almost radioactively contaminating, substance (Harris et al.).

Over the course of the following essay, we advance the argument that progressive social change depends on the condition of a social world predicated not on harmony, but on antagonism; that the vitalization of democratic public engagement can only advance when controversy is allowed to flourish rather than shying away from discord by warehousing the dangerous objects that risk conflict. We suggest that prior to the Exhibit Museum's decision to shutter the diorama installation the condition of possibility existed for just this type of rich and potentially productive antagonism. Indeed, as we show by tracing the competing modalities of magnitude that animated Native and national actors, the stage was set for a fruitful engagement over the state of the nation-state and the contours of our social dialogue. In its insistence on the primacy of the aboriginal authentic, however, those difficult but essential confrontations were interrupted. Ultimately, we suggest, the "success" Native peoples have attained through their particular accent on a celebratory magnitude of presence can only be but a pyrrhic victory, a mere shadow of the agency they may have attained otherwise.

Museums in the Multicultural Moment

It is precisely because the Exhibit Museum controversy, and the ultimate revision of the space, is not singular but instead part of a decades-long initiative to return control of indigenous representation to indigenous peoples themselves that it becomes so worthy of attention. In 1968, the National Congress of American Indians (NCAI) initiated a campaign to combat stereotypical media representations of indigenous people. In 2001, the US Commission on Civil Rights suggested that nonindigenous schools should stop using Native American representations as mascots, which was later enforced by the National Collegiate Athletic Association's (NCAA) ban of these mascots and representations in postseason events (Center for the Study of Sport in Society). Even more recently there have been efforts to strengthen the US Department of the Interior's "Arts and Crafts Board," an agency tasked with overseeing and enforcing consumer protection against the sale of fraudulently marketed "Indian-made" products so as to protect the legitimacy of authentic indigenous art and the commerce of those Native peoples whose livelihood depends on those sales. For all of the energy and often dramatic visibility associated with these endeavors, however, few of the representational redistribution efforts have been as widespread, or as contentious, as the various initiatives to give indigenous populations a voice and veto power in the design of museum exhibits and commemorative sites (Dubin).

This attention to museums and memorials is perhaps not surprising given the air of legitimacy the commemoration industry attains and conveys. Indeed, museums and memorials are presumed to be the accurate and truthful container of a people's history, and by extension, of their potential political agency (Nora). Ivan Karp, curator of African ethnology at the Smithsonian National Museum of Natural History, has put it most clearly when he suggests that "what is at stake in struggles for control over objects and modes of exhibiting them . . . is the articulation of identity. . . . Exhibitions are privileged arenas for presenting images of self and 'other'" (15).

Museums and memorials, in turn, have become critical sites of cultural politics for those seeking to reconfigure representational practices by adjusting the archives both to remember past tragedies and, the hope goes, to offer a bulwark against future intransigence. Across the country, museums exhibiting Native American art and artifacts have faced charges that their installations are replete with factual errors, demeaning stereotypes, and patronizing portrayals. Moreover, charge the critics, museums have been a central force contributing to the ultimately disempowering "vanishing race" syndrome: the concern that nonindigenous patrons leave museum grounds under the impression that Indians are all but extinct, a sense reinforced by their failure to see modern era Indians as "real" since they do not comport to the museological depiction (Bordewich). Ostensibly to set the story straight, then, museums have increasingly sought the guidance of Native American cultural experts in their efforts to present Indian-friendly exhibits by updating inaccurate displays and chronologies that better reflect the history, struggle, and genocide of Native peoples.

This insistence on aboriginal authorship and, it is imagined, the consequently attendant authenticity and authority derived from that lineage have come to dominate the question of "what counts" at a museum or commemorative site. As Bruce W. Ferguson has argued, if exhibits are the speech act of a museum, we might say that what matters today is less the content of that speech than the heritage and identity of the subject authorized to speak; the author has become the content—the thing to behold, to see, and to hear (Ferguson). In a close reading, for example, of one of the original exhibits at the grand opening of the National Museum of the American Indian (NMAI) in 2004, Amanda Cobb writes that perhaps the most remarkable quality of the display was not its design, but its very existence as an Indian-authored discourse:

> An ironic and unspoken aspect of the display was striking; that is, that this argument was being made in a museum, an institutional tool of culture that quite possibly could serve as the fourth major force of col-

> onization after guns, God, and government. I was therefore struck by the fact that in creating the NMAI, Native Americans have *again* turned an instrument of colonization and dispossession into something else—in this case, into an instrument of self-definition and cultural continuance. (486)

No doubt part of Cobb's privileging of author as content comes from her deep suspicions about a non-Native's inability to properly read a modern (i.e., "corrected") museum space. Such patrons, we are told, are not "likely to understand the level of dialogical interaction that is expected of them." They are "resistant" to "trust" the "meaning [that] will be made" from their encounters in the museum in large part because "visitors steeped in Hollywood stereotypes may not realize they have something new to learn" (504).

The crucial element for Cobb, and so many others, is the "indigenizing" (488) of the museum, the incorporation of Indian voices into every stage of the process—or, as Cobb puts it more poetically, the reassurance that their

> "views, voices, and eyes" should be woven into every facet of the museum, literally from the ground up. . . . Each element of the museum . . . stems from these principles all of which are based on Indigenous peoples' knowledge, core values, and definitions of themselves. (489)

These efforts to give indigenous populations the ability to censor or control public representations of themselves are an attempt to provide these communities with a sense of *rhetorical sovereignty.* As Scott Richard Lyons explains,

> Rhetorical sovereignty is the inherent right and ability of peoples to determine their own communicative needs and desires in this pursuit, to decide for themselves the goals, modes, styles, and languages of public discourse. (449–50)

In short, this kind of rhetorical sovereignty provides indigenous communities the rhetorical agency to control and censor detrimental stereotypes and to correct inaccurate representations.

While we can appreciate the desire to have more accurate, humane, and putatively positive representations displayed in public, we should remain cautious that efforts to increase rhetorical sovereignty through the enlargement of a subject's presence, voice, and, in this particular case, physical appearance do not become a discursive form of control and censorship that ultimately harms indigenous communities. Or, as Thomas Farrell once put it in language that forecasts much of our argument to come: "Be careful what you magnify. It may come back to haunt you" ("Love" 103).

As we show, the problem with rhetorical sovereignty when it is conceptualized as veto power—that is, when representation is assumed to be indivisible from the *presence* of particular authors—is that it risks overreaching and opening the door for escalating demands for more changes, revisions, and ultimately the removal of entire sets of histories, narratives, and representations. Under the siege mentality conditions of the present stoked by the belief that control over representation is the linchpin to survival, a type of authenticity arms race may all too easily ensue, which could unleash hyperescalating demands for each subject to demonstrate their zero degree separation from some phantom monolingualism. As John Low, a University of Michigan doctoral student in American Studies and member of the Pokagon Band of Potawatomi Indians, suggested during one roundtable discussion about the diorama controversy, efforts to control and eliminate stereotypical representations may also lead to the erasure of indigenous history if the solution every time there is a complaint about a representation the entire depiction or exhibit goes into storage and is removed from public view (Harris et al.).

Magnitudes of Memory

It is tempting to fixate on the most obvious element of this controversy: the magnification of the Indian subject. To be sure, it would be no arduous task to trace the manner in which activist discourse expressed a near perfect mathematical correlation between the size of the Native figures on display and their corresponding degree of agency. Even the most cursory glance at the commemorative landscape might suggest such a move, for it seems as if, nearly universally, there exists a strident effort to "up size" the Native figure by magnifying its physical presence and force. In addition to the Exhibit Museum, for example, the former Custer Battlefield Memorial was renamed by George H. W. Bush as the Little Bighorn Battlefield Memorial and the grounds were supplemented with a Native-designed memorial circle in order to recognize the loss of Indian peoples during the battle. The aforementioned and recently opened NMAI often gets as much press for its earth-stone exterior and grounds (which contain rock and water features as well as seasonal crops) as it does for its holdings. In nearly all of those accounts, however, the sheer magnitude of the building is a central talking point, as in one travel guide account, which opens by noting, "the building itself is imposing, a large ship-like edifice" (Edwards). None of these, however, hold the proverbial candle to the mountain-sized carving at the Crazy Horse Memorial in the Black Hills of South Dakota, which aims to dwarf its counterpart Mt. Rushmore mere miles away.

As Thomas Farrell went to great pains to help us understand, however, magnitude is not merely about grandiosity in form; rather, it is about establishing significance in whatever fashion might best accomplish that end ("Sizing"). Despite the numerous times he referred to size, weight, scope, dimension, or scale, in Farrell's hands magnitude was less a quality of the object than it was a measure of rhetoricity, even, one might say, the very *sine qua non* of rhetoric itself ("Weight"). Ironically, it is Farrell's concern that excessive magnitude distorts, that it can induce myopia and blindness, that encourages us to shy away from the more direct and obvious connection between our project and that current of his work that most explicitly uses the language of physical magnitude. Instead, we take our cue from his insistence that, for Aristotle at least, magnitude is a type of "inventional logic," a search for the perspective necessary to ground one's discourse with mattering ("Sizing" 7). Or, as James McDaniel has put it, "as every image necessarily articulates a sense of scale and importance, however vague in a given case, so all discourse insinuates a magnitude" (92).

Reconceptualizing magnitude in this manner does not preclude consideration of the attempted enlargement of the Native body (politic) taking place at the Exhibit Museum: it reorders how we consider that excess. Rather than being beholden to the object proper, however, understanding magnitude as an inventional logic more clearly reveals the sentiment circulating through the diorama debate and other examples of commemorative magnification. In its most vulgar form, this sentiment is best described as "size matters," not (merely) because it chimes with a risqué conversation topic, but because it reflects the substance of the argument. Offered as a type of trump card and argument *tout court,* size becomes a register of countervalue.

But, in the Western world at least, gigantism has a long and troubled history of appearing strange or grotesque. The wholly unreliable narrator of Mark Danielewski's novel *House of Leaves,* a modern cult horror classic about a house whose interior grows increasingly larger than its exterior, perhaps best sums up our current sentiment by suggesting that "largeness has always been a condition of the weird and unsafe: it is overwhelming, too much or too big. Thus, that which is uncanny or *unheimlich* is neither homey nor protective, nor comforting nor familiar" (28). Michel-Rolph Trouillot has advanced a similar argument about the daunting and ineffable nature of grandiose commemorative sites:

> The bigger the material mass the more easily it entraps us: mass graves and pyramids bring history closer while they make us feel small. A castle, a fort, a battlefield, a church, all these things bigger than we that we infuse with the reality of past lives, seem to speak of an immensity of which we know little except that we are part of it. Too solid to be unmarked, too conspicuous to be candid, they embody the ambiguities of history. They give us the power to touch it, but not that to hold it firmly in our hands—hence the mystery of their battered walls. We suspect that their concreteness hides secrets so deep that no revelation may fully dissipate their silences. (29–30)

Against the increasingly flamboyant, spectacular, and grandiose extravagance of contemporary ethnic memorialization one could just as easily craft a deft defense of the claim that national archives have turned on a different trajectory altogether, toward a type of de-monumentalization. Indeed, as Carole Blair has argued, today's commemoration is more likely to tender a sober listing of the lost than engage in the triumphal and heroic inscriptions of the fallen's valor typical of earlier eras. The upshot, for Blair, is that current "rhetoric offers no comfort of historical progress and speaks only about loss, not sacrifice," effecting a striking refusal to align with mainstream values, which affords commemoration the status of a "critical" public art, "one that dares to awaken a public sphere of resistance, struggle, and dialogue" (282).

Even as we mark the downshifting of rhetorical embellishment in our contemporary national commemoration, and point to its "critical" potential, we feel the need to locate that shift (well) within a larger historical frame in which it has been quite common for the national subject to accent "the Other's" exotic extravagance against its own putatively temperate and prudent nature. Seen from this vantage, we thus have the appearance of a recalibrated public sphere, but that appears so without having necessarily changed the logics by which that public operates. Following Homi Bhabha, for instance, Deutsche argues that to simply add marginalized groups previously unrepresented in the public arena does nothing more than participate in "masculinism as a position of social authority" in which nostalgia tries to import the excluded into the unchanged ideal (312).

What does all of this have to say about commemoration and the contestation and conflict that are the lifeblood, not the contagion, of a democratic public sphere? Toward answering that question, we return to McDaniel, who has tried to assess the relevance of magnitude and, in particular, of tall talk or self-aggrandizement. McDaniel makes the case that in moments of transformation and the constitution of a new frontier, particular subjects stand as models—or chronotypes—that dictate the style and action of others. And although he is describing a type of style that is more likely to activate public sentiment, he takes pains to note that the style itself is not limited to a singular diachronic expression. In other words, in America's first frontier, he notes, we had figures of magnitude that were "larger than life," such as Davey Crockett, whereas today although the same self-aggrandizement is attainable for someone like the UNIX guru, our new "technological sublime" is fascinated by speed, weightlessness, and the lack of friction.

Even, then, as Native Americans have come to increasingly bank on magnitude as size, the national character seems more interested in sober recitations and remembrances that induce remembrance by overwhelming spectators with the "arithmetic sublime" (Laqueur 5), creating a fundamental disconnect of styles, a tension between what Farrell would call the "moods" of magnitude ("Weight" 485). To put it more directly: there is an asymmetry in the style and tenor of modalities. The Native American accent on a celebratory magnitude of presence may have worked well when the nation was erecting its most triumphant and self-aggrandizing monuments. At present, however, the national commemorative mood is more tragic, more past-oriented. Even still, these varying styles of magnification need not signal the death knell of progressive social exchange. Indeed, as we have attempted to underscore, these variances could well have offered a rich terrain of antagonism spurring debate over the state of the nation, the relation between the universal and the particular, and the substance of our collective memory.

Discourses of Authenticity

It is in this vein that insistence on authenticity as a marker of legitimacy in conversations about the indigenous becomes particularly problematic. This rhetoric has a corrective purpose that seeks to "set the record straight" about indigenous history and practices. While this may be an admirable aim, the problem with this type of discourse is that it seeks to create a perfectible communication and system of representation. However, as Jacques Derrida most notably contends, rhetoric can never have such a pure or perfected meaning because of its iterability, which undermines notions of intent and control (7). Consequently, as these messages are rearranged, edited, packaged, and then consumed, the proper or correct meaning of the message is no longer guaranteed. Besides evoking a celebratory magnitude of presence, attempts to use museum and archeological interactive and visual technologies to present a more correct, modern, or "living" version of indigenous culture demonstrates the superiority of Euro-American culture in preserving and saving near-extinct cultures, which counters the common message indigenous displays hope to present (Dickinson et al., "Spaces" 38). Or, as James Young maintains, once a museum image is created, it almost immediately "appears archaic, strange, or irrelevant altogether" (294). As a result, articulating a correct and truly authentic representation is impossible.

Yet, one of the consequences of this discourse is that the push for an authentic representation can lead to the foreclosure of difference, diversity, and public antagonism. For instance, in an attempt to be authentic, these claims may risk "overwriting the actual complexity of difference [and] may write out that voice as effectively as earlier oppressive discourse of reportage" (Griffiths 237). As Amy Harris, director of the Exhibit Museum, admits, one of the benefits of the dioramas is that they could efficiently represent many different indigenous groups, which is lost with the removal of the exhibits (Harris et al.). But more importantly, once a representation is deemed most accurate, it polices and delegitimizes any other narratives or representations. This is problematic because the very controversy over these representations is a part of the history and the collective memory of Native and non-Native relations. As we struggle to make the past and present collective memory as authentic and accurate as possible, we forget the rather important process of antagonism and controversy that is ultimately a more productive and living type of collective memory. Unfortunately, once an authentic account or representation is presented, all of this controversy is erased and future discussion is shunned; the rhetorical result can be depoliticized historical amnesia.

Discursive Effect of Historical Amnesia

The public debate about the Exhibit Museum highlights the value that public controversy can serve in better understanding a host of contemporary indigenous issues. Museum officials obviously understood this when they created four months of educational programming and placed explanation overlays on the exhibits. While the original exhibits were certainly stereotypical and archaic, their presence and later modification with overlays produced significant public deliberation and education. For example, Harris noted that she learned a great deal about sovereignty conflicts and the spiritual connections between artifacts and people due to the dispute (Harris et al.). Also, the dioramas were the second most popular item in the museum, particularly for school groups (Harris et al.). Thus, they served as important sites for deliberation and education about issues vital to indigenous communities.

The potential benefit of this kind of public debate and continued controversy is that it draws forth a host of contemporary cultural and political issues that typically lie beneath the surface of most exhibits and commemorative acts. As noted earlier, in a multicultural environment, there is no way that any museum can fully represent the sheer cultural, social, and political complexity and diversity of any group it attempts to represent. As a result, "somewhere beneath the surface of all presentations of the past lie the potentially defiant voices of marginalized groups awaiting fulfillment in the crucible of public controversy" (Armada 236). What would be most productive would be to use and channel these controversies to produce sites of dialectical tension. These spaces would allow any underrepresented group to challenge the cultural authority and influence of museums and other commemorative practices and mark themselves and their grievances as important and ongoing (236). When we remove or settle these controversies, we destroy these sites of dialectical tension and public controversy. In doing so, we depoliticize efforts aimed at cultural understanding and produce the discursive effect of historical amnesia (Gallagher 307–08). The sort of living and active memory that indigenous populations seek in order to demonstrate how they are a living and relevant people is triggered by vigorously contested commemorative acts, rather than through an uncritical politics of magnitude (307–08).

In arguing that public controversy and dialectical tension are productive and important, we do not contend that dioramas or other controversial sites or representations should be left untouched. However, we also disagree with decisions to eliminate or erase controversial representations from our collective memory. Instead, these sites of memory should be actively marked and designated as sites of struggle and tension. One example of this kind of politicized marking of memory sites, as examined by Bernard Armada, is Jacqueline Smith's one-woman countermemorial outside of the National Civil Rights Museum (NCRM) in Memphis. For over 15 years, Smith has sat just outside the exit of the museum to protest the museum's commodification and loss of King's ideals and politics (235). Her presence is a constant disruption and critique to the official discourse offered by the NCRM that "opens space for a more critical consumption of the museum's official version of King's memory" (235).

Similarly, James Young has interrogated the development of a number of countermoments throughout Germany that serve as "brazen, painfully self-conscious memorial spaces" that constantly change over time and seek to stimulate memory rather than provide an official or authentic account of history (271). For example, in 1986, a countermonument against fascism was constructed in Hamburg encouraging visitors to write their names on the monument. With the passage of time, the monument sank into the ground. Once completely lowered into the ground, the "burden of memory" was returned to the visitors (276). Rather than provide a singular or authentic account of the history of fascism or the Nazi regime, the countermonument required the public to use its active memory in order to make meaning of the memorial.

In such spaces, there is opportunity for civic engagement and deliberation about issues such as the importance of a living and vibrant culture, the struggles over sovereignty, and spiritual connections to lands and places. One of the primary criticisms of dioramas and other media representations and museums is that they are static and fail to convey a sense of a living culture. Yet in their attempts to police authenticity or express various modes of a magnitude of presence, the burden of remembering and reflecting is transferred from non-Native consumers to the institution, or to the sites or commemorative acts that possess the "correct" representation or presence. By critically interrogating how indigenous commemorative practices produce a politics consumed with magnitude and authenticity, new strategies founded on progressive antagonism and dialectic tension can be discovered that provide more productive sources of agency for indigenous peoples.

Works Cited

Armada, Bernard J. "Memorial Agon: An Interpretive Tour of the National Civil Rights Museum." *Southern Communication Journal* 63 (1998): 235–42.

Balthrop, William V. "Culture, Myth, and Ideology as Public Argument: An Interpretation of the Ascent and Demise of 'Southern Culture.'" *Communication Monographs* 51 (1984): 339–52.

Biesecker, Barbara. "Remembering World War II: The Rhetoric and Politics of National Commemoration at the Turn of the Twentieth Century." *Quarterly Journal of Speech* 88 (2002): 393–409.

Blair, Carole. "Reflections on Criticism and Bodies: Parables from Public Places." *Western Journal of Communication* 65 (2001): 271–94.

Blair, Carole, Brian Dickinson, and Brian L. Ott, eds. Introduction: Rhetoric/Memory/Place. *Places of Public Memory: The Rhetoric of Museums and Memorials.* Tuscaloosa: U of Alabama P, 2010. 1–54.

Blair, Carole, Marsha S. Jeppeson, and Enrico Pucci Jr. "Public Memorialization in Postmodernity: The Vietnam Veterans Memorial as Prototype." *Quarterly Journal of Speech* 77 (1991): 263–88.

Blair, Carole, and Neil Michel. "The Rushmore Effect: *Ethos* and National Collective Identity." *Ethos of Rhetoric*. Ed. Michael J. Hyde. Columbia: U of South Carolina P, 2004: 156–96.

Blight, David W. *Beyond the Battlefield: Race, Memory, and the American Civil War.* Amherst: U of Massachusetts P, 2002.

Bodnar, John. *Remaking America: Public Memory, Commemoration, and Patriotism in the Twentieth Century.* Princeton, NJ: Princeton UP, 1992.

Bordewich, Fergus M. *Killing the White Man's Indian: Reinventing Native Americans at the End of the Twentieth Century.* New York: Doubleday, 1996.

Center for the Study of Sport in Society. "Native American Mascots and Violence." Northeastern University, Center for the Study of Sport. 2007. Web. 9 Jan. 2011.

Cobb, Amanda J. "The National Museum of the American Indian as Cultural Sovereignty." *American Quarterly* 57 (June 2005): 485–506.

Danielewski, Mark Z. *House of Leaves*. New York: Pantheon Books, 2000.

Derrida, Jacques. "Signature Event Context." *Limited Inc.* Ed. Gerald Graff. Evanston, IL: Northwestern UP, 1988. 1–21.

Deutsche, Rosalyn. *Evictions: Art and Spatial Politics*. Cambridge, MA: MIT P, 1998.

Dickinson, Greg, Brian L. Ott, and Eric Aoki. "Memory and Myth at the Buffalo Bill Museum." *Western Journal of Communication* 69 (2005): 85–108.

———. "Spaces of Remembering and Forgetting: The Reverent Eye/I at the Plains Indian Museum." *Communication and Critical/Cultural Studies* 3 (2006): 27–47.

Dubin, Steven C. *Displays of Power: Memory and Amnesia in the American Museum*. New York: New York UP, 1999.

Edwards, Megan. "Something Old, Something New: The Smithsonian's New Museum of the American Indian." *Roadtrip America*. Web. 6 Jan. 2011.

Farrell, Thomas. "Love and Theft after 9/11: Magnification in the Rhetorical Aftermath." *Rhetorical Democracy: Discursive Practices of Civic Engagement, Selected Papers from the 2002 Conference of the Rhetoric Society of America*. Ed. Gerard A. Hauser and Amy Grim. Mahwah, NJ: Lawrence Erlbaum, 2004. 99–103.

———. "Sizing Things Up: Colloquial Reflection as Practical Wisdom." *Argumentation* 12 (1998): 1–14.

———. "The Weight of Rhetoric: Studies in Cultural Delirium." *Philosophy and Rhetoric* 41 (2008): 467–87.

Ferguson, Bruce W. "Exhibition Rhetorics: Material Speech and Utter Sense." *Thinking about Exhibitions*. Ed. Reesa Greenberg, Bruce W. Ferguson, and Sandy Nairne. New York: Routledge, 1996. 175–90.

Gallagher, Victoria J. "Memory and Reconciliation in the Birmingham Civil Rights Institute." *Rhetoric & Public Affairs* 2 (1999): 303–20.

Griffiths, Gareth. "The Myth of Authenticity." *The Post-Colonial Studies Reader.* Ed. Bill Ashcroft, Gareth Griffiths, and Helen Tiffin. London: Routledge, 1995. 237–41.

Harris, Amy, Robert E. Megginson, Raymond Silverman, Frank Ettawageshik, John N. Low, and Lisa C. Young. "Native American Dioramas in Transition." University of Michigan Library. 12 Sept. 2009. Web.

Kammen, Michael. *Mystic Chords of Memory: The Transformation of Tradition in American Culture.* New York: Vintage Books, 1993.

Karp, Ivan. "Culture and Representation." *Exhibiting Culture: The Poetics and Politics of Museum Display.* Ed. Ivan Karp and Steven D. Lavine. Washington, DC: Smithsonian Institution P, 1991. 11–24.

Kratz, Corinne A., and Ivan Karp, eds. Introduction. *Museum Friction: Public Cultures/Global Transformations*. Durham, NC: Duke UP, 2006. 1–31.

Laqueur, Thomas, et al. *Grounds for Remembering: Monuments, Memorials, Texts.* Berkeley, CA: Townsend Center for the Humanities, 1995.

Lyons, Scott R. "Rhetorical Sovereignty: What Do American Indians Want from Writing?" *College Composition and Communication* 51.3 (2000): 447–68.

McDaniel, James P. "Figures for New Frontiers, from Davy Crockett to Cyberspace Gurus." *Quarterly Journal of Speech* 88 (2002): 91–111.

Nora, Pierre. "Between Memory and History: *Les Lieux de Mémoire*." *Representations* 26 (Spring 1989): 7–25.

Olick, Jeffrey K., and Joyce Robbins. "Social Memory Studies: From 'Collective Memory' to the Historical Sociology of Mnemonic Practices." *Annual Review of Sociology* 24 (1998): 105–40.

Taylor, Bryan C. "Radioactive History: Rhetoric, Memory, and Place in the Post-Cold War Nuclear Museum." *Places of Public Memory: Rhetoric of Museums and Memorials*. Ed. Greg Dickinson, Carole Blair, and Brian Ott. Tuscaloosa: U of Alabama P, 2010. 57–86.

Trouillot, Michel-Rolph. *Silencing the Past: Power and the Production of History.* Boston: Beacon Hill, 1995.

Young, James E. "The Counter-Monument: Memory against Itself in Germany Today." *Critical Inquiry* 18 (1992): 267–95.

Zelizer, Barbie. "Reading the Past Against the Grain: The Shape of Memory Studies." *Critical Studies in Mass Communication* 12 (1995): 214–39.

24

"That We Might Become 'A Peculiar People'"

Spatial Rhetoric as a Resource for Identification

Rosalyn Collings Eves

All rhetoric, whether tending toward concord or controversy, emerges from both conceptual spaces and material places. Henri Lefebvre notes: "Every language is located in a space. Every discourse says something about a space (places or sets of places); and every discourse is emitted from a space" (132). Even the language we use to talk about concord and controversy reveals a spatial dimension: when we find ourselves in agreement, we are "on the same page" or "with" someone, we "come together." When we disagree, we often represent others as "outsiders." Material places also matter to the creation of concord or controversy through rhetoric. For one thing, rhetorical persuasion (the move toward concord) cannot take place without some sort of shared material space, whether that space be a physical site (in the case of an audience for a speech), or access to the same text in digital or print form. For another, physical places shape us in ways that matter to our rhetoric, in terms of how we present ourselves and what kind of language, appeals, and evidence are deemed appropriate for particular sites; physical places can limit our options for persuasion and push us toward controversy, particularly in cases where the places invoked by rhetoric contain compelling and contested symbolic value (as in the case of the recent disputes about whether or not to build a mosque near Ground Zero), or in cases where the site of the rhetorical transaction carries significant sociopolitical weight (think of the controversy surrounding Glenn Beck's religious rally at the Lincoln Memorial).

Material spaces and their attendant discourses can also function, however, as powerful rhetorical resources leading to concord and group unity. This material *and* spatial dimension is a crucial, but often unexplored, dimension of rhetoric. As Gregory Clark points out, Kenneth Burke saw place (scene) as a key factor in his pentad, "to the extent that it encompasses as well as shapes and constrains each of the [other terms]" (*Rhetorical* 33). Both Roxanne Mountford and Nedra Reynolds have called for more studies in rhetoric that attend to material space. While scholars have responded to this call, much remains to be done in order to understand how spaces are constructed through rhetoric, how discourses of space are strategically deployed, and how material spaces constrain and enable rhetorical performance.

This essay is part of a larger project in which I explore how geographical space both constrains and enables the rhetorical practices of nineteenth-century women in the American West. By geographical space I mean both the natural and built spaces of a landscape and the cultural discourses surrounding those places. I follow a typical scholarly distinction between space and place, defining space as a conceptual and relational term and place as a more concrete physical location. I understand place in three particular ways: as the physical characteristics of a given site; the cultural discourses that endow particular places with meaning and dictate "appropriate" behavior within that site; and the resulting network of relationships between people, objects, and materials that occupy a given space. Because each of these three aspects of place change over time, places are necessarily dynamic.

As part of this project, I ask: How does geographical positioning (of the rhetor and her audience) constrain and enable rhetors? How do rhetors engage with prominent cultural attitudes toward specific places, both shaping and being shaped by these cultural discourses? How do they use and manipulate conceptions of space into rhetorical appeals on behalf of people and issues that matter to them? In this essay, I examine how the conditions of a physical site can constitute an "invitation to rhetoric" and how discourses about material places can serve as resources for invention—and identification. I use the case study of Eliza R. Snow, a nineteenth-century leader of Mormon women, to show how Snow responded to a geographic exigence by drawing on a shared mythology of space to strengthen Mormon women's positive religious identification.

Rhetorics of Space

Before continuing with the specific analysis, I need to contextualize this project in terms of four basic trends in the broader field of rhetorics of space (although there are arguably more, and many scholarly projects involve elements of more than one of these trends).

First, a number of feminist, postcolonial, and race studies indirectly address space when they explore the ways that women and other minorities were denied access to rhetorically significant sites (pulpits, courtrooms, etc.). Although this situating function of rhetoric is a key element of rhetoric (Nystrand and Duffy), it's not often explicitly recognized as an example of rhetorics of space. Examples of this particular strand might include Cheryl Glenn's *Rhetoric Retold*, Mary Louise Pratt's *Imperial Eyes*, and Shirley Wilson Logan's, *"We Are Coming": The Persuasive Discourse of Nineteenth-Century Black Women*.

Second, the majority of studies that explicitly identify themselves as spatial/rhetorical studies focus on the rhetorical construction of places, examining the ways that discourse shapes the experience and expectations of individuals within a site. In a pair of companion pieces published in *Rhetorical Education in America* (Glenn et al.), Michael Halloran and Gregory Clark ("Transcendence") demonstrate the ways that the educational experience of public spaces, like national parks, are shaped through careful rhetorical framing of the site. Clark's follow-up study, *Rhetorical Landscapes in America*, suggests that as our perspectives of space are shaped through discourse, our experience of particular places becomes rhetorical—that is, particular spaces have the rhetorical power to draw diverse individuals together in a national community through their shared experience of place. Jessica Enoch, Nan Johnson, and Roxanne Mountford all explore the ways that particular spaces are gendered: Enoch looks at the gendering of nineteenth-century schools, Johnson looks at the ways that parlors and other "feminine" sites were rendered appropriate sites for female rhetorical practices, and Mountford looks at the ways that religious pulpits have traditionally been gendered masculine and the problems that presents for women preachers. Some ecocomposition work belongs here as well, particularly studies that examine the ways that discourse shapes perception of the natural environment.

A third trend explores the symbolic operation of space in discourse; for example, Richard Marback's study of narratives about Robben Island, where opponents of apartheid in South Africa were held prisoner, explores the way that the island begins to function as a symbol, "a commonplace for injustices of apartheid" (7), that instructs readers how to emotionally respond to both the site and narratives about the site. Nedra Reynolds similarly offers an insightful critique of the spatial metaphors used in landmark composition studies (particularly the metaphor of a frontier) ("Composition's").

The fourth strand of research on rhetorics of space tends to explore the influence of a particular site on rhetorical performance. For instance, Reynold's *Geographies of Writing* emphasizes the ways that material sites of composition can affect students' writing and learning processes. Similarly, ecocompositionists like Julie Drew and Sidney Dobrin argue that we cannot understand students' writing independent of the places that those students come from. Jerry Blitefield redefines kairos to include place, arguing that rhetorical agency happens when kairos coincides with the right place: "*kairoi* come into existence in places, *as* places" (73). Mountford's study on pulpits would also fit into this category. Because my project tries to understand the ways that places and discourses about those places both constrain and enable rhetorical performance, it falls primarily in the last category. While some of these trends focus more on the discursive than material aspects of space, as John Ackerman notes, it is critical to recognize that linguistic and material dimensions of spaces are linked. Thus, while this paper explores the way discourses of space get leveraged rhetorically (part of the third trend found above), it also attends to the fact that these discourses are rooted in a particular material space (trend number four) and that those same discourses function to shape the way listeners view that landscape (trend number two).

Case Study: Eliza R. Snow

Eliza Roxcy Snow was a prominent member of her Mormon faith, one of Brigham Young's plural wives and widely known among her people as "Zion's poetess." Although born and reared in Ohio, Snow moved west to Utah in 1847 with many other Mormons in response to religious persecution. In 1867, she became the president of the Relief Society, an association for all female members of the Mormon church. As historian Jill Derr argues, "[Snow] was the female voice heard more widely, clearly, and consistently than any other" in contemporary Mormon communities (115).

Although Snow clearly had a significant influence on Mormon women, she and her community remain largely unknown to rhetorical scholars. Despite the recent rise in historiographical projects that recover nineteenth-century American women's rhetoric, there is little recovery work of nineteenth-century Mormon women, including Snow. Anne Ruggles Gere's work on nineteenth-century club women is one of the few published rhetorical texts to treat Mormon women. This neglect may stem from a tendency among feminist rhetorical scholars to identify most strongly with progressive women; Mormon women, belonging as they do to a church now widely recognized as conservative, do not seem to merit the same rhetorical attention. Yet, as Carol Mattingly suggests, focusing solely on women with radical political projects can distort our understanding of nineteenth-century women's political participation, in part because it prevents us from acknowledging other effective rhetorical projects. Moreover, dismissing nineteenth-century Mormon women as conservative on the basis of current representations of Mormonism is a mistake, given the radical origins of Mormonism (Keller et al.). With some justification, Eliza R. Snow could claim that, "No where on the earth has woman so broad a sphere of labor and duty, of responsibility and action, as in Utah" ("An Address" 62). These women believed they were instrumental in creating a revolutionary Kingdom of God on earth; they were among the first to achieve woman's suffrage (in 1870); they established the first enduring women's journal west of the Mississippi called the *Woman's Exponent,* a bimonthly journal written by and for Mormon women (Beecher); and, at one point in the latter half of the nineteenth century, had more women doctors than any other state or territory (Firor).

Snow's life-long rhetorical project was to affirm Mormon women's spiritual identities (Derr), but in the 1870s and 1880s her project took on additional urgency. Following the completion of the transcontinental railroad in 1869, Snow and other Mormon leaders were concerned about the perceived threat to Mormon cultural and religious integrity as growing numbers of non-Mormons moved into Utah territory. Thus, physical conditions in the territory provided Snow with a powerful exigence. In response, Snow increased her rhetorical efforts to strengthen identification among Mormon women. Here, I look at how Snow drew on a specific spatial trope—that of the "desert redeemed"—to invite women to accept the constitutive narrative invoked by the trope and to provide her audience with shared symbols for identity.

The "desert redeemed" mythology held that God had led the Mormons to refuge in the deserts of the West (an isolated, unwanted space where their enemies would not follow them) and made the deserts bloom to support their settlement, thus reaffirming their status as a chosen people. In fact, the language most commonly used by Mormons (and non-Mormons) to describe this phenomenon was that God made "the desert blossom as the rose," a quotation from the Book of Isaiah describing the prophesied renewal of Israel: "the desert shall rejoice, and blossom as the rose" (35:1). Given the dislocation of Mormons, it is not surprising that Snow should turn to space as a powerful resource for symbolic invention. Because land, like other markers of dominant culture identity, often becomes an invisible marker of privilege, land is often only noticed or valued in its absence (Brady). In the wake of their own displacements and dislocations, Mormons (like the Israelites they took as their spiritual predecessors), increasingly invested their physical place with spiritual significance. This narrative of a desert redeemed influenced Mormon settlers and non-Mormon visitors alike in their perception of the Salt Lake Valley. At least one visitor in 1862 noted, "Truly the Mormon prophesy has been fulfilled: already a howling wilderness blooms like a rose" (qtd. in Mitchell 338).

Ironically, this mythology did not accord with the initial perception of Mormon settlers, many of whom (Snow included) found the Great Salt Lake valley more fertile and promising than the Wyoming and Nebraska plains they had crossed. This changing narrative suggests not only the dynamic nature of spaces, but the ways that narratives work to infuse landscapes with meaning. Historian Richard Jackson demonstrates that many of these earlier settlers subsequently modified their narrative accounts of settlement to emphasize God's role in leading them to Utah, including a greater emphasis on the sterility of the valley ("Mormon Perception"). These settlement narratives also downplayed Mormon research on irrigation techniques prior to moving west, in order to suggest that their irrigation practices were also evidence of God's divine blessing. In part, these revised narratives helped Mormons overcome the seeming paradox of God's chosen people being driven out of their assigned Zion (common Mormon belief held Jackson County, Missouri, to be the site of the new American Jerusalem). Moreover, as Jackson argues, the desertification of the Great Plains in these settlement narratives helped Mormons see themselves as spiritual heirs of Israel: "The Great Plains as an American Sinai became the proof that the Mormons were indeed the latter-day inheritors of the Israelites' promises, a chosen people whom God required to be proven by trials through an exodus to an unknown land" ("Mormon Experience" 52).

Snow drew on the image of the desert blossoming to remind her audience of their identity as a chosen people. Thus, her discourse transforms the material facts of the land into a powerful symbol of shared identity. Clark's distinction of land and landscape becomes crucial here: "*Land* is material, a particular object, while *landscape* is conceptual. . . . *Land* becomes landscape when it is assigned the role of symbol, and as symbol it functions rhetorically" (*Rhetorical* 9). In a representative example from 1886, Snow published a description in the *Woman's Exponent* of a meeting she had attended where the predominant audience members were "old folks," of whom she herself (in her eighties at the time) was one. Rather than point to their age or other weaknesses, Snow rejoices in the beauty of these "old folks," and uses the occasion to remind her readers of the importance of their pioneer heritage—a heritage that she links explicitly to the mythology of a desert redeemed:

> I know that many of those whose faces expressed integrity and firmness, had in times gone by, drank freely of the cup of sorrow from the merciless hands of persecution—had from time to time been homeless and destitute—had journeyed over trackless wastes to this Mountain recess, *then the veriest personification of barrenness and desolation* which never would, and never could have been redeemed from its sterility, and utilized, by any other people than such as were before me, whose indomitable courage, nerved by unswerving faith and trust in the living God, which inspired them with more than mortal strength to contend with adverse circumstances and draw forth subsistence from unpropitious elements. *Now that same desert blossoms as the rose.* ("The 'Old Folks'" 20, emphasis added)

For Snow, this narrative demonstrates the faith and courage of those early settlers, a crucial part of Mormon pioneer heritage and identity. Significantly, this identity narrative is tied to the Utah geography: the transformation of the landscape, from the "veriest personification of barrenness and desolation" to a blooming rose, becomes both a symbol of and evidence for their faith and identity.

I would like to analyze in a little more depth how this particular narrative works to interpellate Mormon women into a shared identity. According to Maurice Charland, rhetoric becomes constitutive when it provides an audience with the means for assuming a group identity. As audiences recognize and acknowledge being addressed by a particular discourse, they (consciously or unconsciously) accept the subject position assigned to them by that discourse. Unlike other methods of persuasion, constitutive appeals take effect from the moment of address, prior to the use of any particular appeals. Since most individuals vacillate between a variety of identity positions and are often addressed in a variety of ways, a constitutive rhetoric is most successful when it can best resolve conflicts between subject positions, or when it provides the most compelling narrative of identity. In other words, by asserting the existence of a collective Mormon subject who endured persecution and transformed a desert through divine aid, Snow constitutes her audience as part of that collective. For Snow and her hearers, the myth of a desert redeemed provides a compelling narrative that not only informs their group identity as chosen people, but also confirms their existence as a group (even though the historic group of Mormons was undoubtedly different in composition and, conceivably, values from the group as presently constituted). Snow’s rhetorical texts, which address her Mormon sisters as spiritual beings with extraordinary potential, presume for women the identity she expects them to assume, that of faithful, hard-working women.

In addition to its constitutive function, Snow’s use of the “desert redeemed” trope functions as a powerful symbol for identification. Ernest Bormann, like Kenneth Burke, sees groups as identifying around shared symbols that are charged with meaning. For Bormann, these symbols, or “shared fantasy themes,” represent “the creative and imaginative shared interpretation of events that fulfills a group psychological or rhetorical need” (130). In this sense, shared fantasy themes—like the symbolic trope of a desert redeemed—help individuals understand the identity (in terms of shared history and individual roles within the community) with which individuals are asked to identify. Precisely because these fantasies are shared, they function as “common reference points that enable people to understand themselves as sharing situation and scene” (Clark, *Rhetorical* 39). Sharing group fantasies also “brings about a convergence of appropriate feeling among the participants” (Bormann 130) that motivates listeners to particular group-sanctioned actions. Thus, this symbol (or shared fantasy theme) becomes a shorthand for a particular constellation of symbols and values that constitute identity (Clark, *Rhetorical*). Once a fantasy theme is established, even a cryptic reference to that theme, like the phrase, “a desert blossoming as a rose,” is enough to evoke the full set of meanings and emotional responses embedded in the theme. The pride and sense of spiritual affirmation evoked by the desert redeemed trope allow the women in Snow’s audience to see themselves as strong, courageous, spiritually faithful women and predispose them to orthodox action.

Although I do not have time to describe the other spatial tropes that Snow uses—like the idea of Zion or a mountain home—these tropes outline for Mormon women a rhetorical vision that places even their most mundane actions (child rearing, housekeeping, etc.) as part of a vast spiritual enterprise of Kingdom building. Such invocations of space not only remind listeners of their shared past, they orient listeners toward their future identity and behavior. These tropes remind Mormon women that, as they have separated from the material world in the past, so they are to keep themselves separate in the future, in order to maintain their identity as holy women of God. Such identification is not entirely innocent: as Snow's spatial discourses tend toward concord among her people, they create controversy with outsiders. The identification Snow offers can only be maintained upon terms of exclusion: even as Snow encourages her listeners to identify with one another, she encourages them to withdraw spiritually and economically from the outside world.

In conclusion, I would like to return to a larger vision for this piece. What does Snow's use of a spatial discourse offer to rhetorics of space? First of all, this case study reminds us that exigencies themselves are often spatial, as Snow's geographical positioning provided her with powerful motivation for speech. Second, Snow's use of symbolically laden spatial tropes illustrates some of the ways that material places and their surrounding discourses can be used as resources for invention and powerful methods of persuasion. Snow drew on a shared history and experience of place to offer a spatially rooted identity to Mormon women. As an ideologically laden symbol, place then functioned as a powerful vehicle for group identification. Not only does this symbol help Mormon women understand their place within the broader Mormon culture, but it, in turn, endowed the physical space from which it was derived with significance. Once Snow (and others) established these place-based identifying myths, women had only to experience the landscape around them to be reminded of those myths. In a mutually constitutive turn, Mormon faith and landscape grounded one another: while the faith endowed the landscape with particular significance, the landscape, in turn, became a site for the enactment of faith and an identifying symbol for that faith.

Works Cited

Ackerman, John. "The Space for Rhetoric in Everyday Life." Nystrand and Duffy 84–117.

Beecher, Maureen Ursenbach. "Eliza R. Snow." *Mormon Sisters: Women in Early Utah.* New Edition. Ed. Claudia L. Bushman. Logan: Utah State UP, 1997. 25–42.

Blitefield, Jerry. "*Kairos* and Rhetorical Place." *Professing Rhetoric: Selected Papers from the 2000 Rhetoric Society of America Conference*. Ed. Frederick J. Antczak, Cindy Coggins, and Geoffrey D. Klinger. Mahwah, NJ: Lawrence Erlbaum, 2002. 69–76.

Bormann, Ernest. "Symbolic Convergence Theory: A Communication Formulation Based on Homo Narrans." *The Journal of Communication* 35 (1985): 128–38.

Brady, Mary Pat. *Extinct Lands, Temporal Geographies: Chicana Literature and the Urgency of Space*. Durham, NC: Duke UP, 2002.

Burke, Kenneth. *A Rhetoric of Motives*. Berkeley: U of California P, 1969.

Charland, Maurice. "Constitutive Rhetoric: The Case of the *Peuple Québécois.*" *Quarterly Journal of Speech* 17.2 (1987): 133–50.

Clark, Gregory. *Rhetorical Landscapes in America: Variations on a Theme from Kenneth Burke.* Columbia: U of South Carolina P, 2004.

———. "Transcendence at Yellowstone: Educating a Public in an Uninhabitable Place." Glenn, Lyday, and Sharer 145–59.

Derr, Jill Mulvay. "The Significance of 'O My Father' in the Personal Journey of Eliza R. Snow." *BYU Studies* 36.1 (1996–97): 85–126.

Dobrin, Sidney I. "Writing Takes Place." Weisser and Dobrin 11–25.

Drew, Julie. "The Politics of Place: Student Travelers and Pedagogical Maps." Weisser and Dobrin, 57–68.

Enoch, Jessica. "A Woman's Place is in the School: Rhetorics of Gendered Space in Nineteenth-Century America." *College English* 70.3 (2008): 275–95.

Firor, Anne Scott. Introduction. *Mormon Sisters: Women in Early Utah.* New Edition. Ed. Claudia L. Bushman. Logan: Utah State UP, 1997. xv–xxiii.

Gere, Anne Ruggles. *Intimate Practices: Literacy and Cultural Work in U.S. Women's Clubs, 1880–1920.* Urbana: U of Illinois P, 1997.

Glenn, Cheryl. *Rhetoric Retold: Regendering the Tradition from Antiquity Through the Renaissance.* Carbondale: Southern Illinois UP, 1997.

Glenn, Cheryl, Margaret M. Lyday, and Wendy B. Sharer. *Rhetorical Education in America.* Tuscaloosa: U of Alabama P, 2004.

Halloran, S. Michael. "Writing History on the Landscape: The Tour Road at the Saratoga Battlefield as Text." Glenn, Lyday, and Sharer 129–44.

Jackson, Richard H. "The Mormon Experience: The Plains as Sinai, the Great Salt Lake as the Dead Sea, and the Great Basin as Desert-Cum-Promised Land." *Journal of Historical Geography* 18.1 (1992): 41–58.

———. "Mormon Perception and Settlement." *Annals of the Association of American Geographers* 68.3 (1978): 317–34.

Johnson, Nan. *Gender and Rhetorical Space in American Life, 1866–1910.* Carbondale: Southern Illinois UP, 2002.

———. "Reigning in the Court of Silence: Women and Rhetorical Space in Postbellum America." *Philosophy and Rhetoric* 33.3 (2000): 221–42.

Keller, Rosemary Skinner, Ann Braude, Maureen Ursenbach Beecher, and Elizabeth Fox-Genovese. "Forum: Female Experience in American Religion." *Religion and American Culture* 5.1 (1995): 1–21.

Lefebvre, Henri. *The Production of Space.* Trans. Donald Nicholson-Smith. Oxford: Blackwell, 1991.

Logan, Shirley Wilson. *"We Are Coming": The Persuasive Discourse of Nineteenth-Century Black Women.* Carbondale: Southern Illinois UP, 1999.

Marback, Richard. "The Rhetorical Space of Robben Island." *Rhetoric Society Quarterly* 34.2 (2004): 7–27.

Mattingly, Carol. *Well-Tempered Women: Nineteenth-Century Temperance Rhetoric.* Carbondale: Southern Illinois UP, 2000.

Mitchell, Martin. "Gentile Impressions of Salt Lake City, Utah, 1849–1870." *Geographical Review* 87.3 (1997): 334–52.

Mountford, Roxanne. *The Gendered Pulpit: Preaching in American Protestant Spaces.* Carbondale: Southern Illinois UP, 2003.

Nystrand, Martin, and John Duffy, eds. *Towards a Rhetoric of Everyday Life: New Directions in Research on Writing, Text, and Discourse.* Madison: U of Wisconsin P, 2003.

Pratt, Mary Louise. *Imperial Eyes: Travel Writing and Transculturation*. New York: Routledge, 1992.

Reynolds, Nedra. "Composition's Imagined Geographies: The Politics of Space in the Frontier, City, and Cyberspace." *College Composition and Communication* 50 (1998): 12–35.

———. *Geographies of Writing: Inhabiting Places and Encountering Difference*. Carbondale: Southern Illinois UP, 2004.

Snow, Eliza R. "An Address." *Woman's Exponent* 15 Sept. 1873: 62–63.

———. "The 'Old Folks.'" *Woman's Exponent* 1 July 1886: 20.

Weisser, Christian R., and Sidney I. Dobrin, eds. *Ecocomposition: Theoretical and Pedagogical Approaches*. Albany: State U of New York P, 2001.

25

Malcolm X's Apocalyptic Rhetoric

Esteeming the Disparaged Tragic Frame

Keith Miller

Barry Brummett and Stephen O'Leary analyze American rhetorics that trumpet interpretations of Jewish and Christian scripture about apocalypse. Brummett and O'Leary ascribe the popularity of apocalyptic rhetoric to its adherents' insecurity with social fluctuations and their need for order.[1] Brummett, O'Leary, and other researchers offer a rough distinction between two types of popular apocalyptic rhetoric. The first is agitated rhetors' feverish predictions of a literal, almost imminent doomsday.[2] Those who forecast a literal, impending apocalypse generally explain such an event as cosmically predetermined and inevitable. For that reason, O'Leary argues, such rhetors render their audiences passive and helpless, especially with respect to engagement with social issues. If people become convinced that the world will end very shortly then, O'Leary claims, they will lose any reason to act responsibly and, if anything, might jump into large-scale warfare (220–21). Brummett and O'Leary make their arguments, in part, by analyzing such bestselling books as *The Late Great Planet Earth* by Hal Lindsey, a right-wing, white Christian. O'Leary files this type of apocalyptic rhetoric under the rubric of Kenneth Burke's tragic frame (68–69, 203–28).

For their second type of apocalyptic rhetoric, Brummett and O'Leary identify calm rhetors who predict that biblical apocalypse will arrive in the way-distant future (Brummett 46–85), or who provide an allegorical or contemplative explication of biblical texts about apocalypse (O'Leary 68–76, 200–28). According to O'Leary, such rhetors explain biblical language about the last days as symbolic of individual or ecclesiastical struggle rather than as a forecast of a literal, rapidly approaching doomsday. O'Leary chooses Augustine as his exemplar of the second type of apocalyptic rhetoric (73–76), classifies the second type under the heading of

Burke's comic frame (68–76, 200–28), and endorses what he calls its potentially useful "comic vision" (221).

Brummett and O'Leary clearly disparage the first type of apocalyptic appeal.[3] Through elaborate, nuanced analysis, they portray as either pointless or harmful any effort to predict a literal, imminent drop of the final curtain. Noting the popularity of such apocalyptic predictions over many generations, Brummett observes their inaccuracy: "there has not yet been an apocalypse, despite thousands of years of expectation of one, and whether the world is really on an upward path can certainly be questioned" (172–73). Similarly, O'Leary deprecates popular announcements of a tangible, near-at-hand apocalypse; such rhetoric, he explains, "has survived for thousands of years" despite its "perennially reappearing fallacies" and "despite every imaginable disconfirmation" (218, 221). Brummett and O'Leary indicate that the simple continuation of human life undeniably refutes the many, many predictions of apocalypse that multitudinous rhetors have offered over thousands of years. Inasmuch as you are today sitting, breathing, and smiling as you read this essay, the end time obviously has yet to arrive; for that reason, Brummett and O'Leary note, the plethora of dire apocalyptic prognistications obviously proved inaccurate and even ridiculous. Given the abject failure of literalist apocalyptic predictions, O'Leary contends that those who passively await the cosmically predetermined last days are failing to live wisely. While acknowledging that a specific rhetor who treats apocalyptic themes can, at times, juggle comic and tragic frames, O'Leary strongly favors the second, more allusive, more metaphorical type of apocalyptic rhetoric.[4] In contrast to the first type of apocalypticism, the second type, O'Leary maintains, can prove useful in supplying what Burke terms "equipment for living" because it sometimes prompts self-scrutiny and reflection about social structures, thus creating space for both self-understanding and social reform.

While Brummett's and O'Leary's analysis of Hal Lindsey is helpful, Brummett and O'Leary present a very limited and reductive view of apocalyptic rhetoric as a whole because they fail to examine popular, left-of-center apocalypticism. To investigate African American apocalypticism is to interrogate and problematize Brummett's and O'Leary's overgeneralized disparagement of literalist apocalyptic rhetoric and O'Leary's equally overgeneralized preference for metaphorical, Augustinian apocalyptic rhetoric.[5] To investigate a long, formidable tradition of African American protest rhetoric is to uncover important rhetorical uses for one tradition of hard-edged, literalist apocalypticism of the kind that Brummett, O'Leary, and other scholars categorically disparage. To consider this rhetoric is to problematize their established, overarching theory of apocalyptic language.

Here I pursue this argument mainly by concentrating on the apocalypticism of one exemplar of African American protest—Malcolm X. I interpret Malcolm X's apocalyptic rhetoric as his version of a Burkean "perspective by incongruity," which Burke terms "verbal atom-cracking"

(308). As Burke explains, a rhetor who uses perspective by incongruity "interprets new situations by removing words from their 'constitutional' setting. It is not 'demoralizing,' however, since it is done by the 'transcendence' of a fresh start. . . . It is designed to 'remoralize' by accurately naming a situation already demoralized by inaccuracy" (309). Malcolm X wields apocalyptic rhetoric to introduce a perspective by incongruity in an effort to "remoralize" dominant American culture by renaming it as white supremacist and oppressive.

For most of his oratorical career, Malcolm X served as a minister for the Nation of Islam, an African American separatist organization whose members achieved a measure of self-sufficiency from whites by operating not only their own mosques and schools, but also their own newspaper, grocery stores, restaurants, and other businesses. His oratorical project consisted, in large measure, of disrupting and re-locating African Americans' identification with an exploitative culture that championed whiteness and denigrated blackness.[6] While rejecting the goal of racial integration and promoting psychological withdrawal from pervasive symbols of whiteness, he simultaneously fostered concord by prodding African American listeners—whether light-skinned or dark-skinned, affluent or hungry—to bond with each other. He pursued this project through myriad rhetorical strategies, including such exclamations as "You didn't come here on the *Mayflower*! You came here on a slave ship!" ("Message" 4). And "You're still in prison! That's what America means: prison!" (8). And "I'm not an American!" ("Ballot" 26).[7] His apocalyptic rhetoric can be viewed, in large part, as his effort to intensify his appeal for African Americans to disaffiliate from a culture of patriotic whiteness and to counteridentify with a culture of dissident blackness.

Before exploring Malcolm X, I briefly sketch an African American tradition of apocalyptic rhetoric; then I examine Malcolm X's apocalypticism in some detail; finally, I consider the implications of this investigation for reconceptualizing apocalyptic rhetoric as a whole.

An African American Tradition of Apocalyptic Rhetoric

As Robert Terrill remarks, a robust tradition of apocalyptic rhetoric helped sustain African Americans during the weed-choked centuries of slavery and segregation. Such notable antebellum African American rhetors as David Walker and Nat Turner strongly intensified their antislavery polemics by forecasting a quite literal, close-at-hand apocalypse (46–61). Terrill also analyzes similarly angry, equally literalist apocalyptic rhetoric from Noble Drew Ali, who spotlighted racial oppression during the early twentieth century (73–77). Elijah Muhammad, leader of the Nation of Islam and mentor of the early Malcolm X, announced an upcoming end time when he asserted that a "Battle of Armageddon" would "be waged in the wilderness of North America" (qtd. in Lomax 48). Even Martin Luther

King Jr., in his final speech, announced that, if racial justice does not appear soon, "the whole world is doomed" (209–10). By proclaiming the great likelihood of a palpable, near-at-hand apocalypse, Walker, Turner, Ali, and Elijah Muhammad all supply rhetoric that, according to the analysis of Brummett and O'Leary, would definitely qualify as a species of the first type of literal apocalypticism, the type that O'Leary calls tragic-framed and that both Brummett and O'Leary deprecate.

Malcolm X's Apocalyptic Rhetoric

Although Malcolm X embraced the Nation of Islam and, later in his life, more orthodox Islam, he seldom quoted the Quran publicly. He frequently, however, cited the Bible. Raised in a Christian household, the young Malcolm Little (who later changed his name to Malcolm X) heard his Garveyite father, who was a minister, read the Bible and preach in a Baptist church. Malcolm X's public speeches and statements often reveal a keen awareness of numerous biblical stories, characters, and themes that were also highly familiar to millions within the heavily churched African American community. Terrill observes that the "theology" of Elijah Muhammad, Malcolm X, and the Nation of Islam "explicitly is a program of biblical interpretation" (85). Louis DeCaro adds, "if anyone ever honed Black Muslim biblical application into a fine art, it was Malcolm X" (73).

In 1955, when FBI agents disguised in plainclothes heard the young Malcolm X deliver polemical speeches, the agents recorded his prophecy of a quickly approaching apocalypse (Carson and Gallen 107–09). Later, he preached the same message to audiences in Harlem and to students at Harvard, Yale, and many other universities. In a sympathetic book about Malcolm X, Peter Goldman describes him as a "doomsday fundamentalist" (42). Benjamin Karim, a close associate and confidante of Malcolm X, begins a highly informative, exceedingly thoughtful book by quoting Malcolm X's apocalyptic prophesy:

> In the wilderness of North America, the oppressor shall meet his doom; the evil white enemy will fall ignominiously into destruction while in the East the black Muslims shall rise triumphant to rule forever in freedom, justice, and equality. . . . (7)

Not only did Malcolm X proclaim apocalypse to non-Muslim audiences, he repeatedly emphasized the theme when he spoke inside mosques. Along with Karim, another invaluable chronicler of Malcolm X is his nephew Rodnell Collins, the son of Ella Collins (Malcolm X's favorite sibling). Rodnell Collins reports his participation in a class that his uncle taught inside a mosque. As Collins recalls, standing directly behind Malcolm X was a blackboard adorned with dichotomous images and language:

> We sat there in awed silence. . . . Our classroom always contained a big blackboard on which was drawn an American flag with the words "Slav-

> ery, Suffering, and Death" over it. On the right of the flag was drawn a tree with a black man hanging on a rope from one of its branches. On the other side of that was a Muslim flag with a star and a crescent. In each corner of the Muslim flag was the slogan "I for Islam, F for Freedom, J for Justice, and E for Equality." Written in the center of the blackboard was the question, "Which one will win the War of Armageddon?" (147)

Note that Collins remembers that this classroom of Malcolm X not sometimes, but *always* contained a blackboard with these images and words. On an unpaginated insert in his book about the Nation of Islam, Louis Lomax includes a photo taken inside Temple Number Seven in Harlem that depicts Malcolm X standing on stage beside a blackboard with symbols and words that appear nearly identical to those reported by Collins. Others who entered mosques of the Nation of Islam also observed blackboards with exceedingly similar imagery and wording.[8]

As Manning Marable explains, many people today mistakenly believe that, after Malcolm X completed his pilgrimage to Mecca in 1964, he became a calm, all-loving, nonviolent integrationist—the posthumous image of an unthreatening Malcolm X that is now enshrined on a US postage stamp. But, after his return from Mecca, Malcolm X continued to project a literal, upcoming apocalypse. In his final round of orations and interviews, shortly before his assassination in February 1965, he often altered his normal apocalyptic message by removing biblical references, replacing them with secular language that forecast extremely destructive global warfare.

One can safely observe that predictions of a literal, impending end time constituted one of the most important elements in Malcolm X's rhetoric—both early and late in his career. Responsible scholars of apocalyptic rhetoric, Malcolm X, African American rhetoric, and social change in twentieth-century America should attend to his apocalypticism. What was this rhetoric like?

Many researchers maintain that apocalypticism appeals to disgruntled people who, finding themselves frustrated in an unkempt and unpredictable world, seek recompense and refuge in some account of an Almighty God's grand design for history, a design presumed to lie partly hidden underneath the hurly-burly and jumble of quotidian life. African American apocalypticism works differently. Black Americans confronted not hubbub and confusion, but overly determined, regularly cruel, white supremacist order that was all too clear and all too predictable in the severe restraints that it imposed on subordinated blacks. As many historians have argued, slaves and their descendents responded to grinding degradation by imaginatively claiming that, underlying the exploitative, white supremacist social order lay a more sturdy system of cosmic justice.[9] Whereas southern whites used the Bible to buttress slavery and segregation, African Americans affirmed the possibility of justice by transforming biblical narratives, symbols, and characters into emblems of cosmic fairness and liberty that were achievable by escape to the North or by spiritual and political revolution. Slaves, abolitionists, and civil rights orators—such as Martin Luther King Jr. and Fred Shuttlesworth—regularly interpreted the biblical Exodus typologically, that is, as an event that appears and reappears in history, an engine of past and future emancipation.[10]

As Terrill observes, the task of Malcolm X and other leaders in the Nation of Islam "was to unmask the Bible so that it was no longer understood as a mystical or religious tract, but instead as a reference book of . . . African American history," a book that referred "directly to the Nation of Islam" (86). In 1960, speaking in Harlem, Malcolm X described a Western world "filled with evil and wickedness" and "stumbling blindly" on the "brink of disaster" while risking "fiery destruction" ("Malcolm X on 'Unity'" 130). If whites fail to heed Elijah Muhammad's demand for racial separation and land for blacks, then, Malcolm X announced, God will destroy the American government, just as God destroyed the corrupt kingdoms of ancient Egypt and ancient Babylon (135). In a speech given to many university audiences in 1961 and 1962, Malcolm X interpreted a variety of biblical motifs from Exodus, Ezekiel, Daniel, Malachi, Isaiah, and the gospel of John as typological references to Elijah Muhammad and the Nation of Islam ("Malcolm X's 'University Speech'"). At Yale in 1962, Malcolm X noted that Jesus spoke of the end time or "harvest time" and reiterated the biblical image of an apocalyptic "lake of fire" while claiming that to reject Elijah Muhammad is to invite "divine destruction" ("Malcolm X at Yale" 165–67). In an interview published in 1963, Malcolm X, enraged by the police murder of Ronald Stokes in Los Angeles, equated powerful whites with two prominent biblical figures—the evil Pharaoh of Egypt and the wicked Nebuchadnezzar of Babylon—and claimed that such recent events as the crash of an airplane, irregularities in weather patterns, a rash of deformed newborns, and the loss of an American submarine all served as signs of impending Armageddon, an Armageddon that would be triggered by white arrogance and white supremacy ("Louis Lomax" 176).

According to O'Leary's criteria, this rhetoric would fit within Burke's tragic frame. Although Malcolm X emphasizes the close proximity of the last days, he often mitigates his literal apocalypticism by sketching the *slight* possibility of redemption that will occur *if* whites finally recognize their guilt and the legitimate demands of Elijah Muhammad—a possibility that appeared extremely unlikely, given that the American government had endorsed or tolerated slavery, torture, rape, terrorism, lynching, sharecropping, disenfranchisement, poverty, and segregation during one horrific century after another ("Louis Lomax").[11] By 1963, when this statement was published, Congress had yet to legislate civil rights laws advocated by King, Shuttlesworth, Medgar Evers, Daisy Bates, Fannie Lou Hamer, and other African American leaders who were far more moderate than Elijah Muhammad—more evidence that whites would not respond favorably to Elijah Muhammad.

Malcolm X's secular apocalypticism, if you will, is equally important. In a speech delivered during the final month of his life, Malcolm X told an audience in Detroit:

> And from Washington, D.C. they exercise the same forms of brutal oppression against dark-skinned people in South and North Vietnam, or in the Congo, or in Cuba, or in any other place on this earth where they're trying to exploit and oppress. ("Educate" 86)

The next day, in Harlem, he gave an address that was published twice under the title "There's a Worldwide Revolution Going On." In an address in London, during the same month, he paralleled anticolonialist psychological, political, and military struggles in the Congo, Mozambique, Angola, South Africa, Vietnam, the United States, and the Caribbean ("Oppressed"). In one late interview, he observed, "Oh, yes, we believe that it is one struggle in South Africa, Angola, Mozambique, and Alabama. They are all the same struggle" ("Fight" 70). In his final television interview, a month prior to his death, when asked about Elijah Muhammad's discussion of Armageddon, he explained the possibility of global conflagration:

> I think that an objective analysis of events taking place on this earth today points toward some type of ultimate showdown. . . . [This showdown will] almost boil down along racial lines. I believe that there will be a clash between the oppressed and those that do the oppressing . . . between those who want freedom, justice, and equality for everyone, and those who want to continue the systems of exploitation. . . . [People] can easily be lumped into racial groups, and it will be a racial war. ("Whatever" 187)

Of course, those who had heard or read the orations in which he interpreted biblical texts while forecasting apocalypse could easily understand his later declarations as parallel, tragic-framed apocalyptic predictions, made this time with secular language. These later proclamations seem to resonate with the Pan-African sensibilities of Marcus Garvey and W. E. B. DuBois, except that Malcolm X included in his circle of oppressed peoples not only those of the African diaspora—the major focus of Garvey and DuBois—but Asians as well.

Analyzing Malcolm X's apocalyptic rhetoric—and his rhetoric as a whole—Terrill concludes his thoughtful, book-length study by observing that the Black Nationalist was more concerned with startling his listeners and rearranging their ideas than with advancing specific propositions:

> There is no final product but only a series of provisional constructions perpetually open to change. . . . Malcolm demonstrates an ability to assemble momentarily coherent texts as an exhibition of practical wisdom and would have his audiences assemble similarly coherent texts, motives, and identities. (191)

One of Malcolm X's constructions, however, looms so constantly that it dominates his rhetoric. He never tires of blasting white presumption and white supremacy, regularly coaxing and goading African Americans to resist assimilation into whiteness. With no tentativeness whatsoever and with a rhetorical arsenal that blends everything from extraordinary news commentary to scathing political analysis to biting aphorisms to extended biblical narratives to radical reinterpretations of American history to original animal fables, he brilliantly uncovers and assaults racism regularly throughout his public career. For those long accustomed to unexamined white hegemony, hearing his courageous indictments of white rule meant encountering a Burkean perspective by incongruity.

Malcolm X establishes such a perspective, in part, by realigning familiar biblical symbols into signs pointing toward the impending demise of white imperialism and colonialism throughout the world. Emphasizing tragic-framed apocalypticism, he interprets the end of history as God's ordained, all-consuming cataclysm in which evil whites—including many of the richest and most powerful people in the world—would die for their misdeeds while maids, janitors, laborers, and other long-exploited peoples would reach glory in the new millennium. By sketching what he describes as God's centuries-old, partly hidden plan, he reassures auditors that white supremacy and black suffering could not endure forever. By explaining doomsday as literal, impending, and probably unavoidable, he intensifies his condemnation of Euro-American racism, imperialism, and colonialism. Through such apocalyptic rhetoric, he simultaneously separates African Americans from whiteness, bonds them together, and hands them a dazzling jewel of immediate and certain hope.

Implications for Reconceptualizing Apocalyptic Rhetoric as a Whole

While almost anyone can find examples of Malcolm X's rhetoric that seem hyperbolic, no one should ask someone in his position to shun the powerful appeal of literalist, tragic-framed apocalyptic rhetoric in favor of a comic-framed contemplation of an end time that is merely metaphorical or that is scheduled so far in the future that it fails to impinge perceptibly on the present. Malcolm X demonstrates that, within a culture heavily shaped by Judaism and Christianity, political radicals can sometimes wisely employ tragic-framed apocalyptic rhetoric for the purpose of "verbal atom-cracking." Scholars should not categorically applaud metaphorical, comic-framed apocalyptic language while categorically disparaging and rejecting literalist, tragic-framed apocalypticism. Instead, researchers should reconfigure their theoretical frameworks in order to acknowledge the value of certain kinds of literalist, tragic-framed apocalyptic appeals, especially those appeals that rearrange familiar symbols for the purpose of assaulting oppressed people's psychological affiliation with a dominant, abusive culture and replacing that affiliation with a group-affirming process of counteridentification.

Notes

[1] See, especially, Brummett, pp. 171–75 and O'Leary, pp. 200–24.

[2] Brummett and others use the term "premillennial" to designate this type of apocalyptic rhetoric.

[3] Brummett's attitude is not as explicit as that of O'Leary.

[4] See, especially, O'Leary, pp. 218–28.

[5] Sharon Crowley also analyzes right-wing American apocalyptic rhetoric, but she does overgeneralize her conclusions into a theory about American apocalypticism as a whole.

[6] See Miller, "Plymouth Rock."

[7] Malcolm X's oratorical project proved highly successful, as evidenced, in part, by his large impact on those who initiated the Black Arts Movement, most of whom joined Malcolm X in promoting African American radicalism, solidarity, and counteridentification. See Smethurst.

[8] See Haley (102) and Jamal (132).

[9] See, for example, Raboteau; Berlin, pp. 206–09; and Genovese, pp. 248–55.

[10] For examples of Shuttlesworth's typological appeals, see Shuttlesworth. For analyses of King's typological language, see Miller, *Voice* and Shelby. For "I Have a Dream" as a typological speech, see Miller, "Second Isaiah."

[11] For an example of Malcolm X's softer version of apocalyptic rhetoric, see his "Malcolm X at Harvard."

Works Cited

Berlin, Ira. *Generations of Captivity: A History of African-American Slaves.* Cambridge, MA: Harvard UP, 2003.

Breitman, George, ed. *Malcolm X Speaks: Selected Speeches and Statements.* 1965. New York: Grove, 1990.

Brummett, Barry. *Contemporary Apocalyptic Rhetoric.* New York: Praeger, 1991.

Burke, Kenneth. *Attitudes toward History.* 1937. Berkeley, CA: U of California P, 1959.

Carson, Clayborne, and David Gallen, eds. *Malcolm X: The FBI File.* New York: Carroll and Graf, 1991.

Clark, Steve, ed. *February 1965, Malcolm X: The Final Speeches.* New York: Pathfinder, 1992.

Collins, Rodnell (with A. Peter Bailey). *Seventh Child: A Family Memoir of Malcolm X.* New York: Kensington, 1998.

Crowley, Sharon. *Toward a Civil Discourse: Rhetoric and Fundamentalism.* Pittsburgh: U of Pittsburgh P, 2006.

DeCaro, Louis. *Malcolm X and the Cross: The Nation of Islam, Malcolm X, and Christianity.* New York: New York UP, 1998.

Dower, John. *War without Mercy: Race and Power in the Pacific War.* New York: Pantheon, 1986.

Genovese, Eugene. *Roll, Jordan, Roll: The World the Slaves Made.* New York: Vintage, 1976.

Goldman, Peter. *The Death and Life of Malcolm X.* New York: Harper, 1973.

Haley, Alex. "Mr. Muhammad Speaks." *Reader's Digest* Mar. 1960: 100–04.

Houck, Davis, and David Dixon, eds. *Rhetoric, Religion, and the Civil Rights Movement, 1954–1965.* Waco, TX: Baylor UP, 2006.

Jamal, Hakim. *From the Dead Level: Malcolm X and Me.* New York: Warner, 1973.

Karim, Benjamin (with Peter Skutches and David Gallen). *Remembering Malcolm.* New York: Carroll and Graf, 1992.

King, Martin Luther, Jr. "I've Been to the Mountaintop." *A Call to Conscience.* Ed. Clayborne Carson and Kris Shepard. New York: Time Warner, 2002.

Lindsey, Hal. *The Late Great Planet Earth.* Grand Rapids, MI: Zondervan, 1970.

Lomax, Louis. *When the Word Is Given.* New York: New American Library, 1963.

Malcolm X. "The Ballot or the Bullet." Breitman 23–44.

———. "Educate Our People in the Science of Politics." Clark 75–107.

———. "The Fight against Racism from South Africa to Australia to the U.S.A." Clark 69–72.

———. "Louis Lomax Interviews Malcolm X." Lomax 169–80.

———. "Malcolm X at Harvard." Lomax 112–27. Rpt. as "The Harvard Law School Forum." *Malcolm X: Speeches at Harvard.* Ed. Archie Epps. New York: Paragon, 1991. 115–31.

———. "Malcolm X on 'Unity.'" Lomax 128–35.

———. "Malcolm X's 'University Speech.'" Lomax 136–46.

———. "Malcolm X at Yale." Lomax 153–69.

———. "Message to the Grassroots." Breitman 3–17.

———. "The Oppressed Masses of the World Cry Out for Action against the Common Oppressor." Clark 46–65.

———. "There's a Worldwide Revolution Going On." Perry 111–49. Rpt. in Clark 108–46.

———. "Whatever Is Necessary: The Last Television Interview, with Pierre Berton." *Malcolm X as They Knew Him.* Ed. David Gallen. New York: Carroll and Graf, 1992.

Marable, Manning. "Malcolm X's Life-After-Death." *Living Black History: How Reimagining the African-American Past Can Remake America's Racial Future.* New York: Basic Books, 2006. 121–77.

Miller, Keith D. "Plymouth Rock Landed on Us: Malcolm X's Whiteness Theory as a Basis for Alternative Literacy." *College Composition and Communication* 56 (Dec. 2004): 199–222.

———. "Second Isaiah Lands in Washington, D.C.: Martin Luther King's 'I Have a Dream' as Biblical Narrative and Biblical Hermeneutic." *Rhetoric Review* 26 (2007): 405–24. Print.

———. *Voice of Deliverance: The Language of Martin Luther King, Jr., and Its Sources.* 2nd ed. Athens: U of Georgia P, 1998.

O'Leary, Stephen. *Arguing the Apocalypse: A Theory of Millennial Rhetoric.* New York: Oxford UP, 1994.

Perry, Bruce, ed. *Malcolm X: The Last Speeches.* New York: Pathfinder, 1989.

Raboteau, Albert. *A Fire in the Bones: Reflections on African-American Religious History.* Boston: Beacon, 1995.

Shelby, Gary. *Martin Luther King and the Rhetoric of Freedom: The Exodus Narrative in America's Struggle for Civil Rights.* Waco, TX: Baylor UP, 2008.

Shuttlesworth, Fred. "Address at Medgar Evers Memorial Service." Houck and Dixon 766–68.

———. "Speech at the Meeting of the Fair Share Organization." Houck and Dixon 308–12.

Smethurst, James. "Malcolm X and the Black Arts Movement." *The Cambridge Companion to Malcolm X.* Ed. Robert Terrill. New York: Cambridge UP, 2010.

Terrill, Robert. *Malcolm X: Inventing Radical Judgment.* East Lansing: Michigan State UP, 2004.

Section VI

Argument, Reason, and Rhetorical Theory

How can discussants manage a controversy when disagreement is so deep that concord is not possible and nobody is willing to compromise?

—Beth Innocenti

Can concord and controversy be located within rhetoric itself, within the very textual movement of rhetorical action?

—Jon Leon Torn

At precisely those points where it seems to establish an ideologically and strategically conservative right rhetoric, [Richard Weaver's] rhetoric possesses an equal potential for being an ideologically and strategically conservative left rhetoric.

—Patrick Shaw

Triangulating Burke, de Man, and Nietzsche reveals how it is that Burke and de Man came to their different observations of epistemology while pursuing strikingly similar epistemological trajectories.

—Ethan Sproat

Reading Keller side by side with Burke underscores the extent to which Keller was not simply doing rhetoric; she was living and writing rhetorical theory—theory that often predates Burke's and rivals it in sophistication.

—Ann George

Rational religion was embraced, in different forms, by both Paine and Watson . . . these two old lions of the Enlightenment, both born in the year 1737, played out the contest between deism and rational Christianity on a court governed by reason, each claiming that reason was on his side.

—David C. Hoffman

26

Whately on Pragmatics of Arguing

Beth Innocenti

How can discussants manage a controversy when disagreement is so deep that concord is not possible and nobody is willing to compromise? Is there a viable alternative to agreeing to disagree, and instead getting someone to act as the speaker advocates? An enduring question in rhetorical studies is how rhetorical action begets other symbolic and nonsymbolic action. How does talking get people to act? One answer is that, unlike physical force, talking involves reasoning with people. Throughout its history, rhetoric has been envisioned as an alternative to physical force. In *De Inventione*, Cicero speculates that eloquence originated at a time when humans "did nothing by the guidance of reason, but relied chiefly on physical strength" (I.ii.2). In *The Realm of Rhetoric*, Perelman recommends asking whether a dispute will be settled "by recourse to argumentation, or by recourse to force" (11). In *Norms of Rhetorical Culture*, Farrell suggests that without rhetoric "we have only force" (7). However, scholars have noted that physical force may have discursive analogues. In *Political Judgment*, Beiner laments that the mass spectacle of politics "is commended not by the quality elicited in judgment, but by the force with which it seeks to impress itself upon our sensations" (162). Even persuasion itself has been described as analogous to force (Foss and Griffin 3).

One "normative tendency" in rhetorical traditions is a call to exercise practical reason or judgment (Farrell 8), and one way of exercising practical reason is arguing. As is true for rhetoric, argumentation scholars aim to dissociate arguing from discursive force. Consider two classic accounts of argument in modern research on the topic. First, Douglas Ehninger defined argument as a species of correction distinguishable from another species of correction "designed to compel or coerce conformity with the corrector's view" ("Argument" 101). Second, in an essay entitled "Arguers as Lovers," Wayne Brockriede wrote that "the [argumentative] rapist conquers by force of argument" (4). Yet the fact remains that ordinary use of the word "argument" can involve talk of setting traps, shooting down or cornering opponents, and the like.

Scholars have attempted to define away the issue by describing arguing or "good" arguing as, say, cooperation, resolution of differences, or coalescence of positions (e.g., Gilbert; van Eemeren and Grootendorst; cf. Goodwin "Henry Johnstone"). In contrast, I begin with the fact that arguing can pressure even reluctant auditors to act—that this does not always happen is because the arguers are cooperating, have resolved their differences, or somehow merged their positions or achieved concord. I submit that Whately's account of the pragmatics of arguing helps to explain how this happens and shows that forceful arguing is normative—that its force comes from strategies that bring rhetorical norms to bear in situations. In doing so, this essay addresses scholarly qualms about the force of rhetoric and arguing, because it shows that rhetorical argumentative force is grounded in norms. In addition, it provides a more complete account of Whately's view of argumentation because it transcends logical and psychological elements of his theory.[1] Moreover, it points to a way of integrating logical, dialectical, and rhetorical perspectives on argumentation theory.[2] Finally, it suggests a way of integrating normative and descriptive research on argumentation.[3]

Whately's *Elements of Logic* and *Elements of Rhetoric* are appropriate sources for this analysis because Whately taught and practiced rhetoric and argumentation, his books continue to be canonical in the history of rhetoric and argumentation, and in both he writes about the force of arguments. For example, he writes about those who deny "the evidences of Christianity": "I earnestly hope no force will ever be employed to silence them, except force of argument" (*Rhetoric* xliii–xliv). In addition, in the preface to *Elements of Rhetoric* he remarks:

> if we were to bid an Orator, "use forcible arguments, suited to the occasion," we should be in fact only telling them to "go the right way to work," without teaching them what *is* the right way. (xxxvii)

Moreover, one hallmark of Whately's discussion of rhetoric and argumentation is that he covers adversarial situations in which an arguer addresses reluctant auditors. For example, in *Elements of Logic* he tells arguers:

> The applause of *one's own party* is a very unsafe ground for judging of the real force of an argumentative work, and consequently of its utility. To satisfy those who were doubting, and to convince those who were opposed, are much better tests; but *these* persons are seldom very loud in their applause, or very forward in bearing their testimony. (195–96)

Likewise, in *Elements of Rhetoric* he puts a more cooperative audience on a level with reluctant auditors as he advises arguers to consider "whether the principal object of the discourse be, to give *satisfaction to a candid mind*, and convey *instruction* to those who are ready to receive it, or to *compel* the assent, or silence the objections, of an opponent" (108). In fact, Whately describes the person

> who would claim the highest rank as an Orator . . . [as] the one who is the most successful, not in gaining popular applause, but in *carrying his point*, whatever it be; especially if there are strong prejudices, interests, and feelings opposed to him. (209)

In what follows, I first present Whately's view of the nature and limits of logical and psychological force, and then discuss his insights about the pragmatics of arguing.

Whately on Logical and Psychological Force

One feature of arguments that pressures auditors to act is logic. If an argument has logical force, auditors are pressured by logical elements to accept its conclusion, give it serious consideration, and so on. The pressure is generated by rules of logic: the premises of an argument are acceptable, relevant, and sufficient; and the underlying inference structure is valid. Whately at times uses the term "force" in this sense. For example, in *Elements of Logic* he describes one way of objecting to an enthymeme: "the *force as an argument* of either premiss depends on the *other* premiss: If both be admitted, the conclusion legitimately connected with them cannot be denied" (54–55; see also *Rhetoric* 149). Whately describes the source of the premise's force as its logical relations with another premise; the logical relationships pressure acceptance of a conclusion.

If logic in a narrow sense of sound premise-conclusion structure were a reliable way to make auditors act, then we would expect to frequently see rhetorical strategies featuring logical coherence—presenting a case in a straightforward, claim-evidence or premise-conclusion form. The work of Hamblin, Toulmin, Perelman and Olbrechts-Tyteca, and Johnson, among others, offers compelling reasons for argumentation theory to extend beyond formal logic. Whately offers what may be described as a psychological reason for understanding argumentative force as extending beyond logic when he writes that, to influence the will, reason alone is not sufficient (*Rhetoric* 180).

Whately also uses the term "force" in a psychological sense, which in this case refers to using language to make impressions on individual brains. For example, when discussing conciseness, Whately writes:

> The hearers will be struck by the forcibleness of the sentence which they will have been prepared to comprehend; they will *understand* the longer expression, and *remember* the shorter. But the force will, in general, be totally destroyed, or much enfeebled, if the order be reversed;—if the brief expression be put first, and afterwards expanded and explained; for it loses much of its force if it be not clearly understood the moment it is uttered; and if it be, there is no need of the subsequent expansion. (*Rhetoric* 304; see also 173, 197n., 287, 289, 306–07, 309, 315, 328, 330)

In *Elements of Logic*, Whately uses the term "force" in a psychological sense when he discusses a fallacious use of emotional force:

> Great force is often added . . . by bitterly *reproaching* or *deriding* an opponent, as denying some sacred truth, or some evident axiom. . . . [For example,] a declaimer who is maintaining some doctrine as being taught in Scripture, may impute to his opponents a contempt for the authority of Scripture, and reproach them for impiety, when the question really is, whether the doctrine be scriptural or not. (228–29; see also 233)

However, psychological force may not be a reliable way to pressure auditors to act—especially reluctant ones—since it may be easy enough to dodge such strategies precisely because they are designed to make impressions on one's mind. Whately treats emotion as a motive force, and yet, about emotional appeals writes that "it seems to be commonly taken for granted, that whenever the feelings are excited they are of course *over-excited*" (*Rhetoric* 180; see also 184). Although here he is arguing that emotional appeals are legitimate, his remark points to the suspicion among auditors that they are being manipulated.

Whately on Pragmatic Force

So far we have seen Whately note limits on the force or pressure generated by two design features of arguments: premise-conclusion structure and what may be described as striking in style or emotion. The question remains: how can rhetors design arguments that may be expected to pressure even reluctant addressees to act? To say that an argument has pragmatic force is to say that the actual presentational design of the argument creates practical reasons for addressees to act—to at least tentatively consider an argument, for example. If the argument is designed in a way that makes manifest that the speaker has made a responsible effort to, say, collect evidence and examine different points of view, then—other things being equal—addressees may be vulnerable to criticism for not acting reasonably if they do not give it tentative consideration.[4] Design features (1) make manifest risks openly undertaken by the speaker and (2) generate risks for auditors. The pressure to act to avoid the risks is grounded in rhetorical norms. The following examples illustrate instances when Whately's discussion of argumentative force departs from wholly psychological and wholly logical accounts and toward pragmatics of arguing.

Consider three examples of Whately noting the pragmatic force on the auditor's side of rhetorical transactions. First, Whately discusses the pressure on auditors generated just by giving reasons. He does so during the course of explaining how arguing may go awry, and specifically how an unintelligible argument creates conditions for auditors to act. Whately notes that sometimes an unintelligible discourse can serve as an excuse

> for men to vote or act according to their own inclinations; which they would perhaps have been ashamed to do, if strong arguments had been urged on the other side, and had remained *confessedly* unanswered; but they satisfy themselves, if *something* has been said in favour of the course they wish to adopt. (*Rhetoric* 270)

Whately's analysis points to the pragmatic force generated by the design feature of reason-giving. Other things being equal, auditors who do not at least tentatively consider an argument risk criticism for acting unreasonably. The force is grounded in the rhetorical norm that one ought to act based on good reasons. Of course, as Whately notes, if better, intelligible reasons are given for an alternative position, then the pragmatic force generated by the unintelligible ones is reduced because acting on them makes auditors vulnerable to criticism for acting unreasonably.

Second, Whately discusses pressure on auditors generated by what he describes as "a confident air": "if the speaker with a confident air announces his conclusion as established . . . [listeners often] will take for granted that he has advanced valid arguments, and will be loth to seem behind-hand in comprehending them" (*Rhetorical* 270). Again, the pressure generated is grounded in a rhetorical norm, namely being capable of following and judging arguments. A "confident air" creates conditions that, other things being equal, increase risks of criticism of auditors for not manifesting assent because they will appear to be slow-witted.

Third, Whately discusses pressure on auditors generated by rhetorical questions. He explains that

> the *Interrogative* form . . . calls the hearer's attention more forcibly to some important point, by a personal appeal to each individual, either to assent to what is urged, or to frame a reasonable objection; and it often carries with it an air of triumphant defiance of an opponent to refute the argument if he can. (*Rhetoric* 327)

Whately points to two rhetorical norms that generate pressure: namely appearing reasonable by attending to an argument at all (attention) and by attending to an argument that takes into account one's own interests (personal appeal). Other things being equal, auditors who do not do so risk criticism for failing to act prudently. Whately also points to these norms when he explains why, when arguing with reluctant auditors, a speaker ought to "keep out of sight, as much as possible, the point to which we are tending" and begin with points of agreement or, put differently, "if we thus, as it were, mask the battery, they will not be able to shelter themselves from the discharge" (*Rhetoric* 142): such a strategy "is not only nothing dishonest, but is a point of pacific charitableness as well as of discretion" (*Rhetoric* 142). It is a fallible sign that the speaker is taking into account auditors' positions and thus generates risks to auditors of criticism for not acting prudently, because prudent actors consider positions that take their interests into account.

Now consider examples of Whately's analysis of pragmatic force on the speaker side of the transaction. A speaker may design an argument that affronts auditors by amplifying something that auditors already recognize as significant, or by amplifying something that does not deserve amplification. Whately has this to say about writers who "endeavour to add force to their expressions by accumulating high-sounding Epithets, denoting the greatness, beauty, or other admirable qualities of the things spoken of":

> Most readers, except those of a very vulgar or puerile taste, are disgusted at studied efforts to point out and force upon their attention whatever is remarkable; and this, even when the ideas conveyed are themselves striking. (*Rhetoric* 287)

Whately suggests that the disgust results from a speaker's apparent disdain of auditors' capacity to make a judgment about what deserves attention. On one hand, a speaker may indiscriminately urge upon their attention "whatever is remarkable." On the other hand, a speaker may urge upon their attention ideas that are striking in and of themselves. In both cases, the epithets serve as a fallible sign of the speaker's inability to make a judgment about what deserves amplification, or perhaps the speaker's lack of confidence in auditors' ability to recognize for themselves the significance of a point. Whately recognizes that urging a point on auditors' attention is not simply a matter of making strong impressions in a psychological sense; pragmatic force also involves the speaker making manifest her own assessment of the circumstances and auditors' capacity for judgment and, in doing so, risking criticism for poor judgment. The pragmatic force is grounded in the rhetorical norm that speakers ought to take into account auditors' positions and abilities. This kind of consideration helps to explain why epithets that serve as abridged reasons may have force. Whately provides the following example:

> If any one says, "we ought to take warning from the *bloody* revolution of France," the Epithet suggests one of the reasons for our being warned; and that, not less clearly, and more forcibly, than if the argument had been stated at length. (*Rhetoric* 290; see also 310)

When the epithet serves as a manifest rationale for persuasion—a reason—and when it is presented in an appropriate way that takes into account auditors' knowledge and judgment, then it generates pragmatic pressure to act.

Conclusion

Whately's answer to the question of how arguing pressures auditors to act is inchoate since he is less interested in generating a systematic theory of argumentation than in addressing practical circumstances (Poster). He is also an early nineteenth-century figure writing amidst two intellectual currents: what he considered to be an Aristotelian view of logic and argumentation and eighteenth-century theories of rhetoric described in terms of faculty psychology. As a result, logical and psychological senses of argumentative force are readily apparent. Still, he provides direction in developing an account of the pragmatics of arguing.

Based on this analysis, it is possible to identify three features of pragmatic force: it is distinct from physical force and its discursive analogues; it is compatible with practical reason and judgment; and it is normative. Whately's discussions of the pragmatics of arguing coach readers to effectively participate in controversies without assuming or aiming for concord.

This discussion may help us to reflect on possible relationships between concord and controversy. First, concord and controversy may be considered as opposite endpoints on a continuum. Second, concord may be considered as an outcome of controversy. For both perspectives the ground is agreement: degrees of agreement can constitute a continuum, or agreement can be viewed as an ideal end or purpose of controversy. But one implication of this discussion of Whately is that it is possible to view controversy as an activity regulated and managed by speakers. Concord or agreement need not be possible or desirable; and at the same time a speaker can reasonably pressure addressees to act.

Notes

[1] Scholarship on Whately's theory of argumentation has described his perspective as logical and psychological. For example, scholars have noted that Whately covers both logical and psychological dimensions of argument generally (Einhorn 92) and, more specifically, that for Whately, there are logical and psychological bases of presumption (Sproule 122). They have also noted that for Whately, the force of reasons depends on the degree of probability or certainty with respect to the conclusion and on their intrinsic truth value (McKerrow 266); and that Whately focuses on describing how rhetors may address the understanding more so than the will (Ehninger, Introduction xi). Whately invites these logical and psychological views when he notes the connection and overlap between his *Elements of Logic* and *Elements of Rhetoric* (see *Elements of Rhetoric* xli–xlii), and since he organizes the first two parts of *Elements of Rhetoric* around addressing faculties of mind: understanding and will.

[2] These perspectives have been detailed by Wenzel; for now, it may be enough to note that each involves focusing on a different phenomenon—argument as product, process, or procedure—and, consequently, involves different methods of analysis and different standards of evaluation. One attempt to synthesize the perspectives, the pragma-dialectical, has involved subsuming logical and rhetorical elements under the dialectical. Logical elements are incorporated in attending to the "argumentation" stage of a critical discussion; rhetorical elements are featured in attention to "strategic maneuvering" involved in balancing the goals of a critical discussion and individual success (van Eemeren and Houtlosser). Another attempt, undertaken by Tindale and based on Perelman's work, has involved making a case for the primacy of a rhetorical perspective over the dialectical and logical.

[3] O'Keefe's work has indicated the need to do so, and van Eemeren and Grootendorst have lead the way by proposing to measure argumentative reality against the ideal of a critical discussion.

[4] Examples of scholarship with this perspective include Kauffeld; Goodwin, "Cicero's"; and Innocenti.

Works Cited

Beiner, Ronald. *Political Judgment.* Chicago: U of Chicago P, 1983.

Brockriede, Wayne. "Arguers as Lovers." *Philosophy and Rhetoric* 5.1 (1972): 1–11.

Cicero. *De Inventione*. Trans. H. M. Hubbell. Cambridge: Harvard UP, 1976.

Ehninger, Douglas. "Argument as Method: Its Nature, its Limitations and its Uses." *Speech Monographs* 37.2 (1970): 101–10.

———. Introduction. Whately, *Elements of Rhetoric* ix–xxx.

Einhorn, Lois J. "Consistency in Richard Whately: The Scope of His Rhetoric." *Philosophy and Rhetoric* 14.2 (1981): 89–99.

Farrell, Thomas B. *Norms of Rhetorical Culture*. New Haven, CT: Yale UP, 1993.

Foss, Sonja K., and Cindy L. Griffin. "Beyond Persuasion: A Proposal for an Invitational Rhetoric." *Communication Monographs* 62.1 (1995): 2–18.

Gilbert, Michael A. *Coalescent Argumentation*. Mahwah, NJ: Erlbaum, 1997.

Goodwin, Jean. "Cicero's Authority." *Philosophy and Rhetoric* 34 (2001): 38–60.

———. "Henry Johnstone, Jr.'s Still-Unacknowledged Contributions to Contemporary Argumentation Theory." *Informal Logic* 21.1 (2001): 41–50.

Hamblin, C. L. *Fallacies*. Newport News, VA: Vale P, 1970.

Innocenti, Beth Manolescu. "Norms of Presentational Force." *Argumentation and Advocacy* 41.3 (2005): 139–51.

Johnson, Ralph H. *Manifest Rationality: A Pragmatic Theory of Argument*. Mahwah, NJ: Erlbaum, 2000.

Kauffeld, Fred J. "Presumptions and the Distribution of Argumentative Burdens in Acts of Proposing and Accusing." *Argumentation* 12.2 (1998): 245–66.

McKerrow, Ray E. "Probable Argument and Proof in Whately's Theory of Rhetoric." *Central States Speech Journal* 26 (1975): 259–66.

O'Keefe, Daniel J. "Potential Conflicts between Normatively Responsible Advocacy and Successful Social Influence: Evidence from Persuasion Effects Research." *Argumentation* 21.2 (2007): 151–63.

Perelman, Chaïm. *The Realm of Rhetoric*. Trans. William Kluback. Notre Dame, IN: U of Notre Dame P, 1982.

———, and Lucie Olbrechts-Tyteca. *The New Rhetoric: A Treatise on Argumentation*. Trans. John Wilkinson and Purcell Weaver. Notre Dame, IN: U of Notre Dame P, 1969.

Poster, Carol. "An Organon for Theology: Whately's *Rhetoric* and *Logic* in Religious Context." *Rhetorica* 24.1 (2006): 37–77.

Sproule, J. Michael. "The Psychological Burden of Proof: On the Evolutionary Development of Richard Whately's Theory of Presumption." *Communication Monographs* 43.2 (1976): 115–29.

Tindale, Christopher W. *Rhetorical Argumentation: Principles of Theory and Practice*. Thousand Oaks, CA: Sage, 2004.

Toulmin, Stephen. *The Uses of Argument*. Cambridge: Cambridge UP, 1958.

van Eemeren, Frans H., and Rob Grootendorst. *A Systematic Theory of Argumentation: The Pragma-Dialectical Approach*. Cambridge: Cambridge UP, 2004.

van Eemeren, Frans H., and Peter Houtlosser. "Managing Disagreement: Rhetorical Analysis within a Dialectical Framework." *Argumentation and Advocacy* 37.3 (2001): 150–57.

Wenzel, Joseph W. "Three Perspectives on Argument: Rhetoric, Dialectic, Logic." *Perspectives on Argumentation: Essays in Honor of Wayne Brockriede*. Ed. Robert Trapp and Janice Schuetz. Long Grove, IL: Waveland P, 1990. 9–26.

Whately, Richard. *Elements of Logic*. 8th ed. New York: Harper & Row, 1853.

———. *Elements of Rhetoric*. Ed. Douglas Ehninger. Carbondale: Southern Illinois UP, 1963.

27

<Reason> and the Rhetoric of Rational Religion in Thomas Paine's *The Age of Reason* and Richard Watson's *Apology for the Bible*

David C. Hoffman

This is a study of the rhetorical contest between Thomas Paine's *The Age of Reason; Being an Investigation of True and Fabulous Theology* (henceforth, *Age*), the most important attempt ever made to popularize deism, and Richard Watson's *Apology for the Bible* (henceforth, *Apology*), the most widely circulated reply to Paine.

The Paine–Watson contest is remarkable as one of the last and best expressions of the rhetoric of "natural" or "rational" religion. Natural religion, a concept closely related to Aquinas' natural theology, had received its earliest detailed Protestant formulation in Richard Hooker's *Of the Lawes of Ecclesiastical Politie* (1595), in which it is argued that human conduct is rightfully and naturally governed by a more-or-less self-evident Law of Reason that is universally available to all humans without divine revelation. The theme was developed by Dutch theologian Hugo Grotius and Lord Edward Herbert of Cherbury. From the latter seventeenth through the eighteenth centuries, the comparison between natural and revealed religion became a theological commonplace (Byrne 1–52).

This essay contributes to the literature on the rhetoric of religion through an analysis of how Paine and Watson deploy the ideograph <reason> to construct conflicting rhetorics of rational religion. Rational religion was embraced, in different forms, by both Paine and Watson. Watson was a latitudinarian Anglican bishop who hoped that natural religion might provide a common ground between feuding Protestant sects (on latitudinarianism see

Reventlow 223–85). Paine was a deist who believed that Christian revelation should be discarded in favor of a scientific deism, which he conceived as a pure form of natural religion. On the eve of the Second Great Awakening and nineteenth-century Christianity's turn toward the mystical and the ecstatic, these two old lions of the Enlightenment, both born in the year 1737, played out the contest between deism and rational Christianity on a court governed by reason, each claiming that reason was on his side.

Ideographs, by convention written between angle brackets (< >), were first described by Michael McGee as terms that "are the basic structural elements, the building blocks, of ideology" ("Ideograph" 7), terms that we are "conditioned to believe . . . have an obvious meaning, a behaviorally directive self-evidence" (6). McGee gives <rule of law>, <liberty>, <tyranny>, and <equality> as examples of ideographs. Formally, "an ideograph is an ordinary-language term found in political discourse . . . a high-order abstraction representing a commitment to a particular but equivocal and ill-defined normative goal" (15). It was McGee's dream to "map" ideology in a three-step process: (1) "the isolation of a society's ideographs," (2) the analysis of the "diachronic structure" of each ideograph, i.e., its changing usage over time, and (3) the "characterization of the synchronic relationships among all the ideographs in a particular context" (16).

Since McGee invented ideographic analysis in 1980, the method has been applied to a wide variety of ideographic terms, although the full program outlined by McGee has been pursued only in a piecemeal way. McGee himself elaborated the method in a 1987 analysis of <people> ("Power"). Celeste Condit and John Lucaites have done more to map the diachronic structure of one particularly important ideograph, <equality>, than any other analyst for any other term. Since the publication of their book, *Crafting Equality*, in 1993, ideographic analysis has gained momentum.

By performing diachronic and synchronic analyses of <reason>, I hope to shed light on the definitional strategies that enabled this powerful term to be used by Paine and Watson for conflicting ends. The very boundaries of the discourse about rational religion, in which both Paine and Watson participated, were defined by the possible deployments of the ideograph <reason>. Paine and Watson disagreed, as deists and rational Christians had for a century, on the relative importance of <reason> and revelation. They were able to stake out different positions within the discursive boundaries defined by "rational religion" by employing at least three different constructions of <reason> itself. In *Age*, <reason> is (1) that which will meet the test of legal procedural rationality: Paine argues that the Bible does not stand up to common law rules of evidence. On the positive side, Paine promotes deism by claiming that <reason> is (2) a gift from God given so that humanity might come to know God: Paine argues that the existence and goodness of the Creator are manifest to reason when it contemplates creation. Watson (3) makes <reason> mainly a matter of character: Watson argues that Paine's conclusions should not be trusted because he exhibits certain character flaws that are poor indicators for rationality. Thus, different constructions of <reason> allow for the construction of differing rhetorics of rational religion. In what follows, I will map these three constructions of <reason> in *Age* and *Apology*, saying something about the history or "diachronic structure" and strategic use of each construction. It is my hope that this analysis will shed light on the contest between Paine and Watson.

Legal <Reason> and Paine's Critical Deism

Age, published in two parts in 1794 and 1795, is nothing if not a book with a dramatic and ironic career. Later demonized in the American Federalist press as an atheistic work, according to Paine *Age* was composed to combat the atheistic tendency of the French Revolution with a naturalistic deism. Paine wrote in Paris as he served as a delegate to the National Convention, which was the legislature of the new French republic. The final version of part 1 was finished in late 1793 only hours before Paine, who had run afoul of the Committee of Public Safety, was escorted to palais du Luxembourg with the high expectation that his head would soon be parted from his body. Paine escaped execution through serious illness and administrative error, and lived on to write part 2 (Keane 411–14; Paine 85–88).

Age proved to be another best seller for the popular author of *Common Sense* and *The Rights of Man* (Keane 396), but did not have the kind of impact that Paine had hoped. In France, *Age* had little impact at all amid the tumult of the revolution and the rise of Bonaparte (Davidson and Scheick 88). In England, *Age* was suppressed for more than twenty years (Claeys 188; Prochaska 574–75). In America, *Age* was avidly received by an embryonic network of deistic societies and circulated freely together with numerous replies (Morais 130–38). But the book became embroiled in partisan politics in a way Paine could never have guessed as he was writing in France. Federalists found in Paine a poster boy for all the perceived dangers of the Jeffersonian Republicans, and attacked him ferociously (Hawke 353–58; Keane 455–66; Morais 159–78). All told, about 70 replies to *Age* had been published by 1800, most of them angry (Davidson and Scheick 108–16; Smith n. 43).

"Reason" (including "reasons" and "reasoning," but excluding "reasonable") is used 71 times in the body of the text of *Age*, a frequency that compares favorably with the frequency of the work's other prominent terms, such as "evidence" (114 uses) and "science" (fifty-two uses). However, not every use of "reason" has equal significance. Twenty-one uses in part 2 are simply restatements of the title, for example, "in the Former part of *The Age of Reason* . . ." (Paine 85). Of the uses that remain, thirty are what might be called "justificatory" uses of "reason," for example, "My reasons for not believing them . . ." (22). The remaining twenty uses evoke reason either as a human capacity, for example, "it is only by the exercise of reason, that man can discover God . . ." (47), or as an abstract entity, for example, "it yet remains to reason and philosophy to abolish the amphibious fraud" (25). These uses of "reason" as capacity and "reason" as entity, which I have counted together here because they are frequently difficult to distinguish in practice, are the most "ideographic" because they more strongly and more generally "warrant the use of power," to take McGee's phrase, than the justificatory uses.

Even though "reason" is a relatively frequent term in *Age*, the main argument for viewing <reason> as the controlling ideograph of the text is its place in the title and dedication. The title implies that there is a "true theology" based on reason, and a "fabulous theology" that is not. In the dedication, which is only reproduced in some modern editions, the newly imprisoned Paine puts the work under the "protection" of his "fellow-citizens of the United States of America," saying, "The most formidable weapon against errors of every kind is Reason. I have never used any other, and trust I never shall" (Foner 665). Thus, we gather that *Age* is a work of <reason> that concerns itself with theology. But what is this <reason> really, and how does it fight error? To answer these questions, we must dig into the text.

Part 1 of *Age* was published with seventeen chapter headings in its earliest French edition, headings that are reproduced in translation in the Conway edition cited here. The work can usefully be divided into these five sections:

1. Chapter 1: Paine's profession of faith
2. Chapters 2–8: An attack on Christian revelation
3. Chapters 9–12: A positive case that creation itself is the truest testament of God
4. Chapters 13–16: A comparison of creation and revelation in terms of their appeal as bases of belief
5. Chapter 17: A critique of revealed religion as deceiving people by means of mystery, miracle, and prophecy

Part 2 of *Age* is organized as a book-by-book attack on the credibility and authority of the writers of the Bible.

Age is both a positive case for deism, and an attack on revealed religion. After Paine's profession of faith, in which he declares his faith in God but disavows belief in any organized religion, it is Paine's attack on revealed religion that the reader first encounters. This strain of critical deism is confined mainly to chapters 2–8 and the discussion of miracles in chapter 17 in part 1, but is evident throughout part 2. These sections are dominated by a destructive strategy, based on legal practice, leveled against the Bible's "testimonial evidence" of revelation.

Although the word "reason" is used with relative infrequency in the critical sections of *Age* (just four times from the beginning of chapter 2 until the last two paragraphs of chapter 8, which begin the positive case for deism), the title and dedication authorize a reading of them that takes <reason>, constructed as legal procedural rationality, to be the controlling ideograph: with what else would Paine fight error in a work called *The Age of Reason*? The degree to which Paine relies on a legal construction of "evidence" to do the critical work of <reason> is shown by the sheer number of times "evidence" and related terms are used in *Age*: Paine uses the term "hearsay" four times, "testimony" seven times, "witness" eleven times, and "evidence" 114 times. And, while "evidence" is used throughout the text, the use of "hearsay," "testimony," and "witness" is confined strictly to the critical sections.

In taking a legal approach to the "evidence" of the Bible, Paine is following the lead of a number of prominent early English deists. Anthony Collins, who was a student of law and philosophy and a friend and correspondent of John Locke, first introduced the category of "testimony" into the debate about biblical prophecy in *An Essay Concerning the Use of Reason in Propositions, the Evidence Whereof Depends on Human Testimony* (1707). (On Collins, see Brown 49–50; Herrick 107–08; O'Higgins). After the conviction of one Thomas Woolston for blasphemy in 1729 on account of his having published a number of discourses that promoted an allegorical interpretation of miracles (Brown 50–51; Herrick 77–101; Trapnell), Thomas Sherlock, an Anglican bishop, published *The Trial of the Witnesses of the Resurrection of Jesus* (1729) (see Brown 57–58; Carpenter). This popular work was an elaborate fantasy-restaging of Woolston's trial, in which it was made to seem that Matthew, Mark, Luke, and John are actually on trial as Woolston's counsel tries to "overthrow the evidence of Christ's resurrection" (8). Although the work was ultimately apologetic in aim, and the apostles were "acquitted" at the end, it tended to normalize a legalistic approach to biblical evidence. Thus, when Peter Annet published his scathing, if somewhat belated, response, *The Resurrection of Jesus Considered; in Answer to the Trial of the Witnesses* (1744), it seemed normal that he would employ common law rules of evidence, such as the exclusion of hearsay (see Brown 51–52; Herrick 125–44).

Picking up on this tradition of legalism in the critical deistic tradition, Paine's first line of attack on Christian revelation in chapter 2 of *Age*, "Of Missions and Revelations," is that it is a kind of "hearsay" evidence. "Hearsay" is employed four times in the chapter's ten paragraphs, for example:

> No one will deny or dispute the Power of the Almighty to make such communication if he pleases. . . . [But] it is revelation to the first person only, and *hearsay* to every other; and consequently, they are not obliged to believe it. (23)

Where revelation is at second or third hand, Paine implies, there is no call to treat it with less skepticism than any other human testimony.

Having established that reported revelation in general needs to be treated by the same rules as any other human testimony, Paine turns upon the gospel account of Jesus' life and builds his case against the resurrection on a comparison between what might be expected and what is actually available as evidence. Jesus' "miraculous conception" could not have been expected to produce much evidence. Because it "was not a thing that admitted of publicity . . . [it] was not one of those things that admitted of proof." However,

> The resurrection and ascension, supposing them to have taken place, admitted of public and ocular demonstration, like that of the ascension of a balloon, or the sun at noon day, to all Jerusalem at least. A thing which everybody is required to believe, requires that the proof and evidence of it be equal to all, and universal; and as the public visibility of this last related act was the only evidence that could give sanction to the former part, the whole of it falls to the ground, because that evidence was never given. Instead of this, a small number of persons, not more than eight or nine, are introduced as proxies for the whole world, to say, they saw it, and all the rest of the world are called upon to believe it. (26–27)

Paine argues that because the ascension, unlike the conception, was a public event, one might reasonably expect numerous eye-witnesses who had seen Jesus go into the air. The testimony of just eight or nine is meant to look paltry by comparison. Given the situation, one might have expected stronger proof from extra-biblical sources. Clearly, Paine is occupied with the question of what it would take to prove the story of Jesus in the context of late eighteenth-century legal rules of evidence.

Part 2 of *Age* is completely given over to a legalistic, critical rationality that interrogates the authenticity and character of biblical witnesses and the consistency of their testimony on a book by book basis. Paine argues that, as a whole, the Bible, unlike other ancient writing, is valuable only as testimony.

> . . . with respect to the books ascribed to Moses, to Joshua, to Samuel, etc. Those are books of *testimony*, and they testify of things naturally incredible; and therefore the whole of our belief, as to the authenticity of those books, rests, in the first place, upon the certainty that they were written by Moses, Joshua, and Samuel; secondly, upon the credit we give to their *testimony*. (91)

Having established that the value of the Bible is solely testimonial, Paine proceeds to attack the authority of each book of the Bible in turn using three general strategies: (1) attempting to show that the books were not written by their purported authors, and are therefore untrustworthy; (2) attempting to discredit the character of witnesses and thereby diminish the value of their testimony; and (3) attempting to discredit testimony on internal grounds by finding contradictions and inconsistencies.

To give one extended instance, Paine's main strategy in treating the New Testament is to use inconsistencies between Matthew, Mark, Luke, and John as evidence that none of them can be trusted. Paine notes differences in the genealogies of Jesus Christ at the beginning of Matthew and in the third chapter of Luke (154). He also points to four different versions of the inscription above Jesus on the cross (158), different accounts of which women were present when it was discovered that Jesus had risen and what time of day this discovery took place (161), where the angel who announced the resurrection was (161), and when and where Jesus reappeared (163–66). Paine directly evokes the legal analogy in his handling of the contradictory evidence in what he comes close to calling "the case of the missing body":

> Now if the writers of these four books had gone into a court of justice to prove an alibi, (for it is of the nature of an alibi that is here attempted to be proved, namely, the absence of a dead body by supernatural means,) and had they given their evidence in the same contradictory manner as it is here given, they would have been in danger of having their ears cropt for perjury. (162)

Thus, in the critical sections of *Age*, we find <reason> operationalized as a legal treatment of testimony and evidence.

Sacral <Reason> and Paine's Positive Deism

Paine's positive case for deism is made almost exclusively in what I have labeled the third and fourth sections of part 1 (chapters 9–16, really beginning at the end of chapter 8), with a brief reprise in the conclusion of part 2. It is dominated by a markedly different construction of <reason> than the legal rationality that drives Paine's critical deism: in these passages <reason> is a gift from God that allows humanity to see the Creator in his Creation.

The sacral <reason> employed by Paine in his positive case for deism seems, ironically, to have had its origin in a tradition of Christian apologetic known as physico-theology. Physico-theology was an apologetic movement that arose in the wake of the success of Isaac Newton's *Philosophiae Naturalis Principia Mathematica* (1687) and found a prominent public platform in the Boyle Lecture series at Cambridge. The central thesis of physico-theology was that the existence of an omnipotent and benevolent God could be deduced from the order of creation. Physico-theology was also an apology for science in religious terms: the best way to know the creator is the study of creation, it argued (Reventlow 338–41). Among prominent writers of physico-theology was John Ray, a naturalist elected to the Royal Society in 1667. His *The Wisdom of God Manifested in the Works of the Creation* (1690) is a magisterial panegyric of creation as only a naturalist could write it. Richard Bentley delivered the prototypical physico-theological discourse in a series of sermons entitled *A Confutation of Atheism from the Origin and Frame of the World* (1692). Also prominent were Samuel Clarke (*The Evidences of Natural and Revealed Religion*, 1705) and William Derham (*Physico-Theology, or a Demonstration of the Being and Attributes of God from his Works of Creation*, 1713). The titles say all that need be said here of the nature of the genre.

Physico-theology was already an old tradition when Paine was born in 1737, but his contact with it is demonstrable. In the winter of 1757–1758, the twenty-year-old Paine attended public lectures by two renowned popularizers of Newtonian science, James Ferguson and Benjamin Martin, and became personally acquainted with them (Keane 36–45; Millburn; Paine 63). He renewed his acquaintance with Martin and Ferguson in the winter of 1772–1773 (Keane 40–45). In *Age*, Paine traces the origin of his questioning of Christianity to what he learned of science from these two men (65–66). This is ironic, because neither Martin nor Ferguson were professors of the sort of deism that challenged Christianity. But what Paine did probably pick up from them was the physico-theological justification for the study of science.

Paine turned the sacral conception of <reason>, rooted in physico-theology, to his own deistic purposes. The construction of <reason> as sacred is made explicit in a number of passages in *Age*, and is strongly associated with Paine's positive case for deism. All but five of Paine's twenty uses of "reason" as "capacity" or "abstract entity" in *Age* occur between the last three paragraphs of chapter 8 and the end of chapter 16, the section I have associated with his positive case for deism. Two of the other five uses occur in the conclusion of part 2, as it reprises the positive arguments of part 1.

In the transition from his critical to his positive mode at the end of chapter 8, Paine says that he who accepts revealed religion

> despises the choicest gift of God to man, the GIFT OF REASON; and having endeavored to force upon himself the belief of a system against which reason revolts [i.e., revealed religion], he ungratefully calls it human reason, as if man could give reason to himself. (44)

The real tragedy in rejecting the gift of reason, as Paine sees it, is that those who do so cut themselves off from the only true communion with God available to humanity:

> It is only by the exercise of reason, that man can discover God. Take away that reason, and he would be incapable of understanding anything. . . . How then is it that those people pretend to reject reason? (47)

God is manifest to reason both as the first cause of all things (47) and in the structure of the universe itself. "THE WORD OF GOD IS THE CREATION WE BEHOLD," says Paine in capital letters (45). If God speaks to man through creation, man "hears" God through science:

> The Almighty lecturer, by displaying the principles of science in the structure of the universe, has invited man to study and to imitation. It

> is as if he had said to the inhabitants of this globe that we call ours, "I have made an earth for man to dwell upon, and I have rendered the starry heavens visible, to teach him science and the arts." (55)

Paine gives a lyrical summation of his brand of scientific deism founded on a sacral conception of <reason> at the end of chapter 15 (73), and again at the end of part 2, seemingly to make sure his readers have not forgotten his positive message after so much purely critical material:

> Could a man be placed in a situation, and endowed with power of vision to behold at one view, and to contemplate deliberately, the structure of the universe, to mark the movements of the several planets, the cause of their varying appearances, the unerring order in which they revolve, even to the remotest comet, their connection and dependence on each other, and to know the system of laws established by the Creator, that governs and regulates the whole; he would then conceive, far beyond what any church theology can teach him, the power, the wisdom, the vastness, the munificence of the Creator. He would then see that all the knowledge man has of science, and that all the mechanical arts by which he renders his situation comfortable here, are derived from that source. (191–92)

<Reason> as a Character Trait in Richard Watson's *Apology for the Bible*

"In the beginning of the year 1796," writes Watson in his autobiographical *Anecdotes of the Life of Richard Watson*, "I published *An Apology for the Bible*, being a defense of that Holy Book against the scurrilous abuse of Thomas Paine" (287). Watson's *Apology* responds only to part 2 of *Age*. Watson claims to never even have seen part 1 of *Age* (*Apology* 157). This fact is quite significant, because part 1 includes Paine's profession of faith and much of his positive argument for deism. In spite of this, Watson's *Apology* is generally acknowledged by both scholars and contemporaries to have been the foremost response to *Age*. As searches of Eighteenth Century Collections Online and The Library Company reveal, *Apology* ended up going through at least eight London editions in 1796 alone, and was published or reprinted in a dozen or so other cities. It was still being reprinted as late as 1828. So highly regarded was it that every Harvard student was issued a copy in 1796 as an antidote to *Age* (Claeys 191). Modern scholars also acknowledge the importance of Watson's response to Paine (Conway 243; Davidson and Scheick 90; Morais 166; Prochaska 187).

Apology was written by a man who was, in his own way, as much a champion of rational religion as Paine. Watson, the Bishop of Llandaff, was both a professor of chemistry (*Anecdotes* 28–29) and a professor of divinity at Cambridge (34–38). For Watson "rational religion" meant an imperialistic rational Christianity, which would take the specific form of liberal Anglicanism, advancing on the heels of the civilizing influence of British culture:

> Christianity is a rational religion; the Romans, the Athenians, the Corinthians and others, were highly civilized, far advanced in the rational use of their intellectual faculties, and they all, at length, exchanged Paganism for Christianity; the same change will take place in other countries, as they become enlightened by the progress of European literature, and become capable of justly estimating the weight of historical evidence, on which the truth of Christianity must, as to them, depend. (198)

He believed that science would ultimately bear out, and perhaps even explain by rational means, the truth of most or all of the Bible.

Apology is a work organized as a series of ten letters addressed directly to Paine. Watson's overall strategy in defending Christian revelation against *Age* is to make <reason> a power of the human mind dependent upon character and judgment, and to show that Paine's character is wanting and his judgments ill-formed. Although he is most genteel about it, Watson portrays Paine, in strong language, as someone who is ill-informed and biased—hardly the qualities of a worthy champion of rational religion.

The link between reason and character goes back at least as far as Aristotle, who made *phronesis* an essential part of ethos (*Rhetoric* 2.1.5–7), but has its immediate antecedents in the debate about the ethos of the free thinker in the early eighteenth century. Defenders of free thought, such as Collins and Annet, generally portrayed the free thinker as possessing the ethos of openness and boldness necessary to discover truth. Collins, for instance, in his *A Discourse of Free Thinking* (1713) emphasizes the necessary connection between a disposition that favors thorough and unfettered inquiry, on any subject whatsoever, and the discovery of truth. Such a link between <reason> and the boldness of character necessary to freely pursue thought is amplified in Peter Annet's *Judging for Ourselves; or Free-Thinking, the Great Duty of Religion* (1739).

On the other side, detractors of free thought, such as William Whiston, generally portrayed the free thinker as someone who did not possess the necessary discipline and sobriety for close reasoning. Whiston, a prominent Cambridge mathematician and astronomer who succeeded Newton as Lucasian Chair of Mathematics, and whose writing was certainly known to Watson, wrote one of the many responses to Collins' *A Discourse of Free Thinking*, namely, *Free Thinking, Reflexions on an Anonymous Pamphlet* (1713). But he countered the connection between bold character and <reason> made in the free thought discourse most forcibly in *Of the Temper of Mind Necessary for the Discovery of Divine Truth; and of the Degree of Evidence that Ought to Be Expected in Divine Matters*, which forms the preface of *Astronomical Principles of Religion* (1725). In it he emphasizes the qualities of humility and submission to God's will. It is not enough merely to gather and weigh evidence, one must humbly ask God's help in order to come to the right conclusion.

The dueling constructions of the connection between character and <reason> that can be observed in the pamphlet literature of the early eighteenth century still seem to be at play in the Paine–Watson debate. In *Age*, Paine disparages the character of the sort of person that takes the irrational parts of Christianity on blind faith, ignoring the voice of his own God-given power of reason: "with all this strange appearance of humility, and his contempt for human reason, he ventures into the boldest presumptions . . ." (44). In *Apology*, Watson, for his part, insinuates that Paine is not the sort of unbiased reasoner that should be trusted to be a judge of important matters, but rather a man who "introduces railing for reasoning, vulgar and illiberal sarcasm in the room of argument" (18). Neither man is simply making an ad hominem attack. Rather, both are making the case that his opponent's reasoning is flawed by certain character defects.

Watson starts *Apology* on a positive note, praising Paine's work and giving him credit for his sincerity. The tone of the exchange is really set on the next page as Watson, observing that Paine had intended to put off publication of his religious views until "a later period in life," writes, "I hope there is no want of charity in saying, that it would have been fortunate for the Christian world, had your life been terminated before you had fulfilled your intention" (6). This strikes me as one of the most delicate ways of wishing someone dead that has ever been put to paper. From this point on, and often with the same politely devastating irony, Watson builds the case that Paine's reasoning, although sincere, is warped by ignorance and prejudice.

> I have thought fit to make this remark, with a view of suggesting to you a consideration of great importance—whether you have examined calmly, and according to the best of your ability, the arguments by which the truth of revealed religion may, in judgment of learned and impartial men, be established?—You will allow, that thousands of learned and impartial men, (I speak not of priests, who, however, are, I trust, as learned and impartial as yourself, but of laymen of the most splendid talents)—you will allow, that thousands of these, in all ages, have embraced revealed religion as true. Whether these men have all been in error, enveloped in the darkness of ignorance, shackled by the chains of superstition, whilst you and a few others enjoy light and liberty, is a question I submit to the decision of your readers. (8–9)

Watson's sense of irony is evident in his discussion of priests, who, as a class, Paine invariably associates with "priest-craft" and deceit. Watson, who had some dissenting sympathies himself, trusts that priests are as "learned and impartial" as Paine, who he does not really esteem to be very learned or impartial. The larger point here is to ask whether Paine has taken the trouble to objectively consider the opinions of the multitude of earlier writers on the subject, and to question what would set Paine ahead of such distinguished company.

From this point on, Watson will try to show his readers that Paine's conclusions about religion are not a product of God's gift of reason, but rather of ignorance and prejudice. The closing two sentences of Letter I display this tactic to good effect:

> A philosopher in search of truth forfeits with me all claim to candour and impartiality, when he introduces railing for reasoning, vulgar and illiberal sarcasm in the room of argument. I will not imitate the example you set for me; but examine what you shall produce, with as much coolness and respect, as if you had given the priests no provocation; as if you were a man of the most unblemished character, subject to no prejudices, actuated by no bad designs, not liable to have abuse retorted upon you with success. (18)

Watson says, in effect, that he will treat Paine "*as if*" he could be taken seriously. Watson strongly implies that Paine really should not be trusted because he has a *blemished* character that *is* subject to prejudice.

Although the construction of <reason> as a character trait is perhaps not the only usage of the term that may be found in *Apology*, it certainly represents an organizing principle of Watson's attack on Paine.

Conclusion

It is my hope that the foregoing discussion has provided readers with some insight into the nature of the debate about deism that took place between Paine and Watson. It was a debate whose boundaries were defined by <reason>, an ideograph that both men employed to justify their own positions. Both men embraced the idea that religion could be made to conform completely to the dictates of reason. By employing different constructions of <reason>—namely, legal <reason>, sacral <reason>, and <reason> as a character trait—Paine and Watson defended opposing positions within the discourse of rational religion. It was perhaps the failure of rational religion to unite such men as Paine and Watson that led to its failure as a movement in the early nineteenth century.

Works Cited

Brown, Colin. *Miracles and the Critical Mind*. Grand Rapids, MI: Wm. B. Eerdmans, 1984.

Byrne, Peter. *Natural Religion and the Nature of Religion*. London: Routledge, 1989.

Carpenter, Edward. *Thomas Sherlock 1678–1761*. London: Macmillian, 1936.

Claeys, Gregory. *Thomas Paine: Social and Political Thought*. New York: Routledge, 1989.

Condit, Celeste Michelle, and John Lucaites. *Crafting Equality: America's Anglo-African Word*. Chicago: U of Chicago P, 1993.

Conway, Moncure Daniel. *The Life of Thomas Paine, with a History of His Literary, Political and Religious Career in America, France, and England*. Vol. 2. New York: G. P. Putnam's Sons, 1908.

Davidson, Edward H., and William J. Scheick. *Paine, Scripture and Authority:* The Age of Reason *as Religious and Political Idea*. Bethlehem: Lehigh UP, 1994.

Foner, Eric, ed. *Thomas Paine: Collected Writings*. New York: Library of America, 1995.

Hawke, David Freeman. *Paine*. New York: Harper and Row, 1974.

Herrick, James A. *The Radical Rhetoric of the English Deists: The Discourse of Skepticism, 1680–1750*. Columbia: U of South Carolina P, 1997.

Keane, John. *Tom Paine: A Political Life*. New York: Grove P, 1995.

McGee, Michael Calvin. "The 'Ideograph': A Link between Rhetoric and Ideology." *Quarterly Journal of Speech* 66.1 (1980): 1–16.

———. "Power to the <people>." *Critical Studies in Mass Communication* 4.4 (1987): 432–37.

Millburn, John R. "The London Evening Courses of Benjamin Martin and James Ferguson, Eighteenth-Century Lectures on Experimental Philosophy." *Annals of Science* 40.5 (1983): 437–55.

Morais, Herbert M. *Deism in Eighteenth Century America*. New York: Russell & Russell, 1934.

O'Higgins, James. *Anthony Collins, The Man and His Works.* The Hague: Martius Nijhoff, 1976.

Paine, Thomas. *The Age of Reason; Being an Investigation of True and Fabulous Theology. The Writings of Thomas Paine*. Vol. 4. Ed. Moncure Daniel Conway. New York: Burt Franklin, 1908/1969.

Prochaska, Franklyn K. "Thomas Paine's *The Age of Reason* Revisited." *Journal of the History of Ideas* 33.4 (1972): 561–76.

Reventlow, Henning Graf. *The Authority of the Bible and the Rise of the Modern World*. Trans. John Bowden. Philadelphia: Fortress P, 1984.

Sherlock, Thomas. *The Trial of the Witnesses of the Resurrection of Jesus.* 1729. From the Twelfth London Edition. Boston: John Eliot, 1809.

Smith, Jay E. "Thomas Paine and *The Age of Reason*'s Attack on the Bible." *Historian* 58.4 (1996).

Trapnell, William H. *Thomas Woolston: Deist or Madman*. London: Thoemmes P, 1994.

Watson, Richard. *Anecdotes of the Life of Richard Watson, Bishop of Llandaff.* London, 1817. *Google Book Search*. Web. 23 May 2010.

———. *An Apology for the Bible.* New York, 1796. *Eighteenth Century Collections Online* (Gale Document Number CW3322671017). 23 May 2010.

Whiston, William. *Astronomical Principles of Religion*. London, 1725. *Eighteenth Century Collections Online* (Gale Document Number CW3321350354). 23 May 2010.

28

Augustan Concord, Gothic Controversy, and Models of Empire in *The Spectator*

Jon Leon Torn

If we consider rhetoric as a language art dealing with the political exigencies of concord and controversy, are these aims external to the art itself? Or can concord and controversy be located within rhetoric itself, within the very textual movement of rhetorical action? In the following, I consider how rhetorical style can itself embody, rather than simply respond to the aims of, concord and controversy. I study debates over rhetorical imitation from the formative days of the British Empire, particularly those initiated by Joseph Addison, famous for the epochal London periodical *The Spectator*. These debates raise important issues about the interrelationship of style, politics, and history, and the role of rhetorical imitation in each.

The influence of the style of Addison on modern English was vast. The young Benjamin Franklin was just one of the scores of young writers who developed his own style by imitating Addison's (18). By the end of the eighteenth century, the rhetoric and *belles lettres* movement consistently turned to Addison, as an exemplar of proper English style, rendering him in effect the Demosthenes of the Scottish Enlightenment. Hugh Blair considered him "the safest model for imitation" in the English language (246), while Samuel Johnson wrote that "whoever wishes to attain an English stile, familiar but not coarse, and elegant but not ostentatious, must give his days and nights to the volumes of Addison" (588).

Addison's style may have found such favor because it did not present itself as a creation of the modern world. Indeed, when Thomas Tickell published Addison's collected works in 1721, he describes Addison's contributions as exemplars of the "Augustan" form of writing, a sensibility that combined the scientific knowledge of the modern world with the accessibility of the exalted writers (Vergil, Livy, Horace, Ovid) promoted by

Augustus Caesar, first emperor of Rome. The features of Augustan style listed by Tickell include "good breeding," "gracefulness," "correctness," "propriety of thought," and "chastity of style" (ix). The Augustan style was modern and ancient at the same time, and as such could be seen as an amalgam of all styles of writing prior to it.

If Tickell's list of what it means to be "Augustan" seems decidedly apolitical for a style that names itself after a Roman emperor, this is in keeping with the way *The Spectator* presents itself as detached and aloof from the politics of the day. Indeed, in its very first issue Addison, wearing the eponymous mask of the Spectator, promises to "observe a strict neutrality between the Whigs and the Tories" (*The Spectator* 1:3). Tickell's account of Augustan style, and by implication Addison's performance of the same, places itself generically within our received understanding of Enlightenment thought as ahistorical, acontextual, or apolitical. Of course, few now take this understanding of the Enlightenment seriously nowadays: most accept that *The Spectator*'s detached pose is a mere front for the rise of preindustrial capitalism and see Addison as either the "prophet or ideologue of the bourgeoisie" (Black 22). His complicity with this rise, as with most of his contemporaries, is exemplified by the false neutrality of his apolitical stance, and the false transparency of his written style (Selden 74).

To suggest that Augustan style had a political agenda behind it is nothing new; the issue is whether such an agenda was explicit, implicit, or an unconscious agenda masked by protestations of political neutrality. I suggest that such an agenda was implicit, and that to self-identify a certain kind of writing as "Augustan" could not fail to take note of Augustus Caesar's popularity as a political exemplar in England at the time. Addison's "Augustan style" is better seen not as a "bourgeois" but as an "imperial" style, participating as it did in the active political program in England to create an imperial order modeled after that of Augustus, a project upon which the bourgeoisie and the aristocracy actively collaborated (Cain and Hopkins 6). This project was marked not simply by the advancement of a "bourgeois ideology" in possessive individualism, but also by the creation of overarching systems of political, social, and cultural interconnectivity and incorporation (Walker 68).

If this is the case, what are we to make of Addison's apparent rejection of the political in *The Spectator* #1? There is one qualification he makes, that despite his attempt at neutrality he may "be forced to declare myself by the hostilities on either side" (1:3). When he wrote these words, Addison was serving in Parliament as a member of the Whig Party, and although the mask of the character of the Spectator gives him some wiggle room, Addison's statement of neutrality here seems utter cheek. But rather than considering this a simple (and dishonest) disavowal of politics pure and simple, we should consider how Addison decries a particular kind of politics: the politics of controversy. Indeed, Addison's disavowal of partisan controversy may seem to be a repudiation of politics itself because the era in which he wrote was so saturated with controversy. *The Spectator* appeared in the midst of an unprecedented flood of controversial literature made possible by the lapse of the Licensing Act in 1694 and a culture of partisan wrangling, attack and counterattack. Addison's aim, through promotion of the Augustan style, was to create a harmony or agreement of interests or feelings that would preempt such controversy—"harmony or agreement" being part of the definition of the word "concord" (*American Heritage Dictionary*).

As the critic Frank Kermode once wrote,

> Most people have better things to do than argue about such terms as "Baroque" and "Augustan"—to propose the correct usage for them and then to restrict their employment to a particular and limited period. It is, however, a rational and useful activity to inquire into the ways in which historical persons used such expressions in their own times. (132)

To that end, it is worth noting that "the rise of 'Augustan' as a literary appellative was preceded by and dependent upon . . . political analogues between Rome and Britain" (J. Johnson 512). These analogies were reflected in, among other things, the talk that began to circulate in England about a "new Augustus" shortly after the execution of Charles I, as first Cromwell, then Charles II, then William of Orange (by Addison himself in one of his early poems) were celebrated in panegyrics as new versions of Augustus. These drew on contemporary understandings of Augustus Caesar, who was deemed as a sort of enlightened despot (one who considered himself to be a defender of the ideals, if not the political culture, of the republic) who governed through art and was considered to have brought political stability and cultural glory to Rome after the violent end of the republic. Looking further back in Roman history than advocates of Silver Age Latinity like Bacon and Montaigne, but not quite ready to fully accept the susceptibility to *fortuna* of republican Rome, Addison, like many others in his day, split the difference and chose instead to exalt the Rome of Augustus.

By the time that William took the throne in the "Glorious Revolution" of 1688 the "Battle of the Books" between Sir William Temple and members of the Royal Society was in full swing, and in most circles the question of whether or not the model of Augustan Rome was relevant was no longer an issue. What was at issue was whether or not the English could hope to equal or surpass their ancient masters. Against Temple's claim that ancient knowledge was incapable of being surpassed, William Wotton stated that moderns were not only more knowledgeable than the ancients: they actually knew more about ancient society and ancient literature than the ancients did themselves. "Modern philology and antiquities had given modern scholars an advantage both of method and substance unknown to previous ages. With their help, the whole past could be recovered more fully and accurately than ever before" (Levine 30). It is in the context of this exchange between Wotton and Temple that a young Joseph Addison most likely penned "A Discourse on Ancient and Modern Learning" in the mid-1690s. In this work, in its prudential negotiation of ancient and modern norms, we can detect many tenets that would form the mature Addison's "Augustan style."

"A Discourse on Ancient and Modern Learning" is not, as one might guess, a comparison of ancient and modern systems of knowledge. It is rather a speculation on how ancient readers might have read their own contemporaries in a way that surpasses modern readers in one important ability: sensitivity to the perspicacity of the text. His concern, both as a Christian and a modern admirer of Newton and Locke, is why it should be that ancient writings seem so much more *vivid* than modern ones, and why it is that the world that they depict, devoid of both salvation and physics, should be so attractive to him as a reader, attractive enough to make him yearn for it. What Addison saw in classical writing is evidence of a society whose referential system was firmly anchored in a rich and detailed visual experience.

The exemplars Addison uses for the vividness of classical writing are Homer, Theophrastus, and Vergil. In other words, Addison throws a large net, and his choices reflect widely different historical contexts. To say anything about such disparate figures and to expect it to hang together indicates a youthful hubris (or the programmatic structure of a school essay), but it also serves to caution us that Addison was not beholden to the example of a single epoch to prove his point. Homer is mentioned rather briefly, but Addison's praise of his vivid powers of characterization and description (1:231–32) accurately describes Homer's attention to the telling detail and the dense web of physical and social referents in his work. One of the benefits of this process, claims Addison, is a subconscious complication of form: one that promotes fidelity over mere didactic intent. In the moral character studies of Theophrastus, written when Greek cultural and territorial expansion in the early Hellenic period was at its peak, Addison finds an admirable descriptive roughness that adds to the perspicacity of the text:

> We may observe in most of his Characters something foreign to his Subject, and some other Folly or Infirmity mixing itself with the principal Argument of his Discourse. His eye seems to have been attentively fix'd on the Person in whom the Vanity reign'd, that other Circumstances of his Behaviour besides those he was to describe insinuated themselves unawares, and crept insensibly into the Character. It was hard for him to extract a single Folly out of the whole Mass without leaving a little Mixture in the Separation: So that his particular Vice appears something discolur'd in the Description, and his Discourse, like a Glass set to catch the Image of any single Object, gives us a lively Resemblance of what we look for; but at the same Time returns a little shadowy Landskip of the Parts that lie about it. (1:234–35)

If the "Mixture in the Separation" complicates the didactic intent, it at the same time makes the portrait more vivid and true to life, therefore heightening its potency. Addison also finds in Homer the same insinuating circumstance framing character, an excess of detail that betrays real models, as for example the "honest Cobler, who had been very kind and serviceable to the Poet, and is therefore advanc'd in his Poem, to be *Ajax's* Shield-maker" (1:232). While Vergil's character portraiture in the *Aeneid* is "barren" in comparison, he more than makes up for it in the specificity and richness of his description of place, descriptions that would have situated the ancient reader in familiar space:

> How must a *Roman* have been pleas'd, that was well acquainted with the Capes and Promontories, to see the Original of their Names as they stand derived from *Misenus, Palinurus,* and *Cajeta*? That could follow the Poet's Motions, and attend his Hero in all his Marches from Place to Place? That was very well acquainted with the Lake *Amsanctus*, where the Fury sunk, and could lead you to the mouth of the Cave where *Aeneas* took his descent for Hell? Their being conversant with the Place, where the Poem was transacted, gave 'em a greater Relish than we can have at present of several Parts of it; as it affected their Imaginations more strongly, and diffus'd through the whole Narration a greater Air of Truth. The Places stood as so many Marks and Testimonies to the Veracity of the Story that was told of 'em, and help'd the Reader to impose upon himself in the Credibility of the Relation. (1:238)

While Addison grants the ancient reader an ability to feel the "Air of Truth" more than the modern reader can, he himself by speculatively evoking the context within which those texts were read is responding to the "Air of Truth" that he finds in Vergil, Homer, and Theophrastus, an air representing for him the "truth" of a unified ancient culture. The perspicacity of ancient text invites Addison to insert himself within that ancient context, allowing him to participate speculatively in the visual unity that he sees there. The power of such a coherent visual culture is enough to reach through the ages to incorporate new subjects within its realm. To suggest that such a style of perspicacity is imperial by necessity would be quite wrong of course. Machiavelli offers a republican take on the same phenomenon in his famous letter to Vettori where he says that, through reading, "I enter the courts of the ancients, and am welcomed by them . . . I pass indeed into their world" (qtd. in Sullivan 75). But the great importance Addison places on visual description in Vergil, the way in which ancient readers were enabled to trace the extent of empire through his work, suggests that "putting on courtly dress" and entering into a virtual debate with thinkers past would not be enough for him to enter fully into Vergil's world. When Addison traveled to Italy in 1701, he proceeded to match the poetical descriptions of the ancients with the actual landscape, and his resulting travelogue, *Remarks on Several Parts of Italy,* consisted largely of comparing one with the other, causing Horace Walpole to later complain that "Mr. Addison traveled through the poets, but not through Italy" (qtd. in D. Johnson 32).

Addison keeps coming back to Vergil and the Augustan cultural program as he explores these ideas further. Addison's introduction to Dryden's translation of Vergil's *Georgics*, claiming the piece was "the most complete, elaborate, and finished piece in all Antiquity" (1:229), probably helped to encourage the great neo-Augustan interest in the georgic form and its interest in what Ronald Paulson describes as the "aesthetics of georgic renewal" (*Breaking* 57). Vergil's *Georgics* have been interpreted by some as a typical *speculum principe*, in this case using husbandry precepts to metaphorically give the newly crowned Augustus advice on how to rule (Nappa 3). But Addison also treats the poem more as a popular form that uses poetic devices to make didactic content palatable to the masses. The poem is not only a praise of Augustus but a model for how a ruler may productively communicate with a popular audience. The genius of the georgic style, to Addison, is in how it relates precepts to the imagination through vividness of description:

> Where the Prose-Writer tells us plainly what ought to be done, the Poet often conceals the precept in a description, and represents his Country-man performing the action in which he would instruct his reader. Where the one sets out as fully and distinctly as he can, all the parts of the truth, which he would communicate to us; the other singles out the most pleasing circumstance of this truth, and so conveys the whole in a more diverting manner to the understanding. (1:221–22)

While georgics and pastorals both evoke the countryside, the georgics deal in a poetically enhanced way with the activity of husbandry, not shepherding; it is with an air of productive engagement with the environment rather than a watchful stillness that Vergil describes nature. As in his other essay on ancient writing, Addison focuses on how the richness and complexity of a particular description evokes the world outside of the frame, allowing the imagination of the reader to fill in the context. "[In] the style proper to a *Georgic* . . . the Poet must lay out all his strength, that words may be warm and glowing, and that every thing he describes may immediately present itself, and rise up to the reader's view" (1:224). By focusing on individual details in a way that suggests the presence of greater complexity, as does Theophrastus, Vergil creates descriptions that

> suggest a truth indirectly, and without giving us a full and open view of it, to let us see just so much as will naturally lead the imagination into all the parts that lie concealed. This is wonderfully diverting to the understanding, thus to receive a precept, that enters as if it were through a by-way, and to apprehend an Idea that brings a whole train after it. (1:222–23)

Vergil treats his particulars holographically, in other words, encoding within them the total process of human interaction with nature that husbandry (and by suggestion, human endeavor in general) entails.

Vergil and Theophrastus represent, for Addison, the two poles of a practice of ancient visual eloquence, one that uses description of nature and character respectively to invoke a social, political, and visual totality, making ancient writing more pleasurable, more accessible, and more didactically effective than modern writing. It was a balance Addison strove to master in his own practice. By defending the perspicacity of an ancient style of writing that evokes a collective visual culture, Addison is claiming that the clear superiority of the ancients in verbal arts, acknowledged by all but the most didactic of the moderns, did more than simply produce charming cultural artifacts. To value them as some of the moderns did solely for their charm, their exoticism, their otherness, misses their utility as a model of empire, in their functional aspect of binding a culture together around a shared history of personages and places. It is this way of seeing that the modern attempt to recover the past through the piecemeal work of philology is blind to.

Addison also suggests that the modern attraction to ancient writing provides a glimpse of a perspicacity that is the product, not of an unrecoverable and irreproducible genius of the past, but of writers who were rhetorically committed to the social knowledge of their time, to the task of reflecting accurately the land and the people of ancient Greece or Rome. If this is true, there should be no reason why a modern writer, willing to turn a perspicacious eye to contemporary culture, could not accomplish the same. In an act of self-fulfilling prophecy, the early Addison creates the space for the arrival of a figure that he will eventually come to inhabit.

Opposed to the Augustan style was another whose label was designed to evoke the exact opposite of Rome at its highest influence, power, and self-confidence, which was Rome under Augustus. For Addison, such writing evoked not that great society, but rather the barbarous forces that later brought Rome to its knees: it was "Gothic." The clearest demarcations of Augustan versus Gothic styles of writing can be found in *The Spectator* #409, where after lauding Augustan literature Addison complains that

> Our general Taste in *England* is for Epigram, turns of Wit, and forced Conceits, which have no manner of Influence, either for the bettering or enlarging the Mind of him who reads them, and have been carefully avoided by the greatest Writers, both among the Ancients and the Moderns. I have endeavored in several of my Speculations to banish this *Gothic* Taste which has taken Possession among us. (3:528)

And earlier, in #62:

> This [the Augustan style] is that natural Way of Writing, that beautiful Simplicity, which we so much admire in the Compositions of the Ancients; and which no Body deviates from, but those who want Strength of Genius to make a Thought shyine in its own natural Beauties. Poets who want this Strength of Genius to give that Majestick Simplicity to Nature, which we so much admire in the Works of the

> Ancients, are forced to hunt after foreign Ornaments, and not to let any kind of Wit of what kind so ever escape them. I look upon these writers as *Goths* in Poetry, who, like those in Architecture, not being able to come up with the beautiful simplicity of the old *Greeks* and *Romans*, have endeavored to supply its place with all the Extravagances of an irregular Fancy. (1:268)

Addison was not the first critic to use Gothic as an expletive, or the first to indulge the rather spurious linkage the term evokes between medieval Christian culture and the barbarians who sacked Rome. Alfred Longueil traces the critical term to the early Renaissance and helps to explain the articulation it embodied:

> Because the Goths, being Teutons, conceived and built upon an ideal of beauty foreign to the world they overset; and because medieval men, in fashioning their new world, rebuilt it nearer to the Teutonic than to the classic heart's desire; and because to Renaissance skeptics the Gothic ideal, wrought in castle and cathedral, seemed dark and thwarted beside the measure of a Parthenon, it came to pass, in the early Renaissance, that the term "gothic" took on a new and colored meaning, a meaning that masked a sneer. To the Renaissance, medieval or Gothic architecture was barbarous architecture. By a trope all things barbarous became "Gothic." (453)

By the late seventeenth century the pejorative adjective *gothique* was being used by Nicolas Boileau to designate both old-fashioned, uncouth writing and a similar type of social behavior (Holbrook 498). As Addison was an assiduous reader of that French critic (*The Spectator* 3:529), it is most likely that it was within Boileau's work that he picked it up for this particular use. That his objection was levied not just at a particular style but at those who practiced it is suggested by another distinction made by Addison in *The Spectator* #476, between *method* and *genius*:

> When I read an Author of Genius, who writes without Method, I fancy myself in a Wood that abounds with a great many noble Objects, rising among one another in the greatest Confusion and Disorder. When I read a Methodical Discourse, I am in a regular Plantation, and can place myself in its several Centers, so as to take a view of all Lines and Walks that are struck from them. (4:186)

Addison's main intent in #476 is to extol method at the expense of genius. "I, who hear a Thousand Coffee-House Debates every Day, am very sensible of this want of Method . . . The Man who does not know how to methodize his Thoughts has . . . *a barren Superfluity of Words*. The Fruit is lost amongst the Exuberance of Leaves" (4:187). Addison creates a figure that explicitly links "genius" to the controversial literature of the day in Tom Puzzle, freethinker, radical, atheist, and "one of the most Eminent Immethodical Disputants" to represent "those Schools of Politicks" whose "disputants put me in mind of the Skuttle Fish, that when he is unable to extricate himself, blackens all the Water about him, till he becomes invisible." Tom "has got about half a Dozen common-place Topicks into which he never fails to turn the Conversation," although he seems particularly to harp on "the Unreasonableness of Bigottry and Priestcraft." Puzzle's nemesis, Will Dry, manages to constantly derail this modern sophist by nothing more than "desiring him to tell the Company, what it was that he endeavored to prove. In short, *Dry* is a Man of a clear methodical Head, but few Words, and gains the same Advantages over *Puzzle*, that a small Body of regular Troops would gain over a numberless undisciplined Militia" (4:188).

For Addison the prime adversary in this opposition can be found close to him: his occasional friend and (by the time of *The Spectator*) political adversary, Jonathan Swift. The main protagonist of Addison and Steele's earlier collaboration (*The Tatler*), Isaac Bickerstaff, Esq., astrologer and "Censor of Great Britain," was an invention of Swift's that was borrowed by Steele to serve as the reigning voice of the new paper: a man who used eccentricity as a strategy to be outspoken. The origin of the character lay in a public prank against a certain John Partridge, "a quack astrologer, whose predictions were ridiculously positive yet vague and equivocal" (Bond 7). Swift issued *Predictions for the Year 1708* prophesying Partridge's death, with a follow-up after the predicted date confirming Partridge's demise (*Collected Works*). Partridge's own vehement protests that reports of his death had been greatly exaggerated only added to the popular success of Swift's jest. The figure of Bickerstaff thus came to *The Tatler* with a conceptual pedigree that could go either way on the questions of popularity and genius. In a blow for common understanding against the forces of distortion and obscurity, the fictional Bickerstaff made his name by deflating one who gained a measure of authority through the mastery of an arcane and esoteric lore (astrology). But the macabre humor exhibited in the prank on Partridge was also an example of Swift's tendency to use sharp, personal, even cruel satire to make his points, heir to what Morris Croll has described as the libertine program of "startling 'plebeian intelligences'" (159).

Their friendship appears to be genuine, with Addison labeling Swift the "most Agreeable companion, the Truest Friend and the Greatest Genius of his Age" (although recall the complex feelings Addison had about "genius") and Swift referring to Addison as "*le plus honnete homme du monde*" (McCrea 36). But friendship quickly fell victim to politics, and when the Tories achieved a brief reversal of fortune by winning control of Parliament from 1710–1712, Swift shocked his friends by embracing the new leadership and issuing a paper, *The Examiner,* devoted to applying Swift's corrosive style of satire upon the political positions of his former collaborators. The extent to which this ruined Addison and Swift's friendship is suggested by a pamphlet, "The Late Tryal and Conviction of Count Tariff," in which Addison lampoons Swift as "the Examiner":

> a person who had abused almost every man in *England*, that deserved well of his country. He called Goodman *Fact* [Addison's Whiggish hero] a lyar, a seditious person, a traytor, and a rebel. . . . It was allowed that so foul-mouthed a witness never appeared in any cause. Seeing several persons of great eminence, who had maintained the cause of Goodman *Fact*, he called them ideots, blockheads, villains, knaves, infidels, atheists, apostates, fiends, and devils: never did man show so much eloquence in ribaldry. (2:281)

The copious invective of "the Examiner" figure in "Count Tariff" is inspired by the dizzying vehemence of Swift's attacks upon the temporarily deposed Whigs. Typical of Swift's style is the following passage from *The Examiner* #40, in which he claims the Whigs are the real allies of "Popery, Arbitrary Power, and the Pretender":

> A Dog loves to turn round often; yet after certain *Revolutions*, he lies down to *Rest*: But Heads, under the Dominion of the *Moon*, are for perpetual *Changes*, and perpetual *Revolutions*; like the girl at *Bartholomew-Fair*, who gets a Penny by turning round a hundred Times, with Swords in her Hands. . . . To conclude, the *Whigs*, have a natural Faculty for bringing in *Pretenders*, and will therefore probably endeavor to bring in the great One at last: How many *Pretenders* to Wit, Honor, Nobility, Politicks, have they brought in these last twenty Years? In short, they have been sometimes able to procure a majority of *Pretenders* in Parliament; and wanted nothing to render the Work compleat, except a *Pretender* at their Head. (261)

Addison responded to Swift's betrayal in the summer of 1710 with the *Whig-Examiner*. Much of Addison's work in the *Whig-Examiner* takes a defensive role, as the title indicates. Swift's multiple charges and quickly mutating analogies and metaphors were particularly irksome to Addison, for they could not very well be met with an elevated tone. Like a debater trying to "out tech" his opponent, Swift makes so many charges that to try to answer them point by point would be fruitless. The Examiner represents a genius attempting to dazzle his audience into submission, not an interlocutor trying to find common ground. Addison's main approach is to define the Examiner, not as a legitimate political argument to be refuted, but as "nonsense," albeit "high nonsense":

> Low nonsense is the talent of a cold, phlegmatic temper, that in a poor, dispirited styl creeps along servilely through darkness and confusion. A writer of this complexion gropes his way softly amongst self-contradictions, and grovels in absurdities. *Videri vult pauper, et est pauper*: He hath neither wit nor sense, and pretends to none.
>
> On the contrary, your high nonsense blusters and makes a noise, it stalks upon hard words, and rattles through polysyllables. It is loud and sonorous, smooth and periodical. It has something in it like manliness and force, and makes one think of the name Sir Hercules Nonsense in a play called Nest of Fools. In a word, your high nonsense has

> a majestic appearance, and wears a most tremendous garb, like Aesop's ass clothed in a lion's skin. . . .
>
> Low nonsense is like that [small beer] in the barrel, which is altogether tasteless and insipid. High nonsense is like that in the bottle, which has in reality no more strength and spirit than the other, but frets, and flies, and bounces, and by the help of little wind that got into it, imitates the passions of a much nobler liquor. (1:308)

Addison's exasperation with Swift on the level of style reflects his approach to the political question in the pages of *The Spectator.* Rather than debating the fine points of policy, Addison prefers to attack the lack of good taste and right thinking that leads one away from the "common sense" that would naturally allow one to support Whig policy.

The Whig policy was an imperial one, and the Augustan style coordinated well with its aims of creating a common ground where populations could be coordinated via a shared image of the realm. Through the character of the Spectator, Addison evokes London as a hub of coordinated activity: stock exchanges, cultural activities, and commerce sending capital and reason across the globe and bringing back to England the luxurious goods it could not produce on its own (*The Spectator* 1:288). This evolutionary process was fueled by a providential order, in accordance with the Whig interpretation of history (Butterfield 77). Tory views were not anti-imperialist exactly, but lacking the providential framework and Augustan models underlying Whig values, their writings focused considerable anxiety over the direction England was taking in becoming Great Britain. For Tories and their contemporaries in the "country interest" looking at the centralization of London with dismay, the new imperial England represented a "despotism of speculative fantasy" barely masking social chaos (Pocock 112). From this perspective empire is "less a place where England exerts control than the place where England loses command of its own narrative of identity" (Baucom 3). In asserting a singular eccentric identity through their writings, Swift and his fellow Scriblarians exemplified a Tory response to the incorporating drive of the Whig's imperial ambitions.

But such anxieties were not foreign to Addison and to other Whig writers. As proof of this, for all Addison's politicizing against the Gothic style of the singular genius, he in fact admits in *The Spectator* #435 that he often writes that way himself:

> Most of the Papers I give the Publick are written on Subjects that never vary, but are for ever fixt and immutable. Of this kind are all my more Serious Essays and Discourses; but there is another sort of Speculations, which I consider as Occasional Papers, that take their Rise from the Folly, Extravagance, and Caprice of the present Age. For I look upon my self as one set to watch the Manners and Behavior of my Countermen and Contemporaries, and to mark down every absurd Fashion, ridiculous Custom, or affected Form of Speech that makes its Appearance in the World, during the course of these my Speculations. (4:27)

Here Addison embraces controversy, not on political topics, but social ones. To challenge the political hegemony of the Whigs was to court both political and economic disaster (this is exactly the point of Addison's allegory on Lady Credit in *The Spectator* #3), but social norms, particularly those that isolate imperial subjects from participating in the collective culture, must on the contrary be submitted to relentless critique, which he promises his readers to supply in *The Spectator* #10:

> To the End that their Virtue and Discretion may not be short transient intermitting States of Thought, I have resolved to refresh their Memories from Day to Day, till I have recovered them out of that desperate State of Vice and Folly into which this Age is fallen. The Mind that lies fallow but a single Day, sprouts up in Follies that are only to be killed by a constant and assiduous Culture. (1:44)

But in embracing controversy, Addison also embraces many elements of the Gothic style. His "Occasional Papers that take their Rise from the Folly, Extravagance, and Caprice of the present Age" are meant, as if by homeopathic intent, to model the ephemerality of their subjects. The result, according to Erin Mackie, is "a destabilizing resemblance between the object of criticism—the vain, illusive fetishes of fashion and commodity—and the very forms this criticism takes" (61). By the very loving detail with which he describes these ephemera, Addison in his Gothic mode embodies an essential aesthetic principle of modernity, the taking of pleasure in the uncommon or novel (Paulson, *Beautiful* 71). He reveals that inside the triumphant model of Augustan empire there exists a model of empire's eventual fall, figured as an external threat but really an internal one, a Gothic sense of the fragility and weakness of this bond of common vision the Augustan style promises.

Addison's ability to toggle between the styles of concord and controversy suggests that within the Augustan is enfolded the Gothic, in a kind of return of the repressed. Furthermore the intimate relationship between the rhetorics of concord and controversy in Addison's work suggests provocative conclusions about how these two poles of rhetorical action function in concert, both politically and rhetorically, if those distinctions can even be made. Eventually, there can be no concord without controversy, and vice versa.

Works Cited

Addison, Joseph. *The Miscellaneous Works of Joseph Addison*. 4 vols. London: D. A. Talboys, 1830.

American Heritage Dictionary of the English Language. 4th ed. 2007. Print.

Baucom, Ian. *Out of Place: Englishness, Empire and the Locations of Identity*. Princeton, NJ: Princeton UP, 1993.

Black, Scott. "Social and Literary Form in *The Spectator*." *Eighteenth-Century Studies* 33.1 (1999): 21–42

Blair, Hugh. *Lectures on Rhetoric and Belles Lettres*. London: Charles Daly, 1839.

Bond, Richmond P. The Tatler: *The Making of a Literary Journal*. Cambridge: Harvard UP, 1971.

Butterfield, Herbert. *The Whig Interpretation of History*. New York: W. W. Norton, 1965.

Cain, P. J., and A. G. Hopkins. *British Imperialism, 1688–2000*. Harlow: Longman, 2001.

Croll, Morris W. *Style, Rhetoric and Rhythm*. Ed. John Max Patrick. Princeton: Princeton UP, 1966.

Franklin, Benjamin. *The Autobiography of Benjamin Franklin*. Chicago: Lakeside P, 1903.

Holbrook, William C. "The Adjective Gothique in the XVIIIth Century." *Modern Language Notes* 56.7 (1941): 498–503.

Johnson, Donald R. "Addison in Italy." *Modern Language Studies* 6.1 (1976): 32–36.

Johnson, James William. "The Meaning of 'Augustan.'" *Journal of the History of Ideas* 19.4 (1958): 507–22.

Johnson, Samuel. *Lives of the Poets*. New York: Derby & Jackson, 1857.

Kermode, Frank "Review: The Augustan Idea." *The Kenyon Review* New Series 6.2 (1984): 132–35.

Levine, Joseph M. *Between the Ancients and the Moderns: Baroque Culture in Restoration England*. New Haven, CT: Yale UP, 1999.

Longueil, Alfred E. "The Word 'Gothic' in Eighteenth Century Criticism." *Modern Language Notes* 38.8 (1923): 453–60.

Mackie, Erin. *Market à la Mode: Fashion, Commodity, and Gender in* The Tatler *and* The Spectator. Baltimore: Johns Hopkins UP, 1997.

McCrea, Brian. *Addison and Steele Are Dead*. Newark: U of Maryland P, 1990.

Nappa, Christopher. *Reading After Actium: Vergil's* Georgics, *Octavian, and Rome*. Ann Arbor: U of Michigan P, 2005.

Paulson, Ronald. *The Beautiful, Novel and Strange*. Baltimore: Johns Hopkins, 1996.

———. *Breaking and Remaking: Aesthetic Practice in England, 1700–1820*. New Brunswick, NJ: Rutgers UP, 1989.

Pocock, J. G. A. *Virtue, Commerce and History*. New York: Cambridge UP, 1985.

Selden, Raman. *A Readers' Guide to Contemporary Literary Theory*. Lexington: UP of Kentucky, 1985.

The Spectator. Ed. Donald Bond. 5 vols. Oxford: Clarendon P, 1965.

Sullivan, Vickie B. *The Comedy and Tragedy of Machiavelli: Essays on the Literary Works*. New Haven, CT: Yale UP, 2000.

Swift, Jonathan. *The Collected Works of Jonathan Swift*. Vol. 9. London: George Bell, 1903.

Tickell, Thomas. Preface. *The Miscellaneous Works of Joseph Addison*. 4 vols. London: D. A. Talboys, 1830. v–xxviii.

Walker, William. "Ideology and Addison's Essays on the Pleasures of the Imagination." *Eighteenth Century Life* 24.2 (2000): 65–84.

29

Why Richard Weaver Matters

Patrick Shaw

The RSA call for papers begins with two quotations—one from Cicero, the other from Kenneth Burke—both of which are worth repeating here. The passage from Cicero's *De Inventione* states: "I have often and seriously debated with myself whether men and communities have received more good or evil from oratory and a consuming devotion to eloquence" (3). The passage from Burke: "But put identification and division ambiguously together, so that you cannot know for certain just where one ends and the other begins, and you have the characteristic invitation to rhetoric" (25). Each of these is particularly relevant to Richard Weaver's place in the canon of rhetoric. For good or ill, Weaver displays a consuming devotion to eloquence, and his presence in the history of rhetoric invites identification with other rhetorical theorists of the mid-twentieth century—writers such as Burke, Richard McKeon, Chaïm Perelman, and Wayne Booth—as much as it constitutes a radical departure from these same rhetorical theorists.

Weaver departs from his contemporaries in a number of ways. Perhaps most prominent is his devotion to social and political conservatism and his apparent preference for Platonism in contrast to the more Aristotelian and Ciceronian leanings of the others. His rhetoric is one of division and conflict, assigning ethical values to the very tools of rhetoric. Weaver privileges rhetorical tools associated with conservatives and tradition, while nearly exiling all others from the realm of rhetoric. His radical departure from his contemporaries may be traced to his perspective on the modern era. In keeping with his Southern Fugitive roots, he is anachronistic, privileging his notion of tradition over modern progress, sacred motives over distinctly secular ones, conservative cultural and political ideology over their liberal political counterparts. However, it is not simply that Weaver prefers tradition. Rather, for him, the preference for tradition is ethically correct while entertaining the modern is ethically suspect. At its worst, Weaver's rhetoric becomes an exemplar of the kind of either/or thinking that freshman writing students are admonished to avoid.

For these and other reasons, Weaver's status in the history of twentieth-century rhetoric can therefore seem rather limited. For Weaver to claim a greater place, then, his work would need to contribute in some fashion to the both/and tendencies of other modern rhetorical theorists. I suggest that it does, but in places where such thinking is not frequently looked for. Broadly, Weaver contributes to these tendencies to the extent that his rhetoric adumbrates a cultural position for rhetoric consistent with the cultural position New Critics adumbrate for literature. Writers such as Cleanth Brooks (who directed his dissertation), Allen Tate, Donald Davidson, and John Crowe Ransom were Weaver's mentors and friends (Kimball 4–5). Like theirs, his work is culturally conservative, privileging the sacred over the secular, preferring a lost or at least fading tradition to the modern with a concomitant preference for Culture as opposed to sociological notions of culture. Yet, he shares with his contemporaries in rhetoric a desire to revitalize the study of rhetoric and reassert the importance of rhetoric in politics and ethics. In essence, he aims to construct a rhetoric that, like its New Criticism counterpart in literature, is idealistic and, like the rhetorics of his contemporaries, is pragmatic in the sociopolitical world. Moreover, even though his privileged key terms—terms such as *conservative, sacred, tradition*, and *Culture*—possess the overtones of a stodgy atavism, his definitions of those terms open possibilities for interpretations beyond the politically and socially conservative ideology with which they are associated, thus creating the possibility for a both/and rhetoric. An examination of Weaver's rhetoric and its current reputation reveals ambiguities, or potential moments of both/and, in which the political Left (but not the liberal) may stake an equal claim to the perspectives and methods Weaver constructs on behalf of the Right.

Weaver's current place in the study of rhetoric is overshadowed by prominent figures such as Burke, Booth, and Perelman. And yet, Weaver's reading of Plato's *Phaedrus* established a standard interpretation that many, if not most, other rhetorical interpretations take as their point of departure. Moreover, since the publication for their essay "Looking for an Argument," Weaver and his colleagues (Bilsky et al.) have been credited with suggesting the value of using classical topoi in freshman composition courses (see Johannesen, "Some" 276). Johannesen and several other commentators on Weaver focus on Weaver's choices of classical topoi, namely arguments from definition, analogy, cause and effect, and circumstance, topoi that abound in composition textbooks today, although sometimes in disguise. The choices of topoi in themselves, however, are not as remarkable as are the qualities Weaver attributes to them. In *Language Is Sermonic,* Weaver fashions them into an ethics of argument, placing them in the same order as given above, arguing that the order reflects their ethical value. That is, arguments from definition possess the highest ethical value while arguments from circumstance possess the lowest ethical value, indeed, are ethically suspect. Furthermore, Weaver assigns political identities to these forms of argument, the argument from definition being the higher of the two conservative forms of argument (the other one being the argument from analogy) and the argument from circumstance being the lower of the two liberal forms of argument and the lowest in the hierarchy (*Ethics*).

A more surprising aspect is not the hierarchy itself, but Weaver's illustrations of its highest and the lowest forms. Abraham Lincoln's work is for Weaver the exemplar of conservative argument from definition (which is surprising for reasons that will be discussed shortly), and the work of the English political conservative Edmund Burke is his exemplar of the liberal argument from circumstance. What becomes clear from Weaver's explications of liberal and conservative arguments is that he defines the terms *liberal* and *conservative* in a manner that does not place them in ideological polar opposition to one another. The liberal, for Weaver, is in the middle, a compromiser, which apparently is more abhorrent to him than an ardent leftist. Nonetheless, Roger Gilles asserts that

> while many current rhetoricians would likely reject Weaver's negative appraisal of "liberal" rhetoric and his privileging of a conservative, foundational one, most would agree with Weaver that liberal rhetoric—however broadly we wish to define the word—is and should be both practical and circumstantial. (128)

Gilles analyzed some of the published arguments for and against the first Gulf War using Weaver's ethical and political hierarchy of argumentative forms. What he found is that those on the Far Left, as well as those on the Far Right, tended to employ what Weaver identified as conservative forms of argumentation while more mainstream writers from both the Left and the Right tended to employ arguments from cause and effect and arguments from circumstance, that is, *liberal* arguments. Gilles' analysis reveals, then, that Weaver's ethics values arguments attempt to ground an ideology, be it on the Left or the Right, in either an absolute and eternal truth or a stipulated "truth" of the moment. When combined with the emphasis they have received as basic modes of argument for nearly the past sixty years in freshman composition courses, the ethical and political values attributed to the four topoi indicate that much more is at stake in even the most conventional appearing of courses.

The ethical and political hierarchy of topoi is a practical realization of what Johannesen identifies as three major ideas on rhetoric that Weaver offers "for students as producers and consumers, as designers and evaluators of communication" ("Some" 273). The first of these is that "all human language reflects some element of persuasion. Facts do not speak for themselves: human beings speak" (273). The second is that values play a central role in the rhetorical process. "A value, as a conception of The Good, functions as a goal motivating an individual's general behavior and as a standard the person uses to assess the acceptability of specific means and ends" (274). The third, according to Johannesen, is the stress Weaver places on "the nature and uses of argumentation. For Weaver, skill in argument is an essential tool in contemporary society" (275).

While the three are closely related, each performs a particular function in Weaver's ethics of rhetoric, and each of these can be seen at work in Weaver's interpretation of Socrates' behavior in the *Apology of Socrates.* The first major idea establishes Weaver's conception of the relation between rhetoric and dialectic. While Weaver does place dialectic above rhetoric in terms of its relation to abstract truth, he also notes dialectic's inability to move audiences. Socrates' downfall, Weaver argues in his essay "The Cultural Role of Rhetoric," is his inability or perhaps refusal to argue rhetorically rather than dialectically even when his life is at stake. That is, Socrates clings to his ability to convince through pure reason—through dialectic—when he should realize that in this case he is speaking as a human to other humans, and the facts of his case simply are neither self-evident nor dialectically revealed because even though Meletus (Socrates' chief accuser) responds to Socrates' questions, Meletus does not engage with Socrates in the dialectical search for truth. Meletus and the others desire to be persuaded; Socrates either does not realize this, or he refuses to accept it. Weaver's first major idea, then, overlaps with his third idea, for Socrates' inability or refusal to engage his audience rhetorically suggests that he lacks an essential social skill. What is more, the absence of rhetoric in Socrates' response to his judges illustrates the offense Socrates is accused of in the first place, because, Weaver claims, "*dialectic alone in the social realm is subversive*" (*Language* 163). It is subversive because the appeal to emotion, an appeal the pure dialectician does not use, is "an ultimate source of [social] cohesion" (181). In effect, Weaver's reading of the *Apology* suggests that Socrates' behavior is ethically suspect. Though Weaver remains sympathetic to Socrates, calling him the most virtuous man in Athens and reinforcing his own fealty to Platonist ethics, he nonetheless maintains that Socrates errs when he privileges dialectic over rhetoric in the realm of human society. "Dialectic," he says, "though being rational and intellectual, simply does not heed the imperatives of living, which help give direction to the thought of the man of wisdom. The individual who makes his approach to life through dialectic alone does violence to life through his abstractive process" (174).

To this point, I think there is much with which Weaver's contemporaries may agree. Burke especially would agree that all language use contains some element, some degree, of persuasion. Burke and others also would agree that values are central to the rhetorical process, and it virtually goes without saying that argument is an essential skill in contemporary society. Furthermore, Walter Beale argues that Burke and Weaver share two more "important points of intellectual convergence. First, they were both seeking in the structure of language and the tradition of rhetoric a position beyond modern secular ideology" (628), although Burke was both modernist and secularist while Weaver was neither modernist nor secularist. Second, "is their awareness of the constitutive link between discourse and culture. This involved a view of culture that is . . . 'semiotic.' . . . In this view, culture is, even in its most precise definition, a text, a network of mediating symbols" (628).

Despite these points of overlap, however, the ideological distance between Weaver and his contemporaries is large. The question then becomes, does that ideological distance somehow translate into a rhetorical distance as well? That is, if rhetoric and ideology are, as both he and many of his contemporaries would assert, intimately linked together, and given that the ideological distance between him and his contemporaries is quite significant (not to say vast), then isn't the distance between his notion of rhetoric and their respective notions equally significant? To address this question, I want to turn now to some of his conservative commentators. Their sympathetic perspectives on some of Weaver's more controversial points of view can offer some insights into the relations between rhetoric and ideology, and between Weaver's rhetoric and the rhetorics of his contemporaries.

As recently as September 2006, Roger Kimball wrote admiringly of Richard Weaver as part of a "great pantheon of half-forgotten conservative sages . . ." (4). Weaver, Kimball explains to his readers, was by trade a professor of rhetoric, and he cites an anonymous friend of Weaver's who claimed he was "'a rhetor doing the work of a philosopher'" (4). Kimball corrects this image of Weaver, claiming that "it might be more accurate to say that he was a critic doing the work of a prophet" (4). Kimball's article maintains religious, and reverent, overtones as it recounts Weaver's defense of "the virtues of the Old South," not the least of which was "'its resistance to the spiritual disintegration of the modern world'" (qtd. in Kimball 5), a resistance, ultimately, to science and technology. While Kimball backs away from Weaver's out-of-hand dismissal of the modern—asserting that "part—a large part—of our world today is the world shaped by science," and thus simply cannot be dismissed—he nonetheless admires the way Weaver clings to the "virtues" of the antebellum South. These virtues, it would seem, are in direct conflict with the ideals expressed in Weaver's exemplar of conservative argument, Abraham Lincoln.

More than twenty-five years ago, in the article "Richard Weaver: Rhetoric and the Tyrannizing Image," John Bliese wrote about the connection between Weaver's rhetorical theory and his politics. Bliese acknowledges two basic problems in Weaver's analysis of the relationship between rhetoric and culture. First, is his equivocation on the use of the word *culture*. In some cases it refers to what Bliese terms the "sociological" meaning of culture while in others it refers to what he terms the "honorific" meaning of it. This equivocation makes him wonder "which of the two cultures was open to question" (213). The second problem is that "Weaver treats cultures as far more exclusive than they probably are. He often seems to believe cultures are isolated monads that can only be contaminated by contact with other monads. . . . Overall, however," Bliese concludes, "we must admire Weaver's efforts to revitalize rhetoric as a crucial step in stemming our spiritual decline" (213). For Bliese, Weaver's most important effort in stemming that spiritual decline is Weaver's repeated emphasis on the tyrannizing image, which "unites a community while excluding other communities" (211). Bliese sums up the significance to rhetoric of the tyrannizing image by stating that for Weaver, "rhetoric must function both as a unifying force within a culture and as a divisive force against outside influences" (211). In a later and more academic essay, Bliese continues his defense of Weaver by stressing the relations between rhetor and audience. Bliese states that Weaver suggests poetics "can be used by the rhetor in ways that may take persuasion beyond the limits of rhetorical theory, at least where the problem is one of renewing a decayed value structure in an audience" ("Richard M. Weaver" 324). More importantly, however, Bliese emphasizes Weaver's

> recommendation that conservatives should direct their appeals to each other. . . . A group with serious and significant ideas that are currently out of favor with the public can still build up its own enthusiasm and maintain its cohesion and commitment. It will then be ready to take the offensive if events open up opportunities for it. (324)

While it is debatable as to whether or not conservative ideas are currently out of favor, the strategy Bliese attributes to Weaver is certainly one frequently employed by conservatives today.

Johannesen further reinforces Bliese's conclusion that Weaver is, in essence, preaching to the converted by documenting Weaver's careful choices about where his work was published, preferring conservative publications both inside and outside the academy. While Johannesen does not share Weaver's political leanings or Platonic idealism ("Reconsideration"), he nonetheless expresses a certain admiration for Weaver's ability to interweave and balance the secular and the religious through a synthesis of the Platonic and the Christian in one idealist tradition.

The differences between Weaver and his contemporaries are generally apparent. To take just one comparison, between him and Kenneth Burke, both of them interweave the sacred and the secular. The difference between the two is that Weaver attempts to raise the secular to a level of reverence while Burke secularizes the sacred. Both understand that rhetoric has both unifying and dividing impulses. However, Burke's identification is an effort to emphasize the unifying impulse in rhetoric while Weaver's tyrannizing image places an equal stress on division, separating one culture from another. Both employ the term *culture* equivocally, Weaver using the honorific definition positively, Burke preferring the sociological. Both express a certain skepticism toward science and scientism, but Burke is ready to concede that scientific advancement makes possible our ability to more readily express our objections to science, while Weaver sees it almost exclusively as an assault on traditional values. And both, it can be said, preach to the converted. Burke speaks almost exclusively to liberals more or less to the same extent as Weaver speaks to conservatives.

Sharon Crowley suggests, first, that Weaver's rhetorical theory has been canonized, a perspective I would dispute because, while Weaver typically is acknowledged, his place in the history of rhetoric with respect to the canon is less than secure, to a great extent because of his ideology. However, she poses an important question regarding whether or not a writer of Weaver's (or Burke's, for that matter) status should be presented in such a way as to conceal his or her politics or ideology. The answer to that question clearly is no, and for two reasons. First, as Crowley points out, no rhetorical theory is "generated within an ideological vacuum" (67), so no rhetorical theory should be taught as though it were. But second, ideologies are not isolated: they exist in a realm among other ideologies, and they respond to those other ideologies. Weaver and his contemporaries may be close to the extent that they wish to revive rhetoric, but they are quite far apart with respect to the specific ends to which they would employ rhetoric.

Nonetheless, Weaver's rhetoric is significant historically because it serves as a conservative counterstatement to the more liberal and leftist theories of rhetoric of the mid-twentieth century. As a counterstatement, it demands of its opponents a clearer and more precise articulation of their ideologies than those opponents may otherwise provide. This criticism applies to Weaver's rhetoric as well, for at precisely those points where it seems to establish an ideologically and strategically conservative *right* rhetoric, it possesses an equal potential for being an ideologically and strategically conservative *left* rhetoric. By taking both possibilities into account, it demonstrates that even when a rhetoric asserts an either/or, it implies a both/and. Ultimately, we may choose to continue to preach to the converted. For many in the academy, this would mean ignoring Weaver and those who may be drawn to his work. Or, we may choose to learn from the opposition, an opportunity that may eventually lead to the building of bridges. For without the ambiguities between the conservative (Left and Right) and the liberal, we have a substantially diminished invitation to rhetoric.

Works Cited

Beale, Walter H. "Richard M. Weaver: Philosophic Rhetoric, Cultural Criticism, and the First Rhetorical Awakening." *College English* 52.6 (1990): 626–40.

Bilsky, Manuel, McCrea Hazlett, Robert E. Streeter, and Richard M. Weaver. "Looking for an Argument." *College English* 14.4 (1953): 210–16.

Bliese, John. "Richard M. Weaver and the Rhetoric of a Lost Cause." *Rhetoric Society Quarterly* 19.4 (1989): 313–25.

———. "Richard Weaver: Rhetoric and the Tyrannizing Image." *Modern Age* (Spring/Summer 1984): 208–14.

Burke, Kenneth. *A Rhetoric of Motives.* Berkeley: U of California P, 1969.

Cicero, Marcus Tullius. *De Inventione.* Trans. H. M. Hubbell. Ed. Jeffrey Henderson. Cambridge: Harvard UP, 2000.

Crowley, Sharon. "When Ideology Motivates Theory: The Case of the Man from Weaverville." *Rhetoric Review* 20.1–2 (2001): 66–93.

Gilles, Roger. "Richard Weaver Revisited: Rhetoric Left, Right, and Middle." *Rhetoric Review* 15.1 (1996): 128–41.

Johannesen, Richard L. "A Reconsideration of Richard M. Weaver's Platonic Idealism." *Rhetoric Society Quarterly* 21.2 (Spring 1991): 1–10.

———. "Some Pedagogical Implications of Richard M. Weaver's Views on Rhetoric." *College Composition and Communication* 29.3 (1978): 272–79.

Kimball, Roger. "The Consequences of Richard Weaver." *New Criterion* Sept. 2006: 4–9.

Weaver, Richard M. "The Cultural Role of Rhetoric." Weaver, *Language Is Sermonic.*

———. *The Ethics of Rhetoric.* Davis, CA: Hermagoras P, 1985.

———. *Language Is Sermonic: Richard M. Weaver and the Nature of Rhetoric.* Ed. Richard L. Johannesen, Rennard Strickland, and Ralph T. Eubanks. Baton Rouge: Louisiana State UP, 1970.

30

"To See Our Two Ways at Once"

The Correspondence of Kenneth Burke and Paul de Man

Ethan Sproat

With his typical whimsy, Kenneth Burke once wrote to Paul de Man, "We are so close to each other in our ways of thinking, I keep trying to see our two ways at once. And the effort is fantastically 'dizzifying'" (Letter, 1 Mar. 1982). This was in response to reading a copy of de Man's *Allegories of Reading*, which de Man had sent Burke along with a brief note (both de Man's note and Burke's multidraft response are viewable in the Kenneth Burke Papers housed at the Pennsylvania State University's Pattee Library). Their brief correspondence provides a clear example from Burke's own life of what Burke had elsewhere called "the characteristic invitation to rhetoric."

For Burke, the invitation to rhetoric is not necessarily when two parties completely disagree with each other. Nor can the invitation to rhetoric occur when two parties completely identify with each other. As Burke explains,

> In pure identification there would be no strife. Likewise, there would be no strife in absolute separateness. . . . But put identification and division ambiguously together, so that you cannot know for certain just where one ends and the other begins, and you have the characteristic invitation to rhetoric. (*Rhetoric* 25)

As Burke's response to de Man shows, Burke's "dizzifying" perspective of de Man's work results precisely from Burke's inability to see the clear boundary between his own theories of language and de Man's.

Both Burke's and de Man's theories deal with broad issues of human epistemology in general, and both thinkers rely heavily on principles of rhetoric and literature to help them articulate and describe what it means for humans to think and communicate. Their main epistemological intersection (their particular nexus of identification and division, if you will) extends from their individually nuanced readings of Friedrich Nietzsche. The crisis moment for any epistemology of the last century is arguably Nietzsche's 1873 essay "On Truth and Lying in an Extra-Moral Sense." The problem is this: if all language and thought is irreducibly and subjectively symbolic (as Nietzsche argues) then a universal perspective of epistemological reference is impossible. Epistemological inquiry, thus, disintegrates into a discussion of subjectively experienced thought and language, but could never be about human thought in general. Both Burke and de Man agree with Nietzsche's first premise that all language and thought is symbolic. And certainly, de Man agrees with Nietzsche's dire assessment of epistemology. But Burke tries to salvage epistemological study by arguing for the possibility of a perspective that could involve all other perspectives.

To describe such a perspective, Burke uses the term *dialectic* (which he frequently also identifies with the rhetorical figure of *irony*). Burke defines *dialectic* as "the interaction of terms upon one another, to produce a *development* which uses all the terms" (*Grammar* 512). As such, dialectic is a "perspective of perspectives" in which "none of the participating 'sub-perspectives' can be treated as either precisely right or precisely wrong. They are all voices, or personalities, or positions, integrally affecting one another" (512). In other words, dialectic approaches a complete perspective (and thus salvages epistemological study) because it is a development of all available perspectives.

This sort of dialectic certainly characterizes much of Burke's and de Man's theories of language individually, as well as their theories in regard to each other. But their brief correspondence reveals specific dialectical concerns that cover a staggering range of topics. Most important among these is their shared epistemological interest in Nietzsche and rhetorical tropes like metaphor and metonymy. Their intersection with Nietzsche covers concepts that undergird the very epistemological structure of Burke's dramatism. But their correspondence also alludes to other, more mundane topics including their professional respect for each other and their considerations of each other in regard to thinkers like Bakhtin, Schiller, Kant, and Proust.

Burke and de Man were very aware of each other professionally. Their professional similarities and differences help explain some of the division and identification among their ideas. Over the two weeks after Burke received de Man's note and book, Burke wrote three different drafts of a response. These drafts reveal an almost anxious professional respect for de Man. Some years prior to this in the 1970s, Burke and Malcolm Cowley wrote to one another discussing the merits of de Man's "Rhetoric of Temporality" (which can be found in de Man's collection *Blindness and Insight*). Burke admitted to Cowley that "I ought to read de Man. . . . Obviously, you ought to read him, too" (Jay 406). Further, in one of the drafts to de Man, Burke refers to his familiarity with de Man's work while opining briefly on the nature of rhetoric's disciplinarity vis-à-vis Burke's larger motives project. Using de Man as a representative example of rhetorical studies in English, Burke suggests, "The theory of motives in general can't be reduced (metonymized!) to the virtuosities of your particular field. Your academic job is to say how it all lines up in terms of your specialty" (Letter, 1 Mar. 1982). Pursuing Burke along these lines would probably lead to a project that studies tensions between rhetorical studies in different academic fields in a parallel manner to Steven Mailloux's work (beginning with his 2000 article "Disciplinary Identities: On the Rhetorical Paths between English and Communication Studies").

For his part, Paul de Man's research involved a number of (largely unstated) references to Kenneth Burke. Certainly, central observations in Paul de Man's *Blindness and Insight* play off of Burke's aphorism, "A way of seeing is also a way of not seeing" (*Permanence* 49). He also referred to Burke (along with Northup Frye) as being nearly alone among pre-1960s thinkers who "would have considered themselves theoreticians in the post-1960s sense of the term" (*Resistance* 6). But de Man never wrote an essay expressly devoted to Burke, though he apparently wanted to. Wlad Godzich mentions de Man's unwritten Burke project in his foreword to de Man's *The Resistance to Theory* (Foreword xi). And, de Man himself leaves a tantalizing hint about working on such an essay in the note he wrote to Burke. In its entirety, de Man's note reads: "Dear Kenneth Burke, I have long admired your work and, over the next few months, I'll be trying to write something about it. If it works out, I'll send you a copy. With best wishes for a good year Sincerely yours, Paul de Man" (Letter, 30 Jan. 1982). Sadly, de Man's health deteriorated shortly after this brief exchange and he passed away the following year on December 21, 1983. He never wrote the essay on Burke.

Wlad Godzich, de Man's friend and colleague, spoke with de Man several times about the prospective Burke essay while Godzich was compiling sets of de Man's essays that would eventually comprise the books *Aesthetic Ideology* and *The Resistance to Theory*. Particularly, the collection *Aesthetic Ideology*

> was to be organized around the red thread of denunciation of Schiller's hijacking of Kant, and his promotion of an aesthetic state. KB [i.e., Burke] was to serve as an ambiguous figure embracing state pedagogy but not the Schillerian model. An Auseinandersersetzung [or clashing analysis] between KB and Bakhtin was to be staged, and democracy was its stake, with Bakhtin's dialogism driven back to its Nietzschean roots. . . . It was very clear PdM [i.e., Paul de Man] had the essay formulated in his mind and it was just a matter of sheer physical strength and time to get it done. He ran out of both. (Godzich, "Re: Question")

Structuring de Man's essay in de Man's own words beyond Godzich's recollection will likely be an impossible task. As Godzich explains, de Man did not keep notes for his essays. Instead, de Man "worked them out in his mind and tended to write them out, by hand, in a single session . . . with very few corrections, and a minimum of crossings out" (Godzich, "Re: Question"). Also, Godzich explains in reference to the Paul de Man papers at UC Irvine:

> There are no notes and no files in the sense that most other scholars have them. I do know for a fact that de Man periodically tossed into his fireplace various jottings. This usually was followed by his giving away the books that had elicited them. ("Re: Question")

Though he was unable to write the essay on Burke, de Man did indicate the kind of role that Burke would play in the epic clash with Bakhtin. According to Godzich, de Man personally admired Burke,

> specifically for his having been, in PdM's view, the last American intellectual carrying on a significant project outside of academia. PdM thought this was highly significant about all three: American culture, universities, and KB, and he thought that KB was somewhat of a tragic figure in this respect. ("Re: Question")

In addition to Bakhtin, Schiller, and Kant, there are other critical intersections that Burke and de Man's brief correspondence points us to. Certainly, a triangulation of Burke, de Man, and Proust could be in order. In one of his unsent drafts, Burke summarizes de Man's reading of Proust (from *Allegories of Reading*) involving themes of the "hand," "guilt," and "vocation" of an author. Then Burke posits this outrageously off-color interpretation:

> As judged from the standpoint of my definition of us as bodies that learn language . . . I have no trouble associating the "guilt" with the theme of *vocation* that infuses the whole [Proust] project. I don't know how things are now. But in days like Proust's or mine, the writer's calling as a profession took form at a stage of the body when the HAND performed a *handy function* indeed for helping the performer through a vexingly "problematical" stage in the purely *physiological* development of sexuality, however this motive finally gets lined up. (Letter, 16 Feb. 1982, italics in original)

Certainly, it could be intriguing and fun to rebuild de Man's perspective about Burke, Bakhtin, Schiller, and Kant—just as it would be to rebuild Burke's bawdy perspective about de Man, Proust, and the sexual development of writers. However, as stimulating as such projects would undoubtedly be, formulating them would be extrapolation at best, but most probably only speculation.

The one reliable critical thread that connects all of Burke's letter drafts to de Man's theories, and is substantiated by both Burke and de Man in different published works, is their shared interest in Friedrich Nietzsche. Most notably in his correspondence to de Man, Burke thematically identifies his essay "Four Master Tropes" (*Grammar*) and his interpretation of Nietzsche to de Man's *Allegories of Reading*.

In his first unsent draft to de Man, Burke reflects on his own book *Permanence and Change,* in which "I called the middle section 'Perspective by

Incongruity' in keeping with some things I had written on Nietzsche. But lo! I realized now that, once I had let him in [to my writing], it was impossible to get him out" (Letter, 16 Feb. 1982). But this was not all. Remember the "dizzifying" effect that de Man's *Allegories of Reading* had on Burke. Burke clarifies later in that same draft to de Man,

> here's the kind of discomfiture I'm up against: Your way of presenting the grammar-rhetoric relationship [in *Allegories of Reading*] centers on the difference between metaphor and metonymy. But in my article on the "Four Master Tropes," I cut things a different way by proposing to substitute "perspective" for metaphor and "reduction" for metonymy, when the terms are treated from the standpoint of the principles they embody, as distinct from their blunt literal meaning. . . . Thus whereas everything you say delights me (Gawd! if I could but persuade you to be on my side!), we just haven't made quite the same cuts and the difference shows up for me dizzifying all along the line. (Letter, 1 Mar. 1982)

To understand what is so "dizzifying" about Burke's collision with de Man, it is necessary to understand both *Allegories of Reading* and "Four Master Tropes." But to understand both of them, it is necessary to understand Nietzsche.

Specifically, de Man explicitly connects *Allegories of Reading* to Nietzsche's early essay "On Truth and Lying in an Extra-Moral Sense." As Debra Hawhee illustrates in her article "Burke and Nietzsche," Burke also shows strong predilections to the themes and ideas Nietzsche articulates in that very essay. But while Hawhee's study focuses on Burke's perspective by incongruity, Nietzsche permeates Burke's "Four Master Tropes" as well. Triangulating Burke, de Man, and Nietzsche reveals how it is that Burke and de Man came to their different observations of epistemology while pursuing strikingly similar epistemological trajectories. In the end, de Man believes that the metaphoric nature of language is aberrant, while Burke believes it is normative and the basis of all perspective.

This all begins with Nietzsche's most basic accounting of how humans think:

> The portrayal of nerve stimuli in sounds. . . . What arbitrary deliminations, what one-sided preferences for one trait or another of a thing! . . . He designates only the relations of things to men, and to express these relations he uses the boldest metaphors. First, he translates a nerve stimulus into an image! That is the first metaphor. (248)

In "The Four Master Tropes," Burke specifies that this first kind of metaphor is more accurately a synecdoche. "Sensory representation," he explains, "is, of course, synecdochic in that the senses abstract certain qualities from some bundle of electro-chemical activities we call, say, a tree, and these qualities (such as size, shape, color, texture, weight, etc.) can be said 'truly to represent' a tree" (*Grammar* 508). Burke uses "synecdoche"

> in the usual range of dictionary sense, with such meanings as: part for the whole, whole for the part, container for the contained, sign for the thing signified, material for the thing made, . . . cause for effect, effect for cause, genus for species, species for genus, etc. All such conversions imply an integral relationship, a relationship of convertibility, between the two terms. (*Grammar* 507–08)

Because synecdoche functions in this manner, Burke often interchanges "synecdoche" with "representation"—that is, a perspective is representative if the perspective functions in a synecdochic manner. Nietzsche is correct that the transformation of neuronal stimuli into images or sounds is an irreducibly symbolic overlay. However, the image or the sound as a symbol of neuronal activity is representative in its symbol-quality in that the stimulus is not equitable to the object inducing the stimulus; rather, a nerve stimulus that is transformed into an image or a sound is, at best, a representation of a certain quality or qualities of an object.

Nietzsche continues: after the first metaphor, "then, the image must be reshaped into a sound! The second metaphor" (248). For example, when humans experience the stimulus of their hearts beating, the first metaphor would be observing that stimulus as a "sensation." A second metaphor happens when humans observe that sensation as "heart" (i.e., overlay of the symbol H-E-A-R-T over the sensation). "Each time there is a complete overleaping of spheres—from one sphere to the center of a totally different, new one," Nietzsche observes. He continues, "When we speak of trees, colors, snow, and flowers, we believe we know something about the things themselves, although what we have are just metaphors of things, which do not correspond at all to the original entities" (248–49). This is the problem facing any subsequent epistemological study. Humans cannot refer to anything beyond mere metaphors because those metaphors are the very tools of reference. To refer to anything at all is to only refer to metaphors of things.

However, Burke explains and extends this to a further metaphorical level, namely metonymy. Burke uses metonymy in a usual sense, that is, "the *reduction* of some higher or more complex realm of being to the terms of a lower or less complex realm of being" (*Grammar* 506, italics in original). For Burke, language is a metonymic development in that it

> develops by metaphorical extension, in borrowing words from the realm of the corporeal, visible, tangible and applying them by analogy to the realm of the incorporeal, invisible, intangible; then in the course of time, the original corporeal reference is forgotten, and only the incorporeal, metaphorical extension survives. (*Grammar* 506)

For instance, after a period of separation from a parent, a child may experience a discomfort in the chest in proximity to the organ we call the heart. The child's parent tells the child later that the child felt "sadness." The child grows up to be a poet and writes metonymically about sadness being a "pain in the heart." But notice the poet's metonym here is actually closer in relation to the original stimulus and is therefore less metaphoric than the original metaphor (which was calling the pain in the chest "sadness").

So far so good, but Paul de Man possibly best explains the linguistic urgency of Nietzsche's claims about metaphor and language. After quoting Nietzsche's famous summation of truth (as "illusions about which it has been forgotten they are illusions"), de Man suggests,

> What is being forgotten in this false literalism is precisely the rhetorical, symbolic quality of all language. The degradation of metaphor into literal meaning is not condemned because it is the forgetting of a truth but much rather because it forgets the un-truth, the lie that the metaphor was in the first place. It is a naïve belief in the proper meaning of the metaphor without awareness of the problematic nature of its factual, referential foundation. (*Allegories* 111)

Specifically, this has dangerous epistemological implications for conceptions of the self. As de Man explains, Nietzsche's essay specifically shows

> that the idea of individuation, of the human subject as a privileged viewpoint, is a mere metaphor by means of which man protects himself from his insignificance by forcing his own interpretation of the world upon the entire universe, substituting a human-centered set of meanings that is reassuring to his vanity for a set of meanings that reduces him to being a mere transitory accident in the cosmic order. (*Allegories* 111)

For de Man, the "metaphorical substitution" of every human concept is "aberrant" in that it sublimates "the real" without any observable medium. The only alternative to bleak soul-crushing nothingness, de Man proposes, is to embrace the centrality of language instead of the self in a more accurate conception of cognition. But this is a shallow recovery, he suggests, for while asserting the self as a linguistic reality, it also asserts the self's "insignificance, its emptiness as a mere figure of speech. It can persist as self if it is displaced into the text that denies it. The self which was at first the center of the language as its empirical referent now becomes the language of the center as fiction, as metaphor of the self" (*Allegories* 112). Paul de Man's analysis reaches its own crisis upon the realization of the self as a linguistically structured entity in the midst of a nonlinguistic universe.

Paul de Man's crisis of the self is at the heart of Nietzsche's critique: "How pitiful, how shadowy and fleeting, how purposeless and arbitrary the human intellect appears within nature," Nietzsche writes. "There were eternities when it did not exist; and someday when it is no longer there, not much will have changed. For that intellect has no further mission leading beyond human life. It is utterly human, and only its owner and producer takes it with such pathos as if the whole world hinged upon it" (246). Kenneth Burke, however, follows this same line of thinking with a slightly more positive turn:

> Presumably the realm of nonsymbolic motion was all that prevailed on this earth before our kind of symbol-using organism evolved, and will go sloshing about after we have gone. In the meantime, note that, for better or worse, by evolving our kind of organism, the wordless Universe of nonsymbolic motion is able to comment on itself. ("Questions" 334)

Burke elsewhere suggests that this moment of evolution is "when our primordial ancestors added to their sensations *words* for sensations . . . that's when STORY was born, since words *tell about* sensations. . . . There was no story before we came, and when we're gone the universe will go on sans story" ("Dramatism" 90–91, italics in original).

In this way, Burke both concedes and rejects Nietzsche's and de Man's critique that nothing in the external world ultimately "hinges" on human intellect and symbol use. Burke's concession and rejection rely on different nuances of *world*. In the sense of *world-as-motion* (as in "the world revolves around the sun"), *world* is the nonsymbolic environment in which humans as symbol-using animals find themselves in. In this sense, I doubt Burke disagrees with Nietzsche at all: when humans are extinct, the external world will keep existing in much the same way it did before humans evolved. However, in the sense of *world-as-action* (as in "the world must decide how to end destructive conflict"), *world* is the collection of human society in general. In this sense, Burke rejects Nietzsche's and de Man's critique, for intellect and symbol use are the very stuff out of which the world-as-action is made. So while nothing in the world-as-motion hinges on human intellect, absolutely everything in the world-as-action does.

From Burke's perspective, by following Nietzsche's reasoning to its implied end (i.e., rounding out his terms), de Man's observations are incomplete. Again, for de Man, the "metaphorical substitution" of every human concept is "aberrant" in that it sublimates "the real" without any observable medium. But notice, if *everything* is aberrant, there is *nothing* aberrant about any one thing: being aberrant in such a condition would be the same thing as being normal. As such, the "metaphoric substitution" of thought and language is not aberrant as much as it is normative.

In one of his letter drafts to de Man, Burke asserts,

> I can rescue but one absolute; namely: "We are bodies genetically endowed with the ability to learn verbal behavior," which is to define us in terms of the medium we are using to define us. Logologically we begin from there. And at every step from then on we must keep methodologically going back and starting from there over and over again. (Letter, 16 Feb. 1982)

Burke phrased this conceit more succinctly in an essay about Kant: "We do not thereby obligate ourselves to say that the grounding is 'nothing but' language. We say merely that it is *at least* language (as distinct from 'the senses')" (*Language* 440). In other words, it is not remarkable to lament that all of human reality is composed of nothing but symbols. However, it *is* remarkable to observe all the many ways that humans use symbols to compose everything about reality. The former perspective is saddened that the universe no longer makes (rational) sense. The latter perspective is awed at how (perspectival) *sense* makes the universe.

Now before we get lost down rhetorical rabbit holes of utterly subjective perspectival relativity, we should remember how it is that Burke salvages epistemology via the most complete form of perspective he calls dialectic—the "perspective of perspectives." Since all thought is already (and unavoidably) metaphorically replicated, the pursuit of universal epistemology should concern itself with replicative, rather than applicative, perspectives. If a particular perspective is applicative, it lays itself over a certain subject and thereby views the subject of inquiry in terms of application (in other words, in terms of itself the viewing perspective). However, a perspective that is replicative is a perspective that lays itself over a certain subject and re-presents the subject of inquiry in terms of replication (in other words, in terms of the subject of inquiry). If a particular perspective has a necessary component that induces replication, such a perspective will be better situated to account for other perspectives. It would be, in a word, dialectic. Thus, if a particular perspective, as a dialectic of metaphor and symbol, has the capacity to re-present any other symbol, then its function will be universal even though it has subjective origins.

A perspective with universal representative capability would have a vocabulary adaptable to all meaning or it would otherwise be what Burke calls a "motivational calculus" (*Grammar* 60). Such a perspective would look at all other perspectives (i.e., at all knowledge) from the inside-to-its-extremes (since it could never be from the inside-out much less from the outside-in, for no thought breaks through the barrier that is its metaphoric self). Epistemology thus reconceived would reposition the question "What is knowledge" away from knowledge's relationship to the external world (i.e., knowledge's ultimate container) and nearer to knowledge's relationship with the rest of knowledge (i.e., what is contained in the container).

For those familiar with Burke, it should be evident where all this is leading: Burke's dramatism is a dialectical perspective that "re-presents" because drama (as a metaphor or perspective for the human condition) has sufficient scope to approach all human motives, meaning, and behavior. This is because any perspective that can possibly be presented in any human interaction can be re-presented within a drama. For Burke, drama and dramatism are, thus, dialectical tools with which we can perceive and epistemologically appreciate all other perspectives.

I should note that by the time Burke corresponded with de Man, Burke had nuanced his articulation of dramatism to include logology as well. Burke even noted in the letter he sent de Man that he had included with the letter a copy of his mimeographed "Logology: Over-All View" (Letter, 4 Mar. 1982; the mimeograph is reprinted in Brock et al. 31–32). As for the distinction, Burke asserts that dramatism and logology are "*two* terms for *one* theory" ("Dramatism" 89, italics in original). In Burke's linguistic philosophy, in which humans are symbol-users, Burke believed that dramatism concerns itself with the philosophy's ontological aspect (humans *are* symbol-users), whereas logology concerns itself with the philosophy's epistemological aspect (humans are symbol-*users*). But the difference between the two is more molten than distinct. Aphoristically speaking, I suspect that Burke could say that peoples' ways of knowing *are* their ways of being. At any rate, even if dramatism is ontological, it contains universal *epistemological* assumptions and implications.

But dramatism as a particular perspective of perspectives is not without its pitfalls. While dramatism is a cogent and very likely universal approach to knowledge (because of its dialecticism), those who use it should beware lest they fail to engender a dialectic relationship not just among the dramatistic terms (i.e., the ratios among the pentad), but with other modes of thinking as well. This happens when dramatism is used in applicative rather than replicative manners. Indeed, this is the pitfall for all "systems" of thinking.

Additionally, just because one perspective (like dramatism) may be dialectical does not mean that other perspectives cannot be dialectical as well. Hence, those who are interested in the principles of dramatism should advise themselves as to how dramatism is but one possible mode of universal thinking that could grow too illusive for its epistemological purposes. Thus, the great hope for dramatism is that it could be a linguistic tool (for discovering universal modes of thinking) that could eventually even re-place itself.

Finally, Paul de Man cautions us about the slippery nature of tropes: "not only are tropes, as their name implies, always on the move—more like quicksilver than like flowers or butterflies which one can at least hope to pin down and insert in a neat taxonomy—but they can disappear altogether, or at least appear to disappear" (*Aesthetic* 18). If dramatism begins with the overlay of one metaphor on another, then dramatism's whole structure resides on shifting ground. However, while de Man may be correct in his explanation of how tropes may appear to disappear, I doubt that the tropes may ever "disappear altogether" as long as humans as animals cognize in a way that situates one perspective on another (i.e., metaphorically).

This whole whirlwind of ideas (from metaphor to dialectic and beyond) helps explain Burke's initial contemplative and energetic response to de Man's writing. In one version of his response to de Man, Burke writes, "I am saying, absolutely literally, that as soon as I started to write this letter I became dizzy, not a little bit but a lot" (Letter, 1 Mar. 1982). In the end, Burke and de Man's correspondence (in light of their other published works) reveals Burke experiencing a confounding moment of epistemological awareness while trying "to see [their] two ways at once"—a "dizzifying" dialectical moment involving ideas that undergird the very possibility and culmination of dialectic itself.

Works Cited

Brock, Bernard L., Kenneth Burke, Parke G. Burgess, and Herbert W. Simons. "Dramatism as Ontology or Epistemology: A Symposium." *Communication Quarterly* 33.1 (1985): 17–33.

Burke, Kenneth. "Dramatism and Logology." *Communication Quarterly* 33 (1985): 89–93.

———. "Four Master Tropes." *A Grammar of Motives.*

———. *A Grammar of Motives*. 1945. New York: Prentice Hall, 1952.

———. *Language as Symbolic Action: Essays on Life, Literature, and Method*. Berkeley: U of California P, 1966.

———. Letter to Paul de Man. 16 Feb. 1982. MS. The Kenneth Burke Papers, 1950–1981, Burke-2, Rare Books and Manuscripts. Special Collections Library, University Libraries, Pennsylvania State University.

———. Letter to Paul de Man. 4 Mar. 1982. MS. The Kenneth Burke Papers, 1950–1981, Burke-2, Rare Books and Manuscripts. Special Collections Library, University Libraries, Pennsylvania State University.

———. Letter to Professor de Man. 1 Mar. 1982. MS. The Kenneth Burke Papers, 1950–1981, Burke-2, Rare Books and Manuscripts. Special Collections Library, University Libraries, Pennsylvania State University.

———. *Permanence and Change: An Anatomy of Purpose*. 3rd ed. Berkeley: U of California P, 1984.

———. "Questions and Answers about the Pentad." *College Composition and Communication* 29 (1978): 330–35.

———. *A Rhetoric of Motives*. 1950. Berkeley: U of California P, 1969.

de Man, Paul. *Aesthetic Ideology: Theory and History of Literature*. Minneapolis: U of Minnesota P, 1996.

———. *Allegories of Reading: Figural Language in Rousseau, Nietzsche, Rilke, and Proust*. New Haven, CT: Yale UP, 1979.

———. *Blindness and Insight: Essays in the Rhetoric of Contemporary Criticism*. 2nd ed. Minneapolis: U of Minnesota P, 1983.

———. Letter to Kenneth Burke. 30 Jan. 1982. MS. The Kenneth Burke Papers, 1950–1981, Burke-2, Rare Books and Manuscripts. Special Collections Library, University Libraries, Pennsylvania State University.

———. *The Resistance to Theory*. 1986. Minneapolis: U of Minnesota P, 2002.

Godzich, Wlad. Foreword: The Tiger on the Paper Mat. *The Resistance to Theory*. By Paul de Man. Minneapolis: U of Minnesota P, 2002. ix–xviii.

———. "Re: Question about de Man." Message to Ethan Sproat. 15 Sept. 2009.

Hawhee, Debra. "Burke and Nietzsche." *Quarterly Journal of Speech* 85 (1999): 129–45.

Jay, Paul, ed. *The Selected Correspondence of Kenneth Burke and Malcolm Cowley, 1915–1981*. Berkeley: U of California P, 1990.

Mailloux, Steven. "Disciplinary Identities: On the Rhetorical Paths between English and Communication Studies." *Rhetoric Society Quarterly* 30.2 (2000): 5–29.

Nietzsche, Friedrich. "On Truth and Lying in an Extra-Moral Sense." 1873. *Friedrich Nietzsche on Rhetoric and Language*. Ed. and Trans. Sander L. Gilman, Carole Blair, and David J. Parent. New York: Oxford UP, 1989. 246–57.

31

Mr. Burke, Meet Helen Keller

Ann George

In one sense, of course, Kenneth Burke needs no introduction to Helen Keller. During Burke's lifetime, she was one of the most famous women in the world; Keller also makes a cameo appearance in Burke's discussion of the negative in *Language as Symbolic Action*.[1] But the Helen Keller I want Burke to meet is not the "miracle girl" of cultural mythology first learning language from Anne Sullivan Macy. The Helen Keller I want Burke to meet is one whom surprisingly few have met—the radical Keller, a feminist, early advocate of birth control, and lifelong socialist who supported left-wing political candidates, marched in socialist parades, and cheered on strikers. A large red flag hung in Keller's study, where she penned articles for *Solidarity, The Toiler, Justice*, and the Socialist Party organ *The Call*. By 1916, Keller left the too-tame Socialist Party to join the Wobblies, declaring that she "d[id]n't give a damn about semi-radicals!" ("Why I Became" 84). This Keller was also a powerful rhetor: she published nearly 200 works (including 14 books), gave countless speeches, raised millions of dollars as a lobbyist for the American Federation for the Blind (AFB), and became one of America's most effective goodwill ambassadors.

Analysis of Keller's WWI-era texts and her 1929 memoir, *Midstream*, reveals a striking symmetry between Keller and Burke. Indeed, reading Keller side by side with Burke underscores the extent to which Keller was not simply doing rhetoric; she was living and writing rhetorical theory—theory that often predates Burke's and rivals it in sophistication. Both Keller and Burke sought effective ways to advocate radical change; both argued for socialism by creating identification and "boring from within." As a radical woman constrained by her saintly public persona, Keller understood the power of cultural pieties to blind people to alternative perspectives; as a politically minded citizen, she defended her ability to make informed judgments as well as the sighted, explaining that she learned about things as they do—not firsthand, but through texts. And reading words spelled in her palm, Keller was literally a body that learned language. That is, although Keller never called herself a theorist, she experienced and wrote profoundly about the relationship between individual minds, language, and the social world. What follows is a brief introduction of Helen Keller to Burke as a fellow rhetorician and early contributor to modern rhetorical theory. It begins with a look at Burke's and Keller's analyses of popular resistance to social change. From there, it examines three of their shared rhetorical strategies (boring from within, translation, perspective by incongruity) and ends with a discussion of their shared epistemological and rhetorical theories.

Cultural Piety and Blindness

Burke's and Keller's rhetorical theorizing was bound up with their cultural criticism and their desire to encourage radical social and political change. It was obvious to both Burke and Keller that early twentieth-century capitalist culture was unhealthy and unjust. But what was obvious to them was clearly not as obvious to many Americans. The first step, then, in effecting change, was to explain why so many were seemingly content with so little. "We cannot be free," Keller argues, "until we know the nature of our bondage and examine the chains that bind us" ("Blind Leaders" 60). In *Permanence and Change* (1935), Burke uses the concepts of *trained incapacity* and *piety* to account for people's resistance to change. He argues that Americans have become so well-trained in established cultural values (the pieties of industrial capitalism) that they are incapable of recognizing these pieties as either a cause of their problems or something that might be changed to solve them. Keller's explanation, for a different genre and audience, is more direct, more strikingly ironic—and earlier: in her 1913 *Outlook* magazine article "Blind Leaders" she insists that it is not she, but rather her readers who are truly—that is, spiritually—blind, who think and act in blind conformity to cultural pieties. "Very few people," Keller writes, "open fresh, fearless eyes upon the world they live in. They do not look at anything straight. They have not learned to use their eyes, except in the most rudimentary ways" (57). Keller argues, for instance, that philanthropy, especially from the wealthiest individuals, falsely assures others that those with money are generous and that those in need are being taken care of—by someone else: "[charity] covers the facts [of economic inequality] so that they cannot be seen" (58); likewise, in repeating clichéd complaints that workers are inefficient or unproductive, people lose sight of the fact that these workers "do all the work that is done" in the world (59). Additionally, taking aim at specialist discourse, Keller expresses dismay at how many people are content to hire "'experts' to do their seeing for them" (58).

Burke's and Keller's Rhetorical Praxis

By the early 1930s, Burke and Keller had begun adjusting their rhetoric, though for very different reasons. The antithetical Marxist rhetoric

Burke was hearing from literary leftists seemed designed to appeal solely to true believers, leaving everyone else unconvinced or, worse, antagonized. In Keller's case, when strained finances led her to become a lobbyist and fund-raiser for the AFB in 1924, she, of necessity, adopted a moderate rhetoric better suited to legislators and wealthy donors. Both, however, remained determined to press a leftist agenda and so often used the same three rhetorical strategies for their resistant audiences: what Burke called boring from within, translation, and perspective by incongruity. The first two are essentially means of achieving identification with audiences. Radical language, Burke argued, was not an effective way to promote radical causes: "Zestful antagonism has been the bane of radicals in America. They court resentment. . . . America is the country of 'boring from within.' . . . If you want to attack the Republican party, become a Republican" ("Boring from Within" 327).[2] As a rhetorical strategy, boring from within advances controversial arguments by identifying them with existing cultural values. The more radical the change, the more broadly based an activist's appeals must be. As Burke famously explained in *A Rhetoric of Motives*, "You persuade a man only insofar as you can talk his language by speech, gesture, tonality, order, image, attitude, idea, *identifying* your ways with his" (55). At its most basic, Burkean translation—what he sometimes refers to as "translating English into English" (Jay 202)—is simply this talking the audience's language, expressing ideas in terms the audience will understand and warm to. More elaborate forms of translation might be thought of as "spin" (substituting *death tax* for *estate tax* or inventing the phrase *axis of evil*) or as revealing spin (that is, analyzing the rhetorical effects of specific vocabulary or terministic screens). At its most extreme, translation amounts to redefinition by shifting a term's application or moral weighting or connotations. *Permanence and Change*, which argues for communism and a poetic rather than technological ideology—a hard sell—is built on such translations. For instance, Burke shifts *piety* from the category of religion to social psychology; he discusses Jesus as a master rhetor, and he translates communism, typically associated with class struggle, into its opposite—cooperation, community, communication, poetry. Similarly, when Keller argues for socialism in *Midstream*, she portrays Lenin not as a godless communist but as a Christian prophet who sows the seeds "of a new life for mankind," presaging "salvation" (335, 336), and when she argues for pacifism, she presents it as part of America's heritage via William Penn's brotherly love and Whitman's embrace of difference. Her essay "Blind Leaders" places her in the category of "seer" and sighted leaders in the category of "blind." But as these examples suggest, the rhetorical intent of translation is often an ironic insight, startling juxtaposition, or defamiliarization—the new way of interpreting experience that Keller calls seeing with "fresh, fearless eyes" and that Burke calls perspective by incongruity.

Burke's and Keller's use of new sight/perspective by incongruity is brilliantly displayed in their satires of mechanization and Fordism: Burke's hilarious 1930 *New Republic* essay "Waste—The Future of Prosperity" and Keller's equally hilarious 1932 *Atlantic Monthly* essay, "Put Your Husband in the Kitchen." Their titles emphasize the incongruity of equating waste with prosperity and of putting your husband in the very place he does not belong—the kitchen. Burke's essay is dedicated to Henry Ford for his discovery of the "Theory of the Economic Value of Waste"; if Americans, Burke quips, "can be educated to the full realization of their function as wasters," they can look forward to increased consumption and, hence, increased production and prosperity, for "*though there is a limit to what a man can use, there is no limit whatever to what he can waste*" (228, 229, emphasis in original). Burke prophesizes planned obsolescence—disposable razors, cars and buildings *not* built to last (the "Car of the Future" delivers "super-performance" for exactly one year, then disintegrates [229]), and tap water outlawed in favor of drinks available only in "some manufactured form" (230); war, once thought to be a universal menace, is shown to be "the basis of culture." The trick is "*simply to make sure that the increase in the number of labor-saving devices does not shorten the hours of labor*. . . . If people are to be kept straining at their jobs," he concludes, "the duty of the public as wasters becomes obvious" (229, emphasis in original).

Keller's "Put Your Husband in the Kitchen" similarly satirizes the warped values and false economy of machine culture. Arguing that "[i]n industry, the amazing increase in the use of labor-saving machinery has brought about overproduction, unemployment, and widespread suffering," Keller recounts a hypothetical experiment in which Mr. Jones, "a modern captain of industry," takes over Mrs. Jones's domestic duties to learn, as housewives have, to use machines "for the heretical purpose of saving labor" (141). On his first day, Mr. Jones boasts that he has "revolutionized the business of cooking" (142), baking ten cakes for a family of four simply because the electric mixer and gas range enable him to. The Jones family crams down three cakes, but Mr. Jones faces a net loss when he must pay for the doctor's house call after an outbreak of indigestion later that evening. Next time, Mrs. Jones demands, bake ten cakes "if you must," but throw nine away. "You can't object to that," she says; "I understand such methods are common in your economic world. 'Maintaining the market'—isn't that what you call it? It won't be the first time food has been destroyed to maintain the market" (143). (Here, Mrs. Jones/Keller proves herself to be an expert "translator.") The experiment continues. Mrs. Jones fears her husband will "invent a dish-soiling machine so that the dishwasher may be kept operating at capacity" (144). Later, finding her husband vacuuming, Mrs. Jones sarcastically observes that they have not "realize[d] the productive potentialities" of their vacuum cleaner, which "cries out for new carpets"; she recommends "go[ing] in for 'plant expansion'"—translation: buying a larger house—rather than let the sweeper sit idly in the closet (144). Keller's point is clear: Mr. Jones and other industrialists "forgot that the sole purpose of any economic system is to facilitate the manufacture and exchange of the necessities and luxuries of life, in order that life may be made easier and finer" (143). Burke called this "the good life" (*Permanence* 224). In short, even though Burke is hailed as the modern rhetorician par excellence, Keller, the "miracle girl" and selfless worker for the blind, matches him rhetorical move for rhetorical move.

Burke's and Keller's Epistemology and Theories of Language

At this point, I would like to suggest a perspective by incongruity of my own by arguing that Keller was not only a sophisticated rhetor, but also wrote some sophisticated rhetorical theory. As both Patricia Bizzell and Jane Donawerth observe, sometimes women's rhetorical theory looks very much like that of canonical men, but, more often, it looks very different, perhaps not even directly addressing persuasion (Bizzell 51; Donawerth xv–xvi). The latter is true for Keller. Unlike Burke, Richards, Perelman and Olbrechts-Tyteca, and other canonical new rhetoricians, Keller's theory was not delivered as theory, per se. Instead her rhetorical insights came piecemeal, mixed in with political speeches, memoirs, and other texts in which she attempted to correct the public's false assumptions about the blind, particularly how much—or how—they can know. Popular conflation of physical and mental disabilities caused Keller's critics to question her ability to have or understand experience beyond her immediate sensory perceptions and, hence, to doubt her ability to think or form her own opinions. She might know her feelings, write about her garden or her dogs, and she was, of course, eloquent on the sufferings of the blind. But if she spoke of poverty or war or injustice, she was merely the dupe of unscrupulous radicals. It was Keller's need to defend her right to have a political voice that prompted her to develop sophisticated understandings about the social nature of language, about epistemology and linguistically mediated experience—understandings that rival, and often predate, those of canonical new rhetoricians.

Keller's audiences were often disconcerted by the fact that she wrote as if she were a sighted, hearing person—something they referred to as "verbalism": she wrote elaborately detailed descriptions of landscapes, for instance, or talked about listening to music and watching movies. Thus, after reading her 1929 memoir, *Midstream*, one reviewer complained that

> one does not learn from the book what the world seems like to one who cannot see or hear. Miss Keller, like all the rest of the world, describes by analogy. "The shoulder of the moon turned pink as she threw a scarlet over her head." But Miss Keller has never seen the moon and never seen a scarf. ("Helen Keller Tells")

Charges such as these pushed Keller to explore the social nature of thought and language. So, for instance, just as Burke asserts in *Permanence and*

Change that "we discern situational patterns by means of the particular vocabulary of the cultural group into which we are born" and that "our minds [are] linguistic products" (35), Keller, defending her right to describe colors and all kinds of experience known to sighted people, argues:

> The blind child—the deaf-blind child—has inherited the mind of seeing and hearing ancestors—a mind measured to five senses. Therefore, he must be influenced, even if it be unknown to himself, by the light, color, and song which have been transmitted through the language he is taught, for the chambers of the mind are ready to receive that language. The brain of the race is so permeated with color that it dyes even the speech of the blind. (*World*)

Critics then and now dispute Keller's account of her experience because, in Judith Shulevitz's words, Keller "puts what she has been told on the same epistemological plane as what she has learned through direct observation" (8). "It's as if," Shulevitz remarks, "she had no sense of where she stopped and the world of impersonal information began." Shulevitz criticizes Keller's autobiography *The Story of My Life* because she fails to "locate the boundaries between what was real to her and what she was forced to imagine." In short, Shulevitz finds Keller's autobiography inauthentic, unreflective, and "strangely disturbing" because Keller did not "write about what [she] kn[e]w." And Shulevitz is not alone among fairly recent scholars who maintain this distinction between Keller's mediated and everyone else's supposedly direct experience. For instance, both Paula Cohen and Lois Einhorn, while acknowledging that all experience is mediated to some extent, nevertheless insist that Keller had a greater "dependence on the language of others to translate and integrate perceptions" (Cohen 9). Cohen's claim that Keller's "ground of experience is words" (11) is echoed in Einhorn's argument that "[h]er reality was essentially a linguistic reality because so many of her experiences came to her through the eyes and ears of other people" (59).

Kenneth Burke, of course, argued that everyone's reality is largely linguistic. "Can we bring ourselves to realize," he asked in the early 1960s,

> just how overwhelmingly much of what we mean by "reality" has been built up for us through nothing but our symbol systems? Take away our books, and what little do we know about history, biography, even something so "down to earth" as the relative position of seas and continents? What is our "reality" for today (beyond the paper-thin line of our own particular lives) but all this clutter of symbols about the past combined with whatever things we know mainly through maps, magazines, newspapers, and the like about the present? (*Language* 5)

Keller, however, began arguing against this "naïve verbal realism" (Burke, *Language* 5) as early as 1913. A friend once reported to Keller, "I have heard men say, 'How can one deaf and blind from infancy know about life, about people, about affairs? It is impossible for her to have a first-hand knowledge of what is going on in the world'" ("Blind Leaders" 55). Keller retorts,

> Of course, I am not always on the spot when things happen, nor are you. I did not witness the dreadful accident at Stamford the other day, nor did you, nor did most people in the United States. But that did not prevent me, anymore than it prevented you, from knowing about it. ("A New Light" 95)

Similarly, she maintains that "I have never been a captain of industry or a strike-breaker or a soldier; neither have most people. But I have studied about them, and I think I understand their relation to society" ("Blind Leaders" 56). In other words, she gains knowledge and creates a reality the same way most people do most of the time—through texts, "us[ing] the eye and the ear of the world which the printed page makes mine. . . . If books are not life," she continues, "I don't know what they are. In the writings of poets, sages, prophets, is recorded all that men have seen, heard, and felt" (56). Keller explains that she has visited factories and slums, smelling the poverty she could not see; she has met, studied, and lobbied for the blind. "If this work . . . is not 'first-hand experience,' I do not know where you or I can get it" (57).

Conclusion

The canon of modern rhetorical theory is dramatically and almost exclusively male. With the exception of Ann Berthoff and Lucie Olbrechts-Tyteca, women were, *apparently*, absent from the scene of the New Rhetoric. But only apparently. Keller never called herself a rhetorical theorist, but we can. Should we canonize the woman who, in her lifetime, was often referred to as "the 'patron saint' of the handicapped" ("Miss Keller Seen")? Probably not. Keller's work does not offer the sustained exploration that Burke's does; her material circumstances, her interests, and her commitment to service made that impossible and, perhaps, undesirable. In particular, Keller did not set out, as Burke clearly did, to teach people how to be rhetorical critics, to provide the terms and tools for them to become conscious and conscientious symbol users. But there are certainly other women we might canonize; Arabella Lyon makes an extremely convincing case that Suzanne Langer is one of them. Might we add Keller to our curricula? Certainly. Her fame, her reputation, and the dramatic personal and political exigencies for her theorizing make Keller a compelling (and provocatively incongruous) means of bringing new rhetoric into the classroom. I would suggest, too, that as scholars and teachers of rhetoric, we have our own trained incapacities to overcome as we continue to redefine not just what counts as rhetoric, but what counts as rhetorical theory. Keller's work can help open our eyes to the fact that, as Lyon argues, there could be no modern rebirth of rhetoric without women.

Notes

[1] Burke studied accounts of Keller's language training to verify his belief that the hortatory negative ("thou shalt not" or "don't") is learned before the propositional negative ("it is not") (*Language* 10).

[2] Burke did not coin the phrase *boring from within*, which was a fairly common one during this period. Wendy Sharer notes, for instance, that the term was used by Emily Newell Blair to encourage women to work through established political parties after suffrage (94).

Works Cited

Bizzell, Patricia. "Opportunities for Feminist Research in the History of Rhetoric." *Rhetoric Review* 11.1 (1992): 50–58.

Burke, Kenneth. "Boring from Within." *New Republic* 4 Feb. 1931: 326–29.

———. *Language as Symbolic Action: Essays on Life, Literature, and Method*. Berkeley: U of California P, 1966.

———. *Permanence and Change: An Anatomy of Purpose*. 1935. 3rd ed. Berkeley: U of California P, 1984.

———. *A Rhetoric of Motives*. 1950. Berkeley: U of California P, 1969.

———. "Waste—The Future of Prosperity." *New Republic* 16 July 1930: 228–31.

Cohen, Paula Marantz. "Helen Keller and the American Myth." *Yale Review* 85.1 (1997): 1–20.

Donawerth, Jane. Introduction. *Rhetorical Theory by Women before 1900: An Anthology*. Lanham, MD: Rowan & Littlefield, 2002. xiii–xlii.

Einhorn, Lois J. *Helen Keller, Public Speaker: Sightless But Seen, Deaf But Heard*. Westport, CT: Greenwood P, 1998.

"Helen Keller Tells New Story of Her Life Since Her Graduation." Rev. of *Midstream*, by Helen Keller. *Charleston Daily Mail* 29 Dec. 1929: 8. Access Newspaper Archive. Web. 12 Aug. 2008.

Jay, Paul, ed. *The Selected Correspondence of Kenneth Burke and Malcolm Cowley, 1915–1981*. Berkeley: U of California P, 1990.

Keller, Helen. "Blind Leaders." *Helen Keller: Selected Writings*. Ed. Kim E. Nielsen. New York: New York UP, 2005. 55–66.

———. *Midstream: My Later Life*. Garden City: Doubleday, Doran & Co., 1929.

———. "A New Light Is Coming." Einhorn 95–96.

———. "Put Your Husband in the Kitchen." *Atlantic Monthly* Aug. 1932: 140–47.

———. "Why I Became an IWW." *Helen Keller: Her Socialist Years*. Ed. Philip S. Foner. New York: International Publishers, 1967. 82–86.

———. *The World I Live In*. New York: Century, 1908.

Lyon, Arabella. "Suzanne K. Langer: Mother and Midwife at the Rebirth of Rhetoric." *Reclaiming Rhetorica: Women in the Rhetorical Tradition*. Ed. Andrea A. Lunsford. Pittsburgh: U of Pittsburgh P, 1995. 265–84.

"Miss Keller Seen as Symbol of Hope." *New York Times* 10 Apr. 1940: 33.

Sharer, Wendy B. *Vote and Voice: Women's Organizations and Political Literacy, 1915–1930*. Carbondale: Southern Illinois UP, 2004.

Shulevitz, Judith. "Powers of Perception." *New York Times Book Review* 20 Apr. 2003: 31.

Afterword

In Memory of Michael C. Leff

32

Momentary Civil Religion in Isocrates' "To Philip"

Steven R. Edscorn

In one of his last published essays, Michael Leff compares Pericles' Funeral Oration with Lincoln's Second Inaugural in order to explore how religious principles complicate the relationship between the expedient and the honorable in political rhetoric. While Pericles' encomium may seem to express something similar to a civil religion, Leff argues that it is better seen as an "intensely idealized secular nationalism rather than a civil religion" ("Expedient" 402). By contrast, he finds in the Second Inaugural, which makes use of the American jeremiad form and borrows much from biblical texts, a powerful representation of civil religion (411). Indeed, Leff shows how American civil religion, which tends "to conflate the sacred and secular domains and as a consequence to blur the lines demarcating the honorable from the expedient," provides a crucial backdrop for understanding the force and inventional logic of Lincoln's rhetoric. He concludes, in turn, that Lincoln's address "presents a more complex instance of textual performance" than Pericles' because it creates a mood or attitude that struggles toward an ideal, but fails to attain it. By contrast, Pericles constructs a persona that "is a synecdoche for Athenian political culture," one that is "self-contained and complete" (408).

At the end of his essay, Leff invites further discussion about this dynamic (412). Here, I accept that invitation by offering an analysis of a text that falls somewhere between the secular nationalism of Pericles and the complex civil religion of Lincoln: Isocrates' "To Philip."[1] I hope to bring additional relief to the contrast Leff provided. I also hope to bring to life the ethos and idiosyncrasies of my late mentor, who I came to know during his final years of teaching at the University of Memphis. I will use one of Isocrates' favorite rhetorical forms, the digression, in order to do so.

Leff would likely have approved of my choice of Isocrates to complicate this conversation, even though he occasionally referred to Isocrates as "a real bag of wind," in part because of Isocrates' elitism, and in part because of his habit of digression. I should note, of course, that Leff would not approve of my use of digression here, especially since my purpose in doing so is to make a fuss about him.

Leff's real classical hero was Cicero. But he appreciated Isocrates grudgingly and indirectly, as an important influence on Cicero and, of course, as an influential figure in the history of rhetoric. Leff also appreciated Isocrates for his creative ability to remain in the tension between the ideal and the actual:

> Isocratean paideia looks toward something better than existing political practices and opinions, it does not transcend them altogether, and for this reason, the program stands in the margin between the actual and the ideal. Positioned in this somewhat uncomfortable space, his pedagogical doctrine tends to become opaque, mixed, shifting, and when viewed in detail, apparently inconsistent. ("Isocrates")

Leff was perhaps able to see this because he is not unlike Isocrates in this regard. Both were comfortable with the limitations of human knowledge and with the great complexity of any situation. They could tolerate, even appreciate, creative tension between apparent opposites to the point that they could attract charges of inconsistency. Far from being incoherent, however, both Leff and Isocrates actually embodied a maturity lost on many of their critics. Nowhere is this similarity more apparent than in their relationships to religion and religious rhetoric.

Like Isocrates, Leff did not concern himself with too much metaphysical speculation, and he claimed to be, in this sense, a nonbeliever. He nevertheless identified closely with his Jewish heritage. On the surface, the identification was easy to miss. He did not observe Jewish dietary laws, among other things. He still identified himself as an adherent of the Jewish religion, however, and not as an agnostic, when asked about his religious affiliation while teaching a class that was cross-listed with Memphis Theological Seminary. On the surface, he might appear to be inconsistent, or even to be pandering to a religious audience. However, I think his identification was genuine. Leff was Jewish, even spiritually Jewish; yet, Leff was a skeptic. He allowed these conflicting pieties to coexist, even if Leff the skeptic had the upper hand most of the time.

Even this is too simplistic an understanding of Leff's religious sensibilities. His religious impulse actually transcended Judaism. Leff showed a great deal of interest in Christian theology, whether he was studying Abraham Lincoln or Martin Luther King Jr. King's sermons could move him to tears and he said on more than one occasion that King made him *wish* he was Christian. This was, of course, more an expression of appreciation for King's artful rhetoric than it was an appreciation for Christian dogma. However, there is a suggestion there, since Leff would not have separated content from style, that he found King's religious message deeply touching.

Leff also showed great openness to students with religious commitments, of which he encountered many in Memphis. His nonjudgmental attitude extended well beyond religion, of course. Leff expressed compassion and understanding with misguided or immature student behavior as well. I do not mean to suggest that Leff tolerated bad behavior. He most certainly did correct it. He simply understood that other people have internal tensions as well, and not everyone has made peace with that. This explains why he was open to religiosity as well. In all of this, Leff consistently modeled both an ability to transcend the need for coherence and a level of comfort with incongruity.

Leff's article comparing Lincoln and Pericles exemplifies his interest in this tension between the sacred and the mundane, and his comfort with living in that tension. These two voices, Pericles and Lincoln, represent polar pulls in Leff's own life: the mature idealism of Lincoln and the humanism of Pericles. As this study shows, Isocrates exhibits the same kind of tension in his appropriation from both the Greek enlightenment and ancient Greek religion. Because of this, he actually embodies some of the tensions apparent in Leff's much wider contrast between Pericles and Lincoln.

Leff's approach to Pericles and Lincoln draws on two significant insights. The first he borrows from journalist Tom Wolfe, and that is an attention to the performance of a speech in its opening remarks, an often neglected portion of a speech that gives meaning to what follows. The second insight, the distinction between the empirical and ideal levels of political, he borrows from Harvey Yunis. On the empirical level, according to Yunis, "groups and individuals attempt to advance their interests while (ostensibly) respecting the needs and rules of the community" (Leff, "Expedient" 414). On the ideal level, the rhetor engages "the basic values that determine what a community might find honorable attempt(s) to establish a privileged frame for managing particular conflicts" (402). I approach "To Philip" with these same insights in mind.

I focus on two specific portions of the speech. Following Leff's lead, I examine the prooemium to see how the performance is established. Second, I examine the climax of the speech, at which point Isocrates momentarily breaks into civil religious discourse. I demonstrate how, like Lincoln, Isocrates manages to weave together the honorable and the expedient, but how this happens in a surprising way. The conflation comes not by means of deterministic theology, but through the persona he constructs, which briefly goes beyond the self-contained persona Leff detects in Pericles.

In the prooemium, Isocrates enacts a version of the Athenian orator that is similar to the performance by Pericles (Leff, "Expedient" 404). The difference is that Pericles makes his apologies much more succinctly, conveying an air of confidence, while Isocrates is painfully apologetic. That difference may be attributable to power differentials between the speakers and their audiences. Isocrates is addressing a king, and he must show proper deference. Pericles is a leader addressing citizens, so he only needs to defer to the custom requiring that he give his oration.

This extended prooemium functions to establish Philip as a free agent who has the power to speak and act in any way he deems expedient. The theme of Philip's freedom is apparent throughout the speech. For example, Isocrates writes,

> you and you alone had been granted by fortune free scope both to send ambassadors to whomsoever you desire and to receive them from whomsoever you please, and to say whatever you think expedient, and that, besides you, beyond any of the Hellenes were possessed of both wealth and power, which are the only things in the world that are adapted at once to persuade and to compel. ("To Philip" 15)

The freedom here is one of both speech and action, of persuasion and of coercion. Isocrates never surrenders his own agency, however. For example, the disciples do not prevent Isocrates from or cause Isocrates to publish his speech to Philip. The Greek is very strong here. In my own translation, Isocrates says, "With this in mind, I myself chose to discuss with you . . ." (14). In the next sentence, Isocrates refers to "my decision" to publish the speech. This speech, then, is a discussion between free agents. Isocrates is free to speak. Philip is free to speak or to act.

Throughout the prooemium, Isocrates keeps the discourse grounded in expedient aims, that is, the empirical level according to Yunis. Even when Isocrates reveals the object of his speech, he couches it in pragmatic language. Nowhere to be found in the prooemium is a discussion of the values that make uniting Greece and invading Asia honorable things to do. The discourse is also devoid of religious concepts to this point. The reasons for the mission are entirely to preserve peace within Greece and to secure goods from the Persians (9).

Like Pericles, Isocrates has used the prooemium to construct a persona more than a mood or attitude. The persona is self-contained and complete. It acts entirely from within established frames and serves as a synecdoche for Greek political culture. I say "Greek" rather than "Athenian" as Leff did because of the Panhellenic nature of Isocrates' project. Isocrates, like Pericles, appears to represent the very secular Greek enlightenment tradition here.

The explicit emphasis on free agency provides a sharp contrast to Lincoln. Leff points out that the opening words of the Second Inaugural are "laboriously cast in the impersonal passive," that the Civil War is portrayed as inevitable, and that the theology at work is highly deterministic ("Expedient" 406).

In most of the body of the speech, Isocrates ventures into the ideal realms of political rhetoric, and even uses semireligious historical figures such as Heracles. It should suffice to say that throughout this section, the persona Isocrates constructs remains self-contained and complete like the one constructed by Pericles, and that even the semireligious references do not really provide "a religious way of thinking about politics."

All of this changes as Isocrates reaches the climax of the speech in 149–152, where he adds a significant religious dimension that goes well beyond what he has done up to this point. Isocrates writes:

> Now, if . . . you feel that my discourse is in any part rather weak and inadequate, set it down to my age . . . but if it is up to the standard of my former publications, I would have you believe that it was . . . the divine will (*daimonion*) that prompted it . . . because of its concern for Hellas, and because of its desire to deliver her out of her present distress and to crown you with a glory far greater than you now possess. I think that you are not unaware in what manner the gods (*theoi*) order the affairs of mortals: for not with their own hands do they deal out the blessings and curses that befall us; rather they inspire in each of us such a state of mind that good or ill . . . is visited upon us through one another . . . it may be that even now the gods have assigned to me the task of speech while to you they allot the task of action. . . . Indeed, I believe that even your past achievements would never have reached such magnitude had not one of the gods (*theon*) helped you to succeed; and I believe he did so . . . that, having been trained and having gained experience and come to know your own powers . . . you might set your heart upon the course which I have urged upon you.

Chase has already noted that Isocrates takes the gods themselves a bit more seriously than he does history, both mythical and non-mythical. Chase says that Isocrates "consistently urged respect toward the gods," while "the Greek past was a vast reservoir of moral wisdom, subject to being mined for particular purposes at particular moments." So, while stories about gods and demigods could be interchanged, one must avoid "loose talk against the gods" (251).

Chase also notes that, for Isocrates, piety to logos or alternately to Peitho is performed through the pursuit of rhetoric (250). He makes this case based primarily on the "Antidosis." However, this pattern holds up well in this passage of "To Philip." In fact, it becomes expanded beyond the bounds of rhetoric to encompass other areas of concern. Philip is to perform piety to the gods by using his military power to benefit Greece.

It should be noted that Isocrates does not directly attribute Philip's military power or other abilities to the gods. He says that a god helped him, or set him straight (*katorthosin*), and that he did so in order that Philip might gain valuable experience. The intervention of the gods comes in the form of direct inspiration or inspired messages from others. Abilities and dis-abilities usually come from nature (*physis*). For example, Isocrates' weak voice is attributed to *physis*.

A theology with gods acting through inspiration is consistent with other Isocratean writings, such as his use of Peitho in "Antidosis," and it does not conflict with Isocrates' frequent use of *physis* as a source of actual abilities. Even when one considers the "Hymn to the Logos," the logos that is the source of so much power is identified as part of the "nature of man"

("To Nicocles" 5). So, while Isocrates may use mythical and historical characters and narratives with a great deal of flexibility, his theology remains remarkably stable.

But is this a civil theology? I contend that it is, due to statements that the god or gods that inspire Isocrates and Philip do so out of concern for Greece. The unification of the Greeks and the mission against Asia take on divine importance. This provides a "religious way of thinking about politics," to use Pierard and Linder's definition of civil religion (the same one used by Leff) in a way that goes beyond Pericles' nationalism.

I must acknowledge here that the term "civil religion" belongs to Rousseau, and so applying the term to Isocrates is anachronistic in a way that Leff's application of the term to Lincoln is not. Like Pierard and Linder, I use "civil religion" here as a "scholar's term" in a very flexible way (Pierard and Linder 22). Like Rousseau, however, I would distinguish civil religion, not only from secular nationalism as Leff has, but also from theocracy (Rousseau 45). Civil religion involves some degree of generalization or polysemy that allows the appropriation of religious language in political rhetoric while accommodating religious pluralism. On the other hand, civil religion is distinguished from secular nationalism, as noted by Leff, by language that is explicitly metaphysical.

For Rousseau, civil religion is an idealized solution. This is not the case for Isocrates, who actually seems to favor theocracy on an ideal level. In this passage as elsewhere, the ideal seems to be a society based on religious values. Isocrates' clearest expression of this is in "Busiris," when Isocrates describes religion in his idealized society of Egypt during the reign of the mythical king Busiris. Here he says that the function of the priests is to make rewards and punishments of the gods "seem more certain to the citizens than they really are" (24–27). It also resonates with "On the Peace," where Isocrates says that reward or punishment from the gods is more certain for states than it is for individuals because individuals live only a short time and might die before the immortal gods act, while states, he says, are deathless (120).

This temporal distinction in Isocrates between states and individuals allows Isocrates to accommodate both human skepticism, and by extension Greek enlightenment thought, and Greek religion. This could be seen as a type of religious plurality, and Isocrates' rhetoric is calculated to accommodate both.

Unlike Lincoln, however, Isocrates commits what Reinhold Niebuhr would call "the error of identifying providence with the cause to which the agent is committed" (Leff, "Expedient" 409). The effect of this identification is to make civil religion ephemeral. Greece becomes the direct object of veneration simply because the gods favor Greece. It would not be difficult to cut the gods out of the loop and lapse back into the kind of secular nationalism evident in Pericles.

Furthermore, the conquest of Asia is a much more concrete goal than the millennial expectations that drive a formation such as the American jeremiad. Achieving such a goal or even changing international circumstances could leave the civil religion without a cause. Greece may still be the object of veneration, but it would lack that "errand in the wilderness" provided through the American jeremiad that makes American democracy itself a sacred mission. Of course, if Isocrates were to form a more permanent civil theology, he could not connect it with any particular polity (Konstan 112). The effect of this is that, like Lincoln's speech, "To Philip" "struggles toward" an ideal it does not achieve, but that ideal is much less enduring.

The understanding of piety evident here preserves the strong agency that Isocrates affords to Philip throughout the speech. Even when Isocrates mentions Tyche, translated as "fortune," he describes her as leading the way, and it is clearly still possible for Philip to "refuse to follow." This contrasts sharply with the determinism in Lincoln's Second Inaugural.

Strong agency, the ephemeral character of the civil theology, and the concrete cause, all keep the religious discourse in "To Philip" well-grounded in the expedient. This enables Isocrates to use piety to the gods quite economically, adding considerable force to the speech without sorting out complex doctrine or creating fantastic, otherworldly discourse like one would see in Plato. Isocrates, briefly, achieves the same effect as American jeremiad forms where "virtue and expediency overlap and cooperate; honorable ideals approach realization as they encompass and direct expedient action, and expedient actions become honorable as they advance toward the realization of virtue" (Leff, "Expedient" 412).

What is striking here is that in this case, it is not progressive movement toward a predetermined future that makes this connection possible, but the possibility that divine forces act through the human personality. The construction of the mood or attitude in the audience actually comes through the construction of the persona. Isocrates' performance of piety toward the "divine spirit" (*daimonion*) that inspires his speech exemplifies the attitude Isocrates would like for Philip to adopt toward the god who inspires him to military conquest. With the addition of the *daimonion*, Isocrates' persona is no longer self-contained and complete, and neither is that of Philip. This incompleteness becomes the vehicle for the connection between expedient and honorable.

In conclusion, Isocrates ventures momentarily into civil religious discourse at the end of "To Philip," and that calculated decision adds force to the speech by making the unification of Greece and an expedition against Asia into acts of piety to the gods. Although the civil theology Isocrates constructs is imminently transferrable to other situations that apply to Greece as a whole, it also has an ephemeral, passing quality. "To Philip" lacks the determinism necessary for conflating the honorable and the expedient the way Lincoln does. Instead, Isocrates conflates divine inspiration and human thoughts in a way that renders the speech a hybrid of the secular nationalistic discourse found in "Pericles' Funeral Oration" (Thucydides) and the highly developed civil religious discourse found in Lincoln's Second Inaugural.

In continuing the discussion that Leff started, then, I would suggest that it is worth considering whether a high degree of human agency and a lack of determinism necessarily ground civil religious discourse and render it more ephemeral. From the standpoint of rhetorical invention, must one choose between an undecided future and a self-sustaining civil theology? I would also suggest that it might be worth considering if there are other ways, in addition to participation in a predetermined future (evident in Lincoln) and divine action through inspired human agents (evident in this Isocratean text), in which religious discourse might move to synthesize the honorable and the expedient.

Leff, like others, noted the elitism of Isocrates. Such elitism is quite evident, for instance, in the theocratic idealism of texts such as "Busiris." However, in the religious realm, Isocrates' elitism is tempered by an accommodation of human skepticism on one hand, and religious commitment on the other, which shows up in texts like "To Philip." Here, at least, Isocrates negotiates the tension between humanistic and religious perspectives in a careful and elegant way.

It seems pointless to speculate about whether or not Isocrates really believed in the Olympian religion. Perhaps this should not be a chief concern of rhetoric. Nevertheless, our field can produce insight into historical situations and even persons that should not be ignored. Isocrates may have been careful to use religious language to avoid being accused of impiety, as Socrates was. Or perhaps he faced some kind of social pressure not to be too metaphysical in his rhetoric. He certainly distances himself from sophists who "claim to have exact knowledge" in "Against the Sophists" while expressing concern that such teachers lower the prestige of the whole profession. In any case, as he does in so many other arenas, Isocrates tries to reconcile the two pulls. Here, in "To Philip," he negotiates a tension between humanism and religious belief that might betray his own comfort with such a tension. Is that noble voice inside me the voice of a god? Or is this coming from me as a human? Isocrates' answer appears to be a very human "I don't know. Maybe both."

I do not know whether Leff agreed with Isocrates on this point. He would have been sympathetic to the tension and to Isocrates' attempt to accommodate both skeptics and religious readers. Yet, he would probably have pointed to the conflation of cause and providence and said, "He's a real bag of wind." Leff would have actually preferred the rhetoric of Lincoln, even with, and perhaps because of, its inherent religious dogma, despite his own worldview (which would have found more resonance with Pericles). That tension simply does not need to be resolved for Leff.

With Leff, at least in the years that I knew him, this comfort with incongruity flowed from a kind of maturity that allowed his compassion for human failings to coexist with a very qualified kind of idealism: a hope that the best rhetoric of a Lincoln or a King can make a difference in the world. That difference was not a *cause* for the Memphis Leff, not an overriding *telos* flowing from an adolescent mind-set. Nor were his values and ideas a matter of childish disputation, where his views had to prevail. Leff genuinely learned from his critics and honored them for what they taught him. No, Leff's comfort with incongruity came from a truly adult mind-set achieved at least by the last years of his life. It is not too much of a stretch to imagine that, at 90, Isocrates had reached a similar kind of maturity. It was a comfort in the tension between the ideal and the actual, and, indeed, between concord and controversy, that defined each as a truly mature thinker and an excellent teacher.

Note

[1] In 346 BCE, Isocrates published a speech addressed to Philip II of Macedon, encouraging him to unite the Greeks peacefully and to lead a united Greek attack against Persia. Such a Panhellenic expedition had been a strong theme in Isocrates' speeches throughout his career, but this message was different. In earlier speeches such as the "Panegyricus" and "Helen," Isocrates had encouraged his native Athens to take the lead in such an expedition. Isocrates was now, at over 90 years of age, imploring a Macedonian king to take the initiative. Isocrates encourages Philip to win Greece over through persuasion and diplomacy, no easy task considering that many of the Greek city states were at war with each other including, until just prior to this speech, Athens against Macedon.

Works Cited

Chase, Kenneth R. "Constructing Ethics through Rhetoric: Isocrates and Piety." *Quarterly Journal of Speech* 95 (2009): 239–62.

Isocrates. "Against the Sophists." *Isocrates.* Trans. George Norlin. Vol. II. Cambridge, MA: Harvard UP, 2000.

———. "Antidosis." *Isocrates.* Trans. George Norlin. Vol. II. Cambridge, MA: Harvard UP, 2000.

———. "Busiris." *Isocrates.* Trans. La Rue Van Hook. Vol. III. Cambridge, MA: Harvard UP, 1998.

———. "On the Peace." *Isocrates.* Trans. George Norlin. Vol. II. Cambridge, MA: Harvard UP, 2000.

———. "To Nicocles." *Isocrates.* Trans. George Norlin. Vol. I. Cambridge, MA: Harvard UP, 2000.

———. "To Philip." *Isocrates.* Trans. George Norlin. Vol. I. Cambridge, MA: Harvard UP, 2000.

Konstan, David. "Isocrates' Republic." *Isocrates and Civic Education.* Ed. Takis Poulakos and David Depew. Austin: U of Texas P, 2004.

Leff, Michael. "The Expedient, the Honorable, and the Sacred: Rhetorical Topoi and the Religious Imperative." *New Chapters in the History of Rhetoric.* Ed. Laurent Pernot. Boston: Brill, 2009. 401–14.

———. "Isocrates, Rhetoric, and the Idealization of Civic Education." *The Philosophy of Communication* 2 (2002): 120–25.

Lincoln, Abraham. "Second Inaugural Address." Web. 21 May 2010. <http://www.bartleby.com/124/Pres32.html>

Pierard, Richard V., and Robert D. Linder. *Civil Religion & The Presidency.* Grand Rapids, MI: Academie, 1988.

Rousseau, Jean-Jacques. *The Social Contract*. Book IV, Part 8. "Civil Religion." Web. <http://www.constitution.org/jjr/socon_04.htm>

Thucydides. "Pericles' Funeral Oration." Web. 21 May 2010. <http://www.wsu.edu:8080~dee/GREECE/PERICLES/HTM>

Yunis, Harvey. *Taming Democracy.* Ithaca: Cornell UP, 1996.

Contributors

Ira Allen is a doctoral candidate in Rhetoric and Composition and an Associate Instructor of English at Indiana University, Bloomington. He is the Founding Director of the Bloomington Writing Project, a nonprofit community writing center, and is a professional translator of German. He is the author of articles on rhetorical theory, composition pedagogy, and literary criticism.

Claudia Carlos is Assistant Professor of English and Rhetoric at Carnegie Mellon University. Her research interests include early modern French rhetoric, the art of "safe speaking" in rhetorical theory and practice, and the relationship between figures and argumentation. The journals in which she has published include *Rhetorica, Rhetoric Review, Advances in the History of Rhetoric,* and *Cahiers Naturalistes*.

Lynn Clarke is Assistant Professor of Communication at the University of Pittsburgh.

Sharon Crowley is Professor Emerita at Arizona State University. She is the author of *Toward a Civil Discourse: Rhetoric and Fundamentalism, Composition in the University: Historical and Polemical Essays*, and *The Methodical Memory: Invention in Current-Traditional Rhetoric*. She is a Fellow of the Rhetoric Society of America.

Antonio de Velasco is Assistant Professor of Rhetoric in the Department of Communication at the University of Memphis. He is the author of *Centrist Rhetoric: The Production of Political Transcendence in the Clinton Presidency* (Lanham, MD: Lexington Books, 2010). He wishes to acknowledge Diane Evans of Waveland Press for her editorial skill and wisdom. She was simply indispensable to the fruition of *Rhetoric: Concord and Controversy.*

Zachary Dobbins is Assistant Professor of Rhetoric at Eckerd College. He has received numerous teaching awards, including the Maxine Hairston Prize for Teaching Excellence from the University of Texas, Austin. He wishes to thank Patricia Roberts-Miller and Jeffrey Walker for their invaluable feedback on the argument this paper advances.

Steven R. Edscorn is Library Director and Associate Professor of Theological Bibliography at Memphis Theological Seminary and a doctoral candidate in Communication at the University of Memphis. He is coauthor, with Michael Leff, of "Bibliographie sélective annotée des publications en langue anglaise sur la rhétorique, la critique rhétorique et l'argumentation," *Argumentation et Analyse du Discours* 2 (2009), and author of a forthcoming annotated bibliography of the published works of Michael Leff, *Argumentation et Analyse du Discours* 6 (2011).

Rosalyn Collings Eves is an adjunct lecturer in English at Southern Utah University. Her dissertation, "Mapping Rhetorical Frontiers: Women's Spatial Rhetorics in the Nineteenth-Century American West," won the RSA Award for Best Dissertation in 2009; she has published elsewhere in *Rhetoric Review* and *The Sage Handbook on Gender and Communication*.

Megan Foley is Assistant Professor of Communication Studies at Mississippi State University. Her work has appeared in the *Quarterly Journal of Speech*, *Communication and Critical/Cultural Studies*, and the *Journal of Communication Studies*. She thanks Leslie Hahner, Joan Faber McAlister, and Nathan Stormer for their helpful feedback.

Ann George is Associate Professor of English at Texas Christian University. She is coauthor with Jack Selzer of *Kenneth Burke in the 1930s* and currently serves as President of the Kenneth Burke Society.

Timothy Henningsen is a doctoral candidate in English Studies at the University of Illinois, Chicago. His dissertation examines the little-explored literary relations between the so-called American Renaissance movement and Anglophone Caribbean novelists of the mid-twentieth century. Previously, Tim was an instructor and curriculum developer in UIC's esteemed community-based writing program (CCLCP), and his work appears in *Going Public: What Writing Programs Learn from Engagement* (2010).

David C. Hoffman is Associate Professor at Baruch College, CUNY. He has served as President of the American Society for the History of Rhetoric and has been a Mellon Fellow at the Center for the Humanities at the CUNY Graduate Center. His scholarship has appeared in *Rhetorica*, *Rhetoric Society Quarterly*, *Rhetoric and Public Affairs*, and *Argumentation and Advocacy*. This work was supported (in part) by a grant from The City University of New York PSC-CUNY Research Award Program.

Beth Innocenti is Associate Professor and Chair of the Department of Communication Studies at the University of Kansas.

Jennifer Keohane is a graduate student in the Department of Communication Arts at the University of Wisconsin, Madison. She was awarded a Gerard A. Hauser Graduate Scholarship for this essay at the Rhetoric Society of America's 2010 convention. She would like to thank Angela Ray for her invaluable help and encouragement on this project, which was completed at Northwestern University.

Michael S. Kochin is Professor Extraordinarius of Political Science at Tel Aviv University, and has held visiting appointments at Toronto, Princeton, and Yale. He is the author of *Five Chapters on Rhetoric: Character, Action, Things, Nothing, and Art* (Penn State Press, 2009) and editor, with Yoav Peled, of *The Public Sphere: The Tel Aviv Journal of Political Science.* Thanks to my wife Anna Kochin for her comments and corrections.

Rebecca A. Kuehl is a doctoral candidate in the Department of Communication Studies at the University of Minnesota. She is the author of "Oprah and Obama: Theorizing Celebrity Endorsement in U.S. Politics," in *The Obama Effect: Multidisciplinary Renderings of the 2008 Campaign*, as well as the recipient of a 2010 Gerard A. Hauser Graduate Scholarship for a top student paper at the 2010 RSA conference. She would like to thank Karlyn Kohrs Campbell, Amy Snow Landa, Anthony Nadler, and Kirt Wilson for reading earlier drafts of this essay.

Donald Lazere is Professor Emeritus of English at California Polytechnic State University, San Luis Obispo, and has taught most recently at the University of Tennessee, Knoxville. His latest book is *Reading and Writing for Civic Learning: The Critical Citizen's Guide to Argumentative Rhetoric* (Paradigm Publishers, 2005; Brief Edition, 2009). He has written on literature, literacy, and the rhetoric of politics and media for both scholarly publications and journalistic ones, including *The New York Times* and *The Chronicle of Higher Education*. He is currently writing *English Studies and Civic Literacy: Teaching the Political Conflicts*.

Melody Lehn is a doctoral candidate in the Department of Communication at the University of Memphis, where she was awarded the John Angus Campbell Award for Excellence in Teaching in 2009. She was Assistant to the Conference Director for the fourteenth biennial Rhetoric Society of America conference and would like to express her thanks to Camisha Smith, Mark Nagle, Jack Selzer, Kathie Cesa, and the countless others who helped to make the 2010 convention all that Mike Leff envisioned it would be.

Rebecca Lorimer is a doctoral candidate in the Composition and Rhetoric Program at the University of Wisconsin, Madison. Her research interests include comparative and intercultural rhetoric, second language writing, and community literacy. She is currently conducting research for her dissertation project on immigration and multilingual writing.

Paul Lynch is Assistant Professor of English at Saint Louis University. His work has appeared in *Rhetoric Review, KB Journal,* and *College Composition and Communication*. He is currently serving as President of the Jesuit Conference on Rhetoric and Composition.

Keith Miller is Professor of English at Arizona State University and the author of *Martin Luther King's Biblical Epic: His Great, Final Speech*, which will be published by the University Press of Mississippi in 2011. In 2007, his essay on King's "I Have a Dream" won the Theresa Enos Award for Best

Essay of the Year in *Rhetoric Review.* His essay on Malcolm X and literacy appeared in *College Composition and Communication* in 2004. He thanks ASU for granting him a leave that helped him to complete this essay; he also appreciates encouragement from his ASU colleagues and from Jack Selzer, Keith Gilyard, David Holmes, and Stephen Schneider.

Nancy Myers is Associate Professor of English at the University of North Carolina, Greensboro where she teaches composition, linguistics, and the history of rhetoric. She received the UNCG Alumni Teaching Excellence Award in 2002 and received two teaching awards while at the University of Missouri at Kansas City. She is currently President (2010–2012) of the Coalition of Women Scholars in the History of Rhetoric and Composition. Along with Gary Tate and Edward P. J. Corbett, she is an editor of the third and fourth editions of *The Writing Teacher's Sourcebook* (Oxford University Press). Recent publications include essays in *Silence and Listening as Rhetorical Arts* (Southern Illinois University Press, 2011), *Stories of Mentoring: Theory and Praxis* (Palgrave, 2008), and *The Locations of Composition* (SUNY Press, 2007).

Cezar M. Ornatowski is Professor of Rhetoric and Writing Studies and Associated Faculty in the interdisciplinary Master of Science Program in Homeland Security at San Diego State University. He was Senior Fulbright Research Scholar at the Institute for Philosophy and Sociology of the Polish Academic of Sciences in 1999 and is Honorary Fellow of the Center for Rhetoric Studies at the University of Cape Town.

Alex C. Parrish is a doctoral candidate at Washington State University. He is the founder and current secretary of the student chapter of the Rhetoric Society of America at WSU, and the coordinator of its regional lecture series.

M. Karen Powers is Assistant Professor of English at Kent State University, Tuscarawas.

Ellen Quandahl is Associate Professor of Rhetoric and Writing Studies at San Diego State University. She is the editor, with Patricia Donahue, of *Reclaiming Pedagogy: The Rhetoric of the Classroom.* Her articles appear in *Rhetorica, Rhetoric Society Quarterly, JAC,* and *College English.* She wishes to thank Suzanne Bordelon for reading drafts of this paper. The paper is dedicated to Professor Gracia Grindal.

Heather A. Roy received her BA from Eastern Illinois University in 2010 and is a masters student and Graduate Assistant in the Department of Communication and Rhetorical Studies at Syracuse University. She is the former President of the student chapter of the Rhetoric Society of America at Eastern Illinois University. She would like to thank Dr. Marita Gronnvoll for reviewing earlier drafts of the manuscript.

Kyle Schlett is a doctoral candidate in English at the University of Mississippi. His scholarly interests include popular culture and representations of automotive technology. His presentation of the essay included in this volume received a Gerard A. Hauser Graduate Scholarship at the 2010 conference of the RSA. He would like to extend special thanks to Dr. Felice Coles, Dr. Jonathan Fenno, and Dr. Douglas Robinson for their expertise in and understanding of the issues and potential pitfalls unique to translation.

J. Blake Scott is Associate Chair and Director of Degree Programs in the University of Central Florida's Department of Writing and Rhetoric. His latest book, coedited by Rebecca Dingo and titled *Megarhetorics of Globalized Development*, is forthcoming from the University of Pittsburgh Press.

Jack Selzer has taught scientific and technical communication and a variety of courses in rhetoric and composition at Penn State University since 1978. Currently the Past President of RSA and director of Penn State's Paterno Fellows Program, he has published widely on the rhetoric of science, on the works of Kenneth Burke, and on the conduct of rhetorical analysis. In addition to a third volume on the career of Kenneth Burke, he is now working on a book about the rhetoric of the civil rights movement.

Patrick Shaw is Associate Professor of English and Director of Composition at the University of Southern Indiana. He teaches courses on the history of rhetoric and twentieth-century and contemporary rhetorical theory. His scholarly interests include twentieth-century rhetorical theory, contemporary cultural studies, and writing program administration.

Ethan Sproat is a doctoral candidate in Rhetoric and Composition at Purdue University. His dissertation seeks to reintroduce the term *sympheron* to contemporary rhetorical theory. He is currently serving as President of the Purdue student chapter of the RSA.

Jon Leon Torn is Assistant Professor in the School of Communication at Northern Arizona University.

William Trapani is an Assistant Professor in the School of Communication and Multimedia Studies at Florida Atlantic University. His research and teaching interests include rhetorical theory and criticism, visual rhetoric, and discourses of national identity.

Kelly M. Young is Assistant Professor of Communication and Director of Forensics at Wayne State University. He writes at the intersection of rhetorical and cultural studies with specific interests in: the cultural politics of Native America, collective memory studies, and democratic argument and participation.

Name Index

Subject Index